Defend This Old Town

Defend This Old Town

WILLIAMSBURG DURING THE CIVIL WAR

Carol Kettenburg Dubbs

Louisiana State University Press

Baton Rouge

Designer: Barbara Neely Bourgoyne
Typeface: Adobe Caslon; Cochin
Typesetter: Coghill Composition, Inc.
Printer and binder: Thomson-Shore, Inc.

Library of Congress Cataloging-in-Publication Data

Dubbs, Carol Kettenburg, 1950–
   Defend this old town : Williamsburg during the Civil War / Carol Kettenburg Dubbs.
      p.   cm.
Includes bibliographical references and index.
   ISBN 0-8071-2780-9
   1. Williamsburg, Battle of, 1862.   2. Williamsburg (Va.)—History, Military—19th century.
3. Williamsburg (Va.)—History—19th century.   4. Virginia—History—Civil War,
1861–1865—Social aspects.   5. United States—History—Civil War, 1861–1865—Social
aspects.   I. Title.
   E473.63 .D83   2002
   973.7'32—dc21

2002001863

To my mother and father

CONTENTS

ILLUSTRATIONS

FIGURES

Maps

ACKNOWLEDGMENTS

While I was growing up, my parents took my brother and me on vacations to Williamsburg and Civil War battlefields (not an easy drive from San Diego). I will never forget the time we found my great-grandfather's name on the Sixty-third Pennsylvania Volunteers Monument at Gettysburg. Little did I realize then that I would some day be writing about the battle of Williamsburg, at which the Sixty-third Pennsylvania and my great-grandfather were present.

My interest in the war did not actually begin until I crossed academic paths with Ludwell H. Johnson III, professor of history at the College of William and Mary. Not only did he inspire me in his Civil War class, but he also directed my thesis on the battle of Williamsburg and has constantly been most encouraging. Above and beyond the call of duty, he volunteered to read my manuscript and advised its publication. My debt to him can never be repaid.

A debt of no less magnitude I owe to David F. Riggs, curator at the Colonial National Historic Park, who in 1989 suggested I expand my thesis and join with him as a coauthor on a Civil War history of the Historic Triangle. From that time until now, though he has since published his own study of Jamestown, *Embattled Shrine,* David and his wife, Susan Riggs, in the Manuscripts and Rare Books Department of Swem Library, College of William and Mary, have continued to assist me with my own manuscript in ways too numerous to mention.

I would never have found most of the extant redoubts if it had not been for David and Susan Riggs, Dr. Arthur Eberdt, and Butch Hogge guiding me through the underbrush. Thanks to all.

To Margaret Cook, Stacy Gould, Kay Domine, Ellen Strong, Sharon Garrison, Suzanne Erena, and the rest of the knowledgeable, efficient, and friendly staff, past and present, at Swem Library, I owe another great debt of gratitude. I also appreciate the kind help of Gail Greve, Dale Moore, George Yetter, Doug Mayo, Catherine Grosfils, Marianne Martin, and all the staff at the John D. Rockefeller Jr. Library at Colonial Williamsburg. For assistance with manuscripts and illustrations, I also thank Kitty Deernose and John A. Doerner at the Little Bighorn Battlefield National Monument; R. Blanton McLean and Judy Bell at Eastern State Hospital; Guy Swanson at the Museum of the Confederacy; Richard Shrader at the University of North Carolina, Chapel Hill; William R. Erwin Jr. at Duke University; Bryan Green at the Virginia Historical Society; Nicole Wells at the New-York Historical Society; and Michael Winey and Randy Hackenburg of the U.S. Army Military History Institute. Special thanks go to Will Molineux for sharing his private collection with me; Gregory J. W. Urwin at Temple University for his information on the George Armstrong Custer wedding letter; and to James I. Robertson Jr. at the Virginia Polytechnic Institute and State University for his kind encouragement.

The most enjoyable aspect of this project has been making the acquaintance of descendents of the book's characters. Anne H. Cutler, the great-granddaughter of undertaker Richard Bucktrout, still lives on the family property in Williamsburg and maintains a vital interest in all things historical connected with it. I am indebted to her for many favors, especially for making the Bucktrout Day Book available to me. Her cousin Dorothy Ross, another Bucktrout great-granddaughter, has graciously shared with me the Bucktrout family papers in her keeping. Cynthia Beverley Tucker Coleman's great-granddaughter and namesake, Cynthia Barlowe, inherited her ancestor's interest in history and in helping others, giving me access to family letters not yet in the extensive Tucker-Coleman Papers at Swem Library and allowing me to publish her beautiful family pictures. Thanks also to Lucy Henry for permission to publish the portrait of her namesake, Lucy Anne Tucker. A decade ago Judge Robert Armistead, grandson of Robert T. Armistead, kindly granted me a memorable interview in his lovely Duke of Gloucester Street home, acquired by his grandfather from Lemuel J. Bowden's family after the war.

It has been a pleasure working with Joseph K. Gilley, a talented graphic artist, in preparing the maps, and I thank him profusely for the great job.

I appreciate particularly Robert K. Krick of the Fredericksburg and Spotsylvania National Military Park for taking the time to review part of the manuscript, making helpful recommendations, and pointing me in the right direction.

Editors Sylvia Frank Rodrigue and Gerry Anders at Louisiana State University Press, along with copyeditor Kevin Brock, have made my first venture into publication as smooth as possible, for which I am most grateful.

To my husband, Jack, goes my deepest gratitude for his support, encouragement, and constant cheerful assistance. Joy and Carbon, toddlers when I started this project and now in their teens, have exhibited a gratifying tolerance throughout. And last, but far from least, a word of thanks to Art Harris, who did all the babysitting and cooking while I did research and plugged away on the keyboard. Without all these people and many more, this book would never have been completed.

ABBREVIATIONS

BSE	Benjamin Stoddert Ewell
CBT	Cynthia Beverley Tucker Washington Coleman
CWC	Charles Washington Coleman
CWF	Colonial Williamsburg Foundation
CWM	Earl Gregg Swem Library, College of William and Mary, Williamsburg
DCP	Dorsey-Coupland Papers
EFP	Ewell Family Papers
EYB	Edwin Y. Brown Papers
F/A	Faculty/Alumni File
GFP	Galt Family Papers
HC	Harriette Cary
HCH	Henry C. Hoar Memorial Collection
JLCG	James L. C. Griffin
JRC	John Randolph Coupland
LAT	Lucy Anne Tucker
LM	Lafayette McLaws
MC	Eleanor S. Brockenbrough Library, Museum of the Confederacy, Richmond, Va.
MR-CWM	Manuscripts and Rare Books Department, Earl Gregg Swem Library, College of William and Mary, Williamsburg
OR	U.S. War Department. *The War of the Rebellion: A Compilation of the Official Records of the Union and Confederate Armies.* 128 vols. Washington: Government Printing Office, 1880–1901 (all references are to series 1 unless otherwise indicated)

ORN	U.S. Naval Records Office. *Official Records of the Union and Confederate Navies in the War of the Rebellion.* 30 vols. Washington: Government Printing Office, 1894–1922 (all references are to series 1 unless otherwise indicated)
PSP	Page-Saunders Papers
SMG	Sally Maria Galt
TCP	Tucker-Coleman Papers
UA-CWM	University Archives, Earl Gregg Swem Library, College of William and Mary, Williamsburg
UNC	University of North Carolina, Chapel Hill
VHS	Virginia Historical Society, Richmond
WCP	Williamsburg City Papers
WWG	*Williamsburg Weekly Gazette and Eastern Virginia Advertiser*

Defend This Old Town

Prologue: Dark Days

The news out of northern Virginia was almost "incomprehensible," wrote Williamsburg planter Dr. Robert Page Waller in his diary entry of 21 October 1859. Five days later the editor of Williamsburg's *Weekly Gazette and Eastern Virginia Advertiser,* Edward Henley Lively, termed the report "so startling, indeed, that we do not profess to understand it." By then over a week had passed since a band of abolitionists led by John Brown had seized the federal arsenal at Harpers Ferry for the purpose of arming a slave revolt. The capture, trial, and execution of Brown and his accomplices, carried out under the direction of Virginia's governor, Henry A. Wise, crowded the *Gazette*'s columns for the next few issues. Williamsburg citizens read with horror and dismay how many prominent northerners applauded Brown's actions.[1]

Horror and dismay filled hearts all across the South, but the crisis seemed to have particular significance for Williamsburg, situated just nine miles from the spot where the South and American slavery began. A horse path midway between the James and York Rivers on Virginia's Lower Peninsula developed into Middle Plantation a decade or two after the 1607 founding of England's first permanent American settlement on Jamestown Island. By the time the colonial government decided to move from Jamestown in 1699, Middle Plantation, now called Williamsburg, boasted the brick Bruton Parish Church and the colony's first college, chartered in 1693 by English monarchs William and Mary. The horse path, straightened and broadened, became the new capital's main thoroughfare, named Duke of Gloucester Street. Over the western end of the street loomed the massive college building, and an impressive capitol

1. Robert Page Waller Diary, 21 Oct. 1859, MR-CWM; *WWG,* 26 Oct., 2, 9, 16, 23, 30 Nov., 7, 13, 21, 28 Dec. 1859.

soon faced it from the eastern end almost a mile away. Throughout the first seven decades of the eighteenth century, many more edifices were added to the capital. A royal governor's official residence, dubbed the Palace, was built to the north of Palace Green, which stretched south past Bruton Church. Shops, taverns, and houses large and small lined Duke of Gloucester as well as the parallel Francis and Nicholson Streets, named for the town's planner, Gov. Francis Nicholson. Substantial brick and two-story frame domiciles belonged to Williamsburg's more successful merchants, lawyers practicing in the capital's many courts, and wealthy planters with tobacco farms in adjacent York and James City Counties. As capital of England's largest, wealthiest, and most populous colony, Williamsburg conceived and nurtured some of the great ideas of the day. Concern for the mentally ill, for example, resulted in North America's first public hospital, erected in 1773 on the southwest corner of town. The formal resolution for independence from England, emanating from the capitol in May 1776, led to Williamsburg's downfall four years later, for during the Revolutionary War, Virginia's state capital moved to Richmond, fifty miles to the northwest.[2]

At that time, not only did Williamsburg lose a substantial part of its population of about two thousand, but its stately structures also began to disappear. Two months after Cornwallis's October 1781 surrender at Yorktown, the Governor's Palace burned to the ground, and in 1832 the abandoned capitol likewise fell victim to flames. Few remnants of colonial pomp remained but a marble statue of Virginia's popular royal governor, Norborne Berkeley, Baron de Botetourt, which had earlier been moved from the capitol yard to the college lawn. There it escaped another catastrophic fire in February 1859, the second in William and Mary's history. Only the outside walls of the main building remained, but the college hastily rose from its ashes in a modern configuration to reopen that October. In contrast to the college's struggle to attract students, the public hospital, now called Eastern Lunatic Asylum to distinguish it from Virginia's western institution, was prospering by midcentury and contained about 250 patients in several newly constructed buildings. Churches also flourished in the first half of the nineteenth century as a Methodist and two Baptist churches, one black and one predominantly white, challenged the gentry's favorite Episcopal Bruton Parish and reflected the increasing influence of the working class.[3]

2. Michael Olmert, *Official Guide to Colonial Williamsburg* (Williamsburg: CWF, 1985), 11–4, 76.

3. Olmert, *Official Guide,* 14–6; George Humphrey Yetter, *Williamsburg Before and After: The Rebirth of Virginia's Colonial Capital* (Williamsburg: CWF, 1988), 5, 22–3, 145–6; Norman Dain,

During the progressive 1850s, the white Baptist congregation built a Greek revival–style church next to the octagonal magazine known as the Powder Horn, on Market Square, also called Courthouse Green for the Old Courthouse of 1770. Across Duke of Gloucester, now Main Street, the construction of a new courthouse to service both Williamsburg and James City County courts spanned several years and enriched almost as many contractors as the courts did lawyers. Williamsburg's primary source of wealth, however, even for its many attorneys and doctors, was farming. The land had long since been depleted by tobacco but could still yield a profitable crop of corn, wheat, or oats with improved fertilizing methods and well-managed slaves. Both farmland and the asylum, Williamsburg's largest employer at the state's expense, comfortably supported the community's population, numbering about sixteen hundred, a little more than half black, by midcentury. Most of the old colonial houses remained but had been modernized and expanded to accommodate growing families.[4]

Though dwelling in a backwater isolated from the center of power, many Williamsburg people descended from friends and relatives of George Washington, Thomas Jefferson, and other founding fathers and continued to make their influence felt on the issues of the day. Judge Nathaniel Beverley Tucker— law professor at William and Mary from 1834 to 1851 as his father, St. George Tucker, had been a generation before—wrote a novel in 1836 called *Partisan Leader* advocating southern secession from the Union. His ideas gained popularity through the mid-nineteenth century as the North's growing population and the increasing power of the abolition movement, linked with the rising Republican Party, convinced many southerners that slavery and their entire culture was under siege. More and more began to desire a country of their own.[5]

Thus, when word of John Brown's raid reached Williamsburg, alarmed townspeople immediately took steps for their own defense. The same issue of the *Gazette* that detailed Harpers Ferry announced Williamsburg lawyer Col. Robert H. Armistead's plan to organize a volunteer company. Within two weeks he held a meeting to determine interest. On 8 November a packed house listened to Armistead's lengthy speech "showing the utility and neces-

Disordered Minds: The First Century of Eastern State Hospital in Williamsburg, Virginia, 1766–1866 (Williamsburg: CWF, 1971), 158, 162; *(Williamsburg) Virginia Gazette,* 24 Aug. 1853.

4. *(Williamsburg) Virginia Gazette,* 15 May 1856; *Weekly Williamsburg Gazette,* 10 June 1857; U.S. Bureau of the Census, Williamsburg and James City County Records, 1860.

5. Eric H. Walther, *The Fire-Eaters* (Baton Rouge: Louisiana State University Press, 1992), 8–11, 42–7.

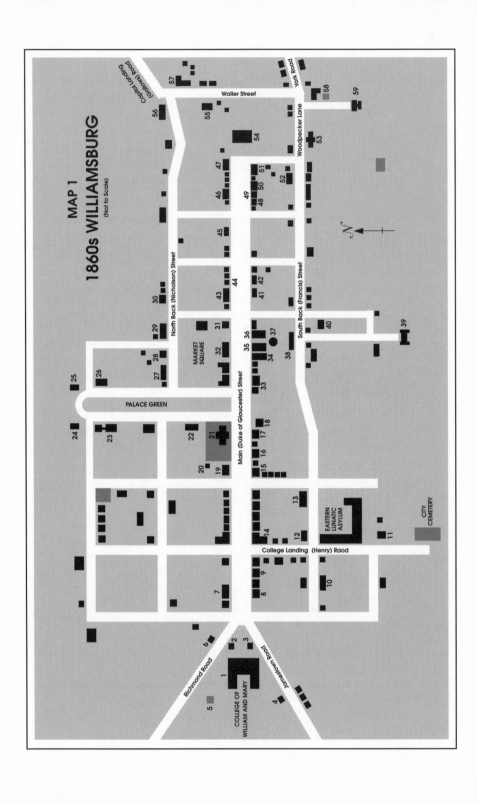

MAP 1
1860s WILLIAMSBURG
(Not to Scale)

Capitol Landing (Gallows) Road

Waller Street

York Road

Woodpecker Lane

North Back (Nicholson) Street

MARKET SQUARE

PALACE GREEN

Main (Duke of Gloucester) Street

South Back (Francis) Street

College Landing (Henry) Raod

EASTERN LUNATIC ASYLUM

CITY CEMETERY

Richmond Road

COLLEGE OF WILLIAM AND MARY

Jamestown Road

N

KEY

(present-day name in parentheses)

1. College of William and Mary Main Building
2. College President's House
3. Brafferton
4. College Steward's House
5. College Cemetery
6. Frog Pond Tavern
7. Lively House and *Gazette* Office
8. Ware House
9. John Charles House
10. Gabriella Galt House (Marshall House)
11. Eastern Lunatic Asylum Tower or Gothic Building
12. Superintendent's House (Travis House)
13. African Baptist Church
14. Charles Waller House
15. Robert Cole House
16. Episcopal Rectory
17. Talbot Sweeney House
18. Maupin House
19. Bowden House (Bowden-Armistead House)
20. Mildred Bowden Cottage
21. Bruton Parish Church and Churchyard
22. Wythe House
23. Saunders House (Robert Carter House)
24. Coleman House
25. Letitia Semple House
26. Sydney Smith House (Brush-Everard House)
27. Tucker House (Tucker-Coleman House)
28. Thompson House (Hay Lodging House)
29. Hansford House (Randolph House)
30. Griffin House (Tayloe House)
31. Boardinghouse and U.S. Commissary
32. Old Courthouse
33. City Hotel and Coach House
34. Methodist Church
35. New Courthouse
36. Baptist Church
37. Powder Magazine or Powder Horn
38. Clerk's Office
39. Tazewell Hall
40. Coke House (Lightfoot House)
41. Peachy House (William Lightfoot House)
42. Deneufville House (George Reid House)
43. Slater House (Ludwell-Paradise House)
44. Peggy Slater Shop
45. Hofheimer Store
46. Vest & Hansford Store
47. Morrison House
48. Young House (Wetherburn's Tavern)
49. Henley House (Charlton House)
50. Bucktrout House
51. Vest House (Palmer House)
52. Galt House (Nelson-Galt House)
53. Custis House (William Finnie House)
54. Female Academy
55. Mercer House
56. Garrett House (Coke-Garrett House)
57. Dr. Robert P. Waller House (Benjamin Powell House)
58. Benjamin Waller House
59. Bassett Hall

sity of reviving the old 68th [militia] regiment of this city." Then, with Clerk of the Circuit Court John A. Henley as chairman and attorney Walker Waller Vest as secretary, eighty-six patriots enrolled. The Williamsburg Junior Guards volunteer company was born.[6]

Hailed by the *Gazette* as defenders of "the Constitution and sectional rights," the volunteers spent a month organizing. Late November reports that local blacks were plotting insurrection may have spurred action, for on the Saturday night of 3 December, the Junior Guards held a meeting to choose officers. The company elected Armistead captain; Henley and Dr. Waller's son, Hugh Mercer Waller, first and second lieutenants; and editor Lively and Henley's brother, Dr. Leonard Henley, two of the four sergeants. On 21 January 1860, Dr. Waller noted that his kinsman Walker Vest came by his home on the eastern end of town and "went after tea with Mercer up town to Company drill," which, weather and circumstances permitting, became a more or less regular exercise the rest of that year.[7]

One frequent interference with drill in 1860 was politics. Meetings started in January when the members of Williamsburg's Democratic Party gathered to elect delegates to the 16 February state presidential convention in Richmond. Armistead, Vest, Mercer Waller, and Dr. Henley were among the ten chosen. With so many officers out of town for a few days, drill was suspended until 20 February. Local rather than national politics absorbed Williamsburg's attention that spring as the annual May elections put Armistead in the office of commonwealth attorney. The following month Armistead, at heart a Unionist and reluctant to take up arms against his country, resigned as captain of the Guards "from a sense of duty as by a principle of self-respect," quoted the *Gazette*.[8]

One month later, on 11 July, the *Gazette* announced that John Henley had been elected captain of the Guards to replace Armistead. Throughout the sultry summer months, drill slackened, but in early September new volunteers, including Dr. Waller's grandson Thomas Hugh Mercer, revived the training pace. On Saturday afternoon, 8 September, Mercer Waller attended a muster in upper James City County at Burnt Ordinary, about twelve miles west of Williamsburg, and that evening Tommy Mercer drilled in town. For the rest of the month and early October, the volunteers, some seventy-odd by Sergeant

6. *WWG*, 26 Oct., 16 Nov. 1859.

7. Ibid., 16, 23 Nov., 7 Dec. 1859; Les Jensen, *32nd Virginia Infantry* (Lynchburg: H. E. Howard, 1990), 6; Waller Diary, 21 Jan. 1860.

8. *WWG*, 25 Jan., 18, 25 Apr., 16, 23, 30 May, 20 June 1860; Waller Diary, 16, 20 Feb., 20 June, 8 Sept., 17 Oct. 1860.

Lively's count, drilled at least three times a week, then declared themselves ready to display their new martial talents. They set the parade date for 19 October. "We sincerely hope they may have a good time," the *Gazette* editorialized, "as it will be their first effort in public."[9]

Of more critical importance at this time was the presidential election coming up in less than three weeks. The North's Republican Party united behind Abraham Lincoln, but throughout the country Democrats had split into two factions, and a third party added further confusion. The Constitutional Union Party's presidential candidate, John Bell, enjoyed the support of many in Williamsburg, though the *Gazette* endorsed Democrat John C. Breckinridge, nominated by Virginia and most of the South. The northern Democratic nominee, Stephen A. Douglas, was generally unpopular among Williamsburg's electorate, numbering just over 120. Only eccentric Albert Gallatin Southall, a close family friend of former president John Tyler, enthusiastically supported him. "Mr. Douglas is the beau-ideal of a democrat in the eyes of Mr. Southall," editor Lively scoffed in September, "but after the 6th of November Douglas will be more of the ideal than anything else." At a political discussion described in the 3 October *Gazette*, "Mr. Southall was so entertaining, and the people wanted to hear him so much, that candles were procured, and he did not conclude until a late hour."[10]

A violent storm forced the Guards to cancel their 19 October parade, as Lively reported in the next *Gazette* before suspending publication indefinitely. Drill immediately resumed the last week of October but took a day off for the presidential election on 6 November—"*The great important day to our country's Institutions,*" Dr. Waller emphasized. The next day the company managed to hold a drill and two more the following week, with a public parade scheduled for 14 November. On Friday night, 16 November, Captain Henley found an anonymous note dropped at his door, Dr. Waller recorded in his diary, "warning them of an insurrection, to *kill* & *destroy* & *burn the town*" the next night. Henley promptly called an emergency meeting of the volunteers Saturday afternoon to form a guard for Williamsburg. To the relief of all, nothing came of the threat. Nevertheless, Dr. Waller received a letter three days later from his son-in-law, Dr. William Morris of Lynchburg, "upon the Subject of sending his Negroes to the South & advising me to do the same on account of the times from Lincoln's election." Reputedly the largest slaveholder in Williams-

9. *WWG*, 11 July, 17 Oct. 1860; Waller Diary, 7–8, 10–12, 16–18, 26, 29 Sept., 2, 4, 17 Oct. 1860.

10. *WWG*, 15 Aug., 12 Sept., 3 Oct. 1860.

burg, Dr. Waller no doubt considered this advice carefully. He had a tendency to worry anyway, exacerbated by a chronic derangement of his nervous system that had caused him great mental and physical suffering for several years. Another parade of volunteers passing his door on the afternoon of 1 December did little to calm his fears.[11]

During the final month of 1860, events began to accelerate. On 20 December South Carolina seceded from the Union. "God only knows what is to be—I hope for the best; and have every faith in a Southern republic," wrote Williamsburg attorney William S. Peachy on New Years Day, 1861, expressing a common feeling among his neighbors. "The first step has been taken by Noble little South Carolina. It is acknowledged that the South has been wronged. Can it be too soon to have an acknowledged wrong redressed? Can it be too soon to have our rights?" President James Buchanan proclaimed 4 January 1861 as "a day of Fasting, Humiliation & Prayer," Dr. Waller noted in his diary, "on account of the horrible situation of our Government induced by the Villainy of the Fanatics of the North urged on by the selfish Villainy of Northern Politicians." In quick succession, Florida, Alabama, Georgia, Louisiana, and Texas seceded. On 11 January a neighbor of Dr. Waller brought up the idea of organizing a mounted home guard, and the following day, the Guards again paraded through the streets of Williamsburg. The next Saturday they held another parade followed by a political meeting. One more political meeting of candidates for the upcoming state secession convention took place on 26 January. On 4 February, the same day southern delegates met in Montgomery, Alabama, to form a new government for the seceded states, Williamsburg held an election of delegates for Virginia's secession convention set to begin 13 February in Richmond. As the speeches and debates unfolded at this convention, Dr. Waller and his fellow townsmen hung on every word reported in the *Richmond Dispatch*, which also printed messages delivered by both new presidents. On 19 February Dr. Waller read "Lincoln's miserable meagre speech at Cleaveland on his way to Washington, then Jefferson Davis's fine speech (Inaugural) at Montgomery Alabama." Meanwhile, the Junior Guards continued to drill.[12]

Not wanting to be left out of the excitement, thirty-five of William and Mary's seventy students petitioned the faculty on 8 January for a military com-

11. *WWG*, 2 Sept., 24 Oct. 1860; Waller Diary, 22–24 Oct., 6, 7, 11–14, 17, 20 Nov., 1 Dec. 1860.

12. William S. Peachy to Tazewell Taylor, 1 Jan. 1861, WCP, MR-CWM; Waller Diary, 4, 11–12, 19, 26 Jan., 4, 14, 16, 19, 26 Feb. 1861.

pany "to be composed of those connected with the College." They obtained permission, though not all professors sympathized with secession. The college's president, Benjamin Stoddert Ewell, affectionately known as "Old Buck," came from a distinguished but impoverished old Virginia family and had graduated from the U.S. Military Academy at West Point. Despite Ewell's strong Unionist sentiments, the company elected him captain. Several local boys in the student body, including Judge Beverley Tucker's son Thomas Smith Beverley Tucker and William Peachy's son, who had not yet joined the Guards, became involved in the college company. Most, however, were out-of-towners like Richard Wise, son of Virginia's former governor Henry Wise. On 9 January Richard wrote his father that the company was raised "merely to train the students while here," but once the fighting started, Richard intended going home to serve under his father. The boys chose a modest uniform of red flannel shirt, homespun pantaloons, and fatigue cap and armed themselves with little more than bowie knives and some outdated double-barreled shotguns or rifles. According to student William Reynolds of Baltimore, a cousin of Ewell, the company never advanced past its first meeting, and "it was the general impression among the students that President Ewell had got himself appointed captain for the express purpose of preventing the company from ever being organized."[13]

Ewell's Unionist leanings were further heralded in February when he selected Reynolds to deliver the traditional Washington's Birthday oration. With the advice and encouragement of Ewell, Reynolds "denounced secession and made a strong appeal for the preservation of the Union." Ewell and several other professors believed secession "unnecessary & inexpedient" yet advocated "the necessity of providing the State in every quarter with the best means of defence, and of educating her sons to that duty." On 5 March the faculty delegated Ewell to request of Virginia's governor, John Letcher, "the loan of two Brass Field guns, with suitable carriages, caissons, accoutrements & ammunition" to drill the college company.[14]

Drill had become more frequent for the Guards, who celebrated Washington's Birthday with another parade through the streets of Williamsburg and trained twice more during the next week for their 2 March trek up Richmond Road to Burnt Ordinary. There they paraded again with companies from New

13. Faculty Minutes, 8 Jan. 1861, UA-CWM; Richard A. Wise to Henry A. Wise, 9 Jan. 1861, William and Mary College Papers, UA-CWM; William Reynolds Deposition, 27 Feb. 1872, Presidents' Papers–BSE, UA-CWM.
14. William Reynolds Deposition, 27 Feb. 1872; BSE, "Autobiography," Presidents' Papers–BSE; Faculty Minutes, 5 Mar. 1861, UA-CWM.

Kent and James City Counties. Two days later Dr. Waller moaned in his diary: *"Dark day for our country Lincoln inaugurated."* Williamsburg residents now feared that "our Villainous President" would replace the town's postmaster with "some Villainous Yankee," and elderly Dr. Samuel Stuart Griffin circulated a petition to prevent such an outrage. On 28 March Dr. Waller reluctantly signed it, fervently hoping "that in a few days, Secession will place us in a different position with the present United States government." He soon had his wish, for on 13 April the U.S. Army surrendered to southern forces at Fort Sumter in Charleston Harbor, South Carolina. Three days later President Lincoln called for 75,000 militia to quell the insurrection and requested permission for them to traverse Virginia. On the seventeenth, Richmond's state convention passed an ordinance of secession, subject to a 23 May vote by the people. Most considered that a mere formality as, once again, Williamsburg embarked on a precarious quest for independence.[15]

15. Waller Diary, 22 Feb., 2, 4, 28 Mar. 1861.

PART 1

Confederate Williamsburg

CHAPTER 1

A Line of Defense

Though Williamsburg lay only fifty miles southeast of Richmond, roads on the Peninsula were so poor that most travelers preferred the speed and comfort of the river route. Side-wheel steamboats regularly plying the James River connected Williamsburg directly with both Richmond and Norfolk. An alternate route between Virginia's old and new capitals used the newly completed York River Railroad from Richmond to the York River, where boats met the cars and continued the trip down to a wharf called Bigler's north of Williamsburg. Those navigating the torturous curves of the James downriver from Richmond had the choice of Jamestown, Kingsmill, or Grove Wharfs servicing Williamsburg. Either way the trip could be made in just three or four hours, and one of these boats probably brought Williamsburg news of the secession vote on 17 April 1861.

The next day, 18 April, students zealous to hoist a secession flag at the college, forbidden until now, put the banner on a pole in the college yard (to prevent damage to the main building's new slate roof). Williamsburg physician Charles Washington Coleman attended this flag-raising event with his sister, bewailing "the destracted condition of our poor, poor Country," where "anarchy rules." Still a bachelor in his early thirties, Dr. Coleman lived with his sister and his mother, Mrs. Catherine Coleman, on the Palace grounds in a brick building that had survived the Palace's burning and had been converted into a private home. As a member of Williamsburg's new mounted home guard, on 24 April he wrote, "We have visited several Yankee encampments or rather settlements in the neighborhood, and have advised them to leave immediately." The ousted northerners could move to Fort Monroe, the closest federally held post, about forty miles southeast of Williamsburg on the tip of the Peninsula. The Williamsburg troopers had also been called down to Yorktown, twelve miles east of Williamsburg, when three U.S. vessels were said to have appeared in the mouth of the York River on the twenty-second. Just before starting they learned it was a false alarm. "There are a thousand and one rumors afloat," Dr. Coleman noted. "By going on the street, you can be enlightened on any doubtful subject." In the excitement of preparing for war, Williamsburg had "many gallant spirits eager for the fray."[1]

Among these eager spirits was Lucy Anne Tucker, widow of Judge Beverley Tucker, and her strikingly beautiful twenty-nine-year-old daughter, Cynthia Beverley Tucker Washington—widow of Henry Washington, a former William and Mary history professor and kinsman of George Washington. During the secession vote Cynthia was visiting Richmond with her brother Tom and younger sisters, Frances Bland Beverley, called Bland, and Henrietta Elizabeth Beverley, shortened to Zettie. Cynthia's efforts to have her father's novel *Partisan Leader* republished failed with excitement over secession running so high. "Now we are going to have war sure enough," she predicted in an 18 April letter to her five-year-old daughter, Sarah Augustine "Sadie" Washington, "and you must get your gun ready, for the Yankees will be down upon us very soon."[2]

Cynthia's mother was already preparing weapons. On 19 April Lucy assured Cynthia that she was "*anxious* but not in the least fearful & if need be will prepare Tom to do battle for Virginia & wish as your Father said that the sword of his brave grand Father could accompany him to the battle field that he might wield it in her cause." Whether she meant Tom's paternal grandfather, St. George Tucker, who served in the Revolutionary War, or maternal grandfather, Gen. Thomas Smith, a distinguished War of 1812 officer, Tom would have to find another unit in which to wield his sword. As soon as Virginia seceded, the college company began to melt away, each student leaving to join his hometown unit. Richard Wise returned to his father, soon to be appointed a brigadier general, and volunteered as his aide-de-camp. Several of the seventeen students from Williamsburg or James City County, along with their young Latin professor, Edwin Taliaferro, joined the Williamsburg Junior Guards and were mustered into Confederate service on 28 April. Col. Robert H. Armistead's son, Robert Travis Armistead, later related that he quit college at the age of seventeen to enlist on 18 April in the Old Dominion Dragoons,

1. William Reynolds Deposition, 27 Feb. 1872, Presidents' Papers–BSE, UA-CWM; CWC to CBT, 18, 24 Apr. 1861, TCP, MR-CWM.
2. CBT to Sarah A. Washington, 18 Apr. 1861, TCP; CBT to James Barron Hope, n.d., TCP.

a cavalry company forming in neighboring Elizabeth City County. Eventually, the entire student body enlisted except two: William Reynolds returned to Baltimore and Thomas Russell Bowden, son of lawyer Lemuel Jackson Bowden, stuck with his father in one of the few Williamsburg families steadfastly opposing secession. Lemuel's mother, Mildred Bowden, alone in the family chose a secessionist stand. Refusing to live with her "Virginia Yankee" son, she moved out of the brick Greek revival mansion he had recently built next to Bruton Church on Main Street and into a small frame cottage in the backyard. As for the Unionist professors, Benjamin Stoddert Ewell later confessed, "when active war waged, resistance became a question of self defense & all whatever were their views united to defend the[ir] homes and firesides, their people & state." On 4 May he received an appointment as major of volunteers for the Peninsula in command of the Williamsburg Junior Guards.[3]

On the same day as Ewell's commission, the Junior Guards received their first official assignment. Federal gunboats had been making forays up both the York and James Rivers, probing the two water avenues to the Confederacy's soon-to-be capital at Richmond. The day before, one fired on a section of the Richmond Howitzers under Lt. John Thompson Brown stationed at Gloucester Point across the York River from Yorktown. The Howitzers drove off the boat, but Brown sent a dispatch to Ewell requesting an infantry force to support his guns. This was asking much of Williamsburg's little company, now numbering only forty-three men rank and file. Yet Ewell "immediately responded by dividing my force into three corps," he later recalled, "sending the first corps under Captain Henley, to the aid of Lieutenant Brown." Edward Lively related that at this early stage in the war, the "servant of each valliant soldier was called on to tote the luggage of his young master." As the heroes started off, their "parents had the old carriages and wagons hauled out and they followed with all the necessary articles of extra clothing, food, &c., not forgetting the lint, splints, salve, &c., always looking for a sharp encounter and the possibility of some one getting hurt. Their mothers had offered them as a sacrifice upon the altar of their Southern country home and fireside, with

3. LAT to CBT, 19 Apr. 1861, TCP; John S. Wise, *End of an Era* (Boston, Houghton Mifflin, 1899), 165; Jensen, *32nd Virginia Infantry*, 6; R. T. Armistead to M. H. Barnes, 7 Dec. 1897, Armistead Papers, MR-CWM; William Reynolds Deposition, 27 Feb. 1872, BSE, "Autobiography," Presidents' Papers–BSE; Parke Rouse Jr., *Cows on the Campus: Williamsburg in Bygone Days* (Richmond: Dietz Press, 1973), 59–60; Victoria King Lee, "Williamsburg in 1861," 1933, John D. Rockefeller Jr. Library, CWF, 19; H. F. Flournoy, ed., *Calendar of Virginia State Papers and Other Manuscripts from January 1, 1836, to April 15, 1869*, 11 vols. (Richmond, 1893), 11:114, 120.

the injunction of the Spartan to return with their shield or on it." These Junior Guards returned with their shields instead of on them, as no more attacks were made on Brown's guns.[4]

While Ewell retained a third corps of Guards in Williamsburg, the second corps set off in the opposite direction. A Federal gunboat had fired on a steamboat near Jamestown Island, where fortifications were being built. Lt. Catesby ap Roger Jones of the Confederate navy, in charge of the island, immediately asked Ewell to send some infantry protection. The major replied on 4 May that he was unable "to send a force sufficient to protect the battery you are erecting," but to "reassure the workmen and thus hasten the construction, a detachment of the Junior Guard is under orders to proceed at once to the island." Seventeen boys set out, arriving at Jamestown Island the evening of 4 May, "without artillery," grumbled Jones. Somehow they had also neglected to bring along rations. After one full day of reassuring the workmen, the seventeen headed back home, "leaving the guns entirely unprotected," Jones complained. The commander of Virginia forces, Maj. Gen. Robert E. Lee, authorized Jones to request two more companies from Ewell on 6 May. Jones did, thanking Ewell "to make the necessary arrangements for subsisting them, as we are entirely without provisions." The navy lieutenant later confided to his superior that "I do not expect to obtain them, as his command are somewhere on York River."[5]

General Lee's impression that Ewell had two companies to send Jones must have been wishful thinking. Since the first of May, Lee had been instructing Ewell to muster six more companies from James City and adjacent counties, a difficult assignment at first, as volunteers came slowly. But recruiting soon picked up, and on 13 May Ewell reported to Lee that he expected to have five or six companies numbering at least twelve hundred men mustered into service by the end of the week. He now needed muskets, rifles, field pieces, horses, and rations to arm and supply these troops. Several cadets, a drummer, fifer, and bugler to train them would also be useful, for, Ewell argued, the recruits were "raw—as much so as possible." Although many of the Junior Guards had been drilling for a year and a half, "their discipline is as imperfect as might by expected, and must remain so until they have been subjected to the discipline and routine of a camp." Ewell had already begun setting up the necessary bivouac, christened "Camp Page," on a field just southwest of Williamsburg on

4. *ORN*, 6:668–9; BSE, "Magruder Reminiscence," EFP, MR-CWM; [E. H. Lively], "Williamsburg Junior Guards," *Southern Historical Society Papers* 18 (1890): 276.

5. *ORN*, 6:669–701.

College Landing Road and was erecting ingenious plank huts on wheels that could be moved from place to place. That temporarily solved one problem, but on 16 May he had over eight hundred volunteers, less than half of them armed, and still no cadets. Four days later Lee informed Ewell, now promoted to lieutenant colonel and given command of the entire lower end of the Peninsula, that he was sending four hundred percussion muskets with ammunition to Kingsmill Wharf on the James River four miles south of Williamsburg. No cadets or musicians, however, were available.[6]

A greater concern to Lee and an even bigger headache for Ewell was the defensive line of earthworks Lee ordered him to build across the Peninsula at Williamsburg to protect this overland route to Richmond. A mathematics professor and former railroad engineer, Ewell had already begun to plan such a line using the area's natural topography. Williamsburg stood about four miles from both the York and James Rivers on a broad plateau deeply cut by ravines reaching toward the outskirts of town like fingers. Tributaries of Queens Creek and College Creek flowing into the York and James, respectively, formed these ravines and left a narrow passage, "the only roads through which were the streets of Williamsburg," Ewell later wrote. Any army marching up the Peninsula from Fort Monroe to Richmond would be forced to traverse these streets. To guard all land access to Williamsburg from the east, Ewell decided to anchor the line's right a mile and a quarter southeast of town on Quarterpath Trace at Tutters Neck, which heads a tributary of College Creek. For the left of the line he chose Capitol Landing Bridge, standing a mile and a half north of town and passing over Queens Creek. The main central work Ewell intended to place "on a commanding position" just east of town overlooking the York Road as it curved down a gentle slope to a fork, which led to Yorktown on the left and Warwick Court House, Newport News, and Hampton on the right. This in Ewell's mind constituted "the strategic point on the Peninsula for defensive purposes in land operations," and he wasted no time in setting his adjunct mathematics professor, Thomas T. L. Snead, to work surveying it.[7]

Ewell was now so busy with military matters that he had little time to devote to the college, which had been "dragging along with a very few students," according to Robert Saunders. Living off of his extensive plantations on Queens

6. BSE to Col. George Deas, 6 July 1861, EFP; *OR,* 51(2): 88, 2:833, 854, 858–9; Robert Saunders to R. L. P. Saunders, 13 May 1861, PSP, MR-CWM; Jensen, *32nd Virginia Infantry,* 9.

7. *OR,* 51(2):174; BSE, "Magruder Reminiscence."

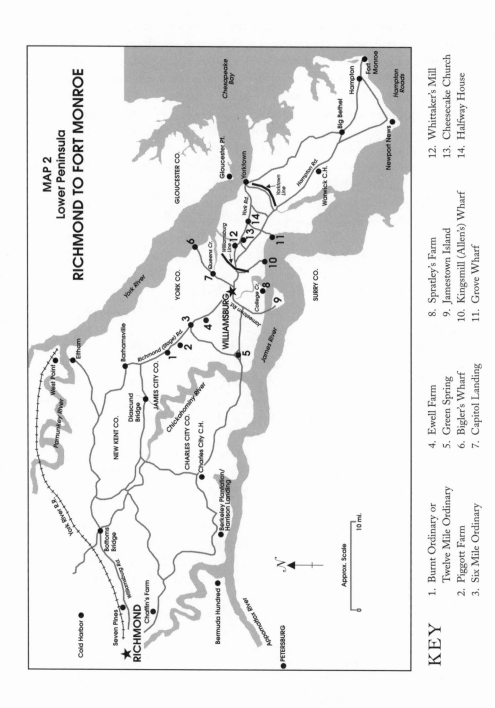

MAP 2
Lower Peninsula
RICHMOND TO FORT MONROE

KEY

1. Burnt Ordinary or Twelve Mile Ordinary
2. Piggott Farm
3. Six Mile Ordinary
4. Ewell Farm
5. Green Spring
6. Bigler's Wharf
7. Capitol Landing
8. Spratley's Farm
9. Jamestown Island
10. Kingsmill (Allen's) Wharf
11. Grove Wharf
12. Whittaker's Mill
13. Cheesecake Church
14. Halfway House

Creek and York River, Saunders had served as magistrate and mayor of Williamsburg, three-term senator in the state legislature, president of the Lunatic Asylum, and president of the York River Railroad. He had attended William and Mary and later was appointed mathematics professor and interim president of the college. On 13 May Saunders wrote his sixteen-year-old son, Bob, away at boarding school, that in Williamsburg "you would merely be idle as most of the boys are and would lose irrecoverable time in receiving that instruction which will render you of more service to your country than merely your body & limbs could afford, which would be very little at your age." Besides, he argued, "there is an abundance of men; what is chiefly required now is *brains*." Only a few local students remained in class at William and Mary, and they were "unable from the excited state of the public mind to pursue their collegiate duties with profit." Thus, on 10 May the faculty voted to suspend all classes, optimistically scheduled to resume in October. The college records and keys were entrusted to the history professor, Robert Morrison, with instructions to superintend the buildings and property of the college from his nearby home in the Old Steward's House and to provide for the safety of the library and apparatus in case of emergency. On 11 May William and Mary closed its doors.[8]

With these collegiate responsibilities off his shoulders, Ewell could focus on his military troubles, which were just beginning. The day after the college shut down, a young engineering officer named Alfred M. Rives showed up along with Richard K. Meade, both sent to Williamsburg by General Lee "to locate and construct the necessary works." Ewell and Rives immediately began to argue. Rives complained that although Ewell had nearly two weeks to work on the line, nothing had been done and no definite points of defense had been selected other than Ewell's estimation that "the lines should rest on Queen's and College Creeks, passing somewhere near Williamsburg." The position that Rives planned retained Tutters Neck on the right but rested the left on Jones Pond, which fed Cub Creek, a tributary of Queens Creek, two and a half miles east of Capitol Landing Bridge. He advanced the central work a mile and a half from town along the York Road almost to its fork, an area known locally as Vineyard Tract, on a section of land belonging to Dr. Waller. Although this line was strategically more sound, Ewell objected that it had been unnecessarily lengthened. All his protests were to no avail, however, as field officers were obliged to yield to engineers in such matters.[9]

8. Robert Saunders to R. L. P. Saunders, 13 May 1861; Mary A. Stephenson, "Robert Carter House Historical Report, Block 30-2, Building 13 Lot 333, 334, 335, 336," John D. Rockefeller Jr. Library, CWF; Faculty Minutes, 10 May 1861, UA-CWM.

9. BSE, "Magruder Reminiscence"; *OR*, 51(2):174–5.

A longer line required more laborers to build, which became another contentious point between the two officers. Rives asserted that for three weeks "Ewell placed scarcely any labor at my disposal, and that consequently scarcely any progress was made." On 25 May Lee still had not heard whether the fortifications were commenced, considering them "of great importance" and reminding Ewell that "no time should be lost in completing these works." Suspecting the work force was insufficient, Lee asked him to report its size and "whether you cannot increase it from the neighboring country." Shortly thereafter, Ewell drafted a circular to the citizens of James City, York, and Warwick Counties informing them that "considerable amount of labor is required immediately—most especially for the country between Williamsburg, Yorktown, & the Grove Wharf. Citizens of those counties living above the line from Yorktown to the former are required to send by the 1st of next week the full quota that can be spared from their farms." Not only slaves must come, but furthermore the "Civil officers will notify the ablebodied Free negroes within the above limits that they are to assist in these works of defence, and that a failure to attend will be visited by a severe penalty." They were to report to Captains Rives and Meade or Professor Snead just below Williamsburg, and more axes, "Spades, & Hoes will be wanted."[10]

Ewell's brief tenure as commander of the Peninsula had already terminated on 24 May, when the newly commissioned colonel John Bankhead Magruder steamed down York River and arrived in Yorktown. Ewell had first met him at West Point in 1828, and since his graduation two years later, Magruder had seen service on the frontier, in the Seminole Wars in Florida, and during the Mexican War, where he won two brevets. Known as "Prince John" for his courtly manners, wig, and dyed mustache, Magruder also had a love for lavish entertaining and a talent for theatrics. Even before disembarking at Yorktown, he was sending dramatic dispatches back to Richmond urgently requesting more troops. He particularly needed four cavalry companies to meet the 2,500 Federals he just heard had invaded Hampton near the tip of the Peninsula. Lee answered promptly the next day by express steamer that his records showed Magruder already had three cavalry troops but that he would order down five more. Four artillery pieces were also on their way down to be used at Yorktown or Williamsburg, where "Colonel Ewell had better be directed to apply all the force he can procure to the erection of those lines." As for the

10. *OR*, 51(2):175, 2:875; BSE, "Magruder Reminiscence"; BSE, "Circular to the Citizens of James City, York, & Warwick Counties," n.d., EFP.

Federal threat at Fort Monroe, Lee did not believe any cavalry had come there or that Magruder faced any immediate danger of an infantry advance.[11]

Actually, more than three thousand blue-clad soldiers were now ensconced at the tip of the Peninsula, many coming shortly after the 22 May arrival of Fort Monroe's new commander, Maj. Gen. Benjamin Franklin Butler, a Massachusetts lawyer and politician. Until then, Union forces at Old Point had been peaceful, even amiable, as Ewell found out during a 14 May visit. But now Butler declared any slaves seeking sanctuary in the fort "contraband of war," and his troops started making threatening moves upon Hampton. When Ewell rode down on 24 May to investigate these developments, he was "unceremoniously dealt with; was taken prisoner and marched into the fort." Quickly released, Ewell hurried back to Williamsburg, where he still commanded the post, to greet a welcome addition to his work force.[12]

On the Friday night of 24 May, Col. Thomas P. August's 3d Virginia (soon to be redesignated the 15th Virginia Regiment) arrived at Kingsmill Wharf after steaming downriver from Richmond. The regiment, except two companies left at Kingsmill to guard the baggage, proceeded directly to Williamsburg. Soon waving over August's commissary department was a "Southern Flag" first raised by editor Lively over the *Gazette* office on 23 May, "the day on which Virginia by the sovereign vote of her Citizens Ratified the ordinance of Secession." The officers found lodgings in the City Hotel, boardinghouses, and private homes, while the men bedded down in the deserted halls of William and Mary. There, one soldier later reminisced, "we certainly rubbed our heads against its honored walls and slept upon its carpeted floors," and, since his company was assigned the library, "I selected some of my favorite authors for a pillow." On Saturday, their first evening in town, the regiment had a dress parade. "Everybody in Wmsburg came to see it, they even closed their stores," a private wrote home. Sunday evening, the two companies that had just come in from Kingsmill held another parade, after which the men sampled the city's feminine society with fervor.[13]

Monday morning, 26 May, they set to work somewhat less enthusiastically

11. *OR*, 2: 36–7, 865, 876; BSE, "Magruder Reminiscence"; Mark Mayo Boatner III, *The Civil War Dictionary*, rev. ed. (New York: David McKay, 1988), 501.

12. *OR*, 2:643, 648–51, 870.

13. Lively, "Southern Flag!" 30 June 1861, *Williamsburg Gazette* microfilm, CWM; Thomas Alfriend to Frank Alfriend, 26 May 1861, Thomas L. Alfriend Papers, MR-CWM; J. Staunton Moore, *An Address Delivered by J. Staunton Moore at the 50th Re-union of the Fifteenth Virginia Regiment at Williamsburg, Virginia, May 24, 1911* (n.p., n.d.), 3–5.

with shovel and pick in throwing up breastworks for the central earthwork already underway at Vineyard Tract. "Our hands were soon covered with blisters," a Virginia soldier later recounted, "and the perspiration exuded freely from our unaccustomed labors." Magruder reported to Lee the next day that he left August's command, consisting of between 600 and 700 men, at Williamsburg because Ewell had only 180 under him and "Williamsburg was very much exposed." Per Lee's instructions, Magruder directed Ewell to employ all his officers as well as men as laborers on the defenses. Magruder sent one company to Yorktown on 29 May despite such a shortage of shoes that August complained to Richmond that many of his men "are now barefooted, and unfitted for service." The same day Ewell reported to Lee that about five hundred hands, "including a part of the volunteer force, are at work." One very important earthwork was "progressing rapidly," he assured the commanding general, but "as to their state of forwardness, the works have not yet been fully planned by the engineers." More troops, "sufficient to repel a serious attack," were necessary to fill them, Ewell stressed to Lee. In another communication that day to Magruder, Ewell promised, "these defenses will be pushed forward with all possible dispatch," but added, "unless artillery is furnished to defend them with, I fear they will avail but little." Ewell needed a minimum of two batteries of light artillery, for "now there is not a piece." Magruder seconded the suggestion as he passed it on to Richmond, requesting at the same time at least two more infantry regiments for Williamsburg. He also wanted a quartermaster stationed there as the main depot for the Peninsula.[14]

Ewell already had someone in mind for this post. Robert Saunders had been lending his horse and buggy to Rives and Meade, and some nights he stayed up until 2:00 A.M. writing business letters for friends and rendering the government "unofficial assistance." So efficient was Saunders that Ewell wrote Lee requesting his appointment as district quartermaster, for he was "better qualified than anyone else I know." Professor Snead likewise received Ewell's recommendation for a position in the civil engineering department due to his surveying experience and service to Rives. In desperate need of a staff, Ewell asked Lee on 21 May for permission to appoint Edwin Taliaferro his adjutant, for though he was still in the ranks, the Latin professor "has great intelligence, is firm and cool, has industry and activity, and is to be depended upon." Lee replied that no matter how talented he was, Taliaferro could not be promoted to adjutant from the ranks but must first be elected lieutenant. At the same

14. Moore, *Address*, 3–5; Thomas Alfriend to father, 2 June 1861, Alfriend Papers; Thomas August to R. S. Garnett, 29 May 1861, Chronology File, UA-CWM; *OR*, 2:886, 891–4, 900.

time, Cynthia Washington was trying to obtain commissions for her brothers by writing on 21 May to one of her father's old admirers, Jefferson Davis. A week later Tom Tucker was nominated for a second lieutenancy in the provisional army, and on 6 June President Davis graciously favored Cynthia with a personal note in reply, suggesting her elder brother, Dr. Beverley St. George Tucker, should "make application in writing for the position he desires."[15]

Communications from the Confederate high command honored other Williamsburg citizens as well. The superintendent of the asylum, Dr. John Minson Galt II, a forty-one-year-old bachelor, and his maiden sister Sarah Maria or Sally, three years his junior, received requests from both Lee and Magruder near the end of May for a copy of the Yorktown battlefield map that belonged to the Galts' grandfather, chief surgeon of Virginia forces under George Washington. "They say it is of unestimable value to them," Sally boasted to a cousin on 30 May, since it "is the only copy extant." She was gratified to note that except for a few runaways in Hampton, "the servants seem to be thus far as much opposed to the enemy as we are" and most "seem anxious to fight for their masters and seem faithful." Sally's time was primarily occupied with keeping track of soldiers "coming in and going out of the house all day as we have many of the officers staying with us" in the Superintendent's House across the street from the asylum. She reckoned she had given out about one thousand asylum visitor permits to the "many thousand soldiers" passing through Williamsburg on their way to Yorktown; "so well behaved a crowd I never saw."[16]

If Williamsburg was not already crowded enough, a few hundred more unexpected guests showed up in the middle of a late-May night. Magruder in Yorktown on the twenty-seventh reported, "women and children have been passing here all day from Hampton." The next morning Williamsburg people awoke to find their Hampton neighbors camped on Courthouse Green, fleeing from Butler's Union troops and carrying little more than the clothes they wore and a few household articles. Wrote Sally Galt on the thirtieth, "I can assure you every door was open to them." The Galts received as many as they could into the Superintendent's House and rented out their family home at the eastern end of town to others. Many more found shelter in other private homes and in the college buildings. Some of these refugees did not feel so welcome, for "with the exception of a few families, the people of Williamsburg

15. Robert Saunders to R. L. P. Saunders, 13 May 1861; *OR*, 2:854, 859, 862, 875; Jefferson Davis to CBT, 6 June 1861, TCP; Flournoy, *Virginia State Papers*, 11:145.
16. SMG to cousin, 30 May 1861, GFP, MR-CWM.

seemed to think we were intruders, and they would have to support us," one asserted. "They showed very little sympathy for our condition." The enemy was still too close for many, prompting them as well as some Williamsburg residents to move on to Richmond and points west.[17]

Among the Hampton refugees who decided to stay in Williamsburg was the family of Dr. John C. King. Upon arriving in town the Kings boarded in a roomy former tavern on Main Street where the Baptist preacher William Young's family lived and Mrs. Young ran a school before the war. Dr. King's daughter Victoria, just entering her sixteenth summer, thought Main Street resembled a country road. Mulberry trees grew along the edge, casting dense shadows and jutting out roots into the footpaths, making "it difficult to walk along the paths after dark." Victoria later recounted how "grass grew from the edge of these paths almost to the center of the street; cows grazed along the street as they pleased, and sometimes the passage of a carriage was delayed while a drove of pigs ran from a mud-puddle in the road." Mud holes that turned into quagmires after heavy rains posed a constant problem for Williamsburg, though every spring slaves plowed up the sides of the street and dragged the dirt to the center. One particularly persistent hole on Richmond Road near the college bred prodigious crops of frogs to entertain patrons of the adjacent Frog Pond Tavern. During the dry season the mud turned into choking dust, coating buildings, vegetation, and animals. The recent addition of a multitude of boots, hooves, and wagon wheels did little to improve these road conditions.[18]

A potentially more serious problem attending Williamsburg's overcrowding was disease. This was early recognized by Letitia Tyler Semple, daughter of President John Tyler and wife of James A. Semple, a U.S. Navy paymaster who had recently transferred to the C.S. Navy. On her way south from New York on the first of May, Letitia stopped in Richmond and with her father's help obtained permission from the secretary of war to establish a hospital in Williamsburg. She had resided off and on in another Palace building facing the Colemans' residence. Upon arriving in Williamsburg she set about transforming the Female Academy, built in 1850 on the site of the colonial capitol, into a hospital with Benjamin Ewell's encouragement and assistance, "making

17. Ibid.; *OR*, 2:886; Lee, "Williamsburg in 1861," 1, 8, 11, 13; George Benjamin West, *When the Yankees Came: Civil War and Reconstruction on the Virginia Peninsula*, ed. Parke Rouse Jr. (Richmond: Dietz Press, 1977), 65.

18. Lee, "Williamsburg in 1861," 2, 13; John S. Charles, "Recollections of Williamsburg, Virginia, as It Was at the Beginning of the Civil War," 1928, John D. Rockefeller Jr. Library, CWF, 65.

the first bed with her own hands." In the words of one observer, "Mrs. Semple's appeal to the ladies of Williamsburg was heartily responded to." With Sally Galt among the ranks, they soon had seventy-five cots to receive the first patients.[19]

The Academy Hospital, one of the Confederacy's earliest, was ready just in time for the war's first so-called battle, which took place on 10 June only a few miles southeast of Yorktown. Hearing rumors that slaves left in charge of Hampton farms were being abducted to work on Williamsburg and Yorktown entrenchments, Butler ordered an assault on Col. Daniel Harvey Hill's 1st North Carolina Volunteers, defending a church called Big Bethel. The Confederates, including Pvt. Bob Armistead in the Old Dominion Dragoons, repulsed their attackers with few casualties, none of whom were treated in the Academy Hospital, but the fight produced a sensation in Williamsburg. The day of 13 June was set apart for fasting and prayer, and Dr. Galt recorded in his diary that the Episcopal Rev. Mr. Thomas M. Ambler at Bruton Church "preached an excellent discourse" affecting, with some hyperbole, "the late battle at Bethel Church, as fully on a par with the Battle of Bunker's Hill." Two weeks after this skirmish, on 24 June, Williamsburg's mounted home guard, organized into the James City Cavalry in May, was mustered into Confederate service and sent down the Peninsula. Dr. Coleman, a private in the company, bade farewell to his mother, sister, and Cynthia Washington, to whom he had been engaged since January. Then off he rode to Yorktown, where the troop was stationed on picket duty the rest of June and into July.[20]

Cynthia's seventeen-year-old sister, Bland, was more fortunate. Her fiancé, Edwin Taliaferro, remained close to Williamsburg, having managed a lieutenancy and appointment as acting adjutant to Ewell. After General Lee inspected much of the defense line, including Tutters Neck, on 5 June and, according to Ewell, "approved of the general plan," Ewell put Taliaferro in charge of rounding up various supplies such as pickaxes and spades. Some he obtained from Dr. Galt and the asylum. These were needed by Ewell's work force, which varied somewhat in June due to Magruder's penchant for moving units from place to place. On the third Magruder reported that Ewell had only about four hundred men but was "to employ, or impress, if necessary, as many

19. Alice Trueheart Buck, "Founder of the First Confederate Hospital," *Confederate Veteran* 2 (1894): 141; Eliza Baker, "Memoirs of Williamsburg," 1933, John D. Rockefeller Jr. Library, CWF, 10; SMG to cousin, 30 May 1861.

20. Buck, "Founder," 141; *OR*, 2:77–8, 91–7; R. T. Armistead to M. H. Barnes, 7 Dec. 1897; John Minson Galt II Diary, 13 June 1861, GFP; James H. Allen, "The James City Cavalry: Its Organization and Its First Service," *Southern Historical Society Papers* 24 (1896): 357.

negroes as he requires for this purpose." That same day Lee sent eight field guns to Jamestown, giving Ewell the responsibility of dragging them into the Williamsburg fortifications. The following week Dr. Galt mentioned in his diary that another Williamsburg company, the Lee Artillery, was hard at work with others throwing up fieldworks at Grove Wharf and on the low bluffs overlooking Kingsmill Wharf. Somehow, Colonel August's 15th Virginia Volunteers found time to entertain Williamsburg's citizenry with parades on Market Square.[21]

In mid-June the Lee Artillery, Peninsula Artillery, Junior Guards, and James City Cavalry became four of the ten local companies Magruder fashioned into a regiment called the Peninsula Guards, numbering some six hundred and placed under Lieutenant Colonel Ewell's command. Except for the cavalry, these men worked mostly on the Williamsburg line. The six hundred effectives of the 15th Virginia were now spread out digging gun emplacements, with one company on the Tutters Neck earthwork, four companies at Kingsmill, and four more at Grove Wharf. Colonel August stationed his last company about two miles upstream from Kingsmill between the mouth of College Creek and the eastern tip of Jamestown Island at Spratley's Farm. Between this farm and Grove Wharf, the shoreline curved, allowing a long-range columbiad an effective enfilading fire all along the shore. For these works, Magruder requested fifteen heavy guns as well as four or five more regiments. Seven of the eight cannon Lee sent on 3 June finally arrived at Spratley's Farm just as an alarming rumor of hostile troops landing at Grove Wharf reached Williamsburg on the nineteenth. The rumor proved false but did emphasize the vulnerability of an area with no completed defenses and only about a dozen soldiers to guard the town. It also elicited another plea from Magruder for more ammunition and, especially, more troops.[22]

On 23 June nine hundred Georgians marched into the earthworks below Williamsburg. These were the 10th Georgia Volunteers led by Col. Lafayette McLaws, a stout former regular-army captain who had graduated in West Point's outstanding 1842 class. He set up camp directly behind the large central redoubt under construction at Vineyard Tract, with the men pitching cotton tents or bunking twelve at a time in Ewell's mobile plank huts, which had been rolled from Camp Page to the entrenchments. Along with the huts came all of Ewell's men and Lively's "Southern Flag" from its third post over the

---

21. Jensen, *32nd Virginia Infantry*, 34; BSE, "Magruder Reminiscence"; Andrew Talcott Diary, 5 June 1861, Talcott Family Papers, VHS; Galt Diary, 12, 21 June 1861; *OR*, 2:900–3.

22. *OR*, 2:931–2; Jensen, *32nd Virginia Infantry*, 32; Galt Diary, 9, 19 June 1861.

headquarters tent at Camp Page. Within a couple days, so much disease had stricken the 10th Georgia's camp that another hospital was established in the college building primarily for the Georgians with Georgia surgeons. Dr. Galt contributed medicine from the asylum stock to treat the thirty cases of measles and mumps, while Sally donated such items as candles, tea, and arrowroot drinks. When staff surgeon Dr. George W. Millen gave him a tour of the facility on 25 June, Dr. Galt found that it contained only two mattresses. By the end of the month, Williamsburg ladies, who had been providing bedding and food for the Yorktown hospitals, began concentrating their energies on the new College Hospital.[23]

The final days of June also brought the organization of the peninsular troops into an official regiment, the 32d Virginia Volunteers, commanded by Ewell after his promotion to colonel on 27 June. He retained Taliaferro for his adjutant and for his regimental quartermaster acquired newly commissioned Capt. Thomas P. McCandlish, a Williamsburg native and instructor of ancient languages and mathematics in William and Mary's preparatory department. The James City Cavalry was not included in the regiment, but the Williamsburg Junior Guards became Company C, and the local artillery companies—Lee Artillery, James City Artillery, and Peninsula Artillery—were designated Companies G, H, and I, respectively. At this time John Henley received his commission as captain of Company C. His brother Leonard served as second lieutenant only a week before transferring to regimental assistant surgeon. Mercer Waller remained second lieutenant in Company C, with his nephew Tommy Mercer a private under him. Also enlisting as privates in the Guards were editor Lively and his brother. Totaling only 670 men in ten companies, all from the Peninsula, the 32d Virginia mustered into Confederate service on 1 July.[24]

Ewell now had his own regiment but had lost control over the defense line. Upon his arrival, McLaws assumed command of the entrenchments and of all forces in and around Williamsburg, including Kingsmill, Grove Wharf, and Spratley's Farm. His orders from Magruder stressed the need to "press the works forward with the utmost possible vigor" that "the defenses in the neighborhood of Williamsburg may be finished without further delay," strongly im-

23. Galt Diary, 22–25 June 1861; Jensen, *32nd Virginia Infantry*, 40; Ezra Warner, *Generals in Gray: Lives of the Confederate Commanders* (Baton Rouge: Louisiana State University Press, 1959), 204; LM to wife, 2 July 1861, LM Papers, Southern Historical Collection of the Manuscripts Department, Wilson Library, UNC; Lively, "Southern Flag!" 30 June 1861, *Williamsburg Gazette* microfilm.

24. Jensen, *32nd Virginia Infantry*, 32–40, 186, 192–4.

plying Magruder's displeasure with Ewell's execution of the job. Directed to "order all the troops to work on the trenches until they are completed," McLaws refused the men a day off even to celebrate the Fourth of July. "I did not wish to have anything in common with the enemy," he explained in a letter to his wife. Williamsburg also ignored the holiday, as Dr. Galt noted in his diary, "Not a gun ushered in this day, so often commemorated with all due ceremony, in this section of country." That evening, while taking his habitual walk to College Landing, Dr. Galt came across a Virginia cavalry troop camped in a fringe of woods beyond the new City Cemetery, about a half mile south of the asylum. He became mesmerized by the "picturesque affect" of "pale blue smoke from the camp fires" curling gracefully above white tents on a spreading lawn with the "deep verdure of the forest, interspersed with the blossoms of the chestnut," in the background. "The sinking sun in the west poured forth a flood of purple and gold; shedding a rich crimson glow over the attractive scene," rhapsodized Dr. Galt. "Notwithstanding the beauty of this landscape, so constant has been recently the influx of the soldiery, that I was the only one from town to view what would a few weeks ago, have called forth the whole population."[25]

As Dr. Galt implied, the war effort had absorbed the entire community. Merchants struggled in the face of the Union blockade to keep their shelves stocked for their booming business, as both soda fountains in town were drained by thirsty troops twice every day. Farmers sold their crops to the government. Many, including Dr. Galt, contributed what they could to aid destitute families of the Junior Guards and to furnish personal articles for convalescent patients at the College Hospital, which was so poorly supplied it had to continue borrowing medicines and other provisions from the asylum. That generous institution also donated its patients' cast-off clothing to needy troops, provided nitric acid for the preparation of percussion caps, converted its old unused buildings into a supply depot for army provender, and allowed army forage mules to graze in its backyard. On 20 July the asylum opened its doors to two soldiers from Louisiana diagnosed as insane. The twin towers on its Gothic Building, high enough to give a view of both the James and York Rivers, were considered "for the locality of telegraphic signals." When Dr. Waller's son-in-law Dr. William Morris, now president of the Southern Telegraph Company, needed a guide "to point out the localities, in relation to laying a telegraph from Richmond down this Peninsula," the asylum's assistant

25. LM to wife, 2, 8 July 1861, McLaws Papers; OR, 51(2):149; Galt Diary, 4 July 1861.

superintendent, Dr. John Galt Williamson, a cousin of Dr. Galt, accompanied him.[26]

Not even the asylum could compare contributions with the energetic Williamsburg ladies doing all they could for the troops. Cynthia Washington arranged "a regular conveyance to take suitable articles of diet, contributed by the benevolent and patriotic in Williamsburg to the sick and convalescent." Professor Morrison's wife sacrificed her wedding gown to fashion a blue and white silk regimental flag for the 15th Virginia, which she took into her heart while those ragged, barefoot boys camped near her home at the college. Others wielded needle and thread for the sick. By 5 July, Sally Galt had completed twenty-seven beds for the York and Williamsburg hospitals, but College Hospital surgeons called for more. During the 7 July Sunday morning service at Bruton Parish, an announcement was made "that a large number of beds were wanted *immediately.*" Thus, instead of attending the usual Sunday afternoon preaching, the church ladies set to work. The next day fifty beds and almost as many pillows had been prepared, but the patient count continued ahead of them. With eighty in the College Hospital by Wednesday, the ladies, dubbing themselves the "Working Society," had to sew through the week and beyond. They also made uniform pantaloons and jackets, tents, and standards. Among the society's hardworking members were Sally Galt, Catherine Coleman, and their president, Cynthia Washington, who declared, "I expect to be very accomplished by the time the War is over."[27]

When the townswomen were not sewing for the troops, they nursed them, either at the Academy or College Hospitals or in their homes. One soldier in the 10th Georgia enjoyed the special care given by Albert Southall's wife, Virginia, and their oldest daughter. "I am indebted to Miss Mary Southall of Williamsburg for the privilege of sending this letter to you," he informed his mother. "She is a sweet lady, and for the many favors extended me by herself and Mother I am under many obligations." Cynthia Washington preferred working as a missionary with the patients at the Academy Hospital, believing "a great deal of good might be done among the poor fellows, in reading to and praying with them." Though McLaws deplored the incompetence of male army nurses, he had nothing but praise for Williamsburg's dedicated ladies, who "are exceedingly kind to the sick, giving all kinds of delicacies indiscrimi-

26. Galt Diary, 1, 10–15, 20–24, 27–29 July, 5, 19 Aug. 1861.

27. Moore, *Address*, 11; Louis H. Manarin, *15th Virginia Infantry* (Lynchburg: H. E. Howard, 1990), 8; Galt Diary, 20 June, 4, 5, 8 July; CBT to CWC, 10, 14 July 1861, TCP; Susan Blain to President of Sewing Society, n.d., TCP.

nately, supplying quantities of bedding of all kinds, clothing of every description, and above all giving their constant *personal* attention." He was gratified to hear that "fifteen ladies at least were from time to time attending in person to the wants of the sick in our hospital alone."[28]

Despite these sewing and nursing duties, the ladies never failed to offer their famous Williamsburg hospitality. Most, except for one woman who callously remarked that she was more "apprehensive" of the Georgians than of the enemy, did their best to make their protectors feel welcome. They sent buckets of tomatoes, baskets of buttered biscuits, gallons of buttermilk, and bouquets of flowers to the camps. Belles took full advantage of this windfall of homesick potential beaux, who were grateful for any kindness shown them. Many ladies, including Sally Galt and Cynthia Washington, invited privates as well as officers into their historic old homes for dinner or tea. Early in July, Cynthia wrote Dr. Coleman in Yorktown that she had "formed the acquaintance of some pleasant Georgians" and on the whole thought "the Georgia Regiment is a very fine looking body of men." Before long, two off-duty officers called on her, the first of many entertained in the Tucker parlor that month. McLaws received numerous invitations to Williamsburg homes but was forced to decline due to his crushing schedule of constructing the defenses, commanding three regiments, and inspecting the College Hospital. He did, however, enjoy the "very sociable clever gentlemen" of the 32d Virginia, especially Ewell and Professor Morrison, now a quartermaster captain, who later appealed personally to President Davis on behalf of McLaws for his promotion to brigadier general.[29]

Already a brigadier since 17 June, Magruder became Williamsburg's most distinguished guest during July. He and the small battalion of aides and orderlies always accompanying him arrived in town early in the morning of the ninth. They found no room available in the City Hotel on Main Street in the center of town, but the Baptist preacher, William Young, generously offered Magruder the house next door to the Tuckers on Market Square. It belonged to Philip Montegu Thompson, a former law student of Beverley Tucker and now the Tucker family's business manager. He and his maiden sister, Julia, were currently out of town, but Young was certain Thompson would want Magruder to occupy his house. Cynthia Washington knew the Thompsons a

28. Charley to mother, 26 Oct. 1863, Civil War Collection, MR-CWM; CBT to CWC, 14 July 1861; LM to wife, 30 July–1 Aug. 1861, McLaws Papers.

29. Galt Diary, 17 July 1861; LM to wife, 2 July, 30 July–1 Aug., 18 Aug. 1861, McLaws Papers; CBT to CWC, 6, 16 July 1861, TCP.

little better than Young did and thought it a good joke. When Montegu returned a few days later, he first "pronounced himself well pleased that Gen. M—— had taken his house," wrote Cynthia, "but now he is furious." Nevertheless, the general's headquarters remained, at least until the end of the month.[30]

Magruder did not come to Williamsburg empty handed. Before leaving Yorktown, where work on an even more extensive defense line was well underway, he collected all the spades that could be spared, as well as Col. William M. Levy's 2d Louisiana Regiment, and presented them to McLaws on his arrival. The Louisianans were assigned to work on the entrenchments alongside the Georgians but found their way into town that weekend to claim their share of social life. On Sunday, 14 July, Cynthia noticed in the Bruton congregation "many soldiers present who had not been in a Church for months. Some of them seemed to look forward with great pleasure to being once more where they could hear sacred music." Several officers along with their men also visited the ladies' Working Society "to invoke our aid, and we have had a great deal more than we could do," Cynthia confessed. "Those poor fellows from Louisiana seem to have lost everything, and to be sadly in want of a little womanly attention." She judged "some of the Officers are very pleasant gentlemen" and by the end of the month was providing the regiment with gaiters and tablecloths.[31]

Meanwhile, work continued on the earthworks. Magruder had long been uneasy about Williamsburg, deeming the place of "extreme importance" but "much exposed" due to its continuing lack of men and defenses. He constantly feared the enemy would land somewhere upriver of the Yorktown line, besiege or turn the Williamsburg line, and march to Richmond virtually unopposed. His first order of business after arriving in Williamsburg, therefore, was an inspection tour of the fortifications. The main central work he found nearly completed. Magruder also found Ewell and Rives still arguing over the length of the line. They did agree, however, along with Magruder and McLaws, that four smaller redoubts were needed. These were immediately commenced while the engineers reported on the artillery necessary to fill them. They already had twelve pieces but required an additional eight howitzers for a minimum of two guns in each of the ten redoubts then under construction plus

30. BSE, "Magruder Reminiscence"; *OR*, 2:970; CBT to CWC, 10, 16 July 1861, TCP; Galt Diary, 29 July 1861.

31. *OR*, 2:970; CBT to CWC, 14, 19 July 1861, William M. Levy to CBT, 1 Aug. 1861, TCP.

three heavy long-range guns for the shore defenses at Grove Wharf and Spratley's Farm. General Lee promised to send the howitzers as soon as carriages
could be completed for them, but the columbiads for shore defense were not
available. He assured Magruder that the batteries farther downriver should
prevent any Federal landing as far up as Spratley's. "Prince John" had not converted the high command to his long-held belief that "the defense of Richmond is here at Williamsburg and Jamestown."[32]

On 21 July, however, the defense of Richmond apparently took place at a
railroad junction known as Manassas near a creek called Bull Run twenty
miles southeast of Washington, D.C. Two wings of the Confederate army
under Brigadier Generals P. G. T. Beauregard and Joseph E. Johnston united
to meet a half-trained Union force marching out of the northern capital. By
day's end, the Federals were in full flight back to Washington as southerners
celebrated and toasted a premature end to the war. When news of this "glorious" Confederate victory reached the Peninsula the next day, salute guns fired
at Yorktown and Gloucester Point, and McLaws ordered the artillery in place
on the Williamsburg line to reply. The noise created a stampede in town, as
many soldiers, both sick and well, rushed down to the entrenchments thinking
the enemy had attacked. Nearly the entire camp turned out to see the guns
fired despite a heavy rainstorm at the time because, boasted McLaws, "our
men are very eager for the fight." Their eagerness had been previously demonstrated on the night of 16 July, when sentries thought they heard persons moving around the entrenchments. As Cynthia described it, the pickets "finally
fired, the alarm was given, and all the Regiments rushed to arms, with a
promptitude quite gratifying, although the enemy did not show himself." The
next day Williamsburg people noticed two tents pitched on the north side of
Courthouse Green opposite the Thompson house. General Magruder had
prudently posted extra sentinels at his headquarters.[33]

Such episodes inspired confidence in the town's defenders if not in its defenses. After the battle of Manassas, alarms ceased for the rest of the month,
"not even a rumor of the advance of the enemy disturbs us," observed
McLaws. This allowed him to concentrate his forces on digging rather than
dispersing all over the countryside chasing down rumored enemy landings.
His black laborers, now numbering nearly four hundred, increased daily as the

32. *OR*, 2:902, 931, 965, 970–1, 975, 51(2):174–5.
33. LM to children, 21–25 July 1861, McLaws Papers; Galt Diary, 16, 17, 22 July 1861;
CBT to CWC, 16 July 1861.

3d Virginia Cavalry, including both the Old Dominion Dragoons and James City Cavalry, scoured the surrounding country and sent all runaway slaves they captured to Williamsburg. In mid-July McLaws commended himself that "more has been done during my short reign than for months previous," but he yet had much to do. The rainstorm the day after Manassas washed out some of the works, which workers soon repaired, and on the far left of the line, soldiers were rebuilding the milldam at Jones Pond in an effort to flood that flank. On the twenty-fourth McLaws "found the dam nearly completed, but the water does not rise as much as I want it."[34]

The following day McLaws rode over the ground on the right of the line, assigning a work party of twenty with axes to cut "down a grove of trees that obstructed the field of fire of one of the batteries, and to entangle a ravine that led up to within a few hundred yards of one of the redoubts." As he explained in a letter to his young son, "by entangling I mean cutting down trees and making them fall across each other and in the direction the enemy is expected to come," preventing "a large number from rushing suddenly upon us, and those who attempt it are exposed a longer time to our fire." McLaws then continued on to Tutters Neck, where he found the earthwork nearly finished and the men lounging on their shovels. Circling back to town, the colonel reported to Magruder, sick in bed with the gout, and pronounced himself well pleased with the progress. Five days later McLaws announced most of the redoubts were either finished or would be within a week. The main fortification, by now christened Fort Magruder, was approaching completion. In his opinion, the earthworks were "fast assuming proportions that will make them exceedingly formidable."[35]

Throughout the month of July, a constant stream of curious townspeople came out to inspect these works and the workers. Cynthia Washington joined a wagonload of sightseers on the afternoon of the fifth, and four days later Dr. Galt "heard incidents shewing that many persons were stopped at the entrenchments" because the "strictness in relation to military passes is represented as very rigid." Yet when he visited the worksite himself on 12 July, he judged security woefully inadequate. "The tents were some of them in the woods; there was a large number of servants employed, troops were drilling, and altogether a scene of vivid life and motion was presented—there being in

34. LM to wife, 18 July, 30 July–1 Aug. 1861, McLaws Papers; LM to children, 21–25 July 1861; Thomas P. Nanzig, *3rd Virginia Cavalry* (Lynchburg, H. E. Howard, 1989), 2.
35. LM to children, 21–25 July 1861; LM to wife, 30 July–1 Aug. 1861.

addition a number of civilians trapsing about, on foot, horseback, in carriages &c.," he jotted in his diary. "I could but think with what facility a spy might have made his approach and departure, unnoticed & unharmed."[36]

Dr. Galt was not alone in his fear of spies penetrating Williamsburg. Albert Southall's son Travis had been in Washington, D.C., the past several months, living and working with his older brother, who joined the Union army. Though Travis had been trying to escape the northern capital since early March, a "deficiency of means" prevented his return to Williamsburg until 2 July. Upon his arrival he intended to join the 32d Virginia, but before he could enlist, he was arrested on suspicion of espionage. In a few days Southall found himself in a North Carolina prison, knowing neither his accusers nor the charges against him. There he languished while his mother appealed directly to President Davis that his case be examined. "If he prove guilty," Virginia Southall pleaded on 2 August, "though his mother I can say let him be punished; if innocent let him be discharged at once and join his company." Dr. Galt and Williamsburg mayor Dr. Robert M. Garrett vouched for young Travis, as did several of Williamsburg's most prominent citizens related to him through his mother. Mrs. Southall's most influential ally, John Tyler Jr., wrote Davis on 3 August that the Southalls, though differing politically from the Tylers, "are no traitors," and that Albert Southall's enemies were apparently striking back at the father through the son. Ewell blamed the arrest on "some of the extremists of Williamsburg who seemed to invect their prejudices towards those who were less enthusiastic than themselves, with the veil of patriotism." Finally, on 9 August, the order came down from Richmond to release Travis Southall immediately. Upon returning home he joined a troop in the 3d Virginia Cavalry, and Williamsburg moved on to its next crisis.[37]

36. CBT to CWC, 6 July 1861; Galt Diary, 9, 12 July 1861.
37. OR II, 2:1362–7, 1371; OR II, 3:701; BSE, "Magruder Reminiscence."

CHAPTER 2

Sickly Season

When Duke of Gloucester became simply Main Street, its parallel companions, Francis and Nicholson, also reverted to the more prosaic South Back and North Back Streets but were lined with the nicer domiciles of Williamsburg's better families. The Galts' old family home stood near the eastern end of South Back Street, which had acquired the sobriquet Woodpecker Lane because, Victoria King later explained, its houses once sported red roofs. Along North Back Street, bordering Courthouse Green, were the Tucker House and Thompson House side by side and, a little farther east, a more modest home belonging to Dr. Samuel Griffin. Descended from an old Virginia family on his father's side and the Scottish royal house on his mother's, Dr. Griffin was born in 1782 in Philadelphia, where his father served as the last president of the Continental Congress. He graduated from William and Mary in 1799, received his medical degree from the University of Edinburgh, and in 1823 settled down on North Back Street to raise his family.[1]

For the past several weeks, Dr. Griffin had been traveling with his son, James Louis Corbin Griffin, also a doctor, though nonpracticing. The younger Griffin made his living as a teacher and Universalist clergyman. Their adherence to this sect, usually associated with New England intellectuals, made the Griffins a target for conversion by their orthodox neighbors. Their kinship ties to other prominent Williamsburg families, notably the Wallers, and the old doctor's involvement as "a leading spirit in all the affairs of this city" endeared

1. Victoria King Lee, "Williamsburg in 1861," 1933, John D. Rockefeller Jr. Library, CWF, 9; JLCG Commonplace Book, Oct. 1862, 19 Dec. 1866, JLCG F/A, UA-CWM; "Letters of William Fitzhugh," *Virginia Magazine of History and Biography* 1 (1893–94): 254; Mary A. Stephenson, "Tayloe House Historical Report, Block 28 Building 3 Lot 262," 1979, John D. Rockefeller Jr. Library, CWF, 7–8.

them to the townspeople nevertheless. Upon returning home in the summer of 1861, James noted in his journal, or commonplace book, that they found the family home "in the hands of strangers!!" It had probably been taken over by Hampton refugees during the Griffins' absence. Rather than evict the intruders, the father and son decided to find shelter elsewhere.[2]

Though several houses in the city took in boarders, most were full of Confederate officers, and the Griffins were fortunate to obtain rooms at a boardinghouse on Main Street belonging to Virginia Southall's sister, the widow Catherine Maupin. There they became acquainted with the 10th Georgia's Lt. Col. Alfred Cumming, whom Col. Lafayette McLaws considered a grumbler. "He thinks he should have been colonel of the 10th Ga Regiment," McLaws confided to his wife, "but says that I should have been Brig Genl." McLaws could not argue with the latter point, for he too had been wondering why he was performing the duties of a brigadier with only a colonel's rank. His hopes rose the evening of 31 July when Brig. Gen. John Magruder visited him in camp and "said that it was his intention to recommend me to the appointment as Brigadier General that he was convinced that it was necessary and would ask that the appointment be made."[3]

In parting, Magruder told McLaws he would be leaving Williamsburg for Yorktown soon, which Dr. Galt confirmed in his 5 August diary entry: "Genl. Magruder reported to have moved his head-quarters below." Two afternoons later, "smoke was very apparent" in the air, followed that night by a glow in the southeast. Learning that Butler planned to fortify Hampton and use it to colonize escaped slaves, Magruder ordered three local cavalry companies to burn the town. Before the end of the month, rumors suggested that Williamsburg was to suffer a similar fate, but by then Magruder was more concerned about telegraphs than destroying towns. He wanted to order a field telegraph from Dr. Morris's company for "use at Williamsburg on the long lines of defense, consisting of detached works." The main telegraph from Richmond, erected in part by a detail from the Williamsburg Junior Guards, was almost completed in early August. It passed down Richmond Road, through town on Main Street, into Fort Magruder, and on to Yorktown over what was now

2. Samuel S. Griffin to JLCG, 3 May 1859, Samuel S. Griffin F/A, UA-CWM; JLCG Commonplace Book, 8 July 1861, 28 Sept. 1862; John S. Charles, "Recollections of Williamsburg, Virginia, as It Was at the Beginning of the Civil War," 1928, John D. Rockefeller Jr. Library, CWF, 37.

3. JLCG Commonplace Book, 25 July, 28 Sept. 1862; LM to wife, 30 July–1 Aug. 1861, LM Papers, Southern Historical Collection of the Manuscripts Department, Wilson Library, UNC.

called Telegraph Road. Soon Magruder would be wired directly to Richmond and no longer dependent on dispatch boats.[4]

The month of August also brought an outbreak of typhoid fever to the area, ushering in the dreaded "sickly season." Dr. Galt recorded several cases of typhoid among soldiers near Williamsburg as early as 3 August. On the twelfth he heard an unconfirmed report that two hundred Georgians had died since coming to the Peninsula, though Williamsburg undertaker Richard Manning Bucktrout had only buried four from the 10th Georgia, along with a few Virginians and one soldier from the 2d Louisiana. All were interred in the City Cemetery and set in orderly rows by state. Within the next two weeks, two more Louisianans and three more Georgians joined their comrades in these rows. One Georgia boy, who "died in Camp Page near WmsBurg from taking mofine," Bucktrout noted in his ledger, traveled home in a metallic coffin. At that time Dr. Galt counted more Virginians than Georgians at College Hospital and heard some talk of converting Williamsburg's churches into hospitals to accommodate the increased numbers of sick on the Peninsula below town. Magruder found deaths occurring at an alarming rate, two a day around Yorktown. At least one regiment was reduced to less than 40 percent of its original strength, Magruder reported on 9 August, before the "sickliest season" had yet arrived. By the twenty-first, Yorktown's supply of quinine became so depleted that he had to send a suffering Louisiana battalion to Williamsburg in search of medicine. The fortification workforce was melting away before his eyes.[5]

To replace these incapacitated soldiers, Magruder had the 3d Virginia Cavalry searching for runaway slaves as far down the Peninsula as the Federal picket lines. One hundred fifty blacks captured early in August were delivered to Williamsburg to work the line, but while these hands were coming in the front door, others were quietly slipping out the back. Some New Kent and Charles City County slaveholders, including ex-President Tyler, who had lent their field hands to the army complained in person to the secretary of war on 26 August that their slaves were being detained in Williamsburg longer than they expected, delaying the wheat crop threshing and causing many to escape or return to their masters without permission. Magruder was also having trouble with the free blacks he had hired for fifty cents a day with the promise of

4. John Minson Galt II Diary, 1, 5, 8, 26 Aug. 1861, GFP, MR-CWM; LM to wife, 30 July–1 Aug. 1861; *OR*, 4:571–3; Rouse, *Cows on the Campus*, 65, illustration.

5. *OR*, 4:572–3, 51(2):246; Galt Diary, 3, 12–13, 23 Aug. 1861; Richard M. Bucktrout Day Book, July–Aug. 1861, MR-CWM.

prompt payment. They were not getting paid, and neither were his troops. The Treasury Department refused to send the money because "they could not get the notes," in Magruder's words, for which "the officers and men evince much dissatisfaction." Rumor had it that the "gentleman officer" entrusted with the payroll four weeks earlier had absconded. "I am afraid," McLaws confided to his wife on 26 August, "that the new confederacy has some agents who are as desirous of making money as were some in the old U.S. army."[6]

In the midst of all these problems, who should march into Williamsburg on the evening of 19 August but Col. Mandeville Marigny and his 10th Louisiana Regiment, having "the reputation of being the most lawless set in existence," according to McLaws. These men had landed on Jamestown Island, where, McLaws heard, within twelve hours they ate "up every living thing on the Island, but the horses, and their own species." Recruited from the tougher segment of Louisiana's population, the ranks contained men representing a dozen different nations and organized like the French army. Many spoke more French than English, even the adjutant who accompanied Marigny to report to McLaws. "The Colonel & Adjutant who have just left my tent, speak English but indiferently well," McLaws remarked to his wife, "the Adjutant did not say much, I think but two words & I do not believe he can talk in English." The Louisianans' unsavory reputation had preceded them to Williamsburg. Dr. Galt mentioned on their arrival, "persons were warned . . . to be on their guard against depredations from them."[7]

Crowding Williamsburg's streets within a couple of days were more Louisiana troops sent up from Yorktown by Magruder. Known as Coppens's Zouaves for their commander, Lt. Col. Georges Auguste Gaston Coppens, they too comprised several nationalities and received their drill commands in French. Their colorful uniforms of baggy red breeches, leggings, blue jackets, and red stocking caps were patterned after the admired French army Zouaves and inspired the nickname "Redlegs." They called themselves "ZuZus," McLaws learned, and rivaled the lawless reputation of Marigny's regiment. These men must have behaved themselves tolerably well while in the area, however, for when Dr. Galt wrote on 10 September that the "Zouaves it is reported, are to have the guarding of the town," he added, "what a sensation such a report would have created a few weeks ago."[8]

6. *OR*, 4:570, 573, 636, 654, 690–1; LM to wife, 26 Aug. 1861, McLaws Papers.

7. LM to wife, 18–20 Aug. 1861, McLaws Papers; Terry L. Jones, *Lee's Tigers: The Louisiana Infantry in the Army of Northern Virginia* (Baton Rouge: Louisiana State University Press, 1987), 30–1; Galt Diary, 19 Aug. 1861.

8. Galt Diary, 23 Aug., 10 Sept. 1861; Jones, *Lee's Tigers*, 3, 252; LM to wife, 18–20 Aug. 1861.

The Zouave battalion would not carry the responsibility of guarding the town alone, for the 5th Louisiana under Col. Theodore G. Hunt shared the duty. A former member of the U.S. Congress from Louisiana, Hunt, McLaws judged, was "an Old Gentleman of independent manners, and an open talker" who "has a considerable opinion of his influence and of his ability both as a soldier and a member of society." A rumor that the Federals were reinforcing the Peninsula below Warwick Court House had just reached Magruder, making his headquarters in Williamsburg again during much of September. He immediately ordered the Academy and College Hospitals in a state of preparation for wounded and sent the 10th Georgia along with the 15th Virginia and 2d Louisiana to Warwick under McLaws. The 5th Louisiana came up from Yorktown to man the earthworks. Besides these Louisiana troops, only the Junior Guards and one other company from the 32d Virginia under Col. Benjamin Ewell, about five hundred soldiers in all, remained to guard Williamsburg.[9]

Cynthia Washington learned about this new arrangement when the 2d Louisiana's Col. William M. Lévy, a former William and Mary student, "came to the Church the day before he left the neighborhood, and made himself very charming—repeating poetry to me—which I really enjoyed," she wrote on 7 September to Dr. Coleman, still on duty in Yorktown. That day she rode out to the entrenchments to deliver some fruit and flowers to McLaws and arrived just in time to see one company of the 10th Georgia receive its marching orders for Warwick, with the rest of the regiment preparing to follow the next day. McLaws insisted upon introducing her to the Zouaves' colonel, probably Coppens, "a very modest unassuming young man," Cynthia playfully remarked to her fiancé, "& I think, I shall take him in hand." She then watched sadly as the troops packed their tents, an ominous sign they would be gone a long time.[10]

Although Cynthia was sorry to see her friends leave, her social life never slackened. On 9 September she wrote Charles, "the house has been full of company, Capts. of Ordnance, and Navy, a Col. and Lieutenants in the Army have been passing in and out all day." Two particularly friendly lieutenants spent an evening with the Tuckers from seven until nearly midnight. The family—augmented by Lt. Edwin Taliaferro, who recently married Cynthia's sis-

9. *OR*, 4:644; Jensen, *32nd Virginia Infantry*, 46; Galt Diary, 8, 12 Sept. 1861; Robert K. Krick, *Lee's Colonels: A Biographical Register of Field Officers of the Army of Northern Virginia*, 4th ed. (Dayton, Ohio: Morningside, 1992), 202; LM to wife, 30 July 1861, McLaws Papers.

10. CBT to CWC, 7 Sept. 1861, TCP, MR-CWM; William M. Levy F/A, UA-CWM.

ter Bland and moved into the Tucker house—had been enjoying "the most charming music from a splendid brass band from Col. Hunt's Regiment, as they play around the neighborhood." Cynthia continued, "of course, we have a full benefit, and we have already had a vocal Serenade from some Virginians." Such entertainment helped her "throw off the sad feelings" she suffered since leaving the deathbed of her friend and former William and Mary student Pvt. James H. Dix at six o'clock that morning. A typhoid victim and the first fatality among the Junior Guards, Dix was buried in Bruton Churchyard.[11]

A large body of cavalry traversing Williamsburg streets early in the morning of 18 September immediately attracted the citizens' attention. These troopers encamped "in unusually peaked tents" across College Landing Road from the original Camp Page and were part of the famed Cobb's Legion, a Georgia unit recruited and led by Col. Thomas R. R. Cobb. Many came out from town to watch the Georgians drill the next day before they continued down the Peninsula to Yorktown, leaving the impression with Dr. Galt "that the enemy could not possibly stand up before them, but would at once be put to flight."[12]

The James City Cavalry under Capt. George Geddy may not have inspired such awe, but the townspeople were happy to see about twenty of its members ride into Williamsburg on 6 September and settle "in the new made enclosure south of the Asylum grounds," Dr. Galt noted. Taking advantage of their proximity to home, the local troopers proved a problem to the new post commander, Colonel Hunt. "You will direct Captain Geddy to keep his company of cavalry together and to drill them twice a day, and particularly to see that his men feed and groom their horses thoroughly," Magruder advised Hunt. "You will please be very sparing of leaves of absence to these men, as it is hard to keep them together."[13]

One James City Cavalry trooper not with this contingent was Dr. Coleman. From the moment Charles left for Yorktown in June, Cynthia had campaigned both for his commission as assistant surgeon and for his transfer to the Williamsburg hospitals. Upon learning of Dr. Leonard Henley's appointment to assistant surgeon of the 32d Virginia, she enlisted her professor friend, Capt. Robert Morrison, to write the surgeon general in Richmond on her fiancé's behalf. A few days later Dr. Coleman's commission arrived at his mother's home. "In order that you may obtain the position of Assist. Surgeon

11. CBT to CWC, 9 Sept. 1861, TCP.
12. Galt Diary, 18–20 Sept. 1861; Warner, *Generals in Gray*, 56.
13. Galt Diary, 6 Sept. 1861; Nanzig, *3rd Virginia Cavalry*, 127; *OR*, 4:666.

of the *Hospitals* in *this place* it is necessary that you should make *immediate* application," Cynthia urged him on 20 July, "by so doing you will get the post, and then we will be fixed." His sister "wrote a note to the Col. of the Va Regiment to send for you." Instead, he was assigned to the Howitzer Hospital located at Bellefield, a plantation near Yorktown belonging to Williamsburg's McCandlish family, to replace the ailing regular surgeon of the Howitzers.[14]

On 4 September Dr. Coleman commenced his new job with the Howitzers, reporting to Maj. (soon to be colonel) George Wythe Randolph, grandson of Thomas Jefferson. The mess he shared there with Randolph and the recently promoted Maj. J. Thompson Brown, one of Cynthia's many distant cousins, was a vast improvement over his old cavalry camp. Nevertheless, Charles pined for Cynthia. They had been hoping to marry since February, but with the twelve-mile separation, they had difficulty even planning a wedding. Charles could obtain leaves only once a fortnight at most, and they could communicate only through letters carried by friends, servants, and relatives who happened to be going to or from Yorktown, as the Peninsula had no regular mail service. At one time they set the date for 19 September 1861. When that day passed with Charles still in Yorktown, they reset it for the twenty-eighth. That did not work out either, but his supervisor promised to transfer him to Williamsburg as soon as possible. Ever since arriving in Yorktown, Dr. Coleman was convinced his "services are really more needed in Williamsburg than here."[15]

Physicians were indeed needed in Williamsburg. On 30 August Dr. Galt mentioned four soldier burials, and before September was over, sixteen graves had been filled in the Georgia row and nine in the Louisiana row of the City Cemetery. Virginia had its share of men dying as well, but many of these Bucktrout packed in sawdust to be sent home. Though the deceased's company captain paid all funeral expenses during the early months of the war, by this time Bucktrout had contracted with the Confederate government to supply plain pine coffins at $10.00 each. The captains still covered all other expenses, however, including $2.00 to dig the grave, $1.00 to convey the coffin to the ground, and another $1.50 for an optional headboard with the name carved in it. Packing and casing to send home usually cost $5.00 or $6.00. One captain in the 5th Louisiana ordered a "1st rate black walnut" coffin at $45.00, "lined & trimed" for his man who died at the Academy Hospital on

14. CBT to CWC, 20 July, 7 Sept. 1861, TCP.

15. CWC to CBT, 7, 9, 22 Sept. 1861; TCP, CBT to LAT, 22 Jan.1861, TCP; CBT to CWC, 16 July, 18, 23 Sept. 1861, TCP; Warner, *Generals in Gray*, 252.

24 September, plus "1 1/2 yds black crape to trim the flag with" at a $1.50. Bucktrout's final notation on this account, however, records that the captain "cleared out without paying."[16]

Despite this overabundance of sick and dying, Cynthia assured Charles, "the chances of your getting up here are 'blue' indeed." One chance evaporated when the Zouaves' surgeon was furloughed home sick early in September and a relative newcomer to Yorktown, Dr. Samuel E. Holt, was assigned to Williamsburg to relieve him temporarily. After an interminable four-hour ambulance ride, Dr. Holt arrived in town about nine o'clock the night of 10 September and checked into the overcrowded City Hotel. He considered himself fortunate that he did not have to sleep in the sitting room with two snoring drunks and two quarreling Zouaves, but he was less than satisfied with a dirty mattress on the parlor floor. Even more disappointing was his morning meal, which he described as "the meanest breakfast I ever beheld set at any table." Though he could eat nothing, he paid his inflated bill of one dollar and "left in disgust." At the Zouave camp, about a mile from town, Dr. Holt found the officers "a nice set of French gentlemen who showed me every attention & kindness." He also found about 150 soldiers suffering from "Intermittant fever Diarrhea Dysenterry, &c," as well as a number "of cases of acute & chronic Rheumatism." Disease soon struck Dr. Holt as well, but he remained at his post until ordered back to Yorktown the first of October.[17]

The order came at a bad time for Dr. Holt. Not only was he still suffering from his malady, but he also did not want to miss the big party being planned. That very day, 1 October, invitations went out from the Zouave camp for a "Ball" or "Soiree" to be given at six o'clock the night of the third by the officers of the 5th Louisiana and Coppens's Zouaves. Dr. Holt, who during his stay in Williamsburg had gained an appreciation for its ladies if not its hostelry, desired "to see the beauty assembled here." The Louisianans went to a great deal of trouble putting up "a most beautiful Hall" at their camp for the occasion, with "the ground around nicely adorned in various ways." The interior decor reflected their elegant French taste, as Dr. Galt described it: "Bayonets acted as reflectors, and the curtains of divisions were flags; the rooms were partly arbours and partly tents. The ladies' room was a perfect gem, being furnished with a bed, lounge and chairs; and cottes also, having a supply of brushes, mirrors (three), essences, soap, &c." Although the refreshments ordered form Richmond did not show up, the Zouaves were able to provide

16. Galt Diary, 30 Aug. 1861; Bucktrout Day Book, Sept. 1861.
17. CBT to CWC, 18 Sept. 1861; Samuel E. Holt Diary, MR-CWM.

sponge cake, butter cake, and fruit cake with wine—everything but plates, which somebody forgot but nobody missed. Even the weather cooperated, becoming beautifully clear and balmy. All agreed that the affair was well attended and a grand success.[18]

The only complaint came from a relative of Dr. Waller named Norborne Blow. The Zouaves, Blow commented in a 10 October letter, "are not very aristocratic in their selection of ladies." He singled out "an old greyheaded major" who was "desperately attentive to a young lass of 16" from a lower social position. "It was a complete dignity ball so far as white amalgamation was concerned for while some of the *porcelain* from the City was present the daughters of the mechanics and shopkeepers had as much attention paid them as any body else," Blow continued. "Perhaps some of the Williamsburg gals and Hampton refugees may adjourn to some Louisiana plantation or palatial residence in New Orleans after the war is over."[19]

Among the aristocrats attending this party were Lucy Tucker, Edwin and Bland Taliaferro, and fifteen-year-old Zettie Tucker, all the adult members of the Tucker family except Cynthia. She stayed home to nurse her daughter's servant suffering with typhoid fever. "After a week of anxiety, and constant nursing, and attention I have been called upon to part with that good, faithful girl Milly," Cynthia wrote Charles two days later on 5 October. Milly died that morning despite the best medical attention from Dr. Waller's son-in-law Dr. John Mercer and the 32d Virginia's surgeon, Dr. George W. Semple. "There never was a more faithful better creature in the World, and I am grieved to my heart to give her up," Cynthia lamented. "But God does all things well, and this is without doubt, intended to work some good end for Sadie and myself." Now Sadie was sick, and Cynthia's thirteen-year-old brother, Berkeley Montegu Beverley, called Monta or Monty by the family, also developed a fever just before he was to leave Williamsburg for school.[20]

Cynthia's seemingly endless nursing duties forced her to postpone their wedding again, she informed Charles in a letter written on 8 October and delivered to Yorktown by his mother. "I have even thought that a *weeks* delay might be better, for some of the servants are sick at your house, and it might be more convenient to your Mother for us to delay our marriage for a week, or more," she suggested, letting him decide. By that time, Sadie had improved

18. Holt Diary; Zouave officers to Tucker family, 1 Oct. 1861, TCP; Galt Diary, 3 Oct. 1861.

19. Norborne Blow to Emma Blacknall, 10 Oct. 1860 [1861], Blow Family Papers, MR-CWM.

20. CBT to CWC, 5 Oct. 1861, TCP.

but Bland had a fever and Monty was diagnosed with typhoid by Dr. Semple. If their illnesses did not force another postponement, Cynthia decided on 17 October for the wedding date.[21]

In any case, she was determined not to miss the second Zouave Ball on 10 October. Due to the inconvenient lack of a dance floor at the Zouave camp, they decided to hold it at Tazewell Hall. This historic old mansion on the southern fringe of town belonged to John D. Munford, a member of a distinguished Richmond family. He was currently a major in the Confederate army commanding a battalion in the western hills of Virginia and could not attend, but most of the town showed up for the party, which commenced in midafternoon and whirled until midnight. Dr. Galt and his sister, Sally, admired the house, adorned with flags and evergreens, again "in the French fashion." Adding more polish to the dance floor were the boys of the 1st Louisiana Battalion, also called the Dreux Battalion, comprised of the first five companies to volunteer from the Pelican State and said to contain the cream of New Orleans society. They were presently camped near the Zouaves southeast of town after spending the summer on the Yorktown line, where in a 5 July skirmish their leader, Lt. Col. Charles Dreux, had been the first Louisiana and Confederate field officer killed in the war. Perhaps not so rowdy as other Louisiana soldiers in Williamsburg, the young men of the 1st Louisiana Battalion nevertheless knew how to have a good time.[22]

So did Cynthia Washington. She spent the night waltzing "with a lady," she assured Charles in a letter dated 11 October, "remembering your objection to seeing any lady for whom you had regard waltzing with a gentleman." She even decided to buy a party dress for all the other "Matinees" the Zouaves were planning throughout that winter, though only after first wearing it as a wedding dress. The wedding would have to be postponed again, however, until 22 or 23 October, as Monty was worsening. Charles was not pleased, either with the postponement or with what he considered Cynthia's unchristian behavior of dancing in public, especially with such disreputable hosts as the Zouave officers. Immediately after receiving his scolding in a 14 October letter, Cynthia dashed off a vigorous defense of dancing ("I never thought it wrong in a religious point of view") and Zouaves ("they are as gentlemanly as any persons you know"). Most of all, she wanted Charles to understand, "I am

21. CBT to CWC, 8, 9 Oct. 1861, TCP.
22. CBT to CWC, 11 Oct. 1861, TCP; *OR* IV, 1:631; Lee A. Wallace Jr., *A Guide to Virginia Military Organizations, 1861–1865* (Lynchburg: H. E. Howard, 1986), 174; Galt Diary, 10 Oct. 1861; SMG to cousin, 31 Oct. 1861, GFP; Jones, *Lee's Tigers,* 250–1.

in all respects your equal, and while, I hope, as a dutiful wife, to be influenced in *all* things by your wishes, I shall expect, in *most* cases, the same from you." What could he do but surrender? "I really enjoyed the racy, saucy style of your letter," he replied on the nineteenth, "it revived my spirits wonderfully." Charles was not sure he was up to "tripping the light fantastic" with her at some future party, as she had suggested, but he was more eager than ever to marry, for the "truth is *old lady,* I love you entirely too much for my own comfort." This letter "acted like champaign" to Cynthia's dark mood when she received it the next afternoon. "I really enjoyed getting a letter from you *so much* that I begin to believe that I must love you more than I sometimes think I do."[23]

Somehow during these busy autumn weeks, Cynthia found time to write to Norfolk poet James Barron Hope about the republication of *Partisan Leader.* The Richmond publisher she contacted in April advised her that since the South had just seceded, it was "unsafe to give any work to the public at that time, as the minds of all persons were engrossed with war." But now she believed the time was right to offer Beverley Tucker's contribution to the secession debate, appended by a biographical sketch from Hope's "graceful pen." She proposed to devote the proceeds of its sale "to our Southern cause. The gallant Soldiers stricken by disease, or wounded in Battle demand my most heartfelt sympathy, and assistance," she assured Hope while requesting his help in contacting a Norfolk publisher. "I feel that in making this effort I am engaged in a holy work that in honouring the dead I am aiding the living."[24]

Aiding the living was consuming most of Cynthia's time in October, both nursing her ever-worsening brother and, despite objections from Charles, distributing cheer and custard among the growing number of sick soldiers. "I went yesterday to the Academy Hospital, and finding I could be of some comfort to some of the poor sick men, I returned again to-day," she wrote him on the seventeenth. "I cannot help looking after the sick, particularly, when I see as I did to-day, grateful eyes following me, and poor wan faces made brighter." She had begun to give up hope Dr. Coleman would ever be transferred to Williamsburg, even though he informed her on the sixteenth that the acting medical director told him "several new Hospitals will be established in Williamsburg, and that he thinks it highly probable that I will be able to winter at home." He promised to be home on the twenty-second or twenty-third at

23. CBT to CWC, 11, 17, 20 Oct. 1861, TCP; CWC to CBT, 14, 19 Oct. 1861, TCP.

24. CBT to James Barron Hope, n.d., TCP; CBT to Ghieslin, n.d., TCP; James Barron Hope to CBT, 28 Oct. 1861, TCP.

the latest to marry. Yet on the twenty-first he learned he could not be there before the twenty-fourth because "Gen Magruder has received news which he concurs to be reliable that the Federals have fifty war vessels at Old Point" near Fort Monroe and "has ordered all of the sick to be removed to Williamsburg immediately, preparatory to an expected attack." That meant converting the town's four churches into hospitals, which Dr. Coleman deplored as desecration but which increased his chances for a transfer to Williamsburg. At least Yorktown's acting medical director, Dr. George W. Millen, formerly at the College Hospital, promised to remember him when surgeons were assigned for duty there.[25]

The following Sunday, 27 October, Cynthia passed along to Charles that "the dear old Church is full of the sick as are all the Churches, and Physicians are much in demand." She had transferred her charitable efforts to Bruton when she was able to leave Monty, who had become so ill she was considering the idea of postponing her wedding indefinitely. "I do not object so much to being married, as to having to send away to ask a Minister to come for *that* purpose, when he may be called upon to officiate on a more solemn occasion and to bury my own Brother," she explained. Two days later Charles journeyed to Williamsburg at long last to wed in a private family ceremony. After becoming Mrs. Charles W. Coleman, Cynthia moved into the old Palace grounds home with her new in-laws and continued to tend the sick, contrary to her husband's wishes, while he returned to Yorktown. She adamantly refused to leave her "post of duty," as she called Bruton Church, hoping it would be Charles's post of duty some day as well.[26]

As the churches began to fill with sick, the pastors, starting with Bruton's Rev. Thomas M. Ambler on 21 October, called upon Dr. Galt, seeking refuge for their displaced flocks. Dr. Galt referred them to the asylum's president, Robert Saunders, who granted them permission to hold religious services in the asylum's chapel. On Sunday the twenty-seventh, both the Baptists and Episcopalians met there as the churches' ladies kept busy providing bedding and "eatables" to the sick soldiery. Sally Galt's servant Arena Baker spent every day baking and "sending articles of food suitable for the sick" to the various churches, especially the African Baptist church next door to the Superintendent's House. The first North Carolina troops seen in town were convalescing there. Ailing officers were generally nursed in private homes, the Superintendent's House sheltering seventeen since the commencement of the war. Sally

25. CBT to CWC, 17 Oct. 1861; CWC to CBT, 19, 21 Oct. 1861, TCP.
26. CBT to CWC, 27, 31 Oct., 7–8 Nov. 1861, TCP.

was thankful all recovered. The church hospitals were placed under Letitia Semple, "an excellent nurse & superintendent" in Sally's opinion. Though the soldiers in her care numbered about 750 by the end of October, not as many died that month as had in September. Bucktrout recorded only eight burials and two shipped home.[27]

At least Williamsburg had no battle casualties to handle, for Magruder's expected Federal attack never materialized. After Colonel Hunt complained that Williamsburg was deficient in "defensive means" and preparation, Magruder outlined on 2 October a contingency plan in case the Federal fleet ascended the James River past the Yorktown line. He directed Hunt to mount in the five redoubts from Tutters Neck to Fort Magruder the three carronades that the navy had lent him plus whatever artillery he could scrape up. The moment Hunt perceived the forts under attack, he was to march the Zouaves from Williamsburg to Spratley's Farm to assist a battalion of the 10th Louisiana in defending that place. Magruder would send up the rest of the 10th Louisiana from Yorktown plus four other regiments, four batteries of field artillery, and six detached companies of the 5th Louisiana. Hunt's other four companies were to man the earthworks between Tutters Neck and Fort Magruder as both artillerists and infantry. Magruder therefore told him to request from Capt. Catesby Jones, still on Jamestown Island, a naval officer to instruct Hunt's battalion in the use of carronades. Jones informed Hunt on 4 October that he had no spare officers to send.[28]

By 7 October, Magruder had become convinced the Federal attack was imminent, and unless he received reinforcements soon, the enemy would be able to turn "all the works on James River and those in front of Williamsburg." He needed at least four more regiments, more guns, and more artillery companies, including three for Williamsburg. Though rains for several days rendered the roads nearly impassable, rumors of "impending hostilities" began seeping into Williamsburg. By the seventeenth, Dr. Galt realized the rumors were "wholly unfounded," but Magruder, now a major general and looking "worn and sick" to McLaws, still expected an attack hourly. On the twenty-first he reported that the 30,000 men brought by the Federal fleet were about to attack his 9,500. That same day some of McLaws's men skirmished briefly "with a considerable body of the enemy," but otherwise the Peninsula remained quiet, and at the end of October, the Federal fleet sailed south.[29]

27. SMG to cousin, 31 Oct. 1861; Galt Diary, 21–27 Oct. 1861; Bucktrout Day Book, Oct. 1861.

28. *OR*, 4:665–6, 668–9; *ORN*, 6:737.

29. *OR*, 4:673–4, 680–1, 684–92; Galt Diary, 15–17 Oct. 1861; LM to Willie McLaws, 18 Oct. 1861, McLaws Papers; LM to wife, 23 Oct. 1861, McLaws Papers.

Williamsburg, however, continued lively all month courtesy of the Zouaves. "I heard on yesterday that Col. Munford's had been broken into at
night—attributed by some, first to no gentleman's being there, and secondly
to many Zouaves frequenting the homes of the neighboring free-coloured
people, who would wash for them, &c.," Dr. Galt recorded on 25 October.
"Recently one of them complained bitterly of a parcel of chickens being pur-
loined." McLaws felt left out on the Yorktown line, while the Zouaves in Williamsburg were "giving parties and picnics, singing and serenading." In an 18
October letter to his son, he told of Zouaves killing Williamsburg hogs and
pulling planks off houses. One Louisiana soldier waiting for a pig to pass by
was "lying flat on the ground for the double purpose of concealing himself
from the pig & from general observation" when a North Carolinian came
along and shot the pig. "The Zouave immediately rose up on his hands and
shouted out, 'Aha de Zouave is not the only one who steals de pig. Some body
else is the d——d rascal besides.'"[30]

Hunt tried to curb such depredations on the Old Burg by declaring war
"on those accused of selling liquor," according to Dr. Galt, but for better or
worse, these Louisiana boys would not be leaving soon. On 3 October Magruder issued General Orders No. 89, organizing the infantry on the Peninsula
into brigades and placing them in winter quarters. Hunt was assigned command of the Second Brigade, comprising only his 5th Louisiana, the 1st Louisiana (Dreux) Battalion, and Coppens's Louisiana Zouaves. All were to
remain in their present positions near Williamsburg except the Dreux Battalion, which shifted to Spratley's Farm to replace the departing 10th Louisiana.
Dr. Galt heard rumors of that destination on 12 October, watched the "battalion moving gradually to Spratley's" the next day, and on the twenty-third reported that six hundred of them were now settled in their new post. Soon they
constructed streets reminiscent of their beloved New Orleans. One "Spratley-
ite" named Herbert Copland had a "flourishing establishment situated at the
corner of Crescent & Canal Sts Spratleyville." The Zouaves too planned to
build "a regular city or town, having its streets" and a jail at their camp near
Williamsburg.[31]

Dr. Galt mentioned on 23 October that one hundred of Benjamin Ewell's
men were at Spratley's as well. Ewell had been named commander of the
Eighth Brigade, consisting of three scattered battalions, only one of which was

30. Galt Diary, 25 Oct. 1861; LM to Willie McLaws, 18 Oct. 1861.
31. OR, 4:668–70; Galt Diary, 11–13, 23 Oct. 1861; Sally Munford to Elizabeth Ewell, 23
July [1862], EFP, MR-CWM.

near Williamsburg, plus the 32d Virginia less its artillery companies. Both the Peninsula Artillery and Lee Artillery had been transferred to the 1st Virginia Artillery, newly organized under Dr. Coleman's friend and messmate Col. George Randolph, currently Magruder's chief of artillery, and were posted with the First Brigade on the Yorktown line. "I am at last a Brigadier General," McLaws crowed in a letter to his wife dated 3 October. "So you may call me General Lafayette at last." A week later he was still trying to put together a staff. Cynthia Coleman's brother, Lt. Tom Tucker, volunteered as one of his aides. Ewell's daughter Lizzie, enamored with certain members of the 10th Georgia, also applied for an appointment as his aide-de-camp, and playing along with the joke, McLaws promised, "I will send one in course of time."[32]

As usual, Ewell had more problems than scattered battalions and a flirtatious daughter. A few grammar schools were starting up again in Williamsburg, including "An English and Classical School" begun by James Griffin on 14 October. But the college could not reopen at its usual time that month since its buildings were still being used for a hospital. Furthermore, on 8 October Ewell reported to the college's governing Board of Visitors that forty-five of the students who enrolled the previous fall had volunteered in the service, and already two had succumbed to disease. Of the professors, Thomas Snead had spent the summer employed as an engineer in the hills of western Virginia with Brig. Gen. Henry Wise, though still without a commission in the engineering corps. The professor of ancient and modern languages and brother-in-law of Walker Vest, Edward S. Joynes, was serving as chief civilian administrator in the War Department in Richmond. Ewell managed to gather three professors, Taliaferro, Morrison, and one other, for a faculty meeting on 28 September, at which time they decided "the interests of the College require that it should be opened if possible" by 1 January 1862. Morrison, now a captain of ordnance, and Taliaferro were appointed a committee to ascertain how soon the college could be vacated by the military, but before they completed their report, Morrison contracted typhoid fever and died on 31 October. "No family could be left more destitute than his," wrote Cynthia to her husband that day. Now, even if the army did move out of the college by January, a new history professor would have to be hired, the rest of the faculty reassembled, and students recruited—an impossible task unless the war ended soon and successfully for the Confederate States of America.[33]

32. Galt Diary, 23 Oct. 1861; *OR*, 4:668–70; LM to wife, 3, 10 Oct. 1861, McLaws Papers.

33. JLCG Commonplace Book, 14 July, 31 Oct. 1862; Board of Visitors Minutes, 8 Oct. 1861, UA-CWM; *OR* IV, 3:1139; Edward S. Joynes F/A, UA-CWM; Faculty Minutes, 28 Sept. 1861, UA-CWM; CBT to CWC, 31 Oct. 1861.

CHAPTER 3

Rumors of War

A full year had passed since Abraham Lincoln won the presidency of the United States. Election day rolled around again on 6 November 1861, sending Williamsburg's electorate to the Old Courthouse to cast votes for the Confederate president, vice president, and their congressman. Interest did not run so high this election with Jefferson Davis entrenched as president of the permanent Confederate government. At the polls Dr. John Galt noticed that of Williamsburg's three election commissioners, only Robert Saunders was present. His son-in-law, former Bruton rector George Wilmer, had become chaplain of the 32d Virginia, "which is at this time rather scattered, but all in this neighborhood," Saunders wrote his son, "so that I hope he will be with us chiefly during the winter." At least Benjamin Ewell was no longer responsible for a fractured brigade. Major General Magruder revoked General Orders No. 89 on 10 November and formed most regiments and battalions on the Peninsula into two divisions, Brig. Gen. Lafayette McLaws commanding the second. Among the troops exempt from this order were those stationed at Williamsburg, although Capt. John Henley's Junior Guards expected to go into winter quarters soon at Spratley's Farm along with the Dreux Battalion.[1]

Early November found Cynthia Coleman also trying to get settled into her new quarters. On Monday the fourth she traveled down to Yorktown to spend the night with Charles. "We were very happy then," she later reminisced about this honeymoon, "and with war all around us dreamed not of its terrors." Several "beautiful Fall tinted leaves" they collected together Cynthia took back to Williamsburg on Tuesday and, with her mother-in-law's assistance, "arranged

---

1. John Minson Galt II Diary, 6 Nov. 1861, GFP, MR-CWM; Robert Saunders to R. L. P. Saunders, 13 Nov. 1861, PSP, MR-CWM; *OR*, 4:697–8.

them in vases for the parlour, and made the room look as gay and bright as possible." The next day Cynthia moved some of her bedroom furniture from the Tucker House into her new Palace building home. Her daughter had not quite adjusted to the move, however. "Sadie has become pretty well domesticated and seems contented and happy—although she is very glad to run off to her 'Ma Tucker's' whenever an opportunity presents itself."[2]

Relieved to remove Sadie from "that typhoid atmosphere" at her mother's, Cynthia continued taking her turn sitting up with Monty, "who improves very slowly if at all." She also continued her efforts to convince her "kind, indulgent Husband" that her place was still at church comforting the sick. "My impulse was to give it up, Charley," she told him in her 7 November letter, but decided this was her "path of duty" and hoped he would "not look upon my continued visits to the Hospital as indifference to your wishes, or disregard of your opinions." Returning to Bruton after her honeymoon, she "found my old friends glad to see me, for they evidently thought I had deserted them" since she had not been there for a week. "To-day I read to some of them parts of the 'Visitation for the Sick,' and was amply rewarded by the interest evinced by one of my auditors, a plain, rough lad but, one who has a soul to be saved, and who feels some anxiety about it." The next day Cynthia announced to Charles that she planned "to act as amanuensis for one poor fellow who wants to write to his wife but is not strong enough to do so."[3]

On Sunday, 10 November, Cynthia conducted two or three morning prayer meetings for the sick in Bruton, then planned to attend church service "at the unheard of hour of 3 1/2 o'clock" in the asylum chapel, as the Baptists had it for morning service. She was going only because her friend George Wilmer was to preach. "But for that I should go home and stay with Mother this afternoon," for Monty was sinking rapidly. Cynthia again worried he would not recover. "Poor Mother—she cannot bear trouble well, and it will go very hard with her to give up her youngest child," she feared. Robert Saunders informed his son on 13 November that "Little Montegue Tucker is exceedingly ill with typhoid fever & not expected to live." He knew of only one other civilian case in Williamsburg, and it was mild.[4]

Military cases, however, were not diminishing. On 4 November, Dr. Galt heard that Williamsburg contained about seven hundred afflicted soldiers.

2. CBT to CWC, 7–8 Nov. 1861, 3 Nov. 1864, TCP, MR-CWM.
3. CBT to CWC, 31 Oct., 7–8 Nov. 1861, TCP.
4. CBT to CWC, 10 Nov. 1861, TCP; Galt Diary, 10 Nov. 1861; Robert Saunders to R. L. P. Saunders, 13 Nov. 1861.

Two days later the estimate elevated to eight hundred, and "five died on yesterday." In November the sick were distributed among ten hospitals, including all four churches, private homes, and the new courthouse. Because William Walker Vest, Walker Vest's father and the town's wealthiest merchant, declined to restock his large new store on Main Street due to the "uncertain" times, it too served as a hospital. On 18 November Dr. Galt learned that Letitia Semple had dropped her nursing duties at the Female Academy to assume the housekeeping responsibilities for all ten. She now lived in the College Hospital, where "accommodations for the sick are as ample as are required," according to its head surgeon, Dr. J. G. Westmoreland. Nevertheless, of the thirty-two soldiers Bucktrout recorded interring throughout November, eleven perished there, while nine died at the academy, three at the African Baptist church, two at the other Baptist church, and one at the Episcopal church.[5]

Private homes too were suffering losses. When Lt. Michel Prud'homme of the 10th Louisiana contracted typhoid fever in mid-October, he was taken into Albert Southall's home and tenderly nursed by Virginia Southall and her four daughters. He seemed to be recovering when suddenly he began to hemorrhage, and on 5 November the regimental chaplain, French Jesuit Father Louis-Hippolyte Gache, hastened up from Yorktown to administer the last sacraments. Father Gache arrived around ten that night, four or five hours too late. Early in the morning the priest obtained permission from Southall to say mass in the parlor and decided to use the Southall's piano top for his altar. Before he started, the four daughters followed by their parents, "all decked out in their Sunday best," stole silently into the room and seated themselves at the far end. Gache never heard another sound from them except for "one distraction which almost made me laugh out loud," he related in a letter to his superior. "Just as I made the sign of the Cross to begin the prayers at the foot of the altar, Mr. Southall tiptoed up behind me and with the greatest solemnity whispered: 'We've just made some hot coffee, wouldn't you like to take a little right now?'" At the conclusion of the mass, Gache was packing his vestments and accessories when the two younger girls charmed him out of picture cards from his breviary book. He left their home with his pockets full of tidbits to take back to camp and his heart full of great admiration and respect for "such a wonderful family."[6]

    5. Galt Diary, 25 June, 4, 6, 18 Nov. 1861; SMG to cousin, 31 Oct. 1861, GFP; Board of Visitors Minutes, 8 Oct. 1861, UA-CWM; Richard M. Bucktrout Day Book, Nov.–Dec. 1861, MR-CWM.
    6. Cornelius M. Buckley, trans., *A Frenchman, a Chaplain, a Rebel: The War Letters of Pere Louis-Hippolyte Gache, S.J.* (Chicago: Loyola University Press, 1981), 67–70, 86.

Gray clouds interspersed with "lurid intervals of a purple tint" hung somberly over Prud'homme's long funeral procession through the streets of Williamsburg late that afternoon, 6 November. With an eye for color, Dr. Galt described the contrast of gray uniforms, "relieved by the red caps of the artillerymen," preceded by several Zouaves carrying a cross wreathed in white flowers and led by Father Gache clothed all in white. "This was probably the first time the city of King William of Orange ever witnessed a Catholic priest, fully vested in cassock, surplice and stole, walking in procession down its historic streets," the Jesuit later reflected. "Wonders never cease. But even more wonderful was the fact that the poor boy was mourned here amongst strangers with no less grief than if he had been buried at home." Prud'homme was buried at home after all, for two days later Bucktrout dug up his grave, number fourteen in the Louisiana row and marked with a cross at his head, and packed the coffin for shipment.[7]

Among Prud'homme's mourners at his Williamsburg funeral was Colonel Ewell, who accompanied Gache from the City Cemetery and invited him to tea and to stay the night in the President's House at the college. The priest gladly accepted. Ewell and his family made him "feel completely at home," even though the colonel and his sister Rebecca were Presbyterians and Lizzie an Episcopalian. "I couldn't have felt more at home with any other family, no matter how Catholic they might be," declared Gache. The next time the chaplain came to Williamsburg a few days later, Ewell lent him his "carriage drawn by two splendid gray horses" to drive the six miles to Spratley's Farm. There Gache improvised a huge tree trunk washed up on the shore as a confessional for the Dreux Battalion. After two days at Spratley's, Gache again used Ewell's carriage to return to Yorktown.[8]

A week later the Jesuit came back to Williamsburg to stay five days with the Ewells and visit the sick, some of whom "expressed the desire to receive Communion." For that he needed a more suitable location to say mass than the Southalls' parlor, and when he mentioned this to Rebecca Ewell, she knew just the place. If the Protestants could use the asylum chapel, why not the Catholics? That Saturday, 16 November, Rebecca first asked permission from asylum president Saunders, then called on Dr. Galt with Gache. "I agreed to let him have the Chapel for mass at 8 o'clock tomorrow morning," Dr. Galt mentioned in his diary, and instructed an officer "to have a fire built up, and

7. Galt Diary, 7 Nov. 1861; Buckley, *A Frenchman, a Chaplain, a Rebel*, 68; Bucktrout Day Book, 8 Nov. 1861.
8. Buckley, *A Frenchman, a Chaplain, a Rebel*, 70–2.

to furnish a table of the necessary height—as to which point, the Father seemed to insist very particularly." Thus, on Sunday, 17 November, Gache could muse, "here it was in the largest and most beautiful building in Williamsburg that I offered mass before a dozen or so Catholic convalescents and some twenty Episcopalian ladies," most of whom, to his surprise, treated him with the utmost kindness and respect.[9]

The genial priest attended a reception that evening at the Ewells', and several ladies paid a visit "with the rather obvious intention of seeing me." Again he found "all were most charming and friendly" except for one whose "manner was rather arrogant and impertinent." The Episcopal Rev. Mr. Thomas M. Ambler also dropped in. As "he greeted me, he put on a mask of sweet innocence which he wore rather unconvincingly during the series of barbed questions and ever-so-polite objections which followed," Gache revealed. Rebecca Ewell came to the father's defense, "showing herself to be a much better theologian than the minister." Many at the mass that morning and in the Ewells' home that night were Lizzie's friends, drawn by the novelty of Catholicism, but Gache soon endeared himself to all. Before leaving he gave Lizzie a "Poorman's Catechism" that she cherished all her life.[10]

Probably not included among the gaggle of Episcopalian ladies was Cynthia Coleman. Charles had been visiting Williamsburg that week and left his wife with a houseful of invalids Sunday morning. Besides Monty, who finally showed signs of recovering, Sadie, Bland, and Lucy Tucker were all sick. Cynthia juggled caring for them with her hospital work and had the added burden of preparing for her eldest brother's impending wedding. At twenty-two, Dr. Beverley St. George Tucker, nicknamed Sainty, was a Confederate surgeon on duty in Richmond and was engaged to Dr. John Mercer's daughter Elizabeth, or Lilie. Most in the Tucker household were well enough on the evening of 26 November to attend the wedding at the Mercers' home near the eastern end of town. Dr. Coleman could not make it, however, having too recently been in Williamsburg, much to Cynthia's disappointment. Many of his friends, including the bride's uncle Lt. Mercer Waller, asked about him and "are very much interested in your transfer," Cynthia informed him, raising her hopes it would happen soon. Lilie's brother Tommy Mercer was probably absent too. He left the Junior Guards for an appointment to the Virginia Military Institute in Lexington the previous month. The next day Cynthia, though "feeling dreadfully" from exhaustion, helped her mother entertain the bride

9. Ibid., 73; Galt Diary, 16, 17 Nov. 1861.
10. Buckley, *A Frenchman, a Chaplain, a Rebel,* 73–4.

and groom and twenty guests at the traditional bridal dinner. Now that the Zouaves were no longer throwing parties, Sainty and Lilie Tucker's wedding provided the high point of Williamsburg's November social calendar.[11]

Not that the Zouaves had entirely ceased to entertain the town, after their own fashion. Their October antics of pilfering pigs and chickens had apparently tapered off in November, due in part perhaps to Colonel Hunt's efforts to cut off their liquor supply and to encourage "playing ball and other games amongst his men" for a diversion. But on 3 November Sally Galt and Letitia Semple requested Bruton Church be railed in "to guard against an excess of desecration." On the ninth Dr. Galt observed "an enclosure of planking being erected around" the Baptist and Methodist churches and the new courthouse, probably for the same reason. Two days earlier Dr. Galt accepted a fourth insane Zouave into the asylum. A Louisiana woman, possibly a nurse, called a "Vivandiere in Bloomer-Zouave dress," visiting the asylum had already captured his attention.[12]

November brought Williamsburg several frosty nights, but the season's first snow arrived on the evening of 1 December. That day the first soldier to die in December, a Louisianan, Bucktrout buried in Prud'homme's vacated plot. Four days later property taxes were due. Only two Williamsburg citizens declined to pay, with Lemuel Bowden refusing "exclusively upon the illegality of the ordinance of secession and consequent want of power to impose or collect any tax." This stand, courageous as it may have been, "greatly excited the ire of the Confederates" and did not enhance Bowden's popularity. Only when his property was advertised for sale on 8 December did Bowden pay, though "not without a written protest against the validity of the tax."[13]

That same day persistent rumors of impending engagements "at last assumed a more positive shape" in the form of a Magruder directive to prepare cartridges and evacuate the hospitals for wounded. This was due to the recent Federal occupation of Virginia's Eastern Shore and the forty thousand Union troops the excitable commanding general believed were massing on the Peninsula for an attack "on all our points simultaneously" within the week. Magruder immediately pulled all his forces down to Yorktown, stripping Williamsburg of its small garrison, which he planned to replace with militia. Although 8 December was a Sunday, the ladies spent the day making car-

11. CBT to CWC, 18, 19, 24, 25, 27 Nov. 1861, TCP; Lee A. Wallace Jr., *1st Virginia Infantry* (Lynchburg, H. E. Howard, 1985), 106.

12. Galt Diary, 11 Oct., 1, 3, 7, 9, 19 Nov. 1861.

13. Ibid., 2, 8 Nov. 1861; Bucktrout Day Book, 1 Dec. 1861; Lemuel J. Bowden F/A, UA-CWM.

tridges. Two days later Cynthia wrote her husband that "the sick who were well enough to be moved have all been sent off to Richmond; this morning but three patients were left in the Episcopal Church, but before dinner they had begun to fill up again and numbered thirteen." The Baptist church still sheltered twenty typhoid cases and on Sunday sent a messenger to Cynthia asking for Dr. Coleman, raising her hopes once more "that something was in the wind and you were coming up." If he did not come up, she determined to go down to Yorktown but then decided to go to Richmond instead to contact a publisher for *Partisan Leader* and do some Christmas shopping.[14]

The day Cynthia was preparing for her Richmond trip, 11 December, Magruder was trying to convince Confederate authorities of his need to call out militia. Secretary of War Judah P. Benjamin did not believe forty thousand Federals could possibly be on the Peninsula. Besides, he reproached Magruder, "It is quite impolitic to call out an unarmed militia, and no call for them can be sanctioned." The general retorted that he could arm two thousand men and calculated his call for militia would not produce more than half that number. He only needed to fill Williamsburg's earthworks in case the Federals broke through his Yorktown defenses. Already placed in depot in Williamsburg and Jamestown were about twenty days' rations for ten thousand men. On 11 December Magruder called out militias from James City, New Kent, and Charles City Counties, but since Williamsburg still had no garrison on the twentieth, he extended the call to an additional twenty counties plus the city of Richmond on Christmas Eve. The militia officers were to muster their regiments, inspect them, and report to Colonel Ewell the number of men and arms available. They could stay home and drill but must "hold themselves in readiness to march to Williamsburg at a moment's warning."[15]

Christmas Day on the Peninsula remained calm enough for Magruder to announce the troops could winter at their current posts. Williamsburg was unusually quiet. Dr. Galt observed that owing "to the deficiency of gunpowder, few or no Christmas-guns were fired off, notwithstanding the many arms now here with the forces of the Confederacy." Sadly, four soldiers died Christmas Day, the most on any one day in a month that saw thirty-four expire, half from Louisiana. At one point during the day, the African Baptist church surgeon sent a messenger next door to Sally Galt to beg some milk on behalf "of a sick brother who will drink nothing but tea or milk. I would not trouble you," he apologized, "but there is no tea in the Hospital and I know not where

14. Galt Diary, 8 Dec. 1861; *OR,* 4:707–8; CBT to CWC, 10, 11 Dec. 1861, TCP.
15. *OR,* 4:708–14, 51(2):431–2.

I can get any but of Miss Gault whose kindness to our sick vols is spoken of by all." Requests to Sally for lemonade, tea, milk, and other "delicacies" continued into the next day.[16]

The last days of 1861 brought such cold weather to Williamsburg that the college millpond froze over, and before long boys were skating on it. On New Year's Eve only 377 soldiers were posted for duty in the city, with another 551 stationed at Spratley's Farm, out of a total of 20,683 Confederates on the Peninsula. The various militias alerted on Christmas Eve, after protesting through Governor Letcher to President Davis, never came to Williamsburg. But then, the 40,000 Federals never made their appearance either. December records reveal only about 13,000 northern soldiers in the entire Department of Virginia. As Dr. Galt remarked on New Year's Eve, "The rumors of skirmishes and impending battles on the Peninsula, seem now to have ceased entirely."[17]

The year 1862 began just as peacefully, so peacefully that Dr. Galt scrawled on 2 January, as "a sign of the times observe that the sentry at the yard below the Asylum, is now often without any weapon." On that day a Georgia soldier became Williamsburg's first death of the year, buried in the thirteenth grave in the Georgia row. Also that day Dr. Coleman, who had been visiting Williamsburg for a few days, returned to Yorktown and wrote Cynthia, "I have heard nothing from Genl Magruder, but if I do not hear from him in a few days, I will give him a reminder, even if I have to get Col Randolph to see him for me for to Williamsburg I must go." On the morning of 9 January, Lt. Edwin Taliaferro penned a note to his sister-in-law announcing that "Dr. Coleman has at length been transferred & ordered to report for duty in Williamsburg." He closed with the understatement, "I know it will be so pleasant a change to both of you."[18]

Another private celebration in Williamsburg took place on 6 January at Catherine Maupin's boardinghouse, where Dr. Samuel Griffin and his son enjoyed a mince pie in honor of his eightieth birthday. That evening Dr. Galt recorded in his diary that the temperature reached only twenty-four degrees with "snow covering a surface of sleet." The next day he observed "that a large portion of the farms on the peninsula would become as a waste, from the rails being used by the troops as fire wood, instead of taking the trouble of cutting

16. *OR*, 4:715; Galt Diary, 25, 26 Dec. 1861; William Kirk to SMG, 25 Dec. 1861, GFP; Bucktrout Day Book, Dec. 1861.

17. Galt Diary, 30, 31 Dec. 1861; *OR*, 4:632, 716.

18. Galt Diary, 2 Jan. 1862; Bucktrout Day Book, 2 Jan. 1862; CWC to CBT, 2 Jan. 1862, TCP; Edwin Taliaferro to CBT, 9 Jan. 1862, TCP.

down trees for the same purpose—one gentleman it was stated, had lost ten miles of fencing from this source." Perhaps that gentleman was Dr. Robert Waller. A company of the 32d Virginia wintering at Camp Waller on his property was costing him, he reckoned, about ten thousand dollars in fencing and "fire wood taken for the army to burn, & timber for building winter Quarters."[19]

Soldiers still found comfort in private homes that frigid January, including the Galts', where dinner parties continued throughout the month. In addition, several military surgeons called to borrow medical books from Dr. Galt, and various soldiers consulted him about medical problems. Hospitality also enlivened the Ewells' household, particularly when Father Gache came to town. On visits to Williamsburg the Jesuit was deeply touched by "a few good and pious ladies there who show me such consideration and esteem and who welcome the opportunity to do little favors for me." He especially appreciated a woolen mattress they made him. No less solicitous were the Protestant ministers, who "are all courtesy in my regard and lavish their kindness upon me," wrote Gache. The Baptist pastor William Young "truly treats me as a brother," and even Ambler insisted on entertaining the Catholic priest, despite their earlier confrontation. "We are almost always arguing with one another—and I don't spare him a bit—but that doesn't spoil our friendship."[20]

Military rather than theological topics absorbed other Williamsburg citizens during January's long winter hours. While watching herds of cattle and droves of hogs pass through town to provision Peninsula troops, Dr. Galt and his friends discussed such topics as whether more life was lost "from active fighting than from the existing inertia." They also debated whether the enemy would ever make "an advance in this direction," whether Magruder's fortifications were "completely worthless," and whether "the war was as good as done with—over." Only a week after two members of the bar presented the latter opinion on 16 January, reports of Confederate reversals in Kentucky began filtering into Williamsburg, providing more grist for the rumor mill and beginning a pattern of depression that gripped the town throughout the following month.[21]

A glimmer of hope came with General Magruder's brief visit to the asylum on 1 February. At that time he announced he "would return the Churches to

19. JLCG Commonplace Book, 7 Jan. 1863, JLCG FA File, UA-CWM; Galt Diary, 6, 7 Jan. 1862; Jensen, *32nd Virginia Infantry*, 54; Robert Page Waller Diary, 4 Oct. 1863, MR-CWM.
20. Galt Diary, 14, 19, 25, 27 Jan. 1862; Buckley, *A Frenchman, a Chaplain, a Rebel*, 95.
21. Galt Diary, 3, 13, 16–18, 25–26, 29 Jan. 1862.

the several denominations" since some of the hospitals were closing for lack of patients. According to Bucktrout's records, the January death count from disease dropped to fourteen. Nevertheless, the four churches continued as hospitals in February, with twelve deaths occurring in them and in the new courthouse and college hospitals. No longer a hospital, the Vest Store was being used as a quartermaster's department by the 32d Virginia's quartermaster, Capt. Tom McCandlish.[22]

Early February also brought rumors of 4,000 more troops landing at Fort Monroe, but Magruder's earthworks were not yet complete to resist them. Reluctant to impress slaves from his own department again, he tried to call on other counties for labor, but the War Department countermanded his orders. Ewell, again commanding the Williamsburg post since Colonel Hunt's transfer to Yorktown, tried to help by writing his former language professor, Edward Joynes, at the War Department. "Not less than 1,000 or 1,500 negroes ought to be at work, and in six weeks, with this force would the defenses be finished and rendered well-nigh impregnable," Ewell insisted in his 7 February letter. "The counties south and west of Richmond can well afford to furnish this labor."[23]

Not only were the works unfinished, but they were also unmanned. In desperation, Magruder ordered Ewell on 15 February to organize on paper all the nurses and government employees "to be ready at a moment's notice to defend the works in front of Williamsburg, and lay aside arms and ammunition for the same." Magruder further directed Ewell to "prepare arms for any citizens, of whatever age, who are willing to turn out and assist in holding the works in front of Williamsburg should the lower defenses at Jamestown be passed." If they could not cover all points, the most important were Fort Magruder and Tutters Neck on the right flank, Magruder stressed. What black labor Ewell could scrape up must prepare "without the slightest delay the forts already constructed for the reception of guns" and complete "such works as may be unfinished."[24]

While Magruder feverishly readied the Peninsula for imminent crisis, the Confederacy's major disaster occurred six hundred miles to the west on the Cumberland River in Tennessee, where the Federals captured Fort Donelson on 16 February. News of the defeat reached Williamsburg three days later, immediately plunging the community into "great despondency" and "constant

22. Ibid., 1–2 Feb. 1862; Bucktrout Day Book, Jan.–Feb. 1862.
23. *OR*, 9:40–3.
24. Ibid., 42–3.

anxiety." Some people talked about removing their families, and "under the gloom" one asylum officer decided not to attend President Davis's inauguration scheduled for the twenty-second. That was also Washington's Birthday, usually a big day in Williamsburg, but the townspeople were so disheartened, Dr. Galt observed, "No attention paid to celebrating the day."[25]

"Everybody here seems to have had a gloom over them, ever since our defeat at Fort Donelson," echoed Robert Saunders's eighteen-year-old daughter, Roberta Page, on 26 February. She was writing to Lizzie Ewell, who had been banished to Richmond by her father, perhaps to remove her from harm's way or from her romance with Louisiana soldier David Levy, among others, of the Dreux Battalion. A rumor was circulating in Williamsburg that Magruder planned to attack the Federals already on the Peninsula. "If the Yankees should whip our men, why they will march up to this place, I can't think of Wmsburg as in the hands of the Yankees, can you?" Page fretted. "I don't believe they will come." Whatever happened, the Confederate units posted locally were sure to be transferred, other rumors indicated. "Well! your beloved David has succeeded in getting a commission," Page informed Lizzie; "he is a Lieut in some company; but—he is going either to Kentucky or Tennessee, I don't know which; he can't leave until it is time for the Battalion to leave the Peninsula." In the meantime, Page enjoyed the attentions of such "Spratleyites" as Levy and Herbert Copland in what for her turned out to be "a delightful week."[26]

For Page and other Williamsburg belles, the fun had just begun. Louisiana boys were not about to let Mardi Gras pass unnoticed, and if they could not be in New Orleans for the festival, they would bring the festival to Williamsburg. With the help of the community, the Dreux Battalion fashioned decorations and confetti from flour balls. "Oh! we are going to have grand doings in town tomorrow night," Page wrote Lizzie on 3 March, "Dreux Battalion will celebrate Mardi Gras." Her family planned to go to the Amblers' house on Main Street across from Bruton Church to watch the procession, if the weather, which had been continuously wet for a month, would cooperate.[27]

It did. "Oh! my dearest Lizzie, how shall I begin to tell you about yesterday," Page continued her epistle on 5 March, "it was the most glorious & charming day, the whole of it, from the morning until nearly one o'clock at night, that I ever spent." She regretted Lizzie and Colonel Munford's daugh-

25. Galt Diary, 19–22 Feb. 1862.
26. R. Page Saunders to Elizabeth Ewell, 24–26 Feb. 1862, EFP, MR-CWM.
27. Galt Diary, 3 Mar. 1862; R. Page Saunders to Elizabeth Ewell, 3–5 Mar. 1862, EFP.

ters, Sallie and Maria, also in Richmond, missed the "carnival," for "everybody in the city of Wmsburg turned out." Rebecca Ewell joined the Saunders family for a picnic, where Page drank four glasses of champagne. Then "some two hundred New Orleans boys got up a wonderful procession, rigged out in as fantastic a manner as it was possible to accomplish," one participant recalled years later. "About eight o'clock the procession entered town, all dressed in the most ridiculous style; some were dressed like devils, some as clowns, some as ladies, goats, some as horses & standing up," Page detailed in her missive. "Mr Copland was a devil or an imp, I don't know which, as he passed us he kissed his hand to me several times. The street was as bright as day, with the torch lights, the procession went up & down town twice, there was a large wagon filled with gentlemen dressed up to look like servants, they were all musicians."[28]

At the close of the parade, townspeople gathered on Courthouse Green to listen to two "very smart & amusing" speakers, while Magruder and his staff, who had come to Williamsburg for the occasion, adjourned to the City Hotel. There they were entertained by members of the Dreux Battalion, one named Billy Campbell convincingly disguised as a young girl. "Magruder, with that gallantry which always characterized him, placed 'Miss' Campbell on his right hand, who partook liberally of everything that was going, including the liquors," a Louisianan recounted. "How far this thing would have gone on it is difficult to say, had not some of the boys ripped up a feather bed belonging to the landlord of the hotel and permitted its contents to fall through an aperture immediately above the dining room, calling out at the same time: 'This is a Louisiana snowstorm.'" The diversion allowed Campbell to escape, leaving a bewildered "Prince John" standing amid the feathers.[29]

Campbell and about twenty of his comrades next showed up at Captain Henley's house, where lived Henley's nieces, Harriette Cary and Mattie Pierce, both twenty-three years old. Needing more female society, Mattie sent Capt. Thomas Powell of the 10th Louisiana to fetch Page Saunders and her sister. "I did have a charming time," Page confided to Lizzie. "I fell in love at least five times." She found most of the gentlemen still in their masquerades—a Greek with "a perfect Grecian face," an Indian whose painted face could not conceal "how handsome he was," and "a Prince of olden times" who "desired to be remembered to your ladyship." Then there was "Mr Campbell,

28. Saunders to Ewell, 3–5 Mar. 1862; R. G. Lowe, "The Dreux Battalion," *Confederate Veteran* 5 (1897): 55–6.
29. Saunders to Ewell 3–5 Mar. 1862; Lowe, "Dreux Battalion," 55–6.

he was a lady & he looked perfectly lovely, he is only seventeen, poor little fellow!" Page declared.[30]

The next morning a sleepy Captain Powell again called at the Saunders House on Palace Green and escorted Page to church for Ash Wednesday. Reality had already begun to set in. Though Dr. Galt pronounced it "a fine exhibition of Mardi Gras," others argued that such "jollification" would never have been permitted had the troops not been so demoralized. "Indeed, Lizzie, things begin to look very serious," Page moaned, having heard a rumor on the morning of 3 March that "Twenty five thousand Yankees have landed at Fortress Monroe! I cried a *little* yesterday when the gentlemen were talking about the people having to leave here & Wmsburg being burnt." Page's eldest sister, Marianne Wilmer, was planning to leave the following week with her husband, George, and family for their home in Pittsylvania County, Virginia, taking some of the Saunders' silver with them. But Page was confident that "if there was any danger Papa would send us away, he has not said a word about our leaving, & has been trying to get Mr Wilmer to stay longer."[31]

The danger at the moment shifted from the Peninsula to Norfolk, toward which the Federals assembling at Fort Monroe since late February were expected to aim their attack. Accordingly, Magruder received orders on 4 March to send 5,000 of his troops with two batteries, more than half his effective strength, south of the James River in support of Norfolk. Though willing to cooperate as fully as possible, Magruder feared the Federals might advance up the Peninsula instead and he would be "forced back to Williamsburg, as there would be three roads to guard with a force of not more than 4,000 men." Nevertheless, on 6 March Magruder reported his men ready to embark at Kingsmill. They were to boat upriver to catch a ride on the railroad south of the James to Suffolk. The next day Dr. Galt learned that seven regiments amounting to 5,000 soldiers were presently in the vicinity, but while they waited, an unexpected development changed the situation entirely.[32]

On Sunday, 9 March, the telegraph operator in Williamsburg received news of the ironclad CSS *Virginia*'s victory over the Union fleet in Hampton Roads the previous day. "Although we were so near to the scene of action, and the Battle began on Saturday, the news did not reach us until Sunday just before going to Church," wrote Cynthia Coleman a few days later, "then we only heard there was a great battle going on." On that Sunday, the *Virginia*

30. Saunders to Ewell, 3–5 Mar. 1862.
31. Ibid.; Galt Diary, 4, 6 Mar. 1862.
32. *OR*, 9:44–5, 50–9; Galt Diary, 7 Mar. 1862.

(formerly USS *Merrimack*) and the new ironclad USS *Monitor* were fighting to a draw in Hampton Roads and changing the course of naval warfare forever. "The excitement here was very great, prayers went up from every heart for Victory," Cynthia reported. On Monday the tenth Dr. Galt found "Rejoicing is general at the late news."[33]

Some firsthand accounts of the engagement reached Williamsburg the following week when a "most proud & happy" young soldier who participated in the shore support came up to visit his mother, an asylum patient spending the day with Sally Galt. Inmates frequently visited Sally, though she was "almost constantly occupied" making jelly and custard for the hospitals, particularly the African church. "Being so near me I do a great deal for it, indeed I call myself the Patron Saint of that Institution," she wrote on 26 March. "Most of the ladies in Williamsburg visit the sick soldiers, but I never do, & consequently think I ought to do as much at home for them as I can." Her African church lost one Louisiana soldier 12 March, number thirty-six in that state's row; a Georgian died the same day at the Southalls', number forty in the Georgia row; and a Virginia boy expired while posted at Lieutenant Taliaferro's Ordnance Department, the eighth in that row. Despite an outbreak of the often-fatal scarlet fever in March, Williamsburg's military mortality that month totaled eleven, the lowest since October.[34]

Along with their continuous nursing duties, Williamsburg ladies busied themselves in March with fundraising. It soon became apparent that the more maneuverable shallow-draft *Monitor* could slip up the river past *Virginia* and threaten not only Williamsburg but also Richmond. On 23 March the ladies, wanting to do their part to "whip the Yankees," met in Dr. Williamson's parlor to discuss sponsoring construction of a gunboat, which they figured would cost between five and six thousand dollars. They planned on "giving Concerts, Suppers, taking up subscriptions in our midst, and invoking the aid of the Ladies throughout the State," Cynthia Coleman revealed. That same day Magruder announced that martial law declared on 19 March for the Peninsula included Williamsburg too, as "great disorder is represented to be at times caused by the sale there of spirituous liquors," he reminded Richmond authorities. This was quickly followed by more irresponsible talk "about the probability of Williamsburg being burnt," Dr. Galt reported, who added skeptically,

33. Galt Diary, 9–10 Mar. 1862; CBT to Lawrence Washington, 13 Mar. 1862, Louis Malesherbes Goldsborough Papers, Special Collections Library, Duke University, Durham, N.C.
34. SMG to cousin, 26 Mar. [1862], GFP; Bucktrout Day Book, Mar. 1862; CBT to Washington, 13 Mar. 1862.

"Some persons seem to present this pleasing idea, simply by way of seeing what effect is induced in the hearer." On the twenty-sixth came tales of a large Federal force landing at Old Point, bringing another "great panic in Williamsburg; many persons moving," observed Dr. Galt three days later, "or preparing to move off with their families and servants."[35]

Dr. Coleman's mother was among those considering relocation. She "has a good many servants," Cynthia wrote at this time, "and the Doct. has been *thinking* of moving them somewhere, the *where* a question of great difficulty." With a married daughter living in Lynchburg, Dr. Waller knew where he could flee, but traveling was hard on his weakened body, and he was burdened with more slaves than he could take along. He finally decided to let many of them stay on his York County farms under one of his overseers. Most of his household staff accompanied him, but, as with many abandoning their homes, at least one trusted servant remained to look after the premises.[36]

About the time Dr. Waller and other refugees were heading up the Peninsula, Lizzie Ewell was on her way down, back to Williamsburg. Sallie Munford, still in Richmond, wrote Lizzie on 27 March that although she enjoyed all her "delightful gentlemen acquaintances" in the capital, "I shall be, not only willing, but most happy to go back to dear old Williamsburg in a few weeks." Whether she would be able to return in a few weeks was beginning to look doubtful, for that large Federal force reportedly landing at Old Point on 26 March was the advance of Maj. Gen. George B. McClellan's Army of the Potomac, and more were sailing toward Fort Monroe for the purpose of marching up the Peninsula to capture Richmond. Directly in the middle of their path lay "dear old Williamsburg."[37]

35. *OR*, 11(3):386, 393, 398, 51(2):503, 505; CBT to Hugh Blair Grigsby, 25 Mar. 1862, TCP; Galt Diary, 23, 26–30 Mar. 1862.

36. CBT to Washington, 13 Mar. 1862; Waller Diary, Oct. 1862–May 1863.

37. Sallie Munford to Elizabeth Ewell, 27 Mar. 1862, EFP.

PART 2

The Battle of Williamsburg

CHAPTER 4

Sunday Skirmish

Ever since its victory at Manassas in July 1861, the southern army under Gen. Joseph E. Johnston had remained camped in that vicinity. The northern Army of the Potomac, meanwhile, stayed in Washington, recruiting, reorganizing, and training under its new commander, George McClellan. After the Federals suffered another humiliating repulse at Ball's Bluff above Washington in October 1861, President Lincoln appointed McClellan, only thirty-five years old, general in chief of all Union armies. By February 1862, Lincoln judged the army ready for the field, but McClellan hesitated, and his overcautious nature and inflated ego brought him into constant conflict with the president. Finally, Lincoln reduced McClellan back to commander of the army, divided it into four corps, and ordered it to move against Richmond.

Again McClellan, affectionately called "Little Mac" by his men, disagreed with Lincoln. The president wanted his army to push overland to Richmond, keeping between the Confederates and Washington in order to protect the capital. McClellan preferred to bypass the southern army by shipping his men to the Rappahannock River before marching to Richmond but found that Johnston beat him to the landing site. Thus, the Peninsular route via Fort Monroe became his next choice. Lincoln consented but held back one corps to guard his capital. In preparation for the transfer of the rest of the army, McClellan received a report on 19 March incorporating information from a Union spy, a Confederate deserter, and some escaped slaves. "On the right of the road, 1 mile below Williamsburg, there is Fort Magruder, a square redoubt with two mounted guns," it stated; "on the left of the road two square redoubts without mounted guns."[1]

1. OR, 11(3):22–3.

Not only was this report grossly incomplete but also totally inaccurate. Fort Magruder actually straddled York, or Telegraph, Road, guarding the fork where York and Hampton Roads merged. An irregular, elongated pentagon, Fort Magruder had nine-foot-thick walls rising fifteen feet out of a flooded moat nine feet deep. Its interior crest measured six hundred yards around, presented a face seventy yards across, and made a platform for eight guns. Several rows of sturdy barracks stood northwest of the fort behind extended ramparts. South of the fort on its right flank were five smaller, roughly square redoubts with ditches, hollowed-out magazines, barbettes cut for gun emplacements, and thirty- to sixty-yard faces. Redoubt One on the far right loomed over the milldam at Tutters Pond and along with Redoubts Two and Three guarded the road called Quarterpath Trace leading from Kingsmill Wharf to Williamsburg. These earthworks stood about a quarter mile apart, as did Redoubts Four and Five, which commanded Fort Magruder. Nearby, timber had been felled with the branches pointing out to form natural abatis. Also chopped down and entangled were all trees standing within artillery range, about one mile, of Fort Magruder, including the first several hundred yards of the dense forest across the plain and down both the York and Hampton Roads. Old grass-covered Revolutionary War breastworks still lay across these roads in and out of thickly matted brush. As a finishing touch, the slope in front of the fort and its nearest redoubts contained numerous rifle pits.[2]

Spreading more than two miles to the left, or northeast, of Fort Magruder (designated number six), were eight more redoubts and open V-shaped redans. Those numbered seven through twelve were arranged on either side of a country road that traversed a cultivated wheat field. Redoubt Eleven stood at the intersection of this country road with a road that crossed the dam over Jones Pond and continued into Williamsburg. Perched on a hill guarding the approach to Jones Pond was Redoubt Fourteen. Dense piney woods lay behind this entire left side of the line and screened its view from Williamsburg. Though Capt. Alfred Rives had planned and built these works with great care, he now considered them "most defective, making a line equally strong it is true, but equally weak at the same time." He particularly feared when "one small redoubt is carried, which can easily be done, the troops cease to have confidence in the whole line." Besides, the line would become useless the mo-

2. Ibid., 19; *New-York Daily Tribune*, 12 May 1862; U.S. War Department, *Atlas to Accompany the Official Records of the Union and Confederate Armies* (Washington: Government Printing Office, 1880–1901), plate XX; LM to children, 21–25 July 1861, LM Papers, Southern Historical Collection of the Manuscripts Department, Wilson Library, UNC; J. H. B. Jenkins to Mary Benjamin, 17 May 1862, HCH, MR-CWM.

ment Federal gunboats could penetrate the river defenses and bypass Williamsburg completely.[3]

To prevent such a disaster, General Magruder suggested in a 20 March letter to General Lee that the James River be obstructed with sunken vessels. Four days later he resumed begging for reinforcements in correspondence to the new secretary of war, his former artillery chief George Randolph, since he was convinced his force of six thousand now faced thirty thousand Federals on the Peninsula. On the twenty-fifth Randolph wired back that two infantry regiments plus Brig. Gen. Henry Wise's legion had been ordered to Magruder, but more substantial reinforcements were planned. That same day Lee wrote Johnston asking how many troops he could send to the Peninsula from their present location on the Rappahannock River. Twenty-five thousand was Johnston's reply on the twenty-sixth.[4]

Many more Federals than that had been steaming down Chesapeake Bay for Old Point throughout late March and early April and were now preparing to march up the Peninsula. Although Dr. John Galt believed the recent wet weather was "unfavourable to the Yankees, by keeping the ground too much saturated with moisture, to allow a facility of advance in the artillery & cavalry," rain would not impede the navy. On 26 March Lee advised Magruder to prepare his retreat in the event Union gunboats managed to force a passage by the James and York river batteries. Consequently, on 4 April Magruder ordered Col. Benjamin Ewell to press all available vehicles in the country to move all sick soldiers from Williamsburg to either Bigler's Wharf or Jamestown for transport to Richmond. Ewell received further instructions that evening through ordnance officer Lt. Edwin Taliaferro. Since the Federal army had appeared by then in front of the Yorktown line, Magruder directed Taliaferro to send down half of all the ammunition in Williamsburg and "have the rest ready for issue." Ewell must prepare the artillery to cover a possible Confederate retreat, and as that could occur at any moment, the men were to remain all night in the works, sleeping on their arms.[5]

The next day, 5 April, McClellan's troops opened fire along the entire Yorktown line. Magruder's army repulsed them, yet he expected blue hordes to break through his position momentarily. On 7 April he instructed Ewell to pile firewood at Kingsmill Wharf and ignite it if Federal gunboats breached

3. *OR Atlas*, plate XX; Richard L. Maury, *The Battle of Williamsburg and the Charge of the Twenty-fourth Virginia of Early's Brigade* (Richmond: Johns and Goolsby, Steam Printers, 1880), 6–7; *OR*, 11(3):388–9.

4. *OR*, 11(3):387, 393, 400–1.

5. John Minson Galt II Diary, 30 Mar. 1862, GFP, MR-CWM; *OR*, 11(3):398, 421.

the lower river batteries. Magruder then turned his attention to his Williams-burg works, considering them "of importance in defending the Peninsula and in securing the best means of safety for the army in case of disaster." But they still contained only the three old carronades left there last October along with two or three old iron guns. "Ten heavy rifled guns and ten batteries of light artillery are required for these works" along with at least two field batteries for Spratley's, and a "large quantity of ammunition is necessary to be deposited at Williamsburg," Magruder implored Lee. He also requested two hundred wag-ons, one hundred horses, and an additional one thousand slaves to finish the earthworks.[6]

Ammunition for Magruder's guns was already on its way downriver, Lee replied on 9 April, but he did not want any more slaves so close to the Union lines and suggested that the troops be put to work instead. "Soldiers cannot be expected to work night and day and fight besides," argued Magruder in his final appeal to the local citizens on 11 April. Defying Lee, he instructed slaveholders to send their laborers "at once, under overseers, to Colonel Ewell, at Williamsburg." On that day the entire garrison at Williamsburg and its vi-cinity numbered only two hundred men. Clearly, Ewell needed more fighters as well as diggers to secure his works and report any progress on them, as Magruder requested of him on 14 April. Again the general urged Ewell to "push forward as much as possible the defenses" at Spratley's Farm and Wil-liamsburg, "completing the works at Williamsburg first."[7]

By that time, Johnston had already assumed command of the Peninsula and his army had begun filling the Yorktown line, relieving Magruder's over-worked troops. On 6 April Ewell received word that the first units would steam down the York River to Bigler's and march directly to Yorktown. Within five days, Magruder's ranks had swollen from about 11,500 to some 31,500, still inadequate to meet the 100,000 northerners McClellan was send-ing up to the Yorktown line. On 16 April the Federals decided to test Confed-erate strength at Yorktown again, and again they were repulsed in a minor skirmish. One Confederate casualty, shot in the arm, was brought up to Wil-liamsburg to recover in the African church as Richard Bucktrout took time out from building coffins to make him a splint. A man in Cobb's Legion, shot through the hip, also came up only to die at the College Hospital on the seventeenth and fill the forty-seventh grave in the Georgia row.[8]

    6. *OR*, 11(3):403–4, 424–31; R. G. Lowe, "Magruder's Defenses of the Peninsula," *Confeder-ate Veteran* 8 (1900): 107.
    7. *OR*, 11(3):434–7, 440.
    8. Ibid., 424–5, 436; Richard M. Bucktrout Day Book, 17, 18 Apr. 1862, MR-CWM.

Though most troops arriving by riverboat at Bigler's and Kingsmill by-passed Williamsburg completely, those coming overland traversed its streets on their way down the Peninsula. "A Regiment of Cavalry, two Brigades of Infantry, several companies of Artillery have passed throught [*sic*] Town to-day, and more are expected to-night," Cynthia wrote on 18 April. "Stewarts Cavalry went down this morning." Soon Brig. Gen. James Ewell Brown Stuart's name would be so famous, she would not likely misspell it again. "We went out to the street and waved our handkerciefs to the poor fellows, who seemed in fine spirits," she continued. The boys in the Hampton Legion of South Carolina appreciated this greeting when they trotted into Williamsburg early one April morning. "The city was clean and very pretty," one trooper later recalled, "and the streets were lined with citizens, who heartily welcomed us." Another cavalryman judged it an "ancient and decayed town," commenting that "the College is not an imposing structure, tho the building seems to be a comparatively modern one. Looks more like a modern female institute than an old university for young men." He was little more impressed with the Eastern Lunatic Asylum, which he considered "a very large and imposing building, but there is nothing beautiful about it." On the way out of town, the legion passed close by Fort Magruder and "could see that there were many large guns planted there."[9]

More guns for the works came with the arrival of Maj. Gen. G. W. Smith's division, marching down from Richmond on 17 April. Some cavalry and artillery had come the day before, and Magruder requested Ewell to guide them from Charles City County to Williamsburg. As Smith's troops approached, the colonel received orders to take four guns from the division for his works and "put them in position with their ammunition and men to serve them." Smith would "examine the works at Williamsburg and place as many men in them as he may deem sufficient to hold the place in case we should fall back upon them." Magruder also instructed Ewell to dispatch a courier to Smith to "inform him and all other troops that they must hurry on in the most rapid manner, as we are struggling against great odds here, and every moment is of importance."[10]

With the arrival of Smith's division on 18 April, the Confederate army was

9. CBT to Sarah and Lawrence Washington, 18 Apr. 1862, Louis Malesherbes Goldsborough Papers, Special Collections Library, Duke University, Durham, N.C.; John Coxe, "With the Hampton Legion in the Peninsular Campaign," *Confederate Veteran* 29 (1921): 415; "Sketches from the Journal of a Confederate Soldier (Samuel Elias Mayes)," *Tyler's Quarterly* 6 (1924): 30–1.

10. *OR*, 11(3):43–6.

fully assembled on the Yorktown line, some 54,000 men to face over 101,000 Federals. A few days later the addition of another Union division brought the northern total to more than 112,000. McClellan, however, believed he was vastly outnumbered and, as an engineering officer, decided on a siege, digging his own entrenchments and hauling massive siege guns up the Peninsula from Fort Monroe. This was no easy task after frequent and heavy spring rains turned roads into bottomless quagmires. Throughout the month of April, the rains never ceased long enough for anything to dry.[11]

As the blue soldiers struggled to move through the Peninsula's muck, those in gray suffered the effects of having to sit in it. Yorktown's badly drained trenches were frequently flooded up to the knees. "The only rest at night was to sleep in the universal mud and water," remembered Johnston's ordnance chief, Lt. Col. Edward Porter Alexander. "Although the men in the worst locations were relieved as often as possible, an unusual amount of sickness resulted." Not surprisingly, the April deaths in Williamsburg hospitals averaged one a day, with a newly opened South Carolina row in the City Cemetery containing four. Before the month ended, Mississippi and Tennessee rows would be added to help accommodate fifty-one bodies. On 21 April Magruder ordered all available private buildings converted into hospitals. Unoccupied houses were taken first, then houses occupied only by men, followed by public offices and the Old Courthouse, after first evicting the guard encamped there. The City Hotel "must also be used before private families are forced to give up their residences," Magruder told Ewell, and family homes used only if the occupants could find shelter elsewhere.[12]

One private home Magruder ordered seized, assuming it abandoned, was Lemuel Bowden's commodious new house. Before McClellan's arrival at Fort Monroe, Bowden had fled with his two sons to a farm belonging to his sister, Mrs. Mary Piggott, nine miles up Richmond Road, "in consequence of the ill usage I had received," he later testified. His old political adversary, Henry Wise, had ordered Bowden's arrest while his cavalry was patrolling the Peninsula above Williamsburg in April. At one point a search party happened to stop at Mrs. Piggott's and discuss plans for Bowden's capture, unaware he was listening in the next room. When Magruder learned that Lemuel's daughter and brother's family occupied the Bowden House, he rescinded the order to seize it. Some Louisiana privates, "influenced no doubt by the tales they heard

11. Ibid., 97, 130, 484, 11(1):18.
12. Edward Porter Alexander, *Military Memoirs of a Confederate: A Critical Narrative* (1907; reprint, New York: Da Capo, 1993), 64; *OR*, 11(3):454; Bucktrout Day Book, Apr. 1862.

from the young officers of the disloyalty of the Bowdens," decided to deal with the "traitors" their own way. They plotted "to attack the house, drive out the inmates, break up the furniture, &c, & do Mr Bowden some bodily harm," Ewell later revealed. "This came by accident to my ears & I appealed to one of the officers, who acknowledged there was some truth in it." After Ewell explained to the officer "that any such attempt should be resisted by the guards in Williamsburg, & of a Company of soldiers camped near there," the threat was averted.[13]

By the end of April, scouting reports of Federal guns in place indicated Yorktown could not be held much longer. Johnston, long anxious to mass his army closer to Richmond, "ordered the Ammunition & Ord Stores in Depot at Wmbg to be shipped to Richmond as soon as possible," as Alexander advised Lieutenant Taliaferro on the thirtieth. Word quickly spread of preparations for the withdrawal, setting off Williamsburg's third panic in as many months. James City County court records were packed and shipped to Richmond for safekeeping. Lizzie Ewell was also shipped to Richmond once more by her father. Her Aunt Rebecca chose to stay and defend the President's House on campus, knowing that Benjamin Ewell would soon be whisked away with the army. Other brave hearts made the same difficult decision to dig in and face the approaching foe as their loved ones marched up the Peninsula. Maj. John Munford's wife, Margaret, though ailing with tuberculosis, bravely continued to occupy Tazewell Hall with her four young children, one a babe in arms.[14]

No less wrenching was the pain of sending a son to war. As Lt. Tom Tucker prepared to march away, Lucy Tucker insisted on "standing her ground in order to save, at least, some of her property," related Cynthia, who could not bear "the idea of leaving her alone under such circumstances." Several lost two sons to the Guards, including the widows Mary Lively, entrusted with the *Gazette*'s presses, and Catherine Maupin. John and Leonard Henley's mother,

13. BSE, "Magruder Reminiscence," EFP, MR-CWM; Henry A. Wise, "The Career of Wise's Brigade, 1861–5," *Southern Historical Society Papers* 25 (1897): 3; U.S. Congress, *The Report of the Joint committee on the Conduct of the War* (Washington: Government Printing Office, 1863), 1:582; Lemuel J. Bowden F/A, UA-CWM.

14. Joseph E. Johnston, *Narrative of Military Operations during the Civil War* (1874; reprint, New York: Da Capo, 1990), 118; E. P. Alexander to Edwin Taliaferro, 30 Apr. 1862, Beverley Randolph Wellford Papers, VHS; Rouse, *Cows on the Campus*, 64; Percy Gatling Hamlin, ed., *Making of a Soldier: Letters of General R. S. Ewell* (Richmond: Whittet and Shepperson, 1935), 107; P. Kearny to A. Kearny, 8 May 1862, WCP, MR-CWM (original in National Archives, Washington, D.C.); M. N. Munford to Henry Naglee, 19 Nov. 1862, WCP; Beverley B. Munford, *Random Recollections* (Privately printed, 1905), 11.

Harriette Henley, also bid farewell to a grandson, Pvt. Miles Cary of the Guards. With two sons fighting on opposite sides, the Southalls likewise elected to remain in Williamsburg.[15]

Others felt bound by duty to remain in town. Dr. Galt would not abandon his patients, nor would his cousin and assistant, Dr. Williamson. And Sally Galt would never abandon her brother. Richard Bucktrout was so busy with burials, he could not leave if he wanted to. His teenage daughter Delia, new wife, and infant son remained with him in their Main Street house, which contained his coffin shop in the basement. The Griffins also decided to stay in town, as James conducted his school until forced to close it on Friday, 2 May. Though Montegu Thompson owned property in Richmond, he and his maiden sister, Julia, preferred to reside in Williamsburg along with their visiting sister, Mrs. Isabella Sully, and her daughter Jennie.[16]

These were among the many who bid sad adieus to friends and relatives beating a hasty retreat ahead of the army. Robert Saunders managed to drag a "so so sad & unhappy" Page with the rest of his family out of Williamsburg and transport them and most of their servants to Pittsylvania County, leaving his trusted butler Edmund Parsons to guard the house and priceless library. Pittsylvania County happened to be the destination too of merchant W. W. Vest, who also relinquished his elegant home to the care of servants. Catherine Coleman and her daughter fled with what slaves they could take but left some hired to the asylum and some to watch their Palace building home. Although Tommy Mercer now served in Johnston's army as drillmaster of the 1st Virginia Regiment, Dr. John Mercer moved his wife and their seven remaining children from Williamsburg to Lynchburg to join Dr. Robert Waller.[17]

By the first of May, General Johnston was ready to move as well. Orders went out for Maj. Gen. D. H. Hill's division to start his train of supply wagons toward Williamsburg early in the morning of 2 May in order to reach town before dark and be out of the way of troops scheduled to march at that time. Only part of the 3d South Carolina Regiment could get underway the morn-

15. CBT to Sarah and Lawrence Washington, 18 Apr. 1862; Samuel Williamson, receipt to Mary Ann Lively, 22 Dec. 1862, Williamsburg *Gazette* microfilm, CWM; JRC to Juliana Dorsey, 26 Apr. 1863, DCP, MR-CWM; Jensen, *32nd Virginia Infantry*, 177; BSE, "The College in the Years 1861–1865," *William and Mary Quarterly*, 2d ser., 8 (1928): 292.

16. Gabriella Galt to Mary Jeffrey Galt, 25 Mar. 1865, GFP; JLCG Commonplace Book, 14 July 1862, JLCG F/A, UA-CWM; Isabella Sully to CBT, 14 Apr. 1863, TCP, MR-CWM.

17. R. Page Saunders to Elizabeth Ewell, [14 May 1862], 30 May [1862]; CBT to CWC, 15 Dec. 1863, TCP; CBT, "Williamsburg during the Occupancy," TCP; Robert Page Waller Diary, 6 Sept. 1863, MR-CWM; Wallace, *1st Virginia Infantry*, 106.

ing of the second, accompanying its trains out of Yorktown and arriving in Williamsburg that afternoon. Now attached to Brig. Gen. Lafayette McLaws's division, the 3d South Carolina formed part of Brig. Gen. Joseph B. Kershaw's brigade along with the 2d, 7th, and 8th South Carolina Regiments, Col. Archibald Gracie's battalion, and one battery. The rest of the army was to follow the night of 2 May, but the next day found it still in the Yorktown trenches casting about for horses and wagons. The scarcity of land transportation forced Johnston on 2 May to implore the navy to pick up Williamsburg's sick at Kingsmill Wharf as soon as possible, for "it is of the greatest importance to have all the sick removed before the troops are drawn back." Only the few too ill to move were allowed to remain, and their burials during the next couple of days brought the total Confederate deaths recorded by Bucktrout since June to some 220. Further hampering the army's movement was the sudden disappearance of Williamsburg's telegraph operator, who deserted his post without Johnston's permission or knowledge.[18]

Finally, about sundown on Saturday, 3 May, the Confederate army began its retrograde movement out of the Yorktown trenches in earnest. It left under a heavy artillery barrage intended to lure the Federals into expecting an imminent attack. The first half of the night, Pvt. James Thomas Petty of the 17th Virginia noticed, was "illumined by the rays of the moon. The air was soft and balmy." Johnston split up his army to use two roughly parallel highways ascending the Peninsula: Hampton Road, also called Lee's Mill or Grove Road, skirting the James River; and York Road, now more often called Telegraph Road, directly from Yorktown. Crossroads connected these thoroughfares in three places along the way. Just below Fort Magruder, Hampton Road merged into Telegraph Road, continuing into Williamsburg. Both routes were more liquid than solid after the rains, and by the time all the infantry had evacuated the trenches around midnight, the moon had set and the intense darkness made the going even more difficult. Porter Alexander remembered "the whole width of the road was filled with either wagons, ambulances, artillery, or infantry plunging & laboring through the mud, with frequent long halts when some gun, or wagon, stalled in some deep spot, & men from the ranks marching near had to swarm in & help the jaded horses pull them out, while everything behind, if the road was at all narrow, had to come to a stop & wait."[19]

18. *OR*, 11(3):479–80, 486–92; F. N. Walker Diary, MR-CWM; Bucktrout Day Book, June–May 1862.

19. James Thomas Petty Diary No. 2, 4 May 1862, MC; Gary N. Gallagher, ed., *Fighting for the Confederacy: The Personal Recollections of General Edward Porter Alexander* (Chapel Hill: University of North Carolina Press, 1989), 78–9.

After wading through twelve miles of this muck all night, averaging less than a mile an hour, the head of the Confederate column pulled into sight of Williamsburg at dawn on Sunday, 4 May. Weary, mud-caked soldiers plodded by Fort Magruder and the Williamsburg line, now abandoned after a full year of backbreaking toil to construct. Up the gentle slope behind the fort and through the city streets they trudged to find their allotted campsites to the west. D. H. Hill's division continued three miles west of Williamsburg before falling out exhausted, but Maj. Gen. James Longstreet's division stayed closer to town. Some of his brigades bivouacked on the asylum grounds and at the City Cemetery, others around the college campus. A few regiments arriving in the early afternoon remained east of town in the field near the redoubts, where "many broad acres were already covered with weary troops cooking, eating, smoking, joking," one observer commented, "but the great majority seeking in profound slumber the rest so greatly needed by all."[20]

Eventually, the artillery began to arrive. One three-gun battery, the Lee Artillery of the 1st Virginia Artillery Regiment, contained many local boys and was commanded by Capt. William Robertson Garrett, son of Williamsburg mayor Dr. Robert M. Garrett. Separated from the rest of his regiment while evacuating Yorktown, Garrett reported to Ewell upon arriving in Williamsburg in midafternoon. "The men, finding that they were expected to march right by their homes without even saying farewell to their families, complained bitterly, and threatened to desert," Garrett divulged. "Under these circumstances, Col. Ewell gave me permission to furlough the men for one day." Garrett placed the three guns in position on Courthouse Green, appointed a guard of five men who did not live in the neighborhood, and permitted the rest of his artillerists to ride the battery horses home to see their families. Lt. John Archer Coke had no need for a horse, for he could walk across the green to his parents' large brick home on South Back Street.[21]

Not so fortunate to have nearby quarters, Johnston looked for private accommodations but, according to Ewell, was refused by a lady who "said she had no room for retreating Generals." He therefore checked into the City Hotel with his staff about two o'clock that afternoon, had a bite to eat, and then stood on the front porch for an informal review of troops. The men of a

20. Alexander, *Memoirs*, 66; John Lawrence Meem to father, 10 May 1862, VHS; Petty Diary No. 2, 4 May 1862; Ervin L. Jordan Jr., *19th Virginia Infantry* (Lynchburg: H. E. Howard, 1987), 15; David Elwell Maxwell to mother, 11 May 1862, David Elwell Maxwell Papers, VHS; Lee A. Wallace Jr., *3rd Virginia Infantry* (Lynchburg: H. E. Howard, 1986), 25; Archibald Gracie, "Gracie's Battalion at Williamsburg in 1862," *Confederate Veteran* 19 (1911): 28.

21. W. R. Garrett to CBT, 15 May 1890, TCP; John A. Coke F/A, UA-CWM.

heavy artillery battalion, which had been the last battery to leave Yorktown at 1:30 that morning, passed the hotel around four o'clock. As they marched by, they were proud to win "an approving smile" from "Grand Old Jo."[22]

At that moment Johnston had good reason to smile, for it appeared his army had slipped away from Yorktown unmolested. The next moment proved otherwise. "About four o'clock P.M.," he related in his memoirs, "the cavalry rear-guard, on the Yorktown road, was driven in, and rapidly followed by the enemy." This was Lt. Col. Williams C. Wickham's 4th Virginia Cavalry, which had been fighting a running battle all afternoon with the Union advance guard. The Confederates' disappearance from Yorktown so took the Federals by surprise, they could not organize their pursuit under cavalry chief Brig. Gen. George Stoneman until late morning. Stoneman, with assurances that Brig. Gen. Joseph Hooker's infantry division would be in close support, initially sent out the 1st and 6th U.S. Cavalry Regiments and Capt. Horatio Gibson's battery of flying artillery from Hays's brigade, all commanded by Brig. Gen. Philip St. George Cooke. Falling into line behind them on Telegraph Road about noon were three other batteries from Hays's brigade and two cavalry regiments. The French noblemen Comte de Paris and his uncle, the Prince de Joinville, both volunteers on McClellan's staff, accompanied Stoneman as did Rhode Island governor William Sprague, who had attached himself to the army to look after his state troops. Sprague later testified, "The column moved with such rapidity that General Stoneman, after stopping to write a despatch to be sent back, would be obliged to trot briskly to resume his place in the column." Possessing no reliable maps or knowledge of the country, they were ordered "to pursue and harass the rear of the retreating enemy, and if possible to cut off his rear guard."[23]

By that time, their quarry was well ahead of them, as the head of Wickham's Virginia cavalry had caught up with the Confederate infantry's rear two miles east of Williamsburg. Within two or three hours, Stoneman's advance made contact with Wickham's rear, and a series of small skirmishes with Cooke's units followed. Still expecting Hooker to be right behind him, Stoneman sent Sprague back to hurry up the infantry. He then ordered Brig. Gen. William H. Emory of the Cavalry Reserve to take some cavalry and artillery units across to Hampton Road, where they tangled with Confederate cavalry

22. BSE, "Magruder Reminiscences"; Gallagher, *Fighting for the Confederacy*, 80; J. W. Minnich, "Incidents of the Peninsular Campaign," *Confederate Veteran* 30 (1922): 54.

23. Johnston, *Narrative*, 119; *OR*, 11(1):423–4, 427; Comte de Paris, *History of the Civil War in America*, 4 vols. (Philadelphia: Porter and Coates, 1876), 2:16; Congress, *Report of the Joint Committee*, 1:568.

and artillery under J. E. B. Stuart. The southerners, outnumbered and blocked on Hampton Road, escaped toward the James River and up a beach path, arriving in Williamsburg later that evening.[24]

Throughout the afternoon Cooke continued pushing cautiously up Telegraph Road until his advance units, emerging from the woods a mile in front of Fort Magruder, were as astonished to discover a line of empty earthworks in front of them as the Confederates were to find a Federal force so close behind. Cooke hurriedly called up the lead section of Gibson's battery to unlimber at the skirt of timber on Telegraph Road. According to Porter Alexander, near Fort Magruder on an errand for Johnston, the artillery "opened fire on everything in sight on the open ground & on the fort—which had no one in it." Immediately, Alexander headed back toward Williamsburg, found Col. Alfred Cumming's 10th Georgia halted on the edge of town, and urged it to Fort Magruder. As tired as the poor fellows were, their lieutenant colonel ordered them to about-face and double-quick past Gracie's Battalion, entering Williamsburg right behind them, full brass band blaring and ladies cheering. "After they passed us," one member of Gracie's Battalion later recalled, "we were about-faced and double-quicked down the same street out into the field and formed in line of battle, while the Georgia brigade had formed on the left of the road, we being on the right."[25]

Captain Garrett had just ridden home and was dismounting at his father's door on the northeastern edge of town when he heard the first shots fired on Fort Magruder. He "immediately rode back to the battery, and found several of the men returning." They did not yet have enough horses to move all the guns but quickly began equipping one. McLaws, also first alerted to the threat by Cooke's opening shot, started for the field. On the way he met Johnston, who had just ordered Brig. Gen. Paul J. Semmes to occupy Fort Magruder and the adjacent redoubts with his command. This, reported Semmes, "was promptly done," requiring his men to traverse the plain behind Fort Magruder exposed to a rapid Federal fire. The artillery attached to his brigade, Capt. Basil C. Manley's battery, "came thundering down the street at a full gallop" past Gracie's Battalion and the Georgians and headed for the fort. Then, detailed one of Gracie's men, "leaving the road, which, in order to lessen the steepness of the grade, makes a wide detour to the right, the battery dashed

24. John Taylor Chappell, "From Yorktown to Williamsburg," n.d., VHS; *OR*, 11(1):424–7, 433–4, 444; Congress, *Report of the Joint Committee*, 1:568.
25. *OR*, 11(1):427, 431; Gallagher, *Fighting for the Confederacy*, 80; Gracie, "Gracie's Battalion," 28, 30.

down the hill in a straight line for the redoubt, over obstructions of briers, bushes, stones, and gullies." Trailing closely behind came Manley's support, the 5th Louisiana, which, along with the 10th Georgia, 10th Louisiana, and 15th Virginia, now composed Semmes's brigade.[26]

As these men scrambled into position, Johnston directed McLaws to turn back another brigade for the lines. Accordingly, Kershaw's brigade west of Williamsburg received marching orders and retraced its steps while "the boom of the enemy's cannon fell upon our ears," a soldier of the 3d South Carolina wrote a few days later. "As we passed through the town," recorded the brigade's historian, "the citizens were greatly excited, the piazzas and balconies being filled with ladies and old men, who urged the men on with all the power and eloquence at their command." One overzealous young maiden came flying out of her house with two pistols buckled around her waist and implored the 17th Mississippi of McLaws's division, still heading west, "to turn and 'Charge the Blue Coats'" and "defend this old town, the cradle of American freedom!" Much to the soldiers' amusement, she cried, "If your Captain won't lead you, I will be your Captain!" Just then the regiment received orders to about-face and double-quick. One Mississippian later reminisced, "the fair heroine, all ablaze with excitement, rushed out of the gate to the head of the charging column, fully convinced that it was her patriotic appeal that had turned the tide backward in defense of her home."[27]

Another interested onlooker was Dr. Galt, who climbed the asylum's observation tower "to see the fight." There he watched as Kershaw's four regiments followed Semmes's brigade onto the field. Captain Gibson's Federal battery found their range "and commenced firing shot and shell at us with an awful rapidity," wrote a private in the 3d South Carolina. "They bursted thick all around us and did but little execution," killing one man and wounding one or two others in the 8th South Carolina. Upon reaching the shelter of Fort Magruder, the Carolinian regiments split up to fill the five right redoubts and place a gun in each. The 10th Georgia stayed in Fort Magruder, with the 15th

26. Garrett to CBT, 15 May 1890; Gracie, "Gracie's Battalion," 28, 30; *OR*, 11(1):442–3, 446; Manarin, *15th Virginia Infantry*, 16.

27. *OR*, 11(1):442–3, 446; D. Augustus Dickert, *History of Kershaw's Brigade with Complete Roll of Companies, Biographical Sketches, Incidents, Anecdotes, Etc.* (Newberry, South Carolina: Elbert H. Aull, 1899), 98; Guy R. Everson and Edward W. Simpson, eds., *"Far, Far from Home": The Wartime Letters of Dick and Tally Simpson, Third South Carolina Volunteers* (New York: Oxford University Press, 1994), 122; C. C. Cummings, "Confederate Heroine at Williamsburg, Va.," *Confederate Veteran* 4 (1896): 91; W. E. Donaldson, "On the 5th Day of May, 1862," *Confederate Veteran* 4 (1896): 164.

Virginia marching into Redoubt Five to the fort's right and half of the 3d South Carolina supporting one of Manley's guns in the next redoubt, number four. The 3d South Carolina's other half plus another of Kershaw's regiments were posted in the woods behind the fort's left. Ewell, "sent by Gen. Johnston to Gen. McLaws to urge him to vigorously repel the attack," arrived on the field soon after the firing began but was appalled to discover none of the left redoubts occupied. "I mentioned the fact to Gen. McLaws," Ewell remarked, "& he agreed with me that it ought to be done, & requested me to take charge of their occupation & lead the troops assigned for the duty." Before Ewell could garrison most of those earthworks with the 10th Louisiana, blue cavalrymen were poised to take advantage of their opponents' oversight.[28]

Cooke had already been informed of these unoccupied redoubts before he arrived on the ground and had sent the 6th Cavalry under Maj. Lawrence Williams to his right along a forest path to attack the Confederate left flank. After a half-mile trot, Williams's men "debouched upon an open but undulating ground in front of the enemy's line of fortifications." About halfway between the woods and these works, a deep ravine cut the field "only passable by file," the major found. All Confederate attention seemed riveted on Gibson's battery near Telegraph Road, allowing the 6th Cavalry to traverse the ravine in file and approach to within one hundred yards of the nearest redoubt. There the blue troopers formed while Williams sent Lt. Daniel Madden ahead to reconnoiter with a platoon partially hidden from Confederate view by several rows of huts nearby and outside of the earthworks. They approached the redoubt with such confidence that McLaws, observing from Fort Magruder, supposed them to be southerners until, wrote the 6th Cavalry's historian, "some of the Confederates looking over the crest called out 'They are Yankees!'" Upon discovering his mistake, McLaws directed Manley to shell them and Col. J. Lucius Davis's 10th Virginia Cavalry nearby to attack. Madden "put his platoon at a gallop," continued the troop's historian, "and by winding in and out of the rows of huts concealed the men from the fire of the fort, but came out facing a brigade of Confederate infantry."[29]

Actually, it was only part of a brigade, Kershaw's, advancing from the woods behind the earthwork. Madden galloped back to report his news to Major Williams, who could see for himself the approaching infantry and pru-

28. Galt Diary, 4 May 1862; Everson and Simpson, *"Far from Home,"* 122; *OR,* 11(1):442–3, 446; BSE's interlinear notes in "Report of Joseph E. Johnston," 19 May 1862, Dispatch Book, Joseph E. Johnston Papers, MR-CWM.

29. *OR,* 11(1):427–8, 436, 439, 442; W. H. Carter, *From Yorktown to Santiago: With the Sixth U.S. Cavalry* (1900; reprint, Austin: State House Press, 1989), 26–9.

dently "determined to retire." Before the retreating blue troopers reached the ravine, gray "artillery began dropping shells into the column with considerable accuracy," hastening the horsemen down as quickly as they could go by twos or file. The final Federal squadron was crossing the bottom "belly deep to the horses in mud" when the 10th Virginia Cavalry appeared on the rim and fired down with pistols and carbines. The blue cavalry kept pushing across, formed column of platoons on the opposite hillside, waited until the Confederates followed up the hill at full gallop, and then wheeled about by platoons and charged. "We became instantly entangled and mixed up and for about ten minutes nothing was heared but the clashing of steel," wrote Pvt. John Taylor Chappell of the 10th Virginia. He had entered the fray armed with two large brass-mounted "Horse pistols," an old sawed-off muzzle-loading musket, and a saber "that might have been made of hoop iron." But he emerged "the happy owner of a brace of Colts Army revolvers, a Sharps Carbine and a handsome basket-hilted English sabre." A few northern troopers "were unhorsed in the deep mud of the ravine, by the plunging and falling of wounded horses, and were captured," their historian recorded. Then as suddenly as they came together, the horsemen parted for their own lines, each side congratulating itself on having routed or repulsed the other.[30]

Meanwhile, the three-gun section of Gibson's battery that had originally opened against Fort Magruder from the woods' edge Cooke moved forward to an open space where it could maneuver more freely. At that time another three-gun section of the battery joined it as well as three squadrons of the 1st U.S. Cavalry under Lt. Col. William N. Grier, placed in a hollow to the battery's right for protection. "The line of the woods around us formed a crescent, partially inclosing the field in which the battery was posted," noted Gibson, and the "ground was very miry and boggy." Manley's guns in the redoubts continued a damaging crossfire on this little Federal force, which furiously continued to return fire for nearly an hour, expending 250 rounds of ammunition.[31]

By that time Stoneman had arrived near the front and, despairing of any infantry support arriving soon, ordered Cooke to withdraw the battery. Section by section the guns were being limbered up and hauled back when the horses of one gun were killed and its wheels sank into a boggy hole near the road, blocking four disabled caissons behind it. While the 1st Cavalry helped wounded artillerists off the field and covered their rear, Grier and one of his

30. *OR*, 11(1):436–7; Carter, *From Yorktown to Santiago*, 26–9; Chappell, "From Yorktown to Williamsburg."

31. *OR*, 11(1):424–32.

sixty-man squadrons stayed behind with the sunken piece to offer advice and assistance to Gibson. Adding to their problems was a battery of Richmond Howitzers under Capt. Edward S. McCarthy, just arrived at Fort Magruder to intensify the fire on Gibson's work party. Ten more horses hitched to the gun and pulling for nearly twenty minutes could not extract it.[32]

Suddenly swooping down upon them at full gallop came the Confederate cavalry. Gibson reluctantly ordered the gun abandoned, as Grier's squadron, entering the timber, wheeled about by fours to meet Lieutenant Colonel Wickham with his 4th Virginia Cavalry and the Hampton Legion. For the second time in less than an hour, horsemen from North and South clashed in fierce hand-to-hand combat. Wickham, turning in the saddle to cheer on his men, took Grier's saber in his back. At the same moment the 4th Virginia's bugler slashed Grier, wounding him only slightly but knocking him off balance and deflecting his fatal sword thrust at Wickham. A Federal artillery private joined the melee and managed to capture the 4th Virginia's battle flag, only to be mistaken for a southerner by his own cavalry. In the tumult he received four saber blows and was compelled to relinquish his trophy. "The charging was perfectly terriffick and overwhelming," gushed young Confederate Lt. Chiswell Dabney Jr. in a letter home, "you cannot form and [sic] idea of it unless you could see it and feel yourself in it, the excitement is tremendous." As the 10th Georgia and 15th Virginia Infantry began to deploy down York Road, the Union cavalry charged once again, ending the day's fighting and allowing Gibson's artillery to escape through the woods. It fell back about a half mile to a large white farmhouse known as the Whittaker House. There it reformed and awaited the arrival of its infantry support.[33]

Where had the Federal foot soldiers been all day? They received orders to march at the same time as the cavalry, but by the time regiments were gathered from dispersed locations, wagons brought up from the rear, and men recalled from inspecting the Confederate works, the columns did not start until nearly an hour later. Passing through Yorktown, some soldiers stumbled upon subterranean shells, or "torpedoes," placed there by the retreating Confederates to impede pursuit, and a few were killed or wounded. From then on they were determined "to avenge the death of their comrades who had been slaughtered in such a cowardly manner," according to one New Yorker. The first

32. Ibid., 424–32, 442; Robert Stiles, *Four Years under Marse Robert* (1903; reprint, Dayton, Ohio: Morningside, 1988), 78.

33. *OR*, 11(1):428–32, 445; Chiswell Dabney Jr. to father, 8 May 1862, Saunders Family Papers, VHS.

infantry to take York Road belonged to General Hooker, commanding the Second Division of the Third Corps. Hooker's corps chief, Brig. Gen. Samuel P. Heintzelman, was an old veteran who had been wounded at Bull Run while heroically but vainly trying to rally his fleeing men. With orders from McClellan to "take control of the entire movement," Heintzelman accompanied Hooker's division. The roads were still wretched, "rendered almost impassable by the passage of the enemy's artillery and trains," grumbled Pvt. Edwin Y. Brown of Hooker's 1st Massachusetts. After they had proceeded out about five miles, Hooker met Governor Sprague, who informed him that Stoneman "had fallen upon the rear of the enemy's retreating column." He left his command and galloped to the front to tell Stoneman his troops were on the way. While there, Hooker learned that his division had halted and upon his return discovered it was blocked by another division filing into Telegraph Road from a crossroad ahead of it.[34]

This was the Fourth Corps's Second Division under Brig. Gen. William F. "Baldy" Smith. It had started several hours earlier up Hampton Road but was stopped by an impassable bridge the Confederates had burned during their withdrawal. Crossing over to Telegraph Road, Smith's men beat Hooker's to the intersection and headed toward Williamsburg by order of Brig. Gen. Edwin V. "Old Bull" Sumner. Another old-timer who had been in the service since 1819, Sumner headed the Second Corps and currently was second in command of the army. At noon "Little Mac" had directed Sumner to take charge of the pursuit without informing Heintzelman of this change.[35]

After waiting three or four hours for Smith's troops to pass, Hooker's men fell in behind them and continued plodding up the highway until they reached the intersection of another crossroad at a landmark called Cheesecake Church. There the aggressive Hooker, chafing at his inability to support Stoneman on Telegraph Road with Smith in the way, "learned from a contraband that by going two or three miles further I could get up to the same position the enemy held, coming in on his right flank." He therefore obtained permission from Heintzelman to cross over and proceed up Hampton Road instead, hoping to arrive at the front that evening. About dusk, word came back of Cooke's re-

34. *OR*, 11(1):456–7, 464; Congress, *Report of the Joint Committee*, 1:348, 576; Allen Nevins, ed., *A Diary of Battle: The Personal Journals of Charles S. Wainwright, 1861–1865* (Gettysburg: Stan Clark Military Books, 1962), 45; Edwin Y. Brown, "Battle of Williamsburg," EYB, MR-CWM; J. W. Ratchford, "More of Gen. Rains and His Torpedoes," *Confederate Veteran* 2 (1894), 283; Fred C. Floyd, *History of the Fortieth (Mozart) Regiment New York Volunteers* (Boston: F. H. Gilson, 1909), 142.

35. *OR*, 11(1):19, 440–1, 444, 449, 526, 534, 558–9.

pulse at Williamsburg, but Hooker's men, "catching the spirit of their gallant leader," declared Private Brown, "uncomplainingly struggled on" through the thickening darkness, with frequent halts to extract artillery from the mud.[36]

Leaving Hooker with instructions "not to let Sumner get into Williamsburg first," Heintzelman trotted on to the Whittaker House. There he arrived about five o'clock and found, to his chagrin, Sumner in command. "Old Bull" was conferring with Generals Smith, Stoneman, and Winfield S. Hancock, commanding the First Brigade of Smith's division, about what to do next as Cooke's bloodied cavalry stood by the road as a warning of what lay ahead. Hancock's men had just arrived after a nine-hour mud march and "stacked arms for a few moments to refresh themselves with rest and food." Stoneman volunteered the misinformation that infantry could traverse the thick forest since cavalry had been riding through it. With that he persuaded Sumner, "feeling the importance of pressing the pursuit as fast as possible," to advance at once. "After giving what few directions the limited time rendered practicable," wrote cavalry lieutenant George Armstrong Custer, accompanying Smith, "General Sumner, that splendid type of veteran soldier, concluded with the remark, 'Gentlemen, at the third tap of the drum the entire command will advance to the attack.'" Two of Hancock's regiments formed in line on the right of the road and two on the left in a field facing the woods, with skirmishers thrown out in front and knapsacks dropped behind. Another of Smith's brigades, led by Brig. Gen. William T. H. Brooks and just now arriving, formed in double columns in the rear. Smith's Third Brigade, temporarily part of Hancock's command, began to form behind Brooks.[37]

While these lines quickly arranged themselves, Hancock detached two companies and went with a guide from Gibson's battery to search for the sunken gun abandoned during the skirmish. They discovered it had already been retrieved, along with the four blocked caissons, by their adversaries. Hancock then sent out another detachment to reconnoiter the Confederate line, but before it could return with any information, "Old Bull" decided to charge blindly and ordered the troops forward. It was now half past six and almost dark. No sooner had they penetrated the woods than the ranks became tangled in the dense undergrowth, blundered into trees and each other in the dark, and eventually lost direction. Smith, commanding the right wing, realized the

36. Ibid., 457, 464–5; Congress, *Report of the Joint Committee,* 1:576; Brown, "Battle of Williamsburg."

37. Nevins, *Diary of Battle,* 56; *OR,* 11(1):451, 457, 534; John S. Carroll, comp. and ed., *Custer in the Civil War: His Unfinished Memoirs* (San Rafael, Calif., 1977), 151.

futility of the movement but could not find Sumner to authorize a halt. Heintzelman sent word that since he was expecting Hooker to attack any minute on
the left, he could not call a halt either. When Hancock saw his left regiments
drifting toward the right wing and intermingling with Brooks's columns, he
took the initiative and stopped them to reform the line. Smith immediately
followed suit, ordering his right wing to bivouac back in the open field where
he had brought it to regroup.[38]

By then it was totally dark. The 6th Maine, leading Hancock's brigade, had
broken out of the dense forest into the fallen timber but could not see to go
forward or back and thus camped on the spot without overcoats or blankets.
Hancock was just settling the rest of his troops down in the woods to await
further instructions when Sumner suddenly appeared and ordered them "to
bivouac on the spot and to defer the assault until daylight." He had become
lost while attempting a personal reconnaissance of the Confederate position
and decided to spend the night with Hancock rather than risk losing his way
back to his Whittaker House headquarters. That dwelling was already becoming crowded with general officers and their staffs anyway. The chief of the
Fourth Corps, Brig. Gen. Erasmus D. Keyes, arrived after dark and "was informed that the enemy had works of strong profiles; that they were in force in
front; and that the position which they had occupied was about the narrowest
part of the peninsula." Concluding "that there must positively be a battle the
next day," Keyes dispatched his adjutant, Capt. C. C. Suydam, back to Halfway House, beside Telegraph Road about halfway between Yorktown and
Williamsburg, with an order for Keyes's Third Division, commanded by Brig.
Gen. Silas Casey and encamped there. It was "to march at dawn of day the
next morning without fail." Suydam arrived at Casey's headquarters shortly
after midnight and wrote a note to Brig. Gen. Darius Couch, whose First
Division of the Fourth Corps had fallen out in rear of Casey's, instructing him
to follow directly behind Casey early in the morning.[39]

Behind Couch lay Heintzelman's Third Division under the aggressive,
one-armed Brig. Gen. Philip Kearny, who had assumed command of it only
the day before. This division did not leave Yorktown until midafternoon and,
though ordered by Heintzelman to advance to Cheesecake Church, had made
just two or three miles. Kearny's fellow division commander, Hooker, after
making a left turn at Cheesecake Church about dark, found his way clear and
continued marching. About ten o'clock Hooker's leading First Brigade turned

38. *OR*, 11(1):446, 451, 526–7, 534–5.
39. Ibid., 451, 511, 535; Congress, *Report of the Joint Committee*, 1:602.

right on to Hampton Road. General Emory, camped at that intersection since his encounter with Stuart, watched the men plod a little way before they fell "down in our blankets, bedraggled, wet, and tired, chewing hard-tack and the cud of reflection," as one infantryman remembered, "the tenor of which was, 'Why did we come for a soldier?'" The 1st Massachusetts found a partial clearing and made beds on the soft earth. There, "sustained by youth and health," wrote Edwin Brown, "our weariness brought us sweet repose."[40]

Once again, as the blue army slept, the gray marched, or at least part of it did. After observing the skirmish from Fort Magruder, Johnston assumed the Federals would ascend the York River to cut off his retreat. He therefore wanted to push Magruder's and G. W. Smith's divisions up the Peninsula as soon as possible and, about sunset, ordered Longstreet to relieve the men in the fieldworks with one of his brigades. The remainder of Longstreet's division was to rest in preparation for an early morning departure. That night Dr. Galt counted "40 or 50 watch or cooking fires" spring up among the regiments camping for the night around the asylum. Since Longstreet's brigades were small, that general sent both Richard Anderson's and Roger Pryor's commands into the earthworks. He also ordered the Richmond Fayette Artillery, under Lt. William I. Clopton, into Fort Magruder about midnight. Captain McCarthy's Richmond Howitzer battery, remaining at Magruder after the afternoon's skirmish, was now augmented by the abandoned Federal gun and caissons dragged in by his men and horses. Robertson Garrett was also still on the field, having managed to bring his brass gun from Courthouse Green down to Fort Magruder before the skirmish ended. McLaws placed him in reserve to the right of the fort, where he was under fire for a short time until the Federal artillery retired. Another Lee Artillery piece arrived at Fort Magruder about sunset and was hauled into Redoubt Five, followed by the battery's third gun, as Garrett and his men settled into camp on the field.[41]

During the night Anderson, the senior brigadier present, took command while his men relieved McLaws's brigades in the right redoubts, Fort Magruder, and two left redoubts barely visible through the darkness. Semmes reported that his troops vacated their positions and retired through

40. OR, 11(1):433, 458, 465, 470; Floyd, Fortieth (Mozart) Regiment New York, 142; Robert Underwood Johnson and Clarence Clough Buel, eds., Battles and Leaders of the Civil War, 4 vols. (1887; reprint, Secaucus, N.J.: Castle, n.d.), 2:196; Brown, "Battle of Williamsburg."

41. Galt Diary, 4 May 1862; James Longstreet, From Manassas to Appomattox: Memoirs of the Civil War in America ([1896]; reprint, New York: Mallard Press, 1991), 72–3; OR, 11(1):442–3, 564, 51(1):85, 88; Johnston, Narrative, 119; Stiles, Four Years under Marse Robert, 78; W. R. Garrett to CBT; 15 May 1890, TCP.

Williamsburg at midnight. Nobody, including Ewell, who remained on the field until nearly 10:00 P.M., thought to tell Anderson about the far left earthworks after Ewell's garrisons departed. And Anderson—described as "a very brave man, but of a rather inert, indolent manner for commanding troops in the field, and by no means pushing or aggressive"—failed to survey the ground. Not expecting to fight in this locale anytime soon, Johnston relaxed by entertaining his staff with "a very pretty exhibition of sabre exercise" in his hotel room that night, recalled Porter Alexander. "At the time it was thought that the army would be on the march by daylight in the morning," Longstreet later explained, "and that the rear-guard would closely follow." Then it began to rain.[42]

42. *OR*, 11(1):446, 580; G. Moxley Sorrell, *Recollections of a Confederate Staff Officer* (1958; reprint, New York: Bantam Books, 1992), 213; Gallagher, *Fighting for the Confederacy*, 80–1; Longstreet, *From Manassas to Appomattox*, 72–3.

CHAPTER 5

Pandemonium Broke Loose

What began as a refreshing drizzle about two o'clock Monday morning, 5 May 1862, had become by breakfast time a cold, drenching rain. Already, fields were transforming into swamps and roads into rivulets as Magruder's troops slogged wearily up the Peninsula all night, progressing only four or five miles toward Richmond. "Prince John," however, was not with them. "Finding that there would be no fighting, at least for a few days," he wrote Secretary of War Randolph from a sick bed southeast of Richmond that morning, "I have seized upon the opportunity to turn myself over to the care of a doctor, to re-establish my health, which sadly needed repair." Rumor had it he was nursing "only the effect of too much Bourbon and chagrin" because General Johnston refused to fight at Yorktown. Also reluctant to abandon the Peninsula, so long and laboriously defended, Colonel Ewell led the 32d Virginia out of Williamsburg and past his James City County farmhouse on Richmond Road. Ordnance officer Edwin Taliaferro, accompanied by wife Bland, departed Williamsburg early Monday morning as well. Bland's brother, Lt. Tom Tucker, tarried behind with General McLaws and the rest of his staff for a farewell breakfast at the Tucker House before heading toward Richmond. Then, wrote Cynthia Coleman, "we the women they left behind them bade them adieu with brave hearts, they to *do* and suffer, we passively to endure."[1]

Another soldier taking one last sample of Williamsburg's hospitality, a young 7th Virginia sergeant named Salem Dutcher, slipped out of camp to breakfast with a lady acquaintance in town. Since supply wagons were sepa-

---

1. *OR*, 11(3):494–5; Everson and Simpson, *Far from Home*, 122; *Battle-Fields of the South, from Bull Run to Fredericksburgh: With Sketches of Confederate Commanders, and Gossip of the Camps* (New York: John Bradburn, 1864), 211; CBT, "Peninsula Campaign," TCP, MR-CWM.

rated from their regiments, most of Dutcher's comrades had meager, if any, rations that morning after a tentless night in the rain. Many had also spent a sleepless night preparing to march. G. W. Smith's division was slated to start at 2:00 A.M., followed by the trains and then D. H. Hill's division. Smith got underway at daybreak, but the trains—parts of which "were stalled on the ground, where they stood during the night," noted Longstreet—could make little progress in his wake. Although Brig. Gen. Jubal A. Early's brigade in Hill's division was ready to go around three o'clock, the gloomy dawn found those men still in camp west of Williamsburg.[2]

Dawn likewise found the widely scattered units of Longstreet's division in the same positions they held the evening before. Brig. Gen. Cadmus Wilcox's brigade, consisting of his own 9th Alabama Regiment as well as the 10th Alabama and 19th Mississippi, waited a mile west of Williamsburg for its turn to depart. The 3d Virginia and 13th and 14th North Carolina Regiments, commanded by Brig. Gen. Raleigh Colston, lingered on the college campus, where the men of Brig. Gen. George E. Pickett's 8th, 18th, 19th, and 28th Virginia, collectively known as the Gamecock Brigade, hastily gulped their last scanty meal before starting their trek westward. Spread around the asylum grounds and City Cemetery, another all-Virginia brigade, Brig. Gen. Ambrose Powell Hill's 1st, 7th, 11th, and 17th regiments, waited impatiently to get moving.[3]

On the other end of town were Brig. Gen. Roger A. Pryor's 14th Louisiana and 8th and 14th Alabama Regiments, distributed with a detached battalion of the 32d Virginia among Redoubts One, Two, Three, and Four. There throughout the drizzly night the men had struggled to keep their muskets and ammunition dry and now watched uneasily as "the grey streak in the eastern horizon gave warning that day was approaching." The 14th Alabama's historian recalled that the "redoubt in which we were posted was dusty when we entered it Sunday night. Monday morning it was ankle deep in mud." That did not facilitate moving Capt. Robertson Garrett's brass piece into Redoubt Four, where he took personal command. Lt. John Coke remained in charge of the iron gun positioned in Redoubt Five since Sunday evening.[4]

2. Salem Dutcher, "Williamsburg: A Graphic Story of the Battle of May 5, 1862," *Southern Historical Society Papers* 17 (1889): 412; Jubal Anderson Early, *Jubal Early's Memoirs: Autobiographical Sketch and Narrative of the War between the States* ([1912]; reprint, Baltimore: Nautical and Aviation Publishing, 1989), 67; Maury, *Williamsburg*, 5; Johnston, *Narrative*, 119–20; Longstreet, *From Manassas to Appomattox*, 72.

3. *OR*, 11(1):584, 590; J. G. de Roulhac Hamilton, ed., *The Papers of Randolph Abbott Shotwell*, 2 vols. (Raleigh: North Carolina Historical Commission, 1929), 1:205.

4. *OR*, 11(1):587, 51(1):88, 90; M. B. Hurst, *History of the Fourteenth Regiment Alabama Vol-*

Also in Redoubt Five, Richard Anderson, commanding the entire line, posted his Louisiana Foot Rifles. Six pieces of Lt. William Clopton's Richmond Fayette Artillery and a two-gun section of Capt. Edward McCarthy's Richmond Howitzers, supported by the Palmetto Sharpshooters and six companies of the 5th South Carolina, occupied Fort Magruder. The first earthwork to the left, number seven, held the other three companies of the 5th South Carolina. Anderson sent three 6th South Carolina companies down to Redoubt Nine and positioned its remaining companies in the skirt of piney woods behind the main fort's left. According to Longstreet, two other earthworks "farther on the left were not seen through the rain, and no one had been left to tell him of them or of the grounds." They and the far left fieldworks therefore remained empty. Pickets from the 4th South Carolina Battalion had been thrown out about six hundred yards in front of Fort Magruder. During the night some of them crawled out another hundred yards to within earshot of the Union lines. "Just at daylight the enemy commenced snapping caps on their guns—to dry the tubes, I suppose," wrote 4th South Carolina private Jesse Reid. "I will admit that I never felt so nervous in my life."[5]

About that time J. E. B. Stuart showed up with his cavalry brigade to survey the skirmish ground of the evening before, regretting he had arrived too late with the 3d Virginia Cavalry and Jeff Davis Legion to participate in that action. Nevertheless, he was determined not to miss any possible fight today. He sent the legion toward Queens Creek to keep an eye on the left flank and the 3d Virginia to the right as far as Kingsmill. The 4th Virginia Cavalry, now commanded by Maj. William H. Payne after Lieutenant Colonel Wickham's severe wounding during the skirmish, Stuart ordered "to proceed cautiously down the Telegraph road and reconnoiter the position and movements of the enemy." Before they had proceeded far into the woods, these gray horsemen ran into some of Brig. Gen. Winfield S. Hancock's blue infantrymen, while

---

unteers, ed. William Stanley Hoole (1863; reprint, University, Ala.: Confederate Publishing, 1982), 9; W. R. Garrett to CBT, 15 May 1890, TCP. John A. Coke stated in his report that the brass gun Garrett personally commanded was in Redoubt Three instead of Five. *OR*, 51(1):88. In his 1890 letter to CBT, Garrett specifically mentioned that Coke was in "the redoubt next to Fort Magruder" and the other piece was "in the next fort to the right." Adding to the confusion is Wilcox's report, saying the guns were in "the second redoubt from the right facing Yorktown," and "the one to its left," which sounds more like numbers two and three. *OR*, 51(1):90. Stuart's report specifies "the two redoubts to the right of Fort Magruder," which agrees with Garrett. *OR*, 11(1): 570.

    5. *OR*, 11(1):580–2, 587; J. W. Reid, *History of the Fourth Regiment of S.C. Volunteers from the Commencement of the War until Lee's Surrender* (1891; reprint, Dayton, Ohio: Morningside, 1975), 80; Longstreet, *From Manassas to Appomattox*, 73.

others closed in behind them on the road to cut off their retreat. "Nothing daunted," Stuart declared, the lead cavalryman "seized the musket of the nearest one and bore it off in triumph, with an entire regiment of the enemy's infantry close to his left. Thus began the battle of Williamsburg."[6]

Stuart notwithstanding, the battle did not open on Telegraph Road, where the Federals were actually moving away from the field. Brig. Gen. Edwin Sumner, after spending all night under a dripping tree, suspected the Confederates had a stronger force and fieldworks in front than Brig. Gen. George Stoneman had led him to believe. At daylight he found his way back to the Whittaker House and received a note from McClellan ordering him "to take charge of operations in front." Since W. F. Smith's men had marched the day before without rations and were too hungry to fight, Sumner decided they should retire. The 6th Maine awoke in the felled timber, or slashing, to discover the line of Confederate redoubts not more than a half mile off and moved back "around a point of woods out of sight of the enemy." The rest of Hancock's brigade fell back to the edge of the trees to retrieve knapsacks they had deposited the previous evening and to receive rations. Replacements for these units were supposedly on the way. Despite "the frightful condition and blocking up of the roads," Brig. Gen. Erasmus Keyes expected his divisions under Silas Casey and Darius Couch to begin arriving at the Whittaker House as early as 9:00 A.M. After all, from their camp around the Halfway House, they had less than four miles to go up Telegraph Road.[7]

Over on Hampton Road, Joseph Hooker awakened his troops "at the earliest signs of dawn," about four o'clock, to resume the march toward Williamsburg. Their last half mile or more lay through a heavy wood, the far side of which they reached about 5:30 A.M. and halted before emerging. Hooker then rode to the front to survey the field. "The landscape is picturesque," he mused, gazing through the mist, "and not a little heightened by the large trees and venerable spires of Williamsburg, 2 miles distant." Fort Magruder stood nearly a mile away. The general looked over log heaps toward Telegraph Road on his right. "Between the edge of the felled timber and the fort was a belt of clear arable land 600 or 700 yards in width," he estimated, and "dotted all over with rifle pits." He could see the line of telegraph poles extending out from Fort Magruder, but much of Telegraph Road and Smith's division were hidden by a spur of woods. Nevertheless, Hooker figured Smith must be poised to attack, and with the rest of the Union army within a four-hour march of his support,

6. *OR*, 11(1):444–5, 570–1; Judge Robert Armistead, interview by author, 22 Apr. 1991.
7. *OR*, 11(1):451, 457, 512, 535, 549–50; Congress, *Report of the Joint Committee*, 1:348.

he decided, without orders, that it was his duty to hold the Confederate army down until reinforcements could capture it.[8]

Though eager to begin the work, Hooker hesitated to attack until his field guns came up. He waited until after 7:00 A.M., when his artillery chief, Maj. Charles S. Wainwright, a farmer from upstate New York, finally joined him. Wainwright had his artillerymen up and moving by three o'clock, but the road "was so terribly cut up that it was with difficulty we could get along," making the four or five miles seem like twenty, he explained in his diary. Hooker's query as to where Wainwright would place his batteries required a ride up the road by both officers until they emerged from the woods. There "the rebs opened on us so sharp," wrote Wainwright, "that we got off our horses, and proceeded out on foot and alone." They walked to the outer edge of the slashing, extending about three hundred yards farther up the left side of the road than the right, and found "a large triangular field having been lately cleared there, and planted in corn last year." Since the open plain in front was too exposed to the guns in Fort Magruder, dimly visible about eight hundred yards away through the thickening rain, Wainwright elected to place most of his pieces in the fallow field with a couple in the road. "Get them in then as quick as you can," Hooker tersely ordered as the two men hurried back to their waiting troops near the edge of the woods.[9]

At half past seven, by Hooker's account, he directed Brig. Gen. Cuvier Grover and his First Brigade to commence the attack. Grover was just bringing his lead regiment, the 1st Massachusetts, out of the woods when he spotted J. E. B. Stuart and his horsemen maneuvering on the right and got their attention with a few shots. Two companies of the 1st Massachusetts he sent out to the edge of the slashing on the left of Hampton Road, and two companies of the 2d New Hampshire he deployed to the right, "with orders to advance as near the enemy's rifle-pits as possible." One of these skirmishers related that the Confederates "immediately opened fire upon us with heavy guns from the fort, while from their rifle-pits came a hum of bullets and crackle of musketry. Their heavy shot came crashing among the tangled abatis of fallen timber, and plowed up the dirt in our front, rebounding and tearing through the branches of the woods in our rear." Although the "little rifle-pits in our front fairly blazed with musketry, and the continuous *snap, snap, crack, crack* was murderous," the skirmishers continued to push their way through

8. Edwin Y. Brown, "Battle of Williamsburg," EYB, MR-CWM; *OR,* 11(1):465.
9. Nevins, *Diary of Battle,* v, 47–9.

the logs, in some places eight to ten feet high, driving back the 4th South Carolina skirmish line before them.[10]

Soon Wainwright's lead battery of six guns, Capt. Charles H. Webber's 1st U.S. Artillery, thundered past the skirmishers up Hampton Road to the far edge of the slashing. There, in the road, Webber began to unlimber his first piece and to place "his second also in the road but some twenty yards to the rear, a slight bend in the road here placing them thus in echelon." His other two sections Wainwright struggled to post in the fallow field to the right, tearing down a fence and urging balky horses to drag all the guns in place. In the process, one horse gave the poor major a swift kick just below his stomach and threw him halfway across the road. At that moment Clopton's Richmond Fayette Artillery stationed in Fort Magruder found the Federal cannoneers' range exactly with two guns, as did McCarthy's Richmond Howitzers. A lieutenant standing beside Wainwright dropped to the ground, wounded in the shoulder, then another lieutenant and two men were hit. The other blue artillerists immediately fled their guns and hid behind the felled trees. Though Wainwright and Webber "slammed at them with our sabres, and poked them out with the point, it was no good," admitted the major; "drive two or three to a gun, and by the time you got some more up the first had hid again. Never in my life was I so mortified, never so excited, never so mad."[11]

Wainwright was also insulted when Hooker offered to man the guns with infantrymen. In desperation he made a frantic appeal to Capt. Thomas W. Osborn's 1st New York Battery, just coming up, for volunteers to serve the guns of "an abandoned regular battery." To the cheers and admiration of the 1st Massachusetts soldiers, and to the immense satisfaction of Wainwright's state pride, every one of Osborn's artillerymen "quickly sprang forward, and gallantly maintained the action of the guns." The rain now falling fast rendered their targets all but impossible to see, but these men, along with some fifteen or eighteen that Webber managed to coax up, worked the battery with good effect. Wainwright now judged "the enemy's shots were not nearly so sure and it became comparatively safe to be about there."[12]

Hooker's infantry had also been successful. Having driven the 4th South Carolina skirmishers back into Fort Magruder, the 1st Massachusetts companies reached the edge of the slashing. "To our left the ground fell away in a

10. *OR*, 11(1):465, 472, 570; Johnson and Buel, *Battles and Leaders*, 2:196.
11. Nevins, *Diary of Battle*, 49–50, 55; *OR*, 11(1):466, 470.
12. Nevins, *Diary of Battle*, 50–1; *OR*, 11(1):466, 470; Brown, "Battle of Williamsburg."

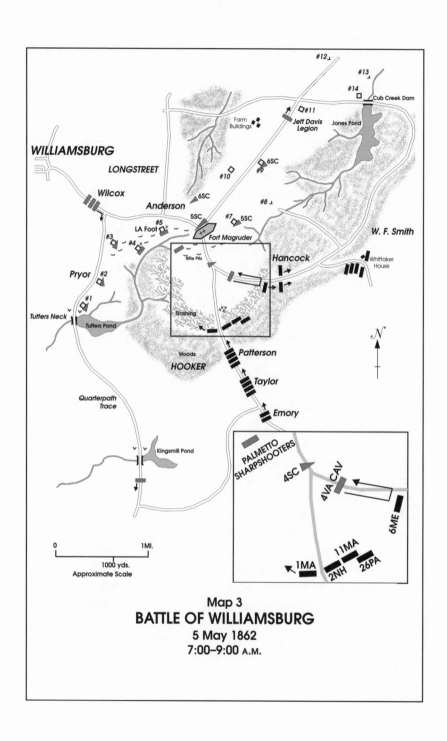

#12

#13

#14
◻ Cub Creek Dam

WILLIAMSBURG

LONGSTREET

Farm
Buildings

◻#11

Jeff Davis
Legion

Jones Pond

Wilcox

Anderson

#10
◻

6SC
◻ #9

6SC

#8 ↵

#7 ◻ 5SC
5SC

W. F. Smith

5SC

LA Foot
#5

#3 #4

Fort Magruder

Rifle Pits

Hancock

Whittaker
House

Pryor
#2

#1

Tutters Neck

Tutters Pond

Slashing

Woods

HOOKER

Patterson

Taylor

Quarterpath
Trace

Emory

Kingsmill Pond

N

PALMETTO
SHARPSHOOTERS

4SC

4VA CAV

6ME

11MA

1MA
2NH   26PA

0   1MI.

1000 yds.
Approximate Scale

Map 3
BATTLE OF WILLIAMSBURG
5 May 1862
7:00–9:00 A.M.

succession of rolling slopes, the whole commanded by a line of rebel redoubts," recounted Edwin Brown, one of the skirmishers. In front of them
the rifle pits were now full of Palmetto Sharpshooters, "busy picking off artillery men and horses," and it fell to Brown's company to dislodge them and
silence the Confederate guns. Clinging "close to the miry earth," Brown fired
from a prone position, somewhat protected from the mud by a rubber blanket
he and his comrade brought along. They were "putting in effective work upon
the rebel artillerists" in Fort Magruder but "were greatly annoyed by a rebel
redoubt far on our left whose shot nearly enfiladed our line."[13]

This was Redoubt Five, slightly sunk in a hollow so the top of its parapet
appeared to be level with the plain. Lieutenant Coke and his 6-pounder field
gun occupied this earthwork and opened a rapid and well-directed fire upon
the Massachusetts skirmishers, splattering them with mud. Brown's bayonet
hanging at his side was struck "and mashed up so as to be useless." He had
just risen on one knee to load "when with a whiz and a thud a solid shot sped
by burying itself in the earth just beyond me and taking away a part of my coat
sleeve and tearing the flesh from my left shoulder as I pitched forward on my
face," Brown vividly narrated. "My comrade was at once bending over me examining my hurt Only a 'flesher' exclaimed he cheerily." With his arm limp
and useless and his comrade loading for him, the plucky New Englander "endeavored to do my best to square accounts of my wounded arm and leave a
little balance in my favor." Coke's constant fire could not discourage these
Federal sharpshooters from raining bullets upon Fort Magruder, forcing the
Palmetto Sharpshooters out of the rifle pits and into the fort to replace the
stricken Fayette Artillerymen and keep the guns booming.[14]

Realizing his troops were up against superior Federal artillery, Anderson
decided to try a flank attack. Cadmus Wilcox had already received instructions
from Longstreet soon after 8:00 A.M. to report to Anderson with his men.
They had been listening to the artillery duel and were not surprised to be
countermarched rapidly through the streets of Williamsburg. There they saw
women "everywhere, some with water for the soldiers, others offering to take
care of blankets, while others still, who had relatives in the army, wept and
wrung their hands in agony." As Wilcox's three regiments arrived on the battlefield, the men paused in a wheat field behind Redoubts Four and Five to

13. *OR*, 11(1):582; Brown, "Battle of Williamsburg"; E. Y. Brown to brother, 10 May 1862,
EYB.

14. Nevins, *Diary of Battle*, 49; Garrett to CBT, 15 May 1890; *OR*, 51(1):88; *OR*, 11(1):472,
582; Brown, "Battle of Williamsburg"; Brown to brother, 10 May 1862.

load their pieces before entering what for most of them would be their first combat. "In front of us and to our right the artillery thundered forth death,—the day dark and gloomy and the rain falling steadily," wrote an Ohio-born corporal named Edmund DeWitt Patterson serving in the 9th Alabama. "The smoke settled down over the hills and valleys and added to the general gloom." In his diary Patterson recorded his meditations during this interlude. "I did not feel at all afraid—the feeling called *fear* did not enter my breast, but it was a painful nervous anxiety, a longing for action, anything to occupy my attention—nerves relaxed and a dull feeling about the chest that made breathing painful," he recalled. "All the energies of my soul seemed concentrated in the one desire for action."[15]

About nine o'clock on the Union side of the field, through the steady rain and smoke now obscuring his vision, Hooker caught a glimpse of Wilcox's brigade drifting beyond his left flank and surmised the Confederates' intentions. He had already reached to his right for support, ordering Grover's 11th Massachusetts to skirmish beyond the 2d New Hampshire and his 26th Pennsylvania to go farther right in an effort to link with "Baldy" Smith's division, which Hooker believed must be forming along Telegraph Road. Ignorant of the terrain to his left, Hooker sent the Third Corps's chief engineer, Lt. Miles D. McAlester, "to reconnoiter the ground and enemy's redoubts to our left," preparatory "to carrying them by assault should a suitable opportunity present itself." The remaining companies of the 1st Massachusetts extended through the felled timber forward and left just before most of Hooker's Third Brigade, consisting of New Jersey regiments under Brig. Gen. Francis E. Patterson, arrived on the field. Patterson immediately detached the 5th New Jersey and sent it to the right of Hampton Road to support Capt. Walter M. Bramhall's 6th New York Battery, which had opened up in the fallow field about a half hour after Webber's. The 6th and 7th New Jersey Regiments Patterson ordered beyond the slashing to the left. There Captain McAlester on his reconnaissance watched them disappear into the woods as they deployed with the 7th to the left of the 6th. The 8th New Jersey had not yet come up.[16]

No sooner had the New Jersey regiments formed in line of battle than they discovered the forest was full of graycoats. Wilcox's 19th Mississippi under Col. Christopher H. Mott was already in battle array just inside the woods, "so dense that a colonel could not see his entire regiment when in line of bat-

15. John G. Barrett, ed., *Yankee Rebel: The Civil War Journal of Edmund DeWitt Patterson* (Chapel Hill: University of North Carolina Press, 1966), 19; *OR*, 11(1):580, 590; *OR*, 51(1):90.
    16. *OR*, 11(1):462, 466–7, 470, 487, 490.

tle." The Mississippians had crossed the field from Redoubt Four through a ravine to shelter them from Federal artillery fire directed blindly toward the woods. Skirmishers sent ahead among the trees to feel for the enemy soon met New Jersey skirmishers, three of whom were captured, and Mott's regiment moved a little farther into the woods. At this point, the 9th and 10th Alabama, having followed the 19th Mississippi through the ravine, formed behind it in a field. To the 19th's right, the 10th Alabama's right wing rested close to a fence enclosing the field. When the 9th Alabama came up on the left, Corporal Patterson noticed that the slashing immediately in front and the "woods on our right were so dense that they completely hid from us the operations of the remainder of the brigade, with the exception of the 19th Mississippi, which was the next regiment to us." More Mississippi skirmishers, under Capt. Jacob M. Macon, went out and, while driving the New Jersey skirmishers back upon their main force, received a volley that mortally wounded Macon in both thighs.[17]

"To the clear and intelligible account of the position and probable force of the enemy, given by this gallant officer while suffering the greatest agony, no small part of our subsequent successes is due," concluded Lt. Col. Lucius Quintus Cincinnatus Lamar, a former U.S. congressman now commanding the right wing of the 19th Mississippi. Macon reported the Union battle line lying about two hundred yards from the Confederate front and nearly parallel to it, partly behind the same rail fence that skirted the 10th Alabama's right but extending beyond that flank. With this information, Wilcox immediately dispatched an urgent request to A. P. Hill to move forward at once to his support. Stuart, ordered by Longstreet to cooperate with Anderson, intercepted the message and delivered it instead to the most convenient brigadier, Roger Pryor, who promptly brought 400 men of his 14th Louisiana and 120 of his 8th Alabama, all he could spare from the four redoubts Anderson had instructed him "to hold at every hazard." Anderson then left Fort Magruder under the command of Col. Micah Jenkins of the Palmetto Sharpshooters and rode over to direct operations personally on the right after first calling on A. P. Hill to join him with his brigade.[18]

Hill's Virginians were ready. They had formed under arms around the asylum early that morning, and after so long a wait their march through the streets of Williamsburg, interrupting Sergeant Dutcher's breakfast date, was a

17. Ibid., 487, 491, 590–1, 596, 51(1):91–2; Barrett, *Yankee Rebel*, 19–20.
18. *OR*, 11(1):571, 580–2, 587–91, 598; Robert S. Holzman, *Adapt or Perish: The Life of General Roger A. Pryor, C.S.A.* (Hamden, Conn.: Achon, 1976), 28.

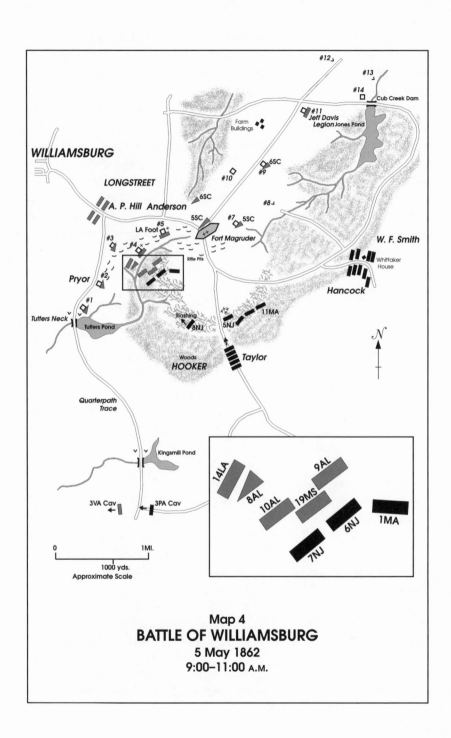

Map 4
BATTLE OF WILLIAMSBURG
5 May 1862
9:00–11:00 A.M.

welcome relief. Dashing out onto Main Street, Dutcher found the sidewalks "full of infantry at double-quick, and artillery, staff officers, and couriers were coming down the roadway at a gallop." The brigade deposited blankets and knapsacks in the street under guard, then halted at the eastern end of town on York Road in position to support either the left or right. While the troops waited there in the pouring rain, a Union "prisoner was brought by dressed up in blue, as if he was going to a ball," the 11th Virginia's adjutant, Lt. Lawrence Meem, later wrote his father. At that moment, "Sam Garland [the 11th's colonel] shouted out, 'boys look at that prisoner, now shoot at all such nice dressed men as that, for you may know they are not your friends' which caused a good deal of merriment at a serious time."[19]

In a more somber mood, Pvt. James Petty of the 17th Virginia pulled out his diary, propped it against his gun, and in a steady hand penciled: "Monday, May 5, 11:30 A.M. In line of battle near 'Fort Magruder'—Bombs have been falling thick and fast but none of us are hurt as yet. The rain is falling heavily and has been ever since about 2 A.M. at which hour I arose. My trust is in God and my Soul is calm and hopeful." Like Petty, Meem also mentioned that "the shells bursted around us in any direction, but without injuring a single man." The right wing of Bramhall's Federal battery had been thrown far forward and was plowing the ground all around Fort Magruder and the road behind the right redoubts with round shot and shell. Return fire came from McCarthy's and Clopton's guns in the fort as well as Garrett's brass piece in Redoubt Four and Coke's gun from Redoubt Five. The Union cannon "were hid from us by an intervening skirt of woods," Garrett remembered years later. "Over this skirt of woods we fired at them, directed by the smoke and our knowledge of the ground; most of us, have hunted over the ground in boy-hood, and being acquainted with its topography." Longstreet at his headquarters in Williamsburg, reckoning Garrett's men could use some help, ordered Capt. James Dearing of the Lynchburg Artillery to take two of his guns into Fort Magruder, accompanied by Powell Hill's infantry. Hill got his men up and moving, but before he and Dearing could find a protected approach to the fort, Anderson sent word that Wilcox was the one who most needed support.[20]

Off across the fields to the right, dodging shells exploding all around, marched Hill's brigade "with all the steadiness of veterans." The 7th Virginia

19. *OR*, 11(1):575–6; Dutcher, "Williamsburg," 412; John Lawrence Meem to father, 10 May 1862, VHS.

20. Petty Diary No. 2, 5 May 1862, MC; Meem to father, 10 May 1862; *OR*, 11(1):576, 51(1):85–8; Nevins, *Diary of Battle*, 51; Garrett to CBT, 15 May 1890.

under Col. James L. Kemper formed in line of battle behind Redoubts Two and Three, and Garland's 11th Virginia stopped in rear of number one. Soon "a shot rang out," recalled Dutcher, "then another, then a sharp rattle" in the distant woods. Wilcox had ordered the 320 men of his 10th Alabama under Col. John H. Woodward on his right flank to attack. As the 7th Virginia began rushing toward the woods to their aid, the Alabamians leaped the fence and engaged the New Jersey troops only fifty to seventy-five yards away. They had been firing about ten minutes when the 10th Alabama was approached from a ravine on its right rear by a man "claiming to belong to the Second Louisiana regiment, saying 'You are firing on your friends.'" Woodward con-sidered this a good possibility with Pryor's Louisiana battalion in the neigh-borhood and ordered a cease fire, immediately upon which the Federals poured a heavy volley into them. "Instantly the word retreat was heard," re-ported Woodward, "and the line commenced retiring." It did not stop, despite the colonel's protests, until it had recrossed the fence and run into General Wilcox seventy-five or eighty yards back. There the general reformed the 10th Alabama behind the just-arriving 7th Virginia, and they "returned to the at-tack with cheers."[21]

These cheers from the throats of Alabamians and Virginians alike reached the 11th Virginia, which at the first sound of musketry had also begun moving through the ravine toward the woods. "As we were going out of the ravine," noted Meem, "a tremendous cheer was sent up in the woods in hearing which I yelled out that we had them, & the whole Regiment commenced double quicknin up the hill cheering as they went, of course making the excitement intense." Three of the 11th's companies came up behind the 7th Virginia, while the other seven companies filed to the right and in the dense under-growth became tangled with Pryor's 14th Louisiana. "We soon got right again," wrote Meem. Then, with the 11th Virginia in front, the 7th Virginia on the left, and the 10th Alabama behind, they all "banged away, might and main, in the direction in which the balls seemed to come," for blue uniforms were not yet visible. Farther to the left, Wilcox ordered the 19th Mississippi, 501 muskets strong, "to fix bayonets and drive the enemy." Thus the advance began.[22]

Through dense undergrowth and over uneven ground, the Confederate line plunged "with the utmost eagerness" toward the rail fence from which the 6th

21. OR, 11(1):576, 588, 591, 596–7; Dutcher, "Williamsburg," 413; Meem to father, 10 May 1862.
22. Meem to father, 10 May 1862; OR, 51(1):92, 11(1):598; Dutcher, "Williamsburg," 413.

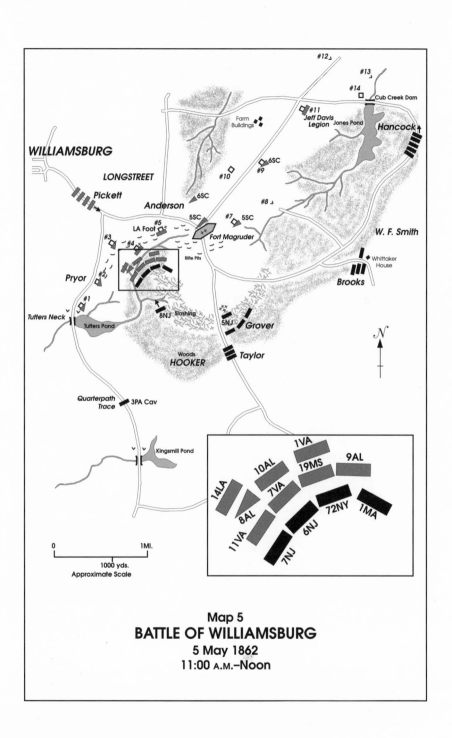

Map 5
BATTLE OF WILLIAMSBURG
5 May 1862
11:00 A.M.–Noon

and 7th New Jersey Regiments were pouring in a heavy and destructive fire. "This was most exciting," asserted Dutcher. "Everybody was yelling, firing, and advancing." The New Jersey volunteers, however, "contested the ground most stubbornly" and did not give an inch until the 19th Mississippi came within thirty yards of them. After a few minutes of close musketry, Colonel Mott of the 19th Mississippi ordered a charge but fell mortally wounded, pierced through the breast by a minié ball while leading his regiment. Lieutenant Colonel Lamar, now in command, expected a hand-to-hand bayonet fight, "but at last, wavering before the impetuosity and undaunted resolution of our men, the enemy began to yield the ground, continuing to fire as they retired." Confederates now possessed the fence, where they found heaps of their slain foes "as evidence of the obstinacy of his resistance."[23]

Immediately to the Mississippians' left, the 333 men of Col. Samuel Henry's 9th Alabama likewise opposed a tough adversary as their ranks, extending to the left out of the woods, pressed forward. With Coke's gun in Redoubt Five covering their left flank, the Alabamians advanced slowly, climbing over the huge pine logs and stumps and through the tangled undergrowth, until they suddenly came within range of Federal sharpshooters. As soon as the firing began, Corporal Patterson saw General Anderson ride up and holler, "*Go forward men, straight forward, don't halt at all.*" The Alabama boys did their best to obey, "though it was impossible to preserve anything like a well formed line," Patterson complained, "and the Yankees being stationed and posted behind the logs had much the advantage of us, for we had to expose ourselves continually in getting over the logs, while we could but seldom get a shot at them." The 9th Alabama's support, consisting of Hill's 1st Virginia placed behind it "with orders to follow closely," had instead drifted to the right into the woods. When the 9th Alabama's right wing became separated from the 19th Mississippi, Patterson, sent over to ask Mott to move his left wing closer, "found that regiment, like our own, without much of a line, and Col. Mott dead." Nevertheless, the 9th Alabama persevered "and slowly drove the enemy back."[24]

Their enemy along this section of the line was the 72d New York from Hooker's Second (Excelsior) Brigade comprised of New York regiments and temporarily commanded by Col. Nelson Taylor. The 5th Excelsior, or 74th New York, halted about two hundred yards from the battlefield along Hampton Road, where Cpl. James R. Burns took the opportunity to prepare a cup

23. *OR*, 11(1):592, 598, 51(1):92; Dutcher, "Williamsburg," 513.
24. *OR*, 51(1):92–3, 11(1):591–2, 594; Barrett, *Yankee Rebel*, 20.

of tea and lunch before entering the fray. "I made a fire by the side of the road," he later reminisced, "took some water from a pool adjoining, and made as good a cup of tea as any soldier need desire." A small company of this brigade was eager to try out a new patent machine gun, nicknamed the "coffee mill" because it fired a hopper-full of bullets cranked through a swiveling single barrel and, asserted one soldier, "was calculated to annihilate an entire regt. at once." It was not practical for use in the felled timber, however, into which the 72d New York was sent to the 6th New Jersey's right with instructions to relieve the 1st Massachusetts and silence Garrett's annoying gun in Redoubt Four. The first of these orders presented no problem, according to Edwin Brown, for the exhausted men of the 1st Massachusetts were only too happy to retire a short distance and "hastily cleanse our muskets which had become foul from the six hours of fighting, and to give us a brief moment to refresh ourselves with a little hard tack and pork coffee." But the New Yorkers had all they could handle in the slashing, with the 9th Alabama relentlessly pressing them back and eventually compelling their Lt. Col. Israel Moses to send Taylor a request for support.[25]

Taylor immediately ordered in his next available regiment, the 1st Excelsior, or 70th New York, commanded by Col. William Dwight. Now Hooker had only the 73d and 74th New York Regiments in reserve and no reinforcements in sight. He had earlier sent the 11th Massachusetts into the woods to the right of Hampton Road to determine whether they contained any Confederates "and, if so, to wipe them out." The 11th's commander, Col. William Blaisdell, reported communicating with General Hancock but found "no enemy in that direction." Neither was there any indication of the support Hooker had long been expecting on Telegraph Road. In desperation Hooker addressed a note at 11:20 to General Heintzelman at the Whittaker House, informing his corps chief that his men were "a good deal exhausted," but "my communication with you by the Yorktown road is clear of the enemy." Hooker handed this message to Capt. Henry Benson, who had come up with his battery earlier that morning and had nothing to do. The captain galloped to the right over open ground in front of the woods. This proved the most expeditious route but was within easy range of Fort Magruder's guns.[26]

When Benson arrived safely at the Whittaker House some ten minutes

25. *OR*, 11(1):466–7, 475, 484, 487, 489; James R. Burns, *Battle of Williamsburgh, with Reminiscences of the Campaign, Hospital Experiences, Debates, Etc.* (New York: Published by author, 1865), iii; David Herbert Donald, ed., *Gone for a Soldier: The Civil War Memoirs of Private Alfred Bellard* (Boston: Little, Brown., 1975), 69; Brown, "Battle of Williamsburg," EYB, MR-CWM.
26. *OR*, 11(1):467, 476, 481, 535; Nevins, *Diary of Battle*, 52.

later, the scene that met him was less than encouraging. The three brigades in W. F. Smith's division sprawled lazily on either side of York Road, "their arms at rest," observed the Comte de Paris, bewildered at headquarters incompetence. Heintzelman had just departed for the front after listening to the rain-muted sounds of combat all morning. In his absence, Benson handed Hooker's message to Sumner. According to de Paris, the Federal field commander seemed disoriented and unable to comprehend the situation. Sumner "is surprised by the firing; he thinks it is Hooker but does not know for sure," that is, until he received Hooker's note. Various officers' repeated entreaties to reinforce Hooker with either Smith's or Casey's division had no discernible effect on Sumner. He merely scribbled on Hooker's envelope "Opened and read" and sent it back without further comment or promise of help.[27]

Sumner had, however, dispatched an order to Gen. Philip Kearny "to pass all others and to proceed to the support of General Hooker." This came as a surprise to the one-armed brigadier, whose division was the last one out of Yorktown Sunday afternoon and then on Monday morning had to wait until nine o'clock for marching orders. Not even Kearny, as eager for a scrap as Hooker, expected to fight that day and therefore mounted his splendid but inexperienced bay colt to lead his men up Telegraph Road. Soon after they came upon the rear of Couch's division, filling the road with troops and trains, Sumner's order arrived. Immediately, Kearny began pushing his men in single file around the obstructions, at times turning "his own guns against laggard captains of other Divisions arresting two for blocking the execution of his orders" to burn mired wagons. A left turn at Cheesecake Church brought them into a road containing no troops and no trains but still plenty of mud.[28]

This omnipresent mud, while hindering Hooker's reinforcements, kept Longstreet's reserves within recall range. "At 12 o'clock it became evident that the trains would not be out of my way before night," Longstreet reported, "and that I could, therefore, make battle without delaying the movement of our army." He had already ordered back George Pickett's Gamecock Brigade after it had progressed but a short distance up Richmond Road from its bivouac behind William and Mary. Returning to the college grounds, Randolph Shotwell of the 8th Virginia and a number of officers took refuge from the

27. *OR*, 11(1):457, 467, 557; Mark Grimsley, ed., and Bernatello Glod, trans., "'We Prepare to Receive the Enemy Where We Stand': The Journal of the Comte de Paris Revealed," *Civil War Times Illustrated* 24 (May 1985): 19–20; Congress, *Report of the Joint Committee*, 1:569.

28. *OR*, 11(1):451, 491; Thomas Kearny, *General Philip Kearny: Battle Soldier of Five Wars* (New York: G. P. Putnam's Sons, 1937), 208; P. Kearny to A. Kearny, 15 May 1862, WCP, MR-CWM.

rain on the second floor of the main building. Shotwell thought "the empty halls, corridors, and lecture rooms had a deserted, depressing look notwithstanding the crowds of soldiers roaming through them." Down on the front lawn he stood examining the weather-beaten old marble statue of Lord Botetourt, Norborne Berkeley, when, coincidentally, Lt. Col. Norborne Berkeley, acting commander of the 8th Virginia, joined him. Rapidly rolling drums suddenly called the brigade forward through Williamsburg. Artillery rattling down the middle of the streets forced infantrymen onto the sidewalks. "Groups of citizens give way to the musket-bearers, and view them with anxious face," noted Shotwell. "Couriers and orderlies dash in and out among the long trains of ambulances and ammunition wagons, guiding them to various points."[29]

Pickett guided his brigade to the point where Quarterpath Trace branched off the main York Road behind the right redoubts. There his men waited and watched as wounded Confederates and grim squads of prisoners passed to the rear. Anderson finally ordered Pickett to take his brigade into the woods to the right and extend far enough over to turn the Union left flank, if possible. Thus the 8th Virginia led the 18th, 19th, and 28th Virginia Regiments behind the redoubts through the field still being raked with heavy artillery fire. "Shells were bursting and solid shot was ploughing mother earth just where we had to go," wrote the 19th Virginia's adjutant, Lt. William Nathaniel Wood. "In front and to the left clouds of dust gave some indication of the danger into which at a double-quick we were rushing." The third full brigade to run this gauntlet that morning, Pickett's men halted when they reached the shelter of "the friendly forest" and, facing the woods, formed their first line of battle as "Pickett's Brigade."[30]

With all but one brigade of his division now deployed and wasting ammunition against the Federals' long-range guns and superior artillery, Longstreet ordered Anderson "to seize the first opportunity to attack the most assailable position of the enemy." Finding a position to assail after the enemy had melted into the woods proved a problem for Kemper's 7th Virginia, now catching its breath at the rail fence. Presently, Dutcher and his comrades could see off to their left "company after company march briskly down a sort of woods road, halt, and face towards us." This was the 8th New Jersey of Gen-

29. *OR*, 11(1):564–5, 584; Hamilton, *Papers of Randolph Abbott Shotwell*, 1:193–4.

30. *OR*, 11(1):584; Hamilton, *Papers of Randolph Abbott Shotwell*, 1:194–6; William Nathaniel Wood, *Reminiscences of Big I*, ed. Bell Irvin Wiley (1895; reprint, Wilmington, N.C.: Broadfoot, 1992), 12.

eral Patterson's brigade, the first northerners seen by either the 7th or 11th Virginia. Adjutant Meem admired the soldiers "drawn up in a beautiful line of battle," the brass buttons on their blue uniforms clearly visible. They were quietly watching the 17th Virginia, commanded by Col. Montgomery D. Corse, coming up on the 7th's left when Kemper called Powell Hill's attention to them. "General Hill leveled his field-glasses on the line," observed nearby Lt. William H. Morgan of the 11th Virginia, "and in a moment said: 'Yes, they are Yankees; give it to them!' Colonel Kemper's clear-ringing voice broke the stillness with, 'Now, boys, I want you to give it to those blue-coated fellows; ready, aim, fire.'" At once the 7th Virginia and three left companies of the 11th Virginia "poured into them a deadly volley" from a distance of only forty-five yards.[31]

Smoke from this volley slowly rose to reveal the entire line of New Jersey men with muskets up. "The long stretch of glittering steel, with a head bent down at the end of each gun-barrel, was a thrilling sight," Dutcher recounted. "A huge cloud of smoke hid them from our view, and a tremendous report rang through the forest." So powerful was the Federals' opening volley that it tore holes in the 17th Virginia's forming ranks and scattered the 8th Virginia, at that moment passing behind. Instantly, the whole Confederate line replied, from Garland's 11th Virginia, backed by the 10th Alabama and 14th Louisiana, on the right to the 19th Mississippi, now supported by Col. Lewis B. Williams's 1st Virginia, on the left. With neither artillery nor cavalry directly involved, "it was," judged Dutcher, "a fair and square stand-up infantry fight at close range."[32]

After a full hour of blazing away without pause, ammunition began to run out, yet the men were too busy loading and shooting to heed Kemper yelling above the roar, "General Hill says the line must be advanced." Finally, Hill himself strode to the front of the line, "waving his pistol over his head, looking back over his shoulder and calling on the men to follow." Bounding over the fence with "a wild cheer," wrote Meem, "the brave Virginians pressed forward to the charge" behind Colonels Kemper, Garland, and Corse. Pickett's brigade also joined in the charge, with the 18th, 19th, and 28th Virginia Regiments behind Hill's brigade. The 8th Virginia, placed on the extreme right, stumbled over Pryor's 14th Louisiana, extending farther to the right in the dense timber.

31. OR, 11(1):565, 576; Dutcher, "Williamsburg," 413–4; Meem to father, 10 May 1862; W. H. Morgan, Personal Reminiscences of the War of 1861–5 (Lynchburg: J. P. Bell, 1911), 104.

32. Dutcher, "Williamsburg," 414; Hamilton, Papers of Randolph Abbott Shotwell, 1:195; OR, 11(1):576–7, 598.

Embarrassed momentarily by overwhelming Federal fire, the Louisianans had reformed and were coming up a ravine behind the 8th Virginia, their left overlapping the Virginians' right. "I and my companions who were somewhat in advance of the majority of our comrades, found ourselves *between two fires!*" exclaimed Shotwell. "Both friends and foes were pouring terrific volleys into and around the spot we occupied!" He promptly tumbled into a Revolutionary War trench "midway between the contestants." Presently, the 14th Louisiana joined him there "and from it gave the Yankees a volcano-like fire."[33]

This fear of "firing into our own friends" seized Meem as well. As the 11th Virginia advanced, he "used every endeavor both by action & word to prevent any such fatal mistake." Colonel Garland joined him in cautioning the men to reserve their fire until they could see the enemy distinctly. At one point another colonel rushed up to a company of the 11th "with hat, pistol, and sword in hand, expostulating against our firing upon his regiment, which he declared was in our front and right, and vehemently ordered us to stop firing," one soldier later related. "This occasioned momentary confusion, as we were horrified at the idea of shooting our own men; but some of our keen-sighted boys shouted back to him, 'Colonel, if that's your regiment, they are facing and shooting this way,' and without further ado we again opened fire and advanced."[34]

Before they had advanced very far, the men of the 11th Virginia commenced falling, including Garland, who soon had his wounded forearm dressed and resumed command. "We keep gradually on," wrote Meem, "scarcely knowing where we are going, but still pressing forward, through ravine & over hill. Some few Yankees are captured & the firing begins to grow terrific, as all the regiments are getting fairly engaged." They lagged a little behind the 7th Virginia, yelling, firing furiously, and slowly driving back the New Jersey boys. The 7th came upon "a double row of knapsacks neatly piled behind" what had been the 8th New Jersey's position, now "bloodily signified by prostrate forms, many dead, others gasping. They lay in every direction, like a rail fence thrown down," Dutcher detailed. "In several instances body lay upon body. It was a wretched sight." The Virginians paused long enough to offer water to the wounded and help themselves to the contents of abandoned knapsacks and haversacks. After replenishing their cartridge boxes from the fallen, they received orders to resume the advance.[35]

33. Morgan, *Reminiscences*, 105; Dutcher, "Williamsburg," 414–5; *OR*, 11(1):565, 575, 585, 588; Meem to father, 10 May 1862; Hamilton, *Papers of Randolph Abbott Shotwell*, 1:196–7.

34. Meem to father, 10 May 1862; T. D. Jennings, "Incidents in the Battle at Williamsburg," *Confederate Veteran* 5 (1897): 477.

35. Meem to father, 10 May 1862; *OR*, 11(1):576; Dutcher, "Williamsburg," 415.

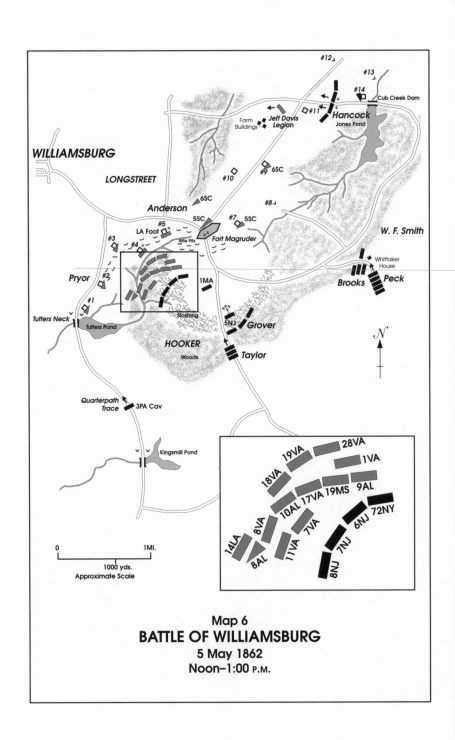

WILLIAMSBURG

LONGSTREET

Anderson

Pryor

Tutters Neck

HOOKER

Woods

Quarterpath
Trace

Kingsmill Pond

#12
#13
#14
Cub Creek Dam
#11
Jeff Davis
Legion
Hancock
Jones Pond
Farm
Buildings

6SC
#10
#9
6SC

6SC
#8
5SC
#5
LA Foot
#7
5SC
#3
#4
Rifle Pits
Fort Magruder

W. F. Smith

Whittaker
House

#2
1MA

Brooks
Peck

#1

Slashing
5NJ
Grover

Tutters Pond

Taylor

3PA Cav

𝒩

0   1MI.

1000 yds.
Approximate Scale

19VA   28VA

18VA   1VA

10AL 17VA 19MS 9AL

14LA   8VA   72NY
7VA   6NJ
11VA   7NJ
8AL   8NJ

Map 6
BATTLE OF WILLIAMSBURG
5 May 1862
Noon–1:00 P.M.

The 11th Virginia swiftly passed the row of knapsacks and became fully engaged. By now "the roar of musketry is terrific," declared Meem. "Bullets are flying like hail through the air & almost every tree is pierced by one or more." Presently the woods grew less dense. The 7th Virginia was the first to emerge at the far edge and discover a belt of felled timber sheltering a new Federal regiment. "The smoke of the previous combats was slowly drifting out of the forest and rising like a thin veil between us and the enemy," Dutcher described. "Through the haze could be seen the long line of infantry, splendidly equipped and motionless as so many statues, the sombre blue of their uniforms relieved by a shining crest of steel, the gold blazonry of the regimental colors, and the gay hues of the national flag."[36]

Grand though they may have looked, these 700 boys of the Excelsior's 70th New York under Colonel Dwight were suffering first-battle jitters. They had spent the morning plodding through rain and ankle-deep mud to get to the battlefield, halting just within range of "screeching shells and whistling bullets" to stack knapsacks and receive instructions from Dwight to "fire low." Between 12:30 and 1:00, the order came from their brigade commander, Colonel Taylor, to support the 72d New York, then being overwhelmed by the 9th Alabama in the slashing. Continuing up Hampton Road, the 70th New York encountered the disquieting sight of Bramhall's 6th New York Battery, its casualties in men and horses littering the ground after two hours of fighting. Dwight then turned his nervous command left off the road and into the slashing. There he noticed wounded New Jersey officers being carried from the field and the 6th, 7th, and 8th New Jersey Regiments—outnumbered, outflanked, and out of ammunition—falling back to the road, having lost over a third of their 1,767 men. As soon as the 70th New York reached the 72d New York's reserves, Lt. Col. Israel Moses briefed Dwight on the situation and position and made a swift exodus with all but four companies of his regiment. The 70th now stood virtually alone against three converging Confederate brigades.[37]

On the advice of Moses, Dwight quickly moved his four right companies diagonally to the right to meet the 9th Alabama, fighting still on that flank. Before long, gray uniforms emerged from the woods sixty yards in front of him, waving their colors and loudly demanding the New Yorkers show theirs. Dwight later learned that "they expected three of their own regiments in the

36. Meem to father, 10 May 1862; *OR*, 11(1):576–7; Dutcher, "Williamsburg," 415–6.

37. A. G. Peterson, "Battle of Williamsburg, May 5, 1862," *Confederate Veteran* 20 (1912): 271; *OR*, 11(1):481, 487.

very position I occupied," but "the moment they saw my national colors the rebels demanded my immediate surrender." Not obtaining it, the 7th Virginia fired a volley that the 70th New York returned. "My limbs were weak so that I could scarcely stand up to the work," one New Yorker confessed. "My gun went off, but I am not sure that I implicitly obeyed the instruction of our colonel to 'fire low.'"[38]

According to Dwight, his regiment's opening volley was so effective, the men were able to advance to within thirty yards of the Confederate line. There A. P. Hill reformed his units, with the 17th Virginia still on the 7th's left. The 11th came up on the right in time to prevent the Federals from flanking Pickett's 18th Virginia, which had already pushed ahead into the slashing and was "fighting desperately." Pickett also brought his 19th Virginia into line on the 18th's left and placed the 28th Virginia slightly in rear as a reserve. Strung out along the edge of the woods, these gray-clad lads ducked down behind the twisted branches to fire buck and ball into the smoke masking the Federal position.[39]

It was now after one o'clock, and in Hooker's words, "the battle had swollen into one of gigantic proportions." He had already thrown in the last of his reserves, placing the 73d New York behind the 70th and 72d New York, with the 74th New York posted to their right. The 1st Massachusetts, after its brief respite, returned to the field to plug the gap between the 72d New York and Hampton Road. Edwin Brown watched as Hooker conversed with Col. Robert Cowdin of the 1st Massachusetts "in those intensely calm and concentrated tones for which he was distinguished in battle, and says Hold these lines Sir to the last man. Brave eyes look back steadily into his, as the dear old Colonel responds proudly, To the last man—Sir—they shall be held," though his ammunition was nearly expended and the supply trains were still mired far to the rear.[40]

To bolster the left, Hooker now ordered the 11th Massachusetts and 26th Pennsylvania to shift across the road from the right. While carrying this message to the 26th Pennsylvania, however, the aide's horse was shot, and these Pennsylvanians, already demoralized, remained on the right, where their commander, Col. William F. Small, had been severely wounded by a rifle ball passing through his leg. The 2d New Hampshire boys, in their original position on the right side of the road, also withdrew "to take post where they could

38. *OR*, 11(1):481–3; Peterson, "Battle of Williamsburg," 271–2.
39. *OR*, 11(1):482, 577, 585; Meem to father, 10 May 1862; Jennings, "Incidents," 477.
40. *OR*, 11(1):467, 475, 485–6; Brown, "Battle of Williamsburg."

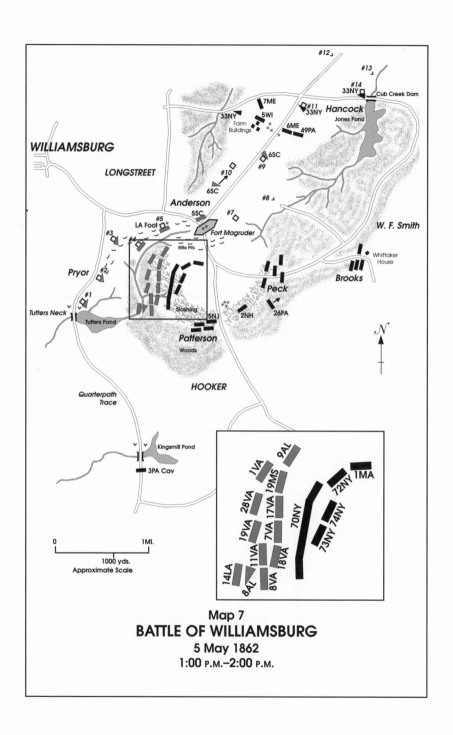

#12

#13

#14
33NY   Cub Creek Dam

7ME
33NY   5WI   #11
Farm   33NY   Hancock
Buildings   6ME   49PA   Jones Pond

WILLIAMSBURG

LONGSTREET   6SC
                              #9

#10
6SC   #8

Anderson   #7
5SC
LA Foot   #5   W. F. Smith
#3
#4   Fort Magruder
                    Rifle Pits   Whittaker
                                                  House
Pryor   #2   Peck
                                                  Brooks
#1
Tutters Neck   Slashing
Tutters Pond   5NJ   2NH   26PA

Patterson
Woods   N

HOOKER

Quarterpath
Trace

Kingsmill Pond

3PA Cav

                                              1VA   9AL
                                          19MS   72NY   1MA
                                    28VA
                            19VA   7VA 17VA 70NY
0   1MI.   11VA   73NY 74NY
                              14LA   18VA
   1000 yds.   8AL   8VA
Approximate Scale

Map 7
BATTLE OF WILLIAMSBURG
5 May 1862
1:00 P.M.–2:00 P.M.

look after the front and left at the same time." They had been lying within "the almost impenetrable thickets," listening to battle sounds coming from the left. "Sometimes the fire seemed to advance and again to recede," the 2d's Col. Gilman Marston reported, "and we were doubtful how the day was going in that part of the field." Their division commander was not much better informed, for Major Wainwright noted, "General Hooker stayed all the time just where the road came out of the wood, and did not go over to the place where our infantry were engaged at all." But Hooker could guess what was happening. "Whenever there would be a regular succession of volleys the General would rub his hands, and exclaim 'That's Dwight, that's Dwight.'"[41]

Shortly after one o'clock, Heintzelman finally arrived at Hooker's position. Captain Benson had ridden from Hooker to the Whittaker House and back in only about twenty minutes and had his horse shot on the return, forcing him to carry his saddle the rest of the way. Yet he never ran into Heintzelman because the general went the long way, a six-mile, two-hour journey by way of Cheesecake Church. Immediately upon learning Hooker's plight, Heintzelman dashed off a plea to Sumner for reinforcements and a diverting demonstration. He sent this note by two orderlies via the shorter but more dangerous route Benson had taken in front of the forest and under Fort Magruder's guns. Both messengers returned safely but with no reply. Heintzelman also dispatched an order back to Kearny "informing him of our pressing need and urging him to hurry up." This reached the general a short distance past Cheesecake Church. He had just given his men a brief rest to close up files, brew some invigorating coffee, and listen to "the ominous booming of distant cannon." Without losing another moment, Kearny ordered knapsacks piled in a nearby open field and the men to resume their march at a double-quick pace through mud holes now knee deep.[42]

While Kearny's division splashed up Hampton Road, Brig. Gen. John J. Peck's Second Brigade of Couch's division made a no less heroic effort to reach the battlefield on Telegraph Road. At 11:00 A.M. Peck, immediately in front of Kearny, came up behind Casey's division at Cheesecake Church, toiled past its wagons and cannon obstructing the road, and pulled in sight of the Whittaker House about one o'clock. "Only the head of the column arrives intact," the Comte de Paris commented; "it is followed by a two-mile stream

41. OR, 11(1):467, 477–9; Nevins, Diary of Battle, 52.

42. OR, 11(1):547–8, 492; Congress, Report of the Joint Committee, 1:353; Floyd, Fortieth (Mozart) Regiment New York, 143; J. H. B. Jenkins to Mary Benjamin, 17 May 1862, HCH, MR-CWM.

of soldiers from all regiments, trying vainly to catch up. But the men arrive full of spirit." Sumner ordered Peck to take his brigade of five regiments forward into the woods, and Peck's corps commander, Erasmus Keyes, directed Peck's division commander, Darius Couch, to post the brigade to the right of Hooker's troops. "General Couch, although quite ill, accompanied me to the field," wrote Peck, "reporting my arrival and advising in the dispositions." Peck and his staff could not locate Hooker, but part of Hooker's 26th Pennsylvania, short of ammunition and with the Confederates pressing in, soon rushed to the rear past Peck's brigade along Telegraph Road. Then a message came from Hooker, and Peck deployed his lead regiment, the 102d Pennsylvania, along the edge of the woods to the right and the 55th New York to the left of Telegraph Road. His other three regiments he held in reserve to the rear. There they lay prostrate for protection from Confederate shells passing over and "canister that beat upon the woods like hail to fall harmless," in Peck's words.[43]

Union soldiers taking refuge in the woods were more impressed with the gray artillery's effectiveness. Dearing's Lynchburg Artillery, now firing from outside Fort Magruder's left, created havoc for stragglers like Pvt. Alfred Bellard of the 5th New Jersey. He observed that "shot, shell and bullets were now flying round lively, and it was about as dangerous to be in the woods on account of the falling trees and limbs that were cut off by the shells, as it was in the front." Around the 74th New York's Corporal Burns, "tree tops dropped as though they had been heads severed from human bodies by the keenest sword." The combination of artillery and small arms produced a din that covered the entire battlefield and was best described by Dutcher as "pandemonium broke loose. It seemed to me as if the brass pieces fairly howled, while the roll of the small arms was something indescribable. Ordinarily heavy musketry rises and falls like the sound of the sea, but here it was one deep, incessant, prolonged deafening roar." This roar continued to crescendo as the battle entered its next phase.[44]

43. Grimsley and Glod, "'We Prepare to Receive the Enemy,'" 20; *OR,* 11(1):513, 517, 520–3.
44. *OR,* 51(1):88–9; Donald, *Gone for a Soldier,* 66; Burns, *Battle of Williamsburgh,* 33; Dutcher, "Williamsburg," 416.

CHAPTER 6

A Hatful of Bullets

Williamsburg had never seen a day like this. Not even during the Revolutionary War was a major battle fought so close to town that people could stroll out
to the battlefield, armed with umbrellas, "to see the smoke, to hear the roar
and smell the gunpowder of the battle more distinctly." A young boy named
John Charles was among several residents who climbed to the top of the asylum's ninety-foot observation tower on the Gothic Building to view the battle's progress that afternoon. Pvt. John Chappell of the 10th Virginia Cavalry,
posted midway between the combatants and the town, noticed that "the top
of every high house in Williamsburg was covered with females who with field
glasses were watching the tide of battle as it ebbed and flowed with the varying
fortunes of the contestants. Our boys had to but turn their backs upon the
enemy to see their white skirts flying in the air, reminding them at once of the
stakes for which they fought." Other girls, including Victoria King, were busy
baking biscuits and frying meat for the hungry soldiers. She was handing out
food in front of a house on Main Street when General Johnston "reined his
horse in, waved in our direction, and shouted to the passing troops, 'That's
what we're fighting for, boys.'"[1]

And fight they did, evidenced by the wounded pouring into Williamsburg
all day and mingling their blood with rainwater flowing in the streets. "Every
available place is open to them," wrote Cynthia Coleman, who tended several

1. David Edward Cronin, "The Vest Mansion: Its Historical and Romantic Associations as
Confederate and Union Headquarters (1862–1865) in the American Civil War," 1908–10, John
D. Rockefeller Jr. Library, CWF, 12; John S. Charles, "Recollections of Williamsburg, Virginia,
as It Was at the Beginning of the Civil War," 1928, John D. Rockefeller Jr. Library, CWF, 25;
John Taylor Chappell, "From Yorktown to Williamsburg," n.d., VHS; Victoria King Lee, "Wil-
liamsburg in 1861," 1933, John D. Rockefeller Jr. Library, CWF, 14.

wounded soldiers in the Tucker House. Dr. Garrett treated wounded from both sides on his expansive front lawn. As the men of the 2d Florida Infantry marched by a house on their way to the battlefield, "a girl young & fair, waved before them a blood-stained cloth, calling out 'go and avenge this blood.' With a yell they passed on at a double quick, and they did avenge it," Cynthia proclaimed, "but with terrible loss to themselves, . . . in defense of the women of Williamsburg."[2]

All this female attention, cavalryman Chappell theorized, underlay many deeds of battlefield valor, for "if there is one thing in the world more than another that will make a man fight it is to know that he is watched by those of the fair sex whose fate depends upon the issue." Although some with only slight wounds required one or two men to assist them from the field, others, "covered with blood, and appearantly shot all to pieces hobbled off the field unattended and yet so weak that they staggered like drunken men on their way to the rear." Chappell barely recognized one of his childhood playmates, now a lieutenant in a Richmond company, stumble by him, "all covered with blood and dirt," holding under his wounded arm three officers' swords and in front of him three Union officers "whom he was quietly conducting from the field as prisoners of war." This spectacle "was so rare that it called forth cheer after cheer as our wounded hero proceeded on his way."[3]

Many on the field witnessed other acts of courage. Longstreet's chief of staff, Capt. Moxley Sorrell, wrote of a loyal servant defying fire and smoke to retrieve the body of his stricken master, Col. Christopher Mott of the 19th Mississippi. "The devoted negro had straddled the stiffened limbs of his master on the saddle before him," Sorrell related, "covered his face with a handkerchief, and thus rescued his beloved master's body for interment with his fathers on the old Mississippi estate." Robert Stiles, an artillerist with the Richmond Howitzers, described "the most inspiring illustration of the noblest traits developed by" war. While working his gun in Fort Magruder during the heat of battle, Stiles saw a member of the Fayette Artillery at the next gun take a bullet first in his calf and another through his skull without removing his thumb from the vent of his gun, nobly saving his fellow-cannoneer "from the loss of his hands by premature explosion as he rammed home the next charge."[4]

2. Eliza Baker, "Memoirs of Williamsburg," 1933, John D. Rockefeller Jr. Library, CWF, 16; CBT, "May 5, 1862," "Peninsula Campaign," TCP, MR-CWM; Cronin, "Vest Mansion," 14.

3. Chappell, "From Yorktown to Williamsburg."

4. Sorrell, *Recollections*, 41; Stiles, *Four Years under Marse Robert*, 80–1.

A Virginia private remarked that many of the boys around him "refused to get behind the trees or to lie down, actuated by a mistaken chivalric sense of manhood." Yet some on the other side of the field complained about the lack of cover. One blue lad admitted that when the heat of battle intensified, "we were none of us too proud, not even those who had the dignity of shoulder-straps to support, to dodge behind a tree or stump. I called out to a comrade, 'Why don't you get behind a tree?' 'Confound it,' said he, 'there ain't enough for the officers.'" That soldier was surprised to find that, unlike pictures of battles he had seen, "in a real battle the officer gets in the rear of his men, as is his right and duty,—that is, if his ideas of duty do not carry him so far to the rear as to make his sword useless."[5]

Even a stout tree or log could not guarantee safety. Salem Dutcher noticed that Col. William Dwight ordered some of the 1st Excelsior's best shots to crawl under the timber and pick off graycoats, and they paid special attention to the 7th Virginia's color bearer. "Time and again as I turned to reload," Dutcher related, "I could see the colors almost jerked out of his hands as a ball tore through the cloth." Men shot in the head or throat while crouching behind logs were falling all around, yet, marveled the 11th Virginia's Lt. Lawrence Meem, "some of us dashed up & down the lines without even a scratch." When Meem urged Col. Samuel Garland to fall back to avoid being outflanked, Garland told him "our orders are to stay" and sent him off to search for three 11th Virginia companies fighting on the right. On this errand Meem ran into the 8th Virginia, which mistook him for a northerner in his personal uniform of blue. No sooner was he set free, after showing his commission to prove his identity, than he was "recaptured" by the 14th Louisiana and released by an old acquaintance, Brig. Gen. Roger Pryor.[6]

Unsuccessful in his search, Meem returned to his own regiment, which "still continues with the 7th Va to fight desperately. The men unlike some other Regiments are firing with great deliberation, for a Yankee cannot show his head from the falling timbers that he is'nt made to suffer while their bullets keep up a continual whiz." The 7th Virginia suddenly began to show signs of strain. Dutcher saw "off on the right one fellow sprang up, dropped his gun to a trail, and made off back into the woods like a quarter-horse. The panic instantly spread, and up and down the line men took to their heels." At first, Dutcher joined them until his conscience reproached him. "I wheeled about and caught at the nearest fugitive," he described the scene. "He tore loose and

5. Jennings, "Incidents," 477; Johnson and Buel, *Battle and Leaders*, 2:197.
6. Dutcher, "Williamsburg," 417; John Lawrence Meem to father, 10 May 1862, VHS.

half knocked me over. A young officer ran up to the rescue, and as he nailed one man I seized another. They, too, broke away. The officer presented his sword to the next man's breast, and throwing my musket arms-a-port I halted two. For one instant there was a rally; the next they surged over us, and made off as if the devil was behind them."[7]

Much of George Pickett's brigade, confusing an order to conserve ammunition for one to withdraw, accompanied the 7th Virginia on this unauthorized retreat. To the general's dismay, "I found the whole line from right to left falling back through the woods, abandoning our dearly-bought position." He and his aides managed to stop the fleeing ranks and reform them, but before sending them forward, he replaced the ammunition-short 18th Virginia with the fresh 28th Virginia. Meeting Col. Thomas Irby and his four companies of the 8th Alabama from Pryor's brigade, Pickett also directed them to move slightly to the right of the 18th Virginia's former position. The 70th New York's Colonel Dwight, eager to take advantage of the crumbling Confederate line, had just ordered "a number of men from each company near me to charge over the timbers with cheers, and drive back the enemy farther and maintain their ground." One of these blue squads came upon Irby leading his 8th Alabama battalion. As Pickett reported, the Federals "called out, 'We are friends; don't fire,' at the same time holding up their hands. While partially turning to caution his men not to fire the accomplished cowards poured in a deadly volley, killing the brave colonel and many of his men, and instantly, upon the fire being returned at such short range, took to their heels."[8]

As New Yorkers pressed forward upon this thinly defended section of the Confederate line, Dutcher "thought I might as well be shot front as rear, and walked back to my tree" to join two or three comrades blazing away there. "The smoke was lifting a little," he recounted, "and the enemy were preparing to advance. Half a dozen heads had already popped up out of the timber." Behind them the 70th New York's main line, lacking colors and showing "marks of the pounding it had received," hesitated when it spotted the 7th Virginia and Pickett's brigade rallying in the rear and returning "at a double-quick, yelling vociferously," much to Dutcher's relief. Dwight repeatedly called for reinforcements, believing his regiment was still holding off the enemy alone. "This skulking contest from opposite sides of logs in front of my main body became in some cases hand-to-hand," Dwight noted, and several of his best officers and men were falling "thick and fast on all sides." He himself

7. Meem to father, 10 May 1862; Dutcher, "Williamsburg," 417.
8. *OR*, 11(1):482, 585–6.

was hit in the right leg. Then, learning that his troops were short of ammunition, he "directed them to fix their bayonets and keep their place." Next, his right companies began to give way, and while endeavoring to check them, Dwight received two more wounds and fell unconscious.[9]

With the loss of its leader, the 1st Excelsior's right wing continued to withdraw. Not only was the regiment almost out of ammunition, but it was also receiving "a sharp enfilading fire of shot and shell" from its right, as were the 73d and 74th New York, now both on the right side of the road trying to advance through the slashing. Bramhall's and Webber's artillerists could no longer take this barrage, for some batteries were completely broken down, their guns disabled or sinking deeper into the muck at every round. While Maj. Charles Wainwright was temporarily absent from the field, his men began filtering back through their infantry support, the 5th New Jersey under Col. Samuel H. Starr, posted in the felled timber behind. Starr then decided that his troops could best protect the deserted batteries by joining the rest of their brigade and pulled the 5th to the left across Hampton Road to connect with the 6th, 7th, and 8th New Jersey Regiments at the woods' edge.[10]

Though Starr withdrew the artillery's support without orders, Hooker assumed full responsibility and "stood there now in the opening to our right unatended and there unmindful of peril to himself as his eye swept along the rebel front with anxious apprehensions," observed Edwin Brown. "Beautiful as a God he seemed to us, so erect and grand, his very attitude eloquent with all that can fire a soldier's heart." Across the lines, Dutcher used the same language to express his admiration for his brigade chief, A. P. Hill, "erect, magnificent, the god of war himself, amid the smoke and the thunder." His brigade had been engaged nearly four hours, more than two in this position, and ammunition was running low. To Hill's left, Cadmus Wilcox's brigade had been under fire for over five hours and was even more exhausted. Lt. Col. Lucius Lamar had pulled his 19th Mississippi's right wing back with the 10th Alabama to within supporting distance of Pickett's 28th Virginia and Hill's 1st Virginia, now occupying the front. The 19th Mississippi's left wing, separated from the right when it reached the slashing, was also almost out of ammunition, and a sudden severe fire from its left threw the far left companies into confusion and a scattered retreat.[11]

9. Dutcher, "Williamsburg," 417; *OR*, 11(1):482–3.

10. *OR*, 11(1):471, 479–80, 485–6, 489; Nevins, *Diary of Battle*, 52–3.

11. Edwin Y. Brown, "Battle of Williamsburg," EYB, MR-CWM; Dutcher, "Williamsburg," 418; *OR*, 11(1):467, 577, 597–9, 51(1):94.

By this time, the left flank of the 9th Alabama had worked its way through the abatis of slashing and approached Hampton Road less than seventy-five yards from Webber's battery in the fallow field across the road, with Bramhall's battery just beyond it. "Then," recorded the 9th's Cpl. Edmund Patterson, "there was a cry from some one, 'They are flanking us on the left.'" Thinking that Col. Samuel Henry had given an order to fall back, the five left companies did just that, retreating nearly a half mile back to the ravine, where Henry met and rallied them to move forward again. The five right companies, however, unwilling to leave the 19th Mississippi's left exposed and seeing the deserted Federal guns immediately in front, charged. They were joined by one company of the 19th Mississippi and its color sergeant, who, when shot, handed the colors to a private, who passed them to another private when he was struck in the arm. Finally, Lt. "Jump" Jones seized the regimental standard and bore it onward.[12]

Right on their heels came the 28th Virginia, directed by Wilcox under General Anderson's orders to advance through the slashing. Pickett sent out his 19th Virginia with an order to its Col. John B. Strange to "advance your regiment at a quick charge when you see the troops on your right move." Simultaneously, Hill gave the signal for his entire brigade to charge with bayonets. The men of the 11th Virginia later remembered that Colonel Garland, "wounded as he was, pushed through our regiment, saying: 'Let's see what's the matter here, boys; we *must* advance.' Some of us said, 'Get back, Colonel; we will go forward,' and, as if by common impulse, our whole line advanced." Overcome by the excitement, Meem penned, "with one wild yell our fellows rush forward to the charge, & pell mell they go together over the timbers." Just to their left, Dutcher found it "confusion worse confounded; now leaping from one tree trunk to another; now running along this, and then crawling under the other."[13]

But, continued Dutcher, "if it was hard for us to get in it was equally hard for the enemy to get out." The 70th New York, nearly half its number killed or wounded, was forced to give way. When the Virginians reached the 1st Excelsior's initial line, they were surprised at how effective their buck-and-ball cartridges were at such short range, even with the protection of the slashing. "The edge of the timber looked as if a cyclone had struck it," marveled Dutcher. "In every angle bodies were huddled." Meem's description agreed:

12. *OR*, 11(1):592–5; Barrett, *Yankee Rebel*, 21.
13. *OR*, 51(1):93, 11(1):577; Wood, *Reminiscences*, 13; Jennings, "Incidents," 477; Meem to father, 10 May 1862; Dutcher, "Williamsburg," 418.

"Heaps of dead are piled up in every direction & more are made to bite the dust, for as they run they are shot like hares by the enthusiastic 11th. Prisoners are taken in quantities & sent to the rear." One of these prisoners was the wounded Colonel Dwight, regaining consciousness just in time to find "the rebels in possession of my position." Soldiers captured from his own regiment were permitted to carry him into Williamsburg while the Confederates pushed forward.[14]

As the 70th New York fell back, the 72d New York behind it yielded as well, leaving the left flank of the 1st Massachusetts open to assault. "The enemy are quick to discover the advantage and pour their musketry in a fierce storm against it," Edwin Brown narrated. "The heavy slashing make it impossible to execute a change of front." The 2d New Hampshire was having the same problem. Its colonel, Gilman Marston, managed to shift his men out of the felled timber on the right side of the road and over to the left, "where our troops seemed to be very hardly pressed. The regiment had become very much broken in making its way through the almost impenetrable thickets in which we had lain for so many hours," Marston explained. "Other regiments were in the same condition, but every man that had a musket to fire went into the fight with whatever regiment or company he happened to fall in with." One of his captains "had collected a company composed of his own men and those of other regiments, and bravely led them on to a body of the enemy, firing his revolver and cheering on his men, when the rebel barbarian in command exhibited a white flag, and cried out to him, 'Don't fire, don't fire; we are friends,' at the same time directing his men to trail their arms." The New Hampshire captain, believing the Confederates were about to surrender, "directed his men not to fire, whereupon the whole body of the enemy suddenly fired upon him, killing him instantly, and also several of his men." The 11th Massachusetts, arriving on the left side of the road to support the New Jersey brigade, had an almost identical ruse pulled on it but managed to retaliate and shoot the Confederate "officer through the heart, thus rewarding him for his mean treachery."[15]

As the gray tide rolled on, Hooker pulled his wavering lines back across Hampton Road from left to right. This maneuver inadvertently aligned the northern ranks with Fort Magruder's guns. Quick to perceive the opportunity, Brig. Gen. J. E. B. Stuart, who had posted his cavalry near Redoubts Four

14. Dutcher, "Williamsburg," 418; OR, 11(1):483; Peterson, "Battle of Williamsburg," 272; Jennings, "Incidents," 477; Meem to father, 10 May 1862.
15. Brown, "Battle of Williamsburg"; OR, 11(1):476–8.

and Five and was directing Garrett's artillery in those works, instructed Micah Jenkins, commanding Fort Magruder, to enfilade the blue line. "That brave and gallant officer Colonel Jenkins replied that he was just going to do it," Stuart commended him. Garrett's gun in Redoubt Four joined in with "an accurate and incessant" crossfire, throwing the Federal units into more confusion as they tried to change front in the slashing.[16]

For the 73d New York (4th Excelsior) under Col. William R. Brewster, this would be the third change of front in the abatis that afternoon. At about one o'clock, these New Yorkers had marched to the left of the road to support their sister regiments; countermarched to the right, "then in imminent danger of being turned"; and returned to the left, where the section of Confederate line occupied by the leftmost 19th Mississippi companies faltered before them. "It seemed to me at this time as though victory was within our grasp," believed Brewster, but then "my ammunition began to give out, the left and center were falling back, and the entire force of the enemy seemed turned upon the point where my regiment and the Seventy-fourth were engaged." His lieutenant colonel, having assumed an advanced position, was taken prisoner as was the wounded Cpl. James Burns of the 74th New York. Burns's regiment retreated about fifty yards, leaving him "in the company of rebels, who, when they saw that I was wounded gave me water to drink; a kindness not expected from rebel hands." The Excelsior Brigade's jammed machine gun was also lost. "While the men were using it, the rebs came on them so suddenly that it could not be dragged away," the 5th New Jersey's Private Bellard wrote, "and in order that the rebels should not use it against us, the barrell was taken out and so rendered useless." The more conventional and reliable pieces of Bramhall's battery, however, were once again manned by volunteers and were again throwing deadly grape and canister at the onrushing southern horde.[17]

To avoid these fire-belchers, A. P. Hill directed his regiments to right oblique before they got too close, but in the smoke and confusion, Dutcher continued straight ahead. Then "a terrific roar and jar and a hot breath as of a furnace warned me of the uncomfortable proximity of a cannon." Throwing himself flat on the ground to avoid the blast, Dutcher saw "fire leap out of the muzzle" and then a "gray wave" sweep over the guns. "Captain Bramhall gallantly fought his pieces until the battery on his left was fairly in the hands of the enemy," Wainwright reported, "when, finding that his men were exposed

16. *OR,* 11(1):570, 583; Brown, "Battle of Williamsburg."
17. *OR,* 11(1):485; Burns, *Battle of Williamsburgh,* iv–v, 35; Donald, *Gone for a Soldier,* 69.

not only to the fire of the advancing foe but also to the return fire of his support on the right, he ordered his men to fall back." With one final dash, the
9th Alabama's leading companies took possession of the guns and were immediately shelled by a Confederate battery mistaking them for Federals. Lt.
"Jump" Jones, still clutching the 19th Mississippi's colors, mounted one of the
captured pieces and waved the flag to announce their identity and triumph.[18]

About that time the 28th Virginia arrived in the captured batteries, closely
followed by General Wilcox, who complimented his men "and was loudly
cheered." Colonel Henry promptly brought up the remaining companies of
his 9th Alabama. Wilcox became apprehensive that the Federals disappearing
into the woods about three hundred yards beyond would attempt to retake the
guns. He therefore ordered Henry to reform his line using the 9th Alabama,
one small company of the 19th Mississippi under Lieutenant Jones, fifteen or
twenty men from the 10th Alabama who had tagged along, and about 150
men of the 28th Virginia—three or four hundred troops in all—and pursue.
The 1st Virginia led by Col. Lewis Williams also passed through the batteries,
where the men picked up a flag inscribed "To hell or Richmond" and a small
blue silk brigade guidon with a gold embroidered "3" as souvenirs before continuing on behind the 9th Alabama toward the woods. Williams was directed
to detail one hundred men to secure the captured guns but protested that he
could not spare that many, having less that two hundred total. That chore
therefore devolved upon Pickett's 19th Virginia, now following Colonel
Strange into the batteries. Meanwhile, the 1st Virginia joined the 9th Alabama and 28th Virginia in charging across the field.[19]

Along with the guns some forty loose Federal artillery horses had fallen
into Confederate possession and were being picked up on every hand. Strange
mounted one and rode off to report the guns had been captured. The 7th Virginia's adjutant grabbed a magnificent dapple-gray horse for himself. Stuart's
aide brought another steed back to his chief near Fort Magruder "and announced the enemy routed and in flight." With this intelligence, Stuart immediately decided "to press the pursuit to the uttermost," ordering forward his
Horse Artillery under Capt. John Pelham. Stuart then galloped his cavalry out
to the left flank of the advancing infantry. Reaching the field "in time to wit-

18. Dutcher, "Williamsburg," 418; OR, 11(1):471, 592; Barrett, Yankee Rebel, 21.
19. Barrett, Yankee Rebel, 21; OR, 11(1):577, 586, 592, 595, 51(1):93–4; Charles T. Loehr,
"The First Virginia Infantry in the Peninsula Campaign," Southern Historical Society Papers 21
(1893): 107.

ness the successful issue of the first grand assault," Longstreet warned Stuart "to move with great caution," for he "did not think that the enemy was yet in confusion." Sure enough, just before his troopers entered the forest near Telegraph Road, they encountered a blue wall materializing behind the trees.[20]

These were the relatively fresh regiments of Peck's brigade. He posted the 102d Pennsylvania on the far right beside Telegraph Road, where it could get a good shot at the left flank of the charging Confederate infantry and cavalry. To the Pennsylvanians' immediate left on the other side of the road stood the men of Regis de Trobriand's 55th New York. They, along with the Zouave 62d New York Regiment, which Peck placed farther left, found themselves the main objective of a loudly yelling gray line. The Confederates had progressed halfway across the field before the 55th New York opened fire on them, but "they continued to advance rapidly, with increased cries," right for de Trobriand's least dependable company on his left flank. At the return volley, that company broke and ran, followed by a second and a third. Thus exposed, the New York Zouaves also began to break and fall back, and, according to de Trobriand, "what is most shameful, some officers ran away with their men, and even without them." The 93d Pennsylvania, placed in line behind them, could not stop the fugitives as they disappeared into the woods. De Trobriand managed to rally one hundred of them and reform his left, which was immediately broken a second time by a strong volley.[21]

This time, instead of fleeing to the rear, these northern boys dashed behind nearby trees and from there rudely welcomed the leading southerners, now at the edge of the abatis and only a few steps away, with "a well-sustained fire." This, along with an oblique fire from de Trobriand's center companies, effectively checked the Confederate advance on that end of Peck's line. At the other end, Stuart's cavalry and Horse Artillery bearing down upon the 102d Pennsylvania were halted by a "brisk fire," unhorsing the 4th Virginia Cavalry's Maj. William Payne with a severe wound through the jaw. As the rest of the troopers retreated, cavalry private Dr. Edmund S. Pendleton noticed Payne bleeding to death and rushed to his assistance amid a hail of bullets. He dragged the major behind a little tree and, thrusting his fingers into his mouth, clamped a severed artery. Together they lay flat between two fires, the air over-

20. Wood, *Reminiscences*, 13; Dutcher, "Williamsburg," 418; *OR,* 11(1):471, 565, 571–4.

21. *OR,* 11(1):521, 523; Richard Wheeler, *Sword over Richmond: An Eyewitness History of McClellan's Peninsula Campaign* (New York: Harper and Row, 1986), 156–7 (quoting Regis de Trobriand, *Four Years with the Army of the Potomac* [Boston: Ticknor, 1889]).

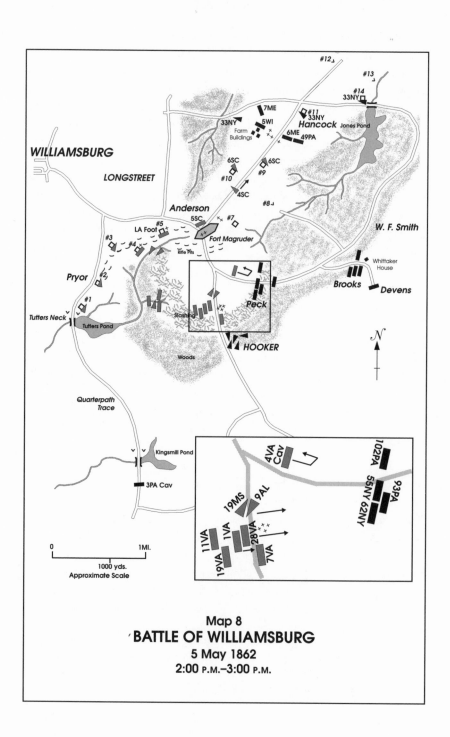

WILLIAMSBURG

LONGSTREET

#12⌐

#13⌐

#14
33NY

7ME
33NY   5WI   #11
            Farm   33NY   Jones Pond
            Buildings 6ME 49PA   Hancock

6SC   6SC
#10   #9

4SC

#8⌐

Anderson
        5SC   #7
LA Foot #5
#3 #4   W. F. Smith
        Rifle Pits
Pryor   #2
                Fort Magruder
#1
Tutters Neck   Whittaker
        Tutters Pond   House
                                        Brooks Devens

                Slashing   Peck

        Woods   HOOKER   N

Quarterpath
Trace

            Kingsmill Pond

        3PA Cav

0   1MI.

1000 yds.
Approximate Scale

4VA
Cav   102PA

                19MS 9AL   55NY 62NY   93PA

            11VA 1VA 28VA
            19VA   7VA

Map 8
BATTLE OF WILLIAMSBURG
5 May 1862
2:00 P.M.–3:00 P.M.

head so filled with bullets "that one could have caught a hatful by holding it up," Payne later recalled.[22]

Not only bullets but solid shot too began flying when Stuart ordered his Horse Artillery into action to the right of Fort Magruder. "Before the order could be given," Stuart boasted, "Pelham's battery was speaking to the enemy in thunder tones of defiance, its maiden effort on the field, thus filling its function of unexpected arrival with instantaneous execution." Pelham's three pieces were soon joined by two field guns and two howitzers of Capt. Robert M. Stribling's Fauquier Artillery, also on the fort's right, supported by six companies of Palmetto Sharpshooters. Dearing's three guns continued to pound away from atop the ramparts.[23]

All this firepower provided cover for the 1st Virginia as it crossed the field to the forest. "While halting in the edge of the woods, we observed several lines of the enemy passing between us and our line which was in the felled timber," recounted Sgt. Charles T. Loehr. "At first we thought they were some of our men until we were fired upon by them." These were the 93d Pennsylvania Volunteers, which Peck brought up to plug the gap in his left center. At this renewed fire, the 1st Virginia staggered back into the slashing, and the rest of the Confederate line, shifting left, came directly in front of the 102d Pennsylvania. "This regiment could not withstand the vigorous onslaught of such superior numbers," admitted Peck, "and retired some distance, so that I greatly feared I should not be able to hold on with the brigade." The brigadier then led his last regiment, the 98th Pennsylvania, also exhibiting a collective case of weak knees, forward to the right and front.[24]

"Now," wrote Loehr, "the enemy having been reinforced, they swarmed all around us. The bullets seem to come from all directions. We lost a good many men," including the 1st Virginia's Colonel Williams, severely wounded through the body. Nevertheless, the regiment tenaciously held on to its position in the slashing. "Most of our muskets had become useless from the continued rain, and our ammunition was nearly all expended," Loehr revealed, "but by supplying ourselves with the enemy's muskets and ammunition, which was abundantly scattered about, the fight was continued."[25]

No such replenishment opportunities existed on the Confederate left of

22. *OR,* 11(1):521–4, 571–2; R. W. Grizzard, "Dr. E. S. Pendleton," *Confederate Veteran* 28 (1920): 177; Mrs. William H. Payne, "Search for My Wounded Husband," 1910, VHS; William H. Payne to CBT, 21 Feb. 1891, TCP, MR-CWM.

23. *OR,* 11(1):572–4, 583, 51(1):85–9.

24. Loehr, "First Virginia Infantry," 107; *OR,* 11(1):521.

25. Loehr, "First Virginia Infantry," 107.

that line, where the 9th Alabama's cartridge boxes emptied within a half hour of engaging Peck. Loath to withdraw through the open field behind, Colonel Henry's men had little choice but to lie low in the undergrowth and wait for at least another half hour. This lull in the firing enabled a crew to come onto the field with a blanket and pick up Major Payne, who had Dr. Pendleton's fingers still clamped over his artery. "When they were taking me to the ambulance," Payne wrote, "the firing rose again, and it was so hot that one of the men dropped his corner of the blanket—Pendleton never faltered." Both major and doctor were lifted into the ambulance together and driven away to Williamsburg about the time Col. George T. Ward arrived on the field with his 2d Florida Regiment and the 2d Mississippi Battalion. These units were detached from Jubal Early's brigade of D. H. Hill's division, earlier called back by Longstreet from its march toward Richmond. "They came up in good style," observed the 9th Alabama's Corporal Patterson, "and were to take our places, and we get out as best we could."[26]

The 2d Florida charged across the field and formed a line at the woods' edge within sixty yards of Peck's position. "We were placed in a rather hard fix," complained one Florida boy, David Elwell Maxwell, with the 9th Alabama "in front of us so we could not fire without shooting our friends & at the same time getting the full force of the enemies fire, which beat any thing I ever imagined." Henry's order to retire reached the 9th Alabama at the same time Ward was directing the 2d Florida to advance into its place. Panic instantly seized both regiments as the Florida boys mistook the withdrawal order to include them and someone shouted they were being flanked. "Then commenced a scene of wild confusion," wrote Patterson; "both regiments broke in perfect disorder and went running through the field to the rear." Ward "rode among his men and cried, 'Floridians, Oh, Floridians, is this the way you meet the enemies of your country?', and fell from his horse dead on the field of honor, his heart pierced by a bullet."[27]

Maxwell and seven comrades stopped to pick up their colonel's body while the rest of their regiment continued running with the Alabamians a mile back to the protection of the ravine. "Just as we came down in the ravine," Patterson recorded in his journal, "I noticed an officer very richly dressed, riding a beautiful and gaily caparisoned horse, coming in full speed toward us, carrying in

26. Barrett, *Yankee Rebel*, 21; Payne to CBT, 21 Feb. 1891; Payne, "Search for My Wounded Husband"; *OR*, 11(1):595, 51(1):94.

27. Maxwell to mother, 20 May 1862, David Elwell Maxwell Papers, VHS; Barrett, *Yankee Rebel*, 21–2.

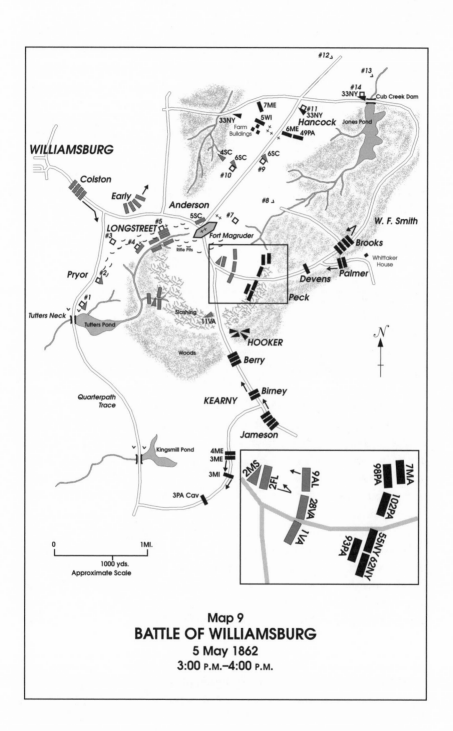

#12

#13

#14
33NY □ Cub Creek Dam

7ME
#11
33NY
5WI   Hancock   Jones Pond
33NY
Farm   6ME 49PA
Buildings

WILLIAMSBURG

Colston

Early

4SC   6SC   6SC
#10   #9

Anderson

5SC   ×× #7 □

#8

LONGSTREET   #5   Fort Magruder
#3   Rifle Pits

#4

W. F. Smith

Brooks   Whittaker
House

Pryor   #2   Devens Palmer

#1   Peck

Tutters Neck

Tutters Pond   Slashing

11VA

HOOKER

Woods

Berry

Birney

KEARNY

Jameson

Quarterpath
Trace

Kingsmill Pond

4ME
3ME

3MI

3PA Cav

2MS
2FL   9AL
98PA   7MA

28VA   102PA

1VA   93PA   55NY 62NY

N

0   1MI.

1000 yds.
Approximate Scale

Map 9
BATTLE OF WILLIAMSBURG
5 May 1862
3:00 P.M.–4:00 P.M.

his hand a slouch hat, in which was a long magnificent plume—he was the very picture of a cavalier." General Stuart imparted "some cheering words" to the Florida lads as they prepared to reenter the contest. Wilcox then "complimented us on the endurance and bravery that we had manifested," continued Patterson, and dismissed the exhausted 9th Alabama to its camp west of Williamsburg. The 19th Virginia, having reformed around the captured Federal batteries, also "marched in the direction of Williamsburg and bivouacked half a mile or more from the scene of action." A. P. Hill halted his 17th Virginia on the ground it had just won and directed the men to refill their "cartridge boxes from those of the enemy's dead, who were plentifully and opportunely strewn around." After similarly resupplying themselves from Union cartridge boxes, the 7th and 11th Virginia Regiments withdrew to the woods' edge and reformed.[28]

Part of the 11th Virginia missed the withdrawal order and upon reaching the abandoned Federal batteries changed "position by the right flank to get in the rear," recited Lieutenant Meem, one of the wayward number. This detour took them down Hampton Road, where "a regiment of Yankees just arrived pours in the most deadly & fatal fire of the day." This little squad of about seventeen Virginians, taking cover in a nearby "ancient line of grass-grown earthworks" they later learned dated from the Revolutionary War, kept up a fierce fight for almost another hour. Dr. Waller's grand-nephew and President John Tyler's grandson, Johnny Waller, "is shot down by me, while not ten feet from me a ball pierces the brain of another of the 11th & he falls back a corpse," Meem wrote. "A moment later another falls dead while the wounded are numerous." He tried to urge his men forward but was nearly cut down by a ball slicing through his pants and another perforating his boot. When a new Federal battery opened down the road, Meem's boys turned their attention to driving off its gunners.[29]

This was Capt. James E. Smith's 4th New York Battery, finally making its appearance. It had camped the night before with Bramhall's battery and had the same distance to travel to the field, but Smith reported midmorning to Hooker that he was blocked by a forage train. At that point the general did not think the battery would be needed. Events proved otherwise early that afternoon, and Wainwright obtained permission from Hooker during a brief

28. Maxwell to mother, 11 May 1862, Maxwell Papers; Barrett, *Yankee Rebel*, 22; Wood, *Reminiscences*, 13; *OR*, 11(1):577.

29. Jennings, "Incidents," 477–8; Meem to father, 10 May 1862.

lull in the action to ride back in search of his still-missing guns. In little clearings among the trees he saw field hospitals giving the wounded their first dressing before sending them another mile or so back to the main hospital. The major picked through ammunition and hospital wagons stuck in the road until he found his lost battery and began heading forward with it. The sound of heavy firing reached him as he approached within a mile of the front, prompting him to push on as fast as he could. "Just as I reached the hospital I met the first of a string of ambulances, waggons, and other vehicles, just breaking into a run," he wrote in his diary; "the men too were starting, hospital attendants and such like." To cut short this stampede to the rear, he drew his saber and threatened the lead driver, who stopped and blocked all behind him on the narrow road. Two squadrons of the 3d Pennsylvania Cavalry arrived a few minutes later to prevent any more outbreaks, and the artillery chief continued on toward the front.[30]

There Wainwright was horrified to find his guns in enemy hands and all of the slashing to the left of Hampton Road occupied by graycoats. Captain Osborn had gathered a dozen of his artillerists to man one piece planted in the road near the edge of the woods. When Smith came up, Wainwright placed two of his Parrott guns and two 6-pounders in echelon on a knoll to the right of the road just inside the woods and ordered them loaded with canister. They did not have long to wait before two Confederate regiments charged in column down the road. "I held fire until the head of the column was well down to within about 150 yards of us," Wainwright detailed. "Three rounds to a gun then blew the whole thing away, except small parties which got into the slashing on the left of the road, and picked off my cannoneers." Twice, Wainwright went back to beg infantry support from Generals Hooker and Grover but with no results.[31]

Before Smith's surviving gunners took refuge behind trees, they divided their fire between Fort Magruder and the redoubts to their left and also raked the southern work party trying to carry off the captured batteries. Three men sent out by Captain Pelham from his Horse Artillery to assist that effort returned in a few minutes on foot, "their horses having been shot down as soon as they made their appearance at the guns." Finally, as John Chappell watched, the captured pieces emerged from the battlefield smoke with their horses at a

30. Walter H. Hebert, *Fighting Joe Hooker* (Indianapolis: Bobbs-Merrill, 1941), 85; Nevins, *Diary of Battle*, 52–3; *OR*, 11(1):434.

31. Nevins, *Diary of Battle*, 53–4; *OR*, 11(1):471.

dead run, "a Confederate soldier standing on the limber of the first gun, crazy with excitement, waving above his head the captured banner, amid the cheers from ten thousand throats, the rattle of musketry and the roar of artillery."[32]

The 19th Virginia had managed to haul off three Parrott guns, one howitzer, and a caisson from Webber's battery, but Bramhall's six guns were stuck in the mud and immovable. With the loss of these pieces, Federal morale sank to its lowest ebb. "The rain, the sight of the wounded, the re-enforcements still behind, all conspired to depress everybody," lamented General Heintzelman. Nothing he could do would move his balky soldiers. "The smoke and rain were driven by the wind into the faces of our men. Even the elements were combined against us." Many, their ammunition exhausted, simply straggled back or carried the wounded to the rear and did not bother to rejoin their regiments. "When the ominous words, 'It is a retreat,' began to be heard among the discouraged New-Jersey troops," one newspaper correspondent observed, Heintzelman's medical director, Dr. John J. Milhau, "packed up his instruments and rapidly began to place his wounded in ambulances and wagons using force and threatening death to the few that refused to assist in the duty." Dr. Milhau was soon "restored to his dreadful labors" on the battlefield by the Third Corps's assistant adjutant general, Capt. Chauncey McKeever, who, anticipating another Bull Run stampede, deployed two squadrons of the 3d Pennsylvania Cavalry on either side of the road in the woods with orders to fire upon stragglers and force them back into battle.[33]

Not all of Hooker's troops were fleeing. Remnants of his division remaining on the field to fight "to the last man," anchored by the staunch 1st Massachusetts, stood at the woods' edge with bayonets fixed as their assailants tore through the abatis shouting "Bull Run—Bull Run." Some graycoats actually penetrated the forest "within a few hundred yards of where I was," Heintzelman later testified, "and on my left they were in the woods beyond me. They were so near that their musket-balls passed over my head." The thought of making a personal withdrawal did cross his mind, the general admitted, but he rejected the idea, fearing its effect on his demoralized troops. Instead, in an effort to inspire them, Heintzelman ordered the drums to beat, but being wet they "did not give forth cheerful sounds." He then found three brass musicians. "'Play,' said he, 'Play! it's all you're good for. Play d——n it. Play some marching tune. Play Yankee Doodle, or any doodle you can think of; only play

32. OR, 11(1):574; Chappell, "From Yorktown to Williamsburg."
33. OR, 11(1):434, 458–9; Edwin Y. Brown to brother, 10 May 1862, EYB; New-York Daily Tribune, 10 May 1862.

something.'" But since they were only a portion of a band, they refused to play. Heintzelman and his staff scurried around looking for more, found a part of another band, and united them with the first three, who then struck up "The Star-Spangled Banner." Reported a satisfied Heintzelman, "The strains were wafted through the old forest, and made themselves heard by our weary troops above the roar of the battle."[34]

As both friend and foe paused to listen, a momentary hush fell over the battlefield, "to be broken an instant later by such a cheer as shook the gloomy forest," wrote Edwin Brown. From "back along the dismal road to our rear, comes a kindred response from ten thousand eager throats." Kearny had arrived at last. Reduced to only about 1,900 after a grueling forced march through knee-deep mud the last three and a half miles from Cheesecake Church, his men came within range of the battlefield shortly before four o'clock. "There was hardly a man who did not tumble headlong at least once," the 2d Michigan's Lt. Charles B. Haydon recorded in his diary. "They looked as little like human beings as any men I ever saw. All were drenched with rain to the skin & cased with mud to the waist at least." Approaching the field, they were greeted by the sight and shrieks of Hooker's wounded being carried to the rear and saw others, as Kearny described them, "hopelessly herded like frightened sheep perfectly discouraged along the road." The brigadier immediately sent an aide to his corps commander for instructions, but Heintzelman, "worthy as stupid," in Kearny's opinion, could only reply "that the enemy was here, there and everywhere; yet he was on foot quite in the rear!" Heintzelman, erroneously assuming that Hooker was the ranking officer, directed Kearny to report to him and suggested that Hooker might be able to "aid him, as he was a stranger to his command." To that Kearny is reputed to have replied, "General, I can make men follow me to hell." Kearny later wrote that upon meeting his fellow division chief, he carefully and pointedly inquired, "General Hooker whilst I reserve my command, as your Senior, I should be happy to know the state of your affairs, and where you want most instant relief."[35]

34. Brown, "Battle of Williamsburg"; Congress, *Report of the Joint Committee,* 1: 353; *OR,* 11(1):458–9; *New-York Daily Tribune,* 13 May 1862.

35. Brown, "Battle of Williamsburg"; Stephen B. Sears, ed., *For Country, Cause, and Leader: The Civil War Journal of Charles B. Haydon* (New York: Ticknor and Fields, 1993), 231; Kearny, *General Philip Kearny,* 243, 250; Congress, *Report of the Joint Committee,* 1:577; Watts de Peyster, *Personal and Military History of Philip Kearny* (New York: Rice and Gage, 1869), 291. Considerable discussion arose immediately after the battle concerning Kearny's actual arrival time. The general believed about two o'clock, but one of his aides said half past two, according to De Peyster (271). Thomas Kearny gives the time as 2:45 P.M. for Berry's brigade, with the rest arriving before four o'clock. *General Philip Kearny,* 217, n. 8. Wainwright recorded General Kearny as saying he

His face "begrimed with mud," Hooker could offer little more information on the situation than Heintzelman. Kearny therefore sent his staff right and left to examine the ground, threw off his India rubber cape to reveal his rank, and spurred his colt up Hampton Road beyond the Federal line, "flourishing a sword in his only arm. Never was our eyes more gladdened than at this sight," exclaimed Edwin Brown. As Kearny rode into full view, the Confederates found him a tempting target and, related an onlooker, "were directed by their officers to take a bead on that 'one-armed devil', as they dubbed him." The gray soldiers rising to fire at him betrayed their concealed positions in the abatis, providing Kearny with the information he desired.[36]

Kearny, miraculously unscathed, returned at a gallop to the head of his column and snapped orders: Third Brigade under Brig. Gen. Hiram G. Berry into line, with Col. Henry D. Terry's 5th Michigan taking the left of the road in timber supported on its left by Col. Samuel B. Hayman's 37th New York. "Owing to Hooker's people occupying the ground, and in trembling packs," Kearny later explained, "I had to come in by a flank movement, very hazardous, instead of by 'Front into Line'." He immediately dealt with a fence impeding this movement. To his men "lined up along the road, he shouted, 'Take down that fence!' Every one near it snatched a rail and it vanished in an instant." An experienced Kearny admonished green troops ducking their heads as shells whizzed by, "Tut, tut; you never can dodge them! You will never hear the one that hits you."[37]

Next came Col. Orlando Poe's 2d Michigan, three hundred strong, which Kearny rapidly arranged with two companies on the right of the road to aid Smith's battery at Wainwright's request, two more companies on the left into the dense pine woods to support the 5th Michigan, and the remaining six companies in reserve. As these Michiganders passed Heintzelman "on the road coming in, he was more enthusiastic than I ever supposed he could be," Lieutenant Haydon observed. "He swung his hat, hurrahed for Michigan most lustily & swore as hard as ever saying 'give them h——l G—d d——n them, give the steel dont wait to shoot.'" More encouragement came from their division commander, whom they had never seen until the moment they

arrived "at two o'clock; I feel very sure it was nearly if not quite four o'clock." Nevins, *Diary of Battle*, 56.

36. De Peyster, *Philip Kearny*, 290; Kearny, *General Philip Kearny*, 225, 243, 249; Brown to brother, 10 May 1862.

37. Kearny, *General Philip Kearny*, 243; *OR*, 11(1):504–7; William Brooke Rawle et al., *History of the Third Pennsylvania Cavalry Sixtieth Regiment Pennsylvania Volunteers in the American Civil War, 1861–1865* (Philadelphia: Franklin Printing, 1905), 49–50.

began forming their line. At that point Kearny "turned to us & said 'Men I want you to drive those blackguards to hell at once. Remember the torpedoes. Will you do it?' He was answered by a yell which reached the enemies' line above the roar of the battle" and propelled his troops into the fray.[38]

"Great Caesar! look!" exclaimed an 11th Virginia lad in the isolated squad. "The woods are black with Yankees." Deploying rapidly among the trees to the rousing refrains of "Yankee Doodle" and "Gem of the Ocean," Berry's brigade advanced without pausing. The 5th Michigan "moved forward in line of battle until the enemy were in full view," reported Colonel Terry, "when a brisk fire was opened on them by our men, who fired very steadily." To their left the 37th New York returned an almost continuous fire upon a concealed foe. Behind them the two supporting 2d Michigan companies "had not advanced a rod into the woods," wrote Haydon, "when Col. Poe was wounded in the hand, Capt. Morse of Co. F. fell shot through the leg & an aide to Gen. Kearney who attempted to show us the way was instantly killed." Kearny himself, on his bay colt, "diving into the deep mud-holes, and leaping over the huge logs of the abatis," personally led the 2d Michigan's two right companies, only fifty or sixty men, in a charge on some one hundred Confederates creeping through the slashing toward Smith's abandoned guns. Kearny's bluff worked, driving back the skirmishers "before they realized how few we were." He later reported, "This duty was performed by officers and men with superior intrepidity, and enabled Major Wainwright, of Hooker's division, to collect his artillerists and reopen fire from several places." To support these guns, all stragglers and survivors from the 5th New Jersey "again came forward with alacrity."[39]

Southerners did not yield ground willingly. The 2d Florida had reformed and returned to the field in time to meet the little 11th Virginia squad prudently retreating before Kearny's advancing division. "We threw in our fortunes temporarily with the Second Florida," one Virginian later recalled, "and 'fit' a while longer." Farther to their right, the 8th Virginia along with Pryor's 14th Louisiana kept Kearny's 37th New York busy on the flank. Soon joining them were three companies of the 14th Alabama under "the gallant little" Maj. Owen K. McLemore, and a battalion of the 32d Virginia, which, as part of Pryor's brigade, had been occupying the right redoubts all day. The Ala-

38. *OR*, 11(1):506–7; Nevins, *Diary of Battle*, 54; Sears, *For Country, Cause, and Leader*, 231–2, 235.

39. Jennings, "Incidents," 478; *OR*, 11(1):492, 505–9; *New-York Daily Tribune*, 13 May 1862; Sears, *For Country, Cause, and Leader*, 232; Kearny, *General Philip Kearny*, 243; P. Kearny to A. Kearny, 15 May 1862, WCP, MR-CWM.

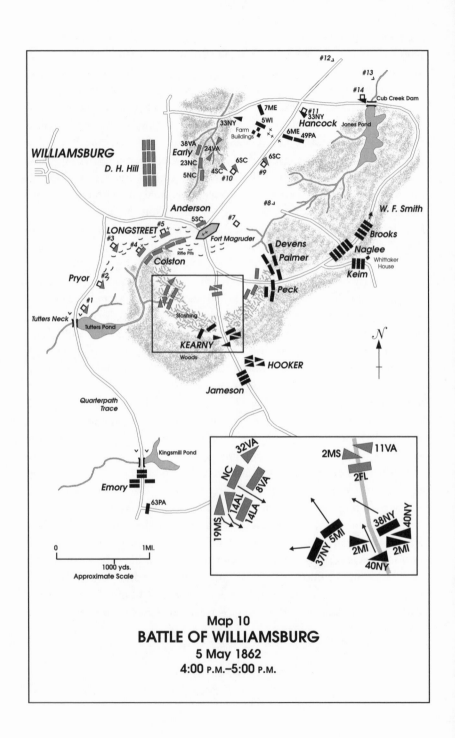

Map 10
BATTLE OF WILLIAMSBURG
5 May 1862
4:00 P.M.–5:00 P.M.

bamians "rushed forward through the drenching rain and deep mud," their regimental historian related. As they entered the woods, "Major McLemore's horse was killed from under him. He dismounted from the already fallen animal, and with a smile, as if nothing had happened, waved his sword, and ordered the men to follow him." These troops extended the line farther right from the 14th Louisiana and met the "extreme fury and pertinacity" of the Federals with "admirable courage and tenacity," holding the ground for a half hour. Lamar then arrived with what companies he had been able to salvage from his 19th Mississippi. After throwing two of these companies right and forward to meet a reported Federal flanking movement, Pryor retained the balance as his rather minimal reserve.[40]

Longstreet's reserves had also dwindled to his last brigade under Gen. Raleigh Colston. Ordered through the woods to the right, Colston reported between four and five o'clock to A. P. Hill and was told to take his 3d Virginia and 13th and 14th North Carolina Regiments forward and farther right. There the 4th North Carolina, detached from D. H. Hill's division, and the 3d Virginia found General Wilcox during a violent rainsquall and were held in the rear. The other two North Carolina regiments continued forward to relieve Powell Hill's and Pickett's brigades. One settled to the right of the 1st Virginia, still fighting Peck in the felled timber, and upon its arrival Sergeant Loehr went over to communicate the 1st Virginia's position. "Just after reaching this regiment and delivering my instructions to the colonel," Loehr wrote, "the enemy made a fierce attack on this regiment. The men were lying behind the trees, and as they commenced to fire their muskets some of the bullets would come out with a stream of fire, then fall to the ground, the powder having become soaked." Other North Carolina boys found their way into the ravine behind the 8th Virginia. They came "marching by the 'right flank' or four men abreast, and passing thro' the lines of the 8th Regiment, despite the warning that the foe was just in front, advanced into the undergrowth," Randolph Shotwell detailed. "'Better not go out there.' cried numbers of our men: to whom the North Carolinians replied.—'Oh you-uns kin stay behind ef you want to; we're able to tote this scrimmage.'" Soon after they disappeared into the dense brush, a "fearful volley burst forth," and unable to resist in their existing formation, the regiment was badly cut up, confused, and partly captured. Observed Shotwell, "They had marched squarely into a nest of hornets."[41]

40. Jennings, "Incidents," 478; *OR*, 11(1):586–8, 599–600; Jensen, *32nd Virginia Infantry*, 63–5; Hurst, *Fourteenth Regiment Alabama Volunteers*, 10.

41. *OR*, 11(1):565, 577, 593; Loehr, "First Virginia Infantry," 108; Hamilton, *Papers of Randolph Abbott Shotwell*, 1:197.

And Kearny's hornets were in a fighting mood. His next unit to arrive on Hampton Road, the Second Brigade commanded by Brig. Gen. David B. Birney, halted in the woods just within range of the battlefield to allow the jaded men to catch their breath for a few minutes and listen to a band "playing the national tunes, which inspired thrills of wildest emotion." Col. Edward J. Riley took the opportunity to address his 40th New York, or the Mozart Regiment, with "'probably the last words he should say to us,'" quoted company clerk J. H. B. Jenkins in a letter to a lady friend a few day later, "'but that any man who did not want to go in, might go back.' Not a man, I believe, refused to 'go in.'" Another Mozarter was so "anxious to confront the enemies of his country" that he stamped his feet, complaining, "What's the use of waiting?" They watched as their sister regiment, the 38th New York under Col. J. H. Hobart Ward, moved to the right of Hampton Road into the woods and advanced cautiously to the edge of the trees. Immediately behind the 38th, Riley led the right wing of the 40th in support, relieving fragments of Hooker's exhausted regiments in the process.[42]

After beating back all the Confederates who had penetrated the woods, Ward's and Riley's men broke out into the felled timber. There two or three companies of Poe's 2d Michigan joined them, but with so many people concealed in the thick brush, they had trouble distinguishing friend from foe. A company of 38th New York skirmishers suddenly gave way and fell back on the 2d Michigan. "The Rebels supposing that the whole line was retreating at once rose to pursue," Haydon wrote, but when they came into an open space, the Michiganders fired at about twenty rods, forcing them back behind the logs for another twenty minutes of "very sharp firing." In that short time Haydon counted more than thirty balls strike within five feet of him and "several within a foot." Ward observed that "our noble officers and men were continually dropping around us, though instead of having a dispiriting effect this nerved our men to desperation." Incensed by the enemy's taunts of "Bull Run, Bull Run," Ward's troops "were determined to 'have no more Bull Runs.'"[43]

At last the 38th New York's three right companies "charged across the road and step by step drove the enemy through the slashing, which was so dense that officers and men had their clothing torn into shreds," Ward asserted. The 2d Michigan, led by Kearny himself, joined in chasing the graycoats out of the felled timber and into the rifle pits in front of the earthworks but was

42. *OR*, 11(1):498, 501; J. H. B. Jenkins to Mary Benjamin, 17 May 1862, HCH, MR-CWM; Floyd, *Fortieth (Mozart) Regiment New York*, 145.

43. Sears, *For Country, Cause, and Leader*, 232; *OR*, 11(1):502.

checked at the edge of the slashing by a Confederate light battery belching shot, shell, and canister. "The heavy-strewn timber of the abatis defied all direct approach" to the rifle pits, expounded Kearny, requiring him to bring up fresh marksmen from Poe's regiment and order Ward "to pursue them across the road and charge them in their rifle pits and endeavor to get a position in their rear." This was not so easily accomplished, despite "the enthusiasm manifested by the men on receiving the order to charge." As Kearny put it, "the wave of impulsion, though nearly successful, did not quite prevail." He then called for the 40th New York's left wing and personally led it up the road. While the Mozarters advanced single file through a roadside ditch to avoid musketry fire from the woods and rifle pits, "Gen. Kearny remained mounted and braved the fusillade of shot, and shell, and bullets, and seemed to bear a charmed life."[44]

Behind their brave though "reckless and imprudent" division chief, the five left companies of the 40th New York passed the old Revolutionary War earthworks and took position in the felled timber now raked by an infantry crossfire and artillery enfilading fire. The Mozarters crouched among the logs and thickly strewn dead soldiers—Jenkins counted fifty bodies within a ten-yard radius while sandwiched between two casualties of the 38th New York—and did their best to fire their balky Austrian rifles. "Not one gun in four of ours would explode," grumbled Jenkins, "so that all that we could do was to stay and be slaughtered with as much fortitude as possible." Another New Yorker noted "the bullets kept up their continual singing, and they came so thick and fast as to give assurance of death in exposed situations." This, added Jenkins, was "agreeably varied by the shell, shot, & grape from the redoubts & Fort Magruder." A solid shot from the fort partially beheaded the Mozarter who waited so impatiently for action, spattering his blood and brains upon nearby comrades. Contributing to their discomfort, the rain was "still pouring in torrents, and we were so saturated that the water ran through our clothes and drained upon the ground."[45]

The 5th Michigan, on the left side of Hampton Road, suffered even more severely while trying to dislodge its adversaries from the rifle pits. Although Colonel Terry had been slightly wounded by a spent ball early in the engagement, he remained on the field and watched a large part of his regiment fall under the Confederates' "brisk fire" until ordered to charge again. This time,

44. *OR*, 11(1):492, 502–3; Sears, *For Country, Cause, and Leader*, 232; Floyd, *Fortieth (Mozart) Regiment New York*, 145.

45. Floyd, *Fortieth (Mozart) Regiment New York*, 145–6; Jenkins to Benjamin, 17 May 1862.

"our men marched up on the double-quick and leaped into the rifle pits and carried the position and retained it," Terry proudly reported. Farther left, the 37th New York, after an hour's contest, compelled the southern army to abandon any flanking plans and retire from that section of woods. Over on Telegraph Road, Peck's right wing managed to hold its ground with the help of the Third Brigade of Couch's division. With the withdrawal of Confederate troops in its front, Peck's brigade recovered Bramhall's battery, which, however, never reopened fire. By this time it was about five o'clock, and the firing had dwindled to a few desultory shots. Thus, after nearly ten hours of continuous savage combat, the Union and Confederate armies once again faced each other from approximately the same ground they possessed when the 1st Massachusetts met the 4th South Carolina in front of Fort Magruder early that morning. The battle of Williamsburg, up to this point, was a draw.[46]

46. *OR*, 11(1):505–8, 521.

CHAPTER 7

Lost Opportunities

Brig. Gen. William Emory, commanding the Union's Cavalry Reserve camped on Hampton Road, already had his men up and marching at five o'clock Monday morning before he received an express order from Hooker. About to face an enemy in force, Hooker thought he could use more artillery and ordered Emory to send Capt. Henry Benson's battery to the front right away. Emory decided to bring along Col. William Averell's 3d Pennsylvania Cavalry as well, leaving only one squadron of Illinois cavalry behind to guard the rear in case Stuart's cavalry or artillery was still in the area. Emory's men saw no sign of Confederates as they struggled over bottomless roads to reach the front, arriving about 9:00 A.M. By that time Hooker realized he could use neither cavalry nor more artillery in the confines of the fallen and standing timber. He worried about Confederate activity around his blind flank, however, and asked Emory to "dispatch a party to reconnoiter and observe the movements of the rebels to the rear of my left."[1]

Averell, the only one available for this assignment, immediately trotted his Pennsylvanians three-quarters of a mile back down Hampton Road to a branch leading to Kingsmill, also called Allen's Plantation. From there they made their way over to Quarterpath Trace, entering it above Kingsmill Wharf, and were soon spotted by Pvt. Bob Armistead and the 3d Virginia Cavalry, posted at Kingsmill to watch that flank. The story Armistead passed down to his grandchildren told of the Virginia troopers, now cut off from town and the main army, mounting their horses and swimming across College Creek to escape. With potential opposition evaporating into the mists, Averell continued up Quarterpath Trace and across the milldam at Kingsmill Pond, guarded

1. *OR*, 11(1):433–5, 466.

by two small, deserted earthworks. He pushed on cautiously, sending ahead one company, which penetrated as far as Redoubt One. There Pennsylvania horsemen surprised a garrison of thirty or forty Confederates, according to one account, and promptly captured them.[2]

From these prisoners and other stray graycoats the Pennsylvanians picked up, Averell learned that Longstreet commanded a force "from 30,000 to 50,000 strong." This dubious information he passed along to General Heintzelman, who, arriving at Hooker's position soon after one o'clock, found Emory standing idle and the chief engineering officer, Lt. Miles McAlester, just returning from a reconnaissance of Hooker's front. McAlester had not been able to see Redoubt One, but he surmised that the open space containing the earthworks extended far enough to the Confederate right to afford "a probable chance of getting at his right or rear." Heintzelman then directed McAlester "to pass around to the enemy's right and see what chances existed of turning his position." Heading toward Kingsmill, the engineer encountered Averell's pickets soon after turning off Hampton Road and went far enough to conclude "that the opening where the enemy's works were and that on Allen's estate were either continuous or very near together, and that a movement around them might be decisive." By the time Heintzelman received this report, he had already ordered Emory to take Benson's guns over to Kingsmill and had sent word to Averell to join them with his troopers.[3]

Whether or not the Confederate retreat could be blocked, Heintzelman reasoned that a diversion on the flank would certainly relieve some of the pressure on Hooker. He therefore ordered Emory to attack, conveying the message through Lt. Walter S. Newhall, a 3d Pennsylvania cavalryman acting as Heintzelman's aide. Newhall raced through field hospitals and woods to the left in search of Emory with his urgent dispatch. He finally found the cavalry general "sitting on his horse half asleep." Upon receiving Heintzelman's orders, Emory asked Newhall to ride a short distance with him and tried to explain "that the brigade had just reported to him, that the men and roads were new to him, etc.," which only disgusted the lieutenant. "I repeated to him General Heintzelman's positive orders, told him a prompt execution of them would certainly turn this flank, and added, 'These men are American soldiers, and will go wherever they are properly led. I will report to General Heintzelman that you are moving rapidly,' and I left him."[4]

2. Ibid., 435–6, 454–5; Judge Robert Armistead, interview by author, 22 Apr. 1991; Burns, *Battle of Williamsburgh*, 23–4.

3. *OR*, 11(1):435–6, 454–5, 463.

4. Rawle et al., *Third Pennsylvania Cavalry*, 53–4.

Despite Newhall's urging, Emory had made no assault before 3:30, when Phil Kearny approached up Hampton Road, leading his mud-spattered, panting troops. Heintzelman immediately dispatched his assistant adjutant general, Capt. Chauncey McKeever, to meet Kearny about a mile from the front and direct him to send three regiments to Emory at Kingsmill. Brig. Gen. Hiram Berry, commanding the lead Third Brigade, detached his 3d Michigan, and Brig. Gen. David Birney, next in line with the Second Brigade, turned over his 3d and 4th Maine Regiments to McKeever, who conducted them to Emory with another order from Heintzelman to attack and turn the Confederate right flank. Still hearing no progress from that quarter by 4:30, Heintzelman again sent McAlester back to Kingsmill to hasten "Emory's proposed movement upon the enemy's right and rear." As an added incentive, McAlester took along with him two batteries from Kearny's division as well as another infantry regiment.[5]

This regiment was the 63d Pennsylvania from Kearny's First Brigade under Brig. Gen. Charles D. Jameson, bringing up the rear and arriving at the front about four o'clock. McAlester guided it and the artillery back to Kingsmill and caught up with Emory and the three other infantry regiments approaching the intersection at Quarterpath Trace. There in an open field, all four regiments formed in line of battle supporting one of the batteries, "doubtless for the purpose of preventing a flank movement on the part of the enemy," the 3d Maine's colonel assumed, since they moved no farther. Emory and McAlester continued up the Trace toward Williamsburg until they came upon the milldam at Kingsmill Pond, which they cautiously crossed and then paused to ponder their next move. "After considerable deliberation, General Emory decided that this force was inadequate to attempt the movement," concluded McAlester. He offered the excuse that Emory at that time was "ignorant of the fact that the road struck the enemy's right at Redoubt No. 1" but did not explain why they failed to ask Averell, who had spent the day "engaged in pushing close reconnaissances up to the enemy's right" and presumably knew where the road led.[6]

When Emory turned his force around and headed back to Hampton Road, he forever lost his opportunity to cut off the Confederate retreat on this flank. He would never know if the three thousand or more men Heintzelman sent him would have been sufficient for the task. Heintzelman, frustrated that his repeated orders to attack were ignored, admitted "there was some risk to run,

5. *OR*, 11(1):458, 463–4, 492, 498–500, 504.
6. Ibid., 435, 463, 496, 499.

but the success would have been great." On the opposite end of the line, another Federal brigadier, far bolder and more aggressive than Emory, likewise recognized the potential benefits of gaining the Confederate rear but spent the entire afternoon trying to convince Edwin Sumner to let him try.[7]

Winfield Scott Hancock's story, like Emory's, began early that rainy Monday morning. At eight o'clock, sixteen contrabands from neighboring farms drifted into Federal headquarters at the Whittaker House and were interrogated by Generals Keyes and Sumner. "Their reports did not agree," remarked Keyes, "but they encouraged the belief that some of the enemy's works on his left were not occupied." Brig. Gen. W. F. Smith had already ordered his engineering officer, Capt. Charles S. Stewart, to reconnoiter the area. While on that mission, Stewart encountered another contraband, who informed "him that there was a road across a dam on our right, leading to Williamsburg, a distance of about 3 miles." Sumner, in consultation with Heintzelman and Keyes, then ordered a more careful examination of the ground. Smith sent Stewart back, accompanied by his assistant adjutant general, Capt. L. D. H. Currie, and four companies of the 4th Vermont from Gen. William Brooks's brigade. At 10:00 A.M. they broke out of the woods upon a space opening on Cub Creek Dam, which they judged practicable for artillery to cross. On the other side of the dam loomed the apparently unoccupied Redoubt Fourteen. Currie immediately carried word of this back to Smith, who promptly passed it on to Sumner.[8]

After confirming this report in a personal interview with Stewart, Sumner gave Smith permission to order a brigade to capture the empty earthwork. It was now nearly eleven o'clock. Hancock, his brigade camped in line of battle at the edge of the woods, had just made contact with Hooker's right wing when the summons came to report to the Whittaker House. Sumner "directed me to take four or five regiments of infantry and a battery of artillery and proceed by a road to the right, crossing Cub Dam Creek, 1½ miles distant," Hancock reported, "and to take possession, if possible, of the enemy's work on the opposite side of the creek commanding the dam at this point." Subsequently, Hancock added, Smith "authorized me to advance farther if I thought any advantage could be obtained, and if I required them to send to him for reenforcements." In Smith's words, Hancock "was ordered by me to go as far as prudent in his own estimation."[9]

7. Ibid., 463–4.
8. Ibid., 451, 457, 512, 527, 545.
9. Ibid., 476, 527, 535.

Happy to be moving at last, Hancock quickly detailed the 5th Wisconsin, 49th Pennsylvania, and 6th Maine of his own First Brigade and the 7th Maine and 33d New York of the Third Brigade, still under his command, as well as Lt. Andrew Cowan's 1st New York Battery of six guns for the expedition. Also tagging along were General Keyes, making his own reconnaissance of the ground, Currie, and Lt. George Armstrong Custer, with permission from Smith to go as a volunteer aide. Falling in without delay, these men headed up the road toward Queens Creek, with the 5th Wisconsin under Col. Amasa Cobb in the lead, followed by Col. Hiram Burnham's 6th Maine and Cowan's artillery. Bringing up the rear was Col. Robert F. Taylor's 33d New York, three companies of which Hancock prudently posted at a junction of a road leading to the right, "not knowing its terminus." Continuing on nearly a mile from the Whittaker House, the columns came "out of the woods into an open country, with York River in view, about 1 mile to our right," wrote Hancock. Another half-mile march to the left brought them, at 11:45, within sight of Redoubt Fourteen, overlooking Cub Creek Dam.[10]

Not a gray uniform could be seen, but playing it safe, Hancock made his "dispositions for an assault under the supposition that the enemy might be present." With high water in both pond and creek, the only way to approach this formidable redoubt was across the dam, about seventy-five yards in length and just barely wide enough to march infantry over in column of fours. A small ridge on Hancock's side of the dam could accommodate Cowan's battery, which unlimbered at a six-hundred-yard range from the redoubt, while Colonel Cobb deployed his 5th Wisconsin on the bank with skirmishers thrown out to the front and left. As these units were forming, Keyes summoned Hancock to meet him nearby and assured him he was not planning to assume command of his brigade but only to "look on and examine the country." Hancock was more concerned about his corps chief wandering around in Confederate territory. "I expressed to him some anxiety on that subject, and requested from him some cavalry, to which he replied that a regiment would be ordered to report to me immediately." Hancock then returned to his troops to make final preparations.[11]

As soon as all were ready, the 5th Wisconsin, with Lieutenant Custer gallantly "leading the way on horseback," charged across the dam, up the road by the redoubt, and through the narrow notch in its rear that served as the only entrance. Its slimy, near-vertical walls rising over twenty feet out of a rain-

10. Ibid., 512, 532, 535, 545, 552; Carroll, *Custer in the Civil War*, 151.
11. *OR*, 11(1):512, 532, 535–6, 554; Carroll, *Custer in the Civil War*, 152.

clogged ditch prevented any other approach, confirming Custer's estimation that "half a regiment stationed in the redoubt could have held the crossing against an entire division." Right behind the 5th Wisconsin, in column of assault, came the 6th Maine. Before the rest of the force crossed over the dam, Hancock sent off two couriers, the first of a long parade of messengers throughout the afternoon. One was Lt. I. B. Parker, who rode directly to the Whittaker House to inform Smith of Hancock's possession of Redoubt Fourteen. The other was Hancock's younger brother and assistant adjutant general, Capt. John Hancock, assigned to find their corps commander. Keyes was on his way back to headquarters, just entering the woods a half mile from the dam, when Captain Hancock caught up with him and reported. With another promise from Keyes to send a cavalry regiment and advice to "move cautiously," Captain Hancock started back to his brother.[12]

From Redoubt Fourteen, General Hancock directed his attention to the next earthwork, number eleven, about twelve hundred yards to the west. Knowing it "commanded the position I was then in," he wrote, "I felt the importance of securing it at once." He garrisoned number fourteen with three companies of the 33d New York and, while waiting for cavalry to show up to scout ahead, formed the rest of his troops in the open field behind that position. On the right of the line of battle stood the 5th Wisconsin with skirmishers in front, the 7th Maine in support, and the 6th Maine coming up on the left. Farther to the left, the 49th Pennsylvania formed in line of battle, and last of all Cowan's battery trundled up into the center. Confident that reinforcements were on the way to guard his rear and flanks, Hancock ordered his troops to advance, whereupon they "took quiet possession of the next redoubt." At the brigade's approach, Colonel Burnham of the 6th Maine noticed some Confederates evacuating, probably a squadron of Stuart's Jeff Davis Legion keeping watch over this end of the line.[13]

Upon reaching Redoubt Eleven, with a crest and natural slope extending from either side into the woods, Hancock turned and faced south toward Fort Magruder. It stood about twenty-three hundred yards across a narrow plain that "was fringed by a dense mass of timber on my right as far as Fort Magruder, and was traversed by a narrow road." Redoubt Nine, visible some thirteen hundred yards to his left front, contained its rightful owners, three companies of the 6th South Carolina under Lt. Col. John M. Steedman. Apparently unoccupied at the moment was number ten, about fourteen hundred

12. Carroll, *Custer in the Civil War*, 152; *OR*, 11(1):544, 547, 550, 554.
13. *OR*, 11(1):536, 550–4, 571.

yards to Hancock's right front. Determined to drive the Confederates out of these earthworks and create a diversion to aid the hard-pressed Hooker, Hancock began to deploy his line on the crest of his earthwork, the 6th Maine supporting Cowan's battery on the right. He stationed three 33d New York companies in the redoubt, having withdrawn the three guarding the road junction, and sent its remaining four companies into the woods on the right as skirmishers. Additional skirmishers he threw out within a few hundred yards of Redoubt Nine. Steedman's companies, unable to identify their new neighbors, signaled them. In reply, Hancock "placed the national colors on the parapet of the redoubt in my possession." Steedman quickly deployed skirmishers in front of his work to exchange shots with the intruders, but the southerners "were soon driven off." Hancock then ordered his skirmishers to lie down behind a fence extending across the plain as Cowan tossed twenty shells and case shot over their heads toward number nine.[14]

Hancock's forces were deploying in front of the redoubt when his brother returned from Keyes with the promise of a cavalry regiment. Calculating that one regiment would not suffice to occupy the next redoubts once they were taken, much less protect his flanks and maintain his position, Hancock immediately dispatched the captain again to both Keyes and Smith to report the occupation of Redoubt Eleven and request sufficient reinforcements. Only a few minutes later, as Cowan's guns shelled number nine, courier Parker returned from General Smith to ask Hancock if any road near his position led "to Williamsburg in the rear of the enemy" and to ascertain how many troops he needed. Hancock sent Parker once again to Smith with the reply, "there was such a road, and that he ought to send up another brigade to cover accidents."[15]

About that time the four guns of Battery E, 1st New York Light Artillery, Capt. Charles C. Wheeler commanding, made their appearance at Redoubt Eleven. Keyes had galloped "with the utmost speed" into the Whittaker House front yard and excitedly announced at the top of his voice that the first earthwork was taken. Smith's artillery chief, Capt. Romeyn B. Ayres, immediately directed his adjutant, Lt. Charles Kusserow, "to lead Captain Wheeler, with his battery as quick as possible to General Hancock's support." With the arrival of Wheeler's battery, Hancock began his preparations for assault. The 49th Pennsylvania he assigned to protect his far left flank, with the 6th Maine to its right. These both advanced to support the batteries, which Hancock

14. Ibid., 532, 536–7, 550–5, 582–3.
15. Ibid., 544, 547.

ordered forward six hundred yards in front of Redoubt Eleven. To the artillery's right came the 5th Wisconsin, two of its companies acting as skirmishers.[16]

This threat at last caught the attention of the Confederates in Fort Magruder. Col. John Bratton of the 6th South Carolina, posted in a skirt of woods to the rear and left of the fort, declared that Hancock's presence "was announced to me by a cannon ball from the enemy's gun, which passed through my line and buried itself in the embankment of Fort Magruder." Steedman with his beleaguered companies in Redoubt Nine had reported the arrival of the Federals to Col. Micah Jenkins, in charge of Fort Magruder. Jenkins "personally reconnoitered" the situation, reported their position and numbers to Longstreet, and ordered Bratton to take his remaining companies to support Steedman. The South Carolinian's small force boldly advanced across the field toward the still-empty Redoubt Ten. "They were nearer to it than we were," as Bratton told the story, "but were advancing cautiously; were receiving a minnie occasionally from my companies in the neighboring work, and were evidently a little suspicious and afraid to believe that things were really as they appeared." Cowan unlimbered his New York battery 350 yards from number nine, straddling the road with two pieces on the right and four on the left. Wheeler came into battery on Cowan's right near some isolated farm buildings and palings that partially screened the 5th Wisconsin, occupying the ground to the right of the batteries. While three of these guns concentrated on Bratton's troops and "serenaded us with shot and shell throughout our advance," two others sparred with a Confederate battery now trained on them from Fort Magruder.[17]

This was Capt. James Dearing's Lynchburg Artillery. Having arrived at Fort Magruder only a half hour before, Dearing was not only the freshest but also the handiest unit available to Jenkins, who ordered him directly into action. The 5th South Carolina deployed in support as Dearing brought his two pieces into battery outside the fort's left "under a heavy fire of artillery from the enemy's battery" and immediately opened on a column of Hancock's infantry still in view crossing between Redoubts Fourteen and Eleven. After firing "about ten rounds of shell and spherical case," Dearing was gratified to "find that I had succeeded in turning the column, which filed to the right and disappeared under the brow of a hill."[18]

16. Ibid., 513, 529, 536–7.
17. Ibid., 532, 537, 582–3; John Bratton, "The Battle of Williamsburg," *Southern Historical Society Papers* 7 (1879): 299–300.
18. *OR*, 11(1):583, 51(1):87–9.

About then another Federal battery set up a crossfire on Dearing, enfilading his position from a small clearing near the edge of the woods eight or nine hundred yards away off Telegraph Road. Capt. Thaddeus P. Mott's four-gun battery, ordered there by General Smith "more to annoy and distract the enemy than with the hope of accomplishing any permanent good," was supported by Brooks's Vermont brigade and had Dearing's range exactly. Dearing lost one Confederate gunner wounded and one horse killed before deciding that his smoothbore field piece and howitzer were no match for Cowan's heavier-caliber, longer-range Parrott guns. He then changed front twenty-five or thirty yards to his right and opened on Mott. Since Dearing's new position was farther from Cowan's battery, the Union gunners "did not succeed in getting my range sufficiently exact for their enfilading fire to do me any damage. Their shells and case-shot burst beautifully, though not close enough, or rather not at the proper distance, to hurt me." Lieutenant Clopton's Richmond Fayette Artillery soon joined Dearing with two pieces, following which Mott figured Hancock was no longer threatened and withdrew his battery. The Lynchburg Artillery likewise retired into Fort Magruder.[19]

Clopton, however, continued firing and turned his attention upon Cowan's guns. Wheeler's battery had opened on their right and, accompanied by volleys from its infantry support, still shelled Bratton's troops after they entered Redoubt Ten. Hancock finally ordered his infantry to cease fire and lie down, and Bratton threw a line of skirmishers on either side of his redoubts into the woods. Cowan's battery, suffering the loss of one gunner killed and another wounded, also ceased firing, while Wheeler pounded the redoubts "preparatory to an assault when the expected re-enforcements should arrive."[20]

What, Hancock was beginning to wonder, had happened to his reinforcements? Wheeler's battery was helpful but hardly the cavalry and infantry he had twice sent his brother and Parker to request at headquarters. General Smith had been trying to send additional forces since Parker first reported to him but could not obtain permission from Sumner. All through the morning one officer after another had implored "Old Bull" to send Hooker a brigade of reinforcements until, finally, an exasperated Governor Sprague rode back to Yorktown to hasten General McClellan forward. Even with the crescendo of musketry and artillery from his left, Sumner's primary concern was the center of the line directly in front of him. "The maintenance of that point seemed to me of the utmost importance," he later explained, "for if they had pierced

19. Ibid., 11(1):513, 527–9, 532, 556, 51(1):89.
20. Ibid., 51(1):87, 11(1):532–3, 537, 583; Bratton, "Battle of Williamsburg," 300.

the center it would have been impossible to have prevented a serious disaster." After Hancock's departure to the right, all Sumner had left to hold this vital section were Stoneman's cavalry and light artillery, part of Smith's Third Brigade, and his Second Brigade under Brooks, posted at the edge of the woods to the right of Telegraph Road. Sumner at last consented to send Brooks's Vermonters to Hooker on the left, but by then Hancock also needed them. Smith went back to Sumner "to expostulate against the breaking up of my command, and to ask that I might go with the two remaining brigades of the division to re-enforce General Hancock."[21]

At that moment Captain Hancock galloped into headquarters to report General Hancock had taken Redoubt Eleven and needed immediate support. Sumner agreed to let Smith take Brooks over to Hancock, but only after ordering up another brigade of Keyes's corps to take the Vermonters' place as headquarters guard. Silas Casey's First Brigade under Brig. Gen. Henry M. Naglee was chosen. Before it could start from its camp below Cheesecake Church, Sumner countermanded his own order, sending Naglee to the left to support Hooker instead. Sumner further instructed Casey, who had spent the morning bringing up supply wagons for his starving men, to accompany his brigade. "The men seized their arms, and moved off with alacrity," wrote Col. William W. H. Davis of Naglee's leading 104th Pennsylvania, "for any change was preferable to standing in the timber and fields in the rain. Passing by the old church, we struck across the country, through thickets and marshes, over hills and valleys and across water courses, the mud and mire being every where deep." Brooks's men were also preparing to march as Smith and Keyes hurried Captain Hancock off with assurances they were sending his brother a cavalry regiment and infantry brigade, "some of which were on the road moving forward."[22]

Captain Hancock had not yet returned with this welcome news to Redoubt Eleven when Wheeler's battery, accompanied by Lieutenant Kusserow, arrived in the midst of the Cowan-Dearing artillery duel and Bratton's advance into Redoubt Ten. "Having disposed of all his staff officers," related Kusserow, Hancock "ordered me to ride as quickly as I could, reporting to General Smith what I had seen, and asking him at once for larger supports." On the road to the Whittaker House, Kusserow met Parker returning to Hancock with the

21. *OR*, 11(1):452, 527, 537, 544–7, 556; Grimsley and Glod, "'We Prepare to Receive the Enemy,'" 19–20.

22. *OR*, 11(1):527, 544–5, 556–9; W. W. H. Davis, *History of the 104th Pennsylvania Regiment from August 22nd, 1861, to September 30th, 1864* (Philadelphia: Jas. B. Rodgers, 1866), 64.

message that Smith was sending four regiments. Smith subsequently gave Kusserow the same promise when he arrived at headquarters, but no sooner had this lieutenant galloped off to convey the news to Hancock than Sumner again changed his mind. Bounding out of the woods toward him from the left came Captain Bramhall and his artillerists abandoning their guns. The head of Peck's brigade had just arrived at the Whittaker House and was immediately sent forward. Battle sounds continued to approach from the left, and the Comte de Paris confessed that everyone at headquarters "expect at any time to see Hooker's right flank emerge from the woods in disorder with the enemy right behind." Sumner therefore ordered Smith to pull Brooks's brigade off the road as it was about to start for Hancock and place it "in a position to resist an attack on the ground we then occupied."[23]

Unaware that his reinforcements were not coming, since Parker, Kusserow, and Captain Hancock all confirmed they were on the way, General Hancock prepared for their imminent arrival. The 49th Pennsylvania still held down the left flank, some companies patrolling the woods to his left and front. He deployed skirmishers from the 7th Maine "to my right and rear to protect me from assault from that direction, concerning which I was very anxious," Hancock admitted, "as the space from my right through the woods to the creek which skirted the other side of the woods toward Williamsburg was greater than I could occupy with my troops, and I had serious apprehensions of an attack from that quarter by troops from that place or from Fort Magruder." He advanced the rest of the 7th Maine on the right behind Wheeler's battery one hundred paces from the crest of the redoubt and diagonally to his line of battle to protect his right flank. Finally, 33d New York skirmishers swept the woods on the right for a mile in front of the 7th Maine flankers. Encountering no opposition, they returned and took position as an advanced line of flankers.[24]

Hancock's promised support still had not appeared when, on the parapets of Redoubts Nine and Ten, "the enemy suddenly formed line of battle," observed Kusserow, "and General Hancock ordered me to report this fact to General Smith, asking again for re-enforcements." During his second ride to the Whittaker House, Kusserow saw no infantry on the road but ran into Brooks and learned that his Vermont regiments had been ordered back to the center. More bad news met the courier when he found Smith and Sumner

23. *OR,* 11(1):527, 529, 547; Grimsley and Glod, "'We Prepare to Receive the Enemy,'" 20; Nevins, *Diary of Battle,* 53–4.
24. *OR,* 11(1):537.

together. "Stating the fact of General Hancock's position dangerous in case of a retreat, and at the same time expressing General Hancock's hope of great success when sufficiently re-enforced," Kusserow wrote, "I received General Sumner's order for General Hancock to retire." In disbelief, Kusserow turned to Smith, who repeated the order, "explaining to me that he wanted General Hancock to occupy his first position." That meant nothing less than a withdrawal under fire back to Redoubt Fourteen.[25]

Dutifully, Kusserow started back to Hancock with this order. Before he returned, the Confederates in front of Hancock had been reinforced by the 4th South Carolina Battalion, which Jenkins sent to Bratton in an attempt to drive the Federals out of Redoubt Eleven. As 4th South Carolinian Cpl. Jesse Reid described the fiasco, "a corporal's guard undertook to storm a fort well supplied with artillery and perhaps ten times our numbers of infantry to back them." Wheeler's battery pounded the redoubts, and Hancock's advanced skirmishers forced the Carolinians out of their works, "killing many of them as they debouched from the gorges which were on the right side of each work as we stood with reference to them," related Hancock. The 4th South Carolina then took position to the left of Bratton's skirmishers and extended his line farther into the woods. At this point, Hancock realized, "there was now no apparent obstacle to prevent us from taking possession of these redoubts had the re-enforcements arrived."[26]

Instead of reinforcements, disappointment arrived soon after two o'clock in the person of Kusserow, bearing Sumner's directive to fall back and expect no support. "Never at a loss for expletives, and with feelings wrought up by the attendent circumstances," according to Lieutenant Custer, at the general's side just then, "Hancock was not at all loath to express his condemnation of the policy which from his standpoint was not only plainly unnecessary, but in the end must prove disastrous." Rather than comply, Hancock, "knowing General Smith's disposition to strengthen me and to make a movement in this direction," decided to send back yet another messenger. An ordnance officer on Smith's staff accompanying this expedition, Lt. C. R. Crane, took off with Hancock's instructions to "please tell General Smith that I think he ought to send me re-enforcements at once, as the enemy are getting very thick in front." Then turning to Custer, Hancock took out his watch and remarked, "It is now

25. Ibid., 529–30.
26. Ibid., 531, 537, 583; Reid, *Fourth Regiment of S.C. Volunteers,* 81; Bratton, "Battle of Williamsburg," 300.

two o'clock. I shall wait till four: if no reply reaches me from headquarters, I will then withdraw."[27]

It was nearly three o'clock before Crane found Sumner, who merely repeated his previous order. Smith told Crane to "Go at once to General Hancock and tell him that I have wanted and have tried to re-enforce him, but that General Sumner has positively forbidden to allow any re-enforcements to be sent to him until more troops come up from the rear." Sumner had just sent Keyes down Telegraph Road to hunt for these troops. Before reaching Cheesecake Church, Keyes encountered Couch's First Brigade, delayed by the necessity of returning to Yorktown for supplies, and "urged them on with all speed." Keyes then came upon five regiments from Casey's division with arms stacked near Cheesecake Church and "put them on the march without a moment's delay."[28]

At last Keyes found the rear of Naglee's brigade, still slogging through the swamps toward Hooker, turned it around, and dispatched it to the front center. The staff officer he sent to Generals Casey and Naglee at the head of the column with the 104th Pennsylvania caught up with them just in time. "After a march of two hours, the artillery half of the time up to the axles in the mud, the cavalry horses plunging, and the men in mud to their ankles, we arrived immediately in the rear of General Hooker at 3:30 P.M., the very moment he was driven back by the enemy," Naglee reported. "We were preparing to support him, when another order came for all to countermarch and return in haste." Riding back to convey this order to his rear battalions, Naglee discovered Keyes had already halted them more than two miles behind. He then accompanied Keyes and his rear battalions to the front, leaving the 104th Pennsylvania, chagrined at being the only regiment sent on this "wild goose chase several miles out of the way," grumbled Colonel Davis, to return as best it could.[29]

Neither was Hancock any happier on the opposite side of the battlefield. Since Crane did not return by 3:15, he sent Smith's aide-de-camp, now acting as his aide, Capt. Fred A. Aiken, to Sumner to explain his occupation of the redoubt and request reinforcements one more time. Fifteen minutes later Crane showed up with Smith's confirmation that he must fall back and could not be reinforced because of "movements on the left." It then occurred to

27. *OR*, 11(1):530, 537–8, 548; Carroll, *Custer in the Civil War*, 153–4.
28. *OR*, 11(1):514–5, 519, 548.
29. Ibid., 514–5, 557–9; Davis, *104th Pennsylvania*, 64–5.

Hancock that "Old Bull" needed a more detailed explanation of the situation. He picked a young engineering lieutenant named Francis U. Farquhar and instructed him "to represent to General Sumner my position, with a view of showing the disadvantage of falling back at that time and giving up the advantages we had already secured, for which we might have to fight again the next day in order to recover, besides the bad impression it would make on my troops, and the inspiriting effect it would have upon the enemy." Furthermore, Farquhar was to state Hancock's exact position and inform Sumner "that I would obey the order to fall back if no answer should arrive when a reasonable time had elapsed."[30]

At the Whittaker House, Farquhar recited all this to the first general he found, "Baldy" Smith, who told him to go to Sumner and, after detailing Hancock's exact position, "to respectfully suggest that the remaining two brigades of his (Smith's) division might be sent as re-enforcements." Though Sumner had just sent Aiken back to Hancock with emphatic instructions to withdraw, he finally relented and ordered Farquhar to direct Smith to support Hancock. One more time, Brooks got his brigade up and moving to the right guided by Kusserow, on his third visit to headquarters. This time the 3d Vermont at the head of the column advanced almost eight hundred yards up the road before Sumner did it again. "The crisis of the battle in front of Fort Magruder appeared to have arrived," Hancock described this moment, "and in order to furnish all the assistance possible our battery threw percussion shell into that fort." Unknown to Sumner, interpreting the noise coming through the forest as "a furious attack upon my center," it was actually Kearny's whirlwind assault on the Confederate line. According to the Comte de Paris, an anxious "Sumner, followed only by his aide-de-camp, gallops left and right and wants to put the cannon on the edge of the wood and the cavalry where it cannot charge." And Sumner once again called Brooks back "to resist an attack upon the position then occupied."[31]

Four o'clock came and went and still no word of reinforcements arrived at Redoubt Eleven. Fully aware of his risk in disobeying Sumner's repeated direct orders to fall back, Hancock decided to put one last request in writing, perhaps for the benefit of any future court-martial. Farquhar had not yet returned by 4:20, at which time Hancock addressed a note to Smith reiterating his intention to "allow a reasonable time to get an answer to my previous message to

30. OR, 11(1):538, 547–8.
31. Ibid., 451, 528–30, 538, 546–8, 556; Grimsley and Glod, "'We Prepare to Receive the Enemy,'" 20.

General Sumner before falling back to the fort with the creek in my rear." If the "reasonable time" phrase was not vague enough to protect him, he added, "General Sumner has ordered me to fall back to my first position, which I believe to be the first fort occupied; if not, please correct me." This communication Hancock placed in Aiken's hands with verbal instructions to hand it to Sumner if he could not find Smith. Aiken took off again for headquarters "as quickly as possible," delivered it to Smith, and started back with an equally vague reply "that in regard to falling back or occupying the position you then held you could exercise your discretion," but Hancock should not expect any reinforcements.[32]

As Aiken galloped away from the Whittaker House, de Paris and others around headquarters noticed "an odd movement among the troops behind us. Everyone turns. A group of riders are advancing rapidly along the road. We recognize the General." McClellan had finally reached the field, thanks to Governor Sprague, who had departed the front for Yorktown shortly before noon. He found the general supervising the transport of Brig. Gen. William Franklin's division up the York River, hoping to cut off the Confederate retreat before Richmond. Despite Sprague's entreaties and clearly audible battle sounds from the west, "Little Mac" was reluctant to leave Yorktown. He later testified that this was "the first intimation I had that there was anything at all serious" happening in Williamsburg. Sprague finally convinced him that his "presence in the front was necessary," and with a large escort of aides and orderlies, McClellan started up Telegraph Road. About five o'clock he arrived at Sumner's headquarters. To his wife the next day McClellan wrote without false modesty, "As soon as I came upon the field the men cheered like fiends & I saw at once that I could save the day." Noted de Paris, "everyone senses that we finally have a leader and each of us feels reassured."[33]

After the cheers died down, reality struck. "I found everything in a state of chaos and depression," McClellan recounted, for "there was no plan of action, no directing head." His designated directing head, Sumner, "expecting another burst of the enemy to force the center" at that moment, was busy pushing troops forward as they straggled in to support Peck's brigade still hotly engaged near Telegraph Road. From Charles Devens's brigade in Couch's division, the 7th Massachusetts had entered the contest about three o'clock and

32. Carroll, *Custer in the Civil War*, 153; *OR*, 11(1):538, 545–6.

33. Grimsley and Glod, "'We Prepare to Receive the Enemy,'" 20; Congress, *Report of the Joint Committee*, 1:430, 569–70; Stephen W. Sears, ed., *The Civil War Papers of George B. McClellan: Selected Correspondence, 1860–1865* (New York: Da Capo, 1992), 255, 257.

the 2d Rhode Island an hour later. The Rhode Islanders, posted about six hundred yards from Fort Magruder, "could see the Rebel gunners load and fire the cannon from the fort," Sgt. Elisha Hunt Rhodes wrote in his diary, "and we had to stand it, for we were ordered for some reason not to fire." Soon, elements of Casey's brigade began to arrive from Cheesecake Church, Brig. Gen. Innis N. Palmer's 92d and 93d New York just ahead of Brig. Gen. William H. Keim's 85th, 101st, and 103d Pennsylvania Regiments. Since Keim was lagging behind due to a "severe indisposition," Couch directed Palmer to take command of all five regiments and send a couple to Peck. Palmer accordingly detailed both of Keim's regiments, the 85th Pennsylvania leading, "over the fence into the woods under a brisk fire of the enemy." Close behind them were Palmer's three regiments to relieve three of Peck's that were now out of ammunition.[34]

Naglee's brigade was the next up Telegraph Road, preceded by its commander. After Keyes showed him the position his troops would occupy in the woods, Naglee returned to the head of his column and met McClellan coming up the road. Keyes lingered in the woods long enough to deliver "a few spirit-stirring remarks" to Keim's men, "who heartily cheered the general and resumed the work of destruction with more zeal." He then attended a meeting of general officers McClellan called in a clearing near the Whittaker House. "The general quickly comprehended the state of the field and gave many directions to the fresh troops," wrote Keyes. With the sound of heavy firing coming just then from their right, McClellan ordered Smith, "chafing like a caged lion, to move as rapidly as possible to Hancock's support." Once again, Brooks's Vermonters turned around and for the third time that afternoon headed up the road toward Redoubt Eleven. Immediately behind Brooks came Naglee, his men starting "off amidst the pelting rain, with the mud to their ankles, at a double-quick step." At long last someone in authority was paying attention to General Hancock.[35]

34. George B. McClellan, *McClellan's Own Story* (New York: Charles C. Webster, 1887), 328–30; *OR*, 11(1):451, 521, 524–5, 561–3; Robert Hunt Rhodes, ed., *All for the Union: The Civil War Diary and Letters of Elisha Hunt Rhodes* (New York: Orion, 1985), 64.

35. *OR*, 11(1):515, 528, 559–62; McClellan, *Own Story*, 330.

CHAPTER 8

Magnificent Blunder

The Confederate high command first became aware of the threat on its far left flank shortly before Cowan's New York battery opened on Fort Magruder. The Jeff Davis Legion galloped in from Redoubt Eleven to report Hancock's presence to J. E. B. Stuart, but the cavalry general was not unduly alarmed at first. "The force on the left could not be ascertained, as it was entirely screened by the woods" from Stuart's vantage point, though Hancock's lack of aggressiveness "convinced me that *there* he was either weak, timid, or feigning, and in neither contingency to be feared." Stuart did send in Dearing's unemployed artillery and detached three companies from Roger Pryor's 14th Alabama to strengthen the apprehensive Colonel Jenkins. He also kept Longstreet, still in Williamsburg, "informed of every stage of the action and my impressions of it." As the fighting grew hotter and all readily available troops became engaged, Stuart dispatched a messenger into town to summon Longstreet. The commanding general was on his way out to the field anyway, having "concluded that it would be well to ride to the front" after hearing "the swelling noise of battle." At Fort Magruder Longstreet realized Jenkins needed more help on the left and immediately sent back to town for more troops.[1]

With his own division entirely committed, Longstreet sought assistance from D. H. Hill. Most of Hill's division had started for Richmond early that morning and "had waded but a few miles through the mud and slush when the heavy firing in our rear announced that Longstreet was engaged." Jubal Early's brigade, however, had remained under arms about two miles west of Williamsburg since three that morning. About noon Early was ready to join the march to Richmond, but Hill sent him an order "not to move" followed

1. *OR*, 11(1):565, 571, 583; Longstreet, *From Manassas to Appomattox*, 74.

shortly by directions to march back to town and report to Longstreet. His troops accordingly countermarched to the open space behind the college, stacked arms, and waited in the rain. "The music of battle sounded continually in our unaccustomed ears, and wounded friends and ambulances, and squads of prisoners passed frequently by," wrote Maj. Richard L. Maury of the 24th Virginia, a regiment raised in the western hills of Virginia by Early. "Every one looked for orders 'to the front!' each moment." With every passing hour "the tension of expectation and excitement became more and more intense."[2]

Since another division was about to become involved, Longstreet notified General Johnston of the situation. That morning Hooker's attack evinced "so little vigor" that Johnston became convinced "it was a mere demonstration, intended to delay our march—that the Federal army might pass us by water." Therefore, about ten o'clock he departed his headquarters in the Vest House to accompany his troops pushing up the Peninsula. He turned back upon receiving Longstreet's message, arrived on the battlefield in midafternoon, and found Longstreet near Fort Magruder. "Mounted on his celebrated roadster, Sam Patch," Johnston appeared to one of his staff officers "as calm as a May morning," chatting with his men as they passed from the battlefield and offering "an occasional valuable suggestion" to Longstreet.[3]

Longstreet had also requested that D. H. Hill return with the balance of his division and between three and four o'clock ordered Early forward to support Gen. Richard Anderson. Sending his aide, Lt. Samuel H. Early, ahead to tell Anderson he was coming, Early put his "command in motion, moving as rapidly as the condition of the streets would permit." The men hastily threw their knapsacks in a yard as they hurried down Main Street at the double, urged on by "the cheers and the tears of the women and maidens, whose pallid faces appear at every window and door, waving adieu to the eager soldiers as they pass so quickly by." Down York Road they ran. Before reaching the field, Early detached the 2d Florida and the 2d Mississippi Battalion to Longstreet's support.[4]

The other four regiments in the brigade continued by the left flank into a wide wheat field to the left and rear of Fort Magruder. There Early formed them on the crest of a ridge in the field, near a barn and some houses, facing

2. *OR*, 11(1):565, 602, 606; Early, *Memoirs*, 67–8; Richard L. Maury, "The Battle of Williamsburg, Va.," *Southern Historical Society Papers* 22 (1894): 110.

3. Johnston, *Narrative*, 120–1; *OR*, 11(1):275, 565; Longstreet, *From Manassas to Appomattox*, 77; E. J. Harvie, "Gen. Joseph E. Johnston," *Confederate Veteran* 18 (1910):521; Gallagher, *Fighting for the Confederacy*, 81.

4. *OR*, 11(1):565, 602, 606–7; Maury, "Williamsburg, Va.," 110–2.

dense piney woods two or three hundred yards away. While they scrambled into position, the unmistakable booming of a battery emanated from the other side of the woods, drawing Hill's attention as he rode over to his command. Early suggested to Hill "the propriety of moving through the woods to attack" the Federal battery, though neither general knew the battery's exact location. A cursory examination of the ground convinced them that a small stream "skirted by very dense undergrowth difficult to penetrate" at the edge of the woods in front of Early's right wing would offer no obstacle to the advance. With that, Harvey Hill galloped off to consult Longstreet.[5]

Both Longstreet and Johnston were already aware of Hill's interest in the battery, as he had sent an officer over "to ask that he be allowed" to attack it. Finding both generals together, the messenger was bounced back and forth between the two, who apparently could not decide. Longstreet was against it. "We were only fighting for time to draw off our trains," he reasoned. Besides, "we could not risk being drawn into serious delay by starting new work so late in the day." Hill, upon his arrival, argued that "he could get through before night, and would not be likely to involve delay of our night march." Longstreet still hesitated. "The brigade you propose to use is not in safe hands," he told Hill, displaying his lack of confidence in Early. Finally, after consulting with Johnston, Longstreet gave him permission to attack, but only if Hill would "go with it, and see that the troops are properly handled." In his report, Hill admitted that "neither Longstreet nor myself knew the precise position of the battery, and both were entirely ignorant of the ground." Apparently, nobody thought to consult Colonel Bratton, still keeping a close watch on Hancock with his 6th South Carolina posted in Redoubts Nine and Ten. With a final caution from both Longstreet and Johnston, D. H. Hill rode off to the left.[6]

During his division chief's absence, Early finished forming his brigade. The 5th North Carolina under his senior colonel, Duncan McRae, took position on the right, in line with Col. John F. Hoke's 23d North Carolina to its left. Next on the left stood the 38th Virginia commanded by the giant six-foot, four-inch Lt. Col. Powhatan B. Whittle. The 24th Virginia led by Col. William R. Terry came up on the far left of the line. The ranks of the 24th, bringing up the rear of the brigade, had become "open and much extended" during their run down from town and were just getting into position when the command to load and fix bayonets was given. Then, gesturing toward the

5. Maury, "Williamsburg, Va.," 112; *OR*, 11(1):603, 607; Early, *Memoirs*, 69.
6. Longstreet, *From Manassas to Appomattox*, 77–8; Johnston, *Narrative*, 122; *OR*, 11(1):565, 603; Bratton, "Battle of Williamsburg," 300.

woods, Early announced to the men they were to capture a battery "over there," adding grimly "that the safest place after getting under fire will be at the guns themselves, and so I advise you to get there as quickly as you can." Gen. Gabriel Rains's brigade soon lined up close behind Early's along with the 2d Richmond Howitzers. Hill returned from Longstreet while Early placed these guns in position. "After informing me that the attack was to be made," Early reported, Hill "posted the artillery so as to cover the retreat of my brigade if it should be compelled to fall back."[7]

The boys of the 24th Virginia were still catching their breath as they watched Early, his staff, and field officers, all mounted, take position on the far left in front of the regiment, contrary to "the rule which places commanding officers in *rear* of the line in a charge." D. H. Hill, after making his own "short address to the command" and "instructing the men to use the bayonet as the most efficacious mode of attack," took charge of the North Carolina regiments on the right and ordered them to move forward. "The order was not heard by me or the regiments on the left," asserted Early; "but seeing the regiments on the right moving and General Hill with them, I ordered the other two regiments to move forward, and the whole brigade was thus put in motion." Across the wheat field they advanced, maintaining their alignment, and entered the woods. As soon as the right wing crossed the little stream and penetrated the undergrowth, Hill halted it to align the entire brigade. He could not see his left wing through the thick brush and sent his adjutant over to determine whether it too had reached this marshy ravine.[8]

The 24th Virginia, however, had not halted but forged straight ahead. "Here the miry ground, the dense and tangled undergrowth, dripping with wet, and the large fallen timber, somewhat impaired the line," Major Maury detailed. The Virginians "have left the field whence they started, they have traversed the tangled woods down the hill, across a country road, into the forest again and up another slope, but heavy, weary, breathless, and almost broken down, and still no foe is found, although half a mile and more has been passed." The 38th Virginia to their right, facing even worse terrain, lost its place in line, the left companies becoming detached from the rest and causing Whittle to march the remaining seven by the left flank and thus fall fifty yards behind the others. Both North Carolina regiments remained back at the

7. *OR*, 11(1):607; Maury, "Williamsburg, Va.," 113; Maury, *Williamsburg*, 10; Krick, *Lee's Colonels*, 396.
8. Maury, *Williamsburg*, 10; D. K. McRae, "The Battle of Williamsburg—Reply to Colonel Bratton," *Southern Historical Society Papers* 7 (1879): 368; *OR*, 11(1):603, 607.

stream. But the 24th Virginia behind Early, who calculated his wing would come out directly on the battery, pressed on until light appeared ahead and the trees thinned.[9]

In a moment the 24th Virginians broke through the edge of the forest and ran into a rail fence separating them from a half-grown wheat field. There they beheld "as a picture, the open plateau of Magruder's entrenchments, the contour of the Confederate redoubts stretching away to the right to Fort Magruder, about three-quarters of a mile distant." The other three regiments of the brigade were nowhere in sight, but directly in front of several large companies detached from the right wing of the 24th stood Redoubt Ten, still occupied by Bratton's South Carolinians. Off the 24th's left flank stood Captain Wheeler's Federal four-gun battery about seven hundred yards away and Lieutenant Cowan's six guns in reserve behind it. From the 24th's perspective, all were partially masked by farm buildings. Infantry regiments supporting these batteries were lying down in position, the 6th Maine in front of the 49th Pennsylvania on the left, and the 5th Wisconsin on the right, with the 7th Maine to the right rear and the 33d New York watching the woods on that wing. Most had "their oil-cloths over them, to protect them from the pelting rain," one soldier revealed. Some were dozing, while others chatted in squads and watched the weather thicken.[10]

"The clouds had become very heavy over us and the rain was drenching the troops," Hancock observed from Redoubt Eleven, and "I concluded to make my dispositions for the night." He had been waiting since 4:20 for Lieutenant Farquhar's return with an answer to his written communication to Gen. W. F. Smith saying he would wait a "reasonable time" to hear from Sumner before falling back. Ten minutes after five was as long as Hancock dared stall, and the weather, now providing some cover, gave him an excuse for having waited until then. Not ready to give up hope that reinforcements might yet arrive, Hancock began issuing orders to pull his troops back to the crest of his redoubt preparatory to a further withdrawal. Wheeler was on his way to Hancock to report that one of his guns was disabled when Custer met him with Hancock's order to retire the batteries one at a time. Wheeler instantly started back to his guns.[11]

9. Maury, *Williamsburg*, 11–2; Maury, "Williamsburg, Va.," 113–4; *OR*, 11(1):603, 607, 613.

10. Maury, "Williamsburg, Va.," 114–5; Maury, *Williamsburg*, 12; Early, *Memoirs*, 69–70; *OR*, 11(1):531, 550–5, 607–8; William DeLoss Love, *Wisconsin in the War of the Rebellion: A History of All Regiments and Batteries the State Has Sent to the Field* (Chicago: Church and Goodman, 1866), 270.

11. *OR*, 11(1):531, 538; Carroll, *Custer in the Civil War*, 154.

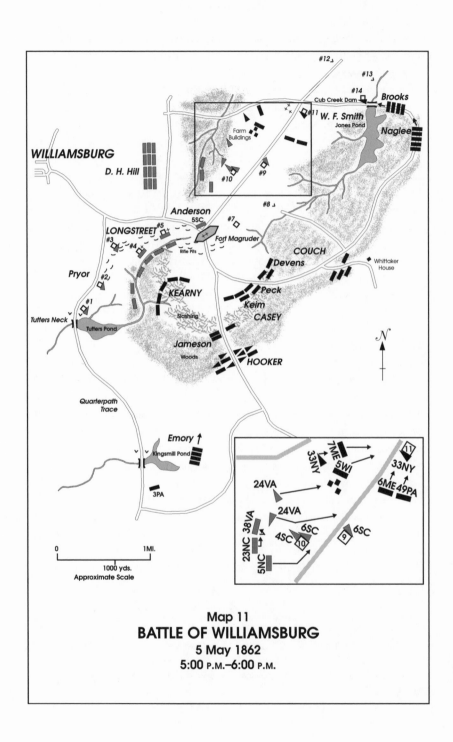

#12 ↲

#13 ↲

#14

Cub Creek Dam

Brooks

W. F. Smith #11

Jones Pond

Naglee

Farm Buildings

WILLIAMSBURG

D. H. Hill

#10

#9

#8 ↲

Anderson 5SC

#7

LONGSTREET #5

Fort Magruder

#3

#4

Rifle Pits

COUCH

Devens

Whittaker House

Pryor

#2

#1

KEARNY

Peck

Keim

CASEY

Tutters Neck

Tutters Pond

Slashing

Jameson

Woods

HOOKER

𝒩

Quarterpath Trace

Emory ↑

Kingsmill Pond

3PA

0   1MI.

1000 yds.
Approximate Scale

7ME
33NY

5WI

11

33NY

24VA

6ME 49PA

24VA

23NC 38VA

4SC 6SC

10

9   6SC

5NC

Map 11
BATTLE OF WILLIAMSBURG
5 May 1862
5:00 P.M.–6:00 P.M.

Just then a "sharp, quick rattle of musketry" issued from the woods on Hancock's right as 33d New York skirmishers collided with 24th Virginia boys springing over the fence and into the field. "There they are," cried Early, leading the charge upon Wheeler's guns: "Follow me." Early and his mounted officers were apparently so numerous they were mistaken for cavalry by the startled Federals. Right behind them came gray foot soldiers, each intent on being the first to reach the coveted guns. The 24th's detached right companies were unable to see the artillery around a spur of woods and instead headed straight for the redoubts occupied by Bratton, who rushed "out to stop them and change their direction before they were exposed to the fire of the enemy." From Hancock's vantage point, these stray companies appeared to be reinforcing the South Carolinians in Redoubts Nine and Ten. He quickly dispatched his brother to Smith "to notify him of the state of affairs" and resubmit his request for reinforcements, then ordered his artillery to throw shell at the attackers now attempting to reform.[12]

Despite this barrage, the wayward Virginians found their places in the ranks and swiftly changed front. Meanwhile, the bulk of the regiment, "alone and unsupported, with both flanks in the air," started toward the 5th Wisconsin skirmishers, who were delivering "steady volleys at most uncumfortably short range" from a rail fence four hundred yards away. "Clinging instinctively to the timber, bordering the field on its left flank, so as to mask its weakness as well as might be, and opening out its files to cover the foe's broad front," narrated Maury, leading that wing, "these fearless mountaineers break at once into the double and charge with a wild cheer that thrills through every heart." The 5th Wisconsin's withering fire was augmented by Wheeler's three serviceable guns belching case shot and Cowan's six pieces contributing spherical case, tearing great holes in the Virginians' ranks. "None halt or hesitate," Maury marveled, "but all rush forward with a vigor hardly to be paralleled," though "not so quickly, perhaps, as they would have done had they not been exhausted by their run through field and forest, but still without delay."[13]

A few minutes after the commencement of this onslaught, Hancock sent Captain Currie back to Smith with one final desperate plea for support. The sight of gray uniforms pouring out of the woods toward his right front reminded Hancock they could just as easily be debouching on his right or left rear. He therefore "directed the artillery to retire rapidly, piece by piece, to my

12. Love, *Wisconsin in the War,* 270; Maury, "Williamsburg, Va.," 114–5; *OR,* 11(1):538–9, 545, 552, 603, 607–8; Early, *Memoirs,* 70; Bratton, "Battle of Williamsburg," 300.

13. Maury, "Williamsburg, Va.," 115; *OR,* 11(1):531–3.

second line," and began to pull back his infantry, starting with the two regiments to the left of the artillery. The men of the 6th Maine, closest to Wheeler's battery on the left, slowly fell back about halfway to the fort to collect their skirmishers and to hold "the ground in front with the greatest pertinacity against" the Confederate skirmishers from Redoubt Nine. On their left, the 49th Pennsylvania's Col. William Irwin noticed the 6th Maine's withdrawal, then faced his men by the rear rank and marched them "at the parade step" back toward the left side of Redoubt Eleven.[14]

On the extreme right of the redoubt, about three hundred yards behind the batteries, Col. Edwin Mason's 7th Maine also received Hancock's orders to fall back "with its right thrown back against the woods, in order to be ready to meet an assault from that quarter." Halting frequently, Mason's regiment slowly retired to the rear. This left only the main body of Col. Amasa Cobb's 5th Wisconsin to protect the batteries near the farm buildings. Cobb, seeing only the mounted officers at first, quickly formed his men "in square to resist cavalry" but soon found the "cavalry" effectively checked by his skirmishers and turning back to direct the infantry. Within a few minutes, Early himself received "a very severe wound in the shoulder from a minie ball," and his horse was also "very badly shot, having one of his eyes knocked out."[15]

Wondering what had happened to his other regiments, still not in view after he sent them orders to advance, Early turned back down the field on his spunky half-blind steed to look for them. Just at that moment he saw a gray wave arising in the distance: the 5th North Carolina boys were finally on their way. They had not halted five minutes to reform at the marshy stream before they heard shouting and firing in front. D. H. Hill ordered his Carolinians forward, then hurried off ahead of them through the dense undergrowth. Upon emerging from the woods, he could "see nothing of General Early or the Yankees" due to the spur of trees blocking his view. Hill moved off to the left through the trees as the 5th North Carolina reached the edge of the woods. "On the verge of the field beyond," McRae reported, "I halted and reformed the line and examined for the enemy's battery." McRae was also blinded by the spur of trees and thus advanced his line about one hundred yards into the field for a better look.[16]

From that point the vista before the North Carolinians opened to their left, where Bratton's closest redoubt, number ten, could be seen a couple of hundred

14. *OR,* 11(1):538–9, 545, 550, 553.
15. Ibid., 539, 551, 555, 608–9; Early, *Memoirs,* 70.
16. Early, *Memoirs,* 70; *OR,* 11(1):603, 608–10.

yards away. What caught their immediate attention, however, was a battery seven to nine hundred yards on their left sending a barrage of shells their way. A quick change of face in that direction revealed a broken line, as both the 23d North Carolina and 38th Virginia, which should have been filling the field on their left, were still in the woods. Only the 24th Virginia was visible far to the left front of the 5th North Carolina as it now started off through the open field of soft earth. Colonel McRae doubted his troops were heading in the proper direction and felt "great anxiety" because they had no cover. He therefore dispatched Maj. P. J. Sinclair to Hill to tell him he had found the enemy battery and "to inquire of him if that was the battery he desired us to assail." Sinclair was also instructed to urge Hill, respectfully, "to expedite the advance of the two regiments" that had not yet appeared.[17]

At almost the same moment that Sinclair found General Hill in the woods with the two missing regiments, one of Early's aides came galloping up to report that Early was "in the open field chasing the Yankees; that he was wounded and needed re-enforcements, and had ordered a regiment in the earthwork to his support." This regiment was the 6th South Carolina, which Early came across when he approached Bratton's redoubt "for the purpose of dismounting and directing the operations from that point." Bratton begged to join the charge, and Early, finding himself too weak and in pain to dismount, told him to take his men "and go toward the enemy." The wounded brigadier then "rode from the field, to the hospital at Williamsburg," he later wrote, "passing by Fort Magruder, and informing General Longstreet, whom I found on the right of it, of what was going on with my command."[18]

Early's command, Maury asserted, was doggedly continuing without him, although "the ground is soft and yielding; the wheat half-knee high, drenched with rain, clings heavily to the legs, and many trip and stumble and sometimes fall." The 24th Virginia's colors were "already pierced with many a bullet," the flagstaff shattered, but the color bearer "grasps the broken staff and cheerily waves the silken folds in front." On and on, down a slope and up the other side, the stalwart Virginians approached the fence just abandoned by 5th Wisconsin skirmishers and found a wounded Wisconsin captain left behind in the confusion. He was almost bayoneted by a private "frantic at the fall of his brother" but was rescued by Maury, who accepted the captain's surrendered sword and waved it while leading on his men. As they neared the fence, the Virginians came within canister range of Wheeler's and Cowan's guns and

17. *OR,* 11(1):610; McRae, "Williamsburg," 364, 369.
18. *OR,* 11(1):603; McRae, "Williamsburg," 369; Early, *Memoirs,* 71.

promptly received a full load. Suddenly, away off to their right, they beheld the 5th North Carolina "coming up at the double-quick to our aid," related Maury, "led by that preux chevalier, Colonel Duncan McRae, his horse trotting briskly in advance."[19]

The 5th North Carolina broke into double-quick as soon as Sinclair returned from Hill with the order "to move on the battery rapidly and use only the bayonet." Capt. Sam Early informed McRae that General Early was wounded and the command of the brigade had devolved on him. Seeing no sign of the 38th Virginia or the 23d North Carolina, McRae realized his boys must traverse the ground those regiments should have been filling in order to make the necessary connection with the 24th Virginia. He therefore obliqued his line to the left to pass between Bratton's two redoubts, first sending ahead his lieutenant colonel, John C. Badham, on the right of the regiment to Redoubt Nine "to communicate to the officer in charge who we were," McRae wrote, "and that he did so I am sure, for the men in that redoubt cheered the regiment lustily as we passed." He briefly halted his troops for not obliquing sufficiently and ordered them to lie down to compose themselves. About that time Hancock's infantry began firing on the Carolinians, and Captain Early, now some distance ahead, was waving them on, and so on they pushed. "My color-bearer was first struck down," McRae detailed, "when his comrade seized the flag, who fell immediately. A third took it and shared the same fate." Finally, a captain "carried it until the staff was shivered to pieces in his hands."[20]

Riding forward to put himself in command of the 24th Virginia, McRae could see the Federal troops steadily falling back. The 6th Maine, still halfway to the redoubt, allowed the 49th Pennsylvania to precede it to the fortification, pausing frequently on the way "until it came to the crest, when it halted, faced to the front, called its colors and guides on the line, and dressed as if on parade" under Hancock's watchful eye. Colonel Irwin of the 49th reported that his Pennsylvanians immediately "commenced firing on the enemy, who were rapidly and boldly advancing, and were then in good rifle range." Again the 6th Maine turned its back to the field and resumed its retreat. "The enemy were now close upon us," wrote Colonel Burnham. "Seeing us fall back they fancied that we were in full retreat and their exultation knew no bounds. They poured out from the cover of the woods and rushed on toward us, crying out,

19. Maury, "Williamsburg, Va.," 116, 121–2; Maury, *Williamsburg*, 20; *OR*, 11(1):531–3, 556.
20. McRae, "Williamsburg," 369–70; *OR*, 11(1):610.

'Bull Run,' 'Ball's Bluff,' &c. It was with difficulty that I restrained my men from facing about and taking vengeance for these taunts upon the spot."[21]

Still heavily engaged with the left wing of the 24th Virginia, the 5th Wisconsin maintained its original position but reduced its square and formed in line of battle behind the rail fence enclosing the farm buildings. From there it fired on the Virginia infantry bearing down on its right. "Our men stood their ground manfully, notwithstanding their comrades were falling fast and thick under the fire of the advancing foe," recounted one Wisconsin soldier. The farm buildings, Colonel Cobb noted, both protected the Wisconsin regiment's left flank and diminished the effectiveness of its fire. "The firing at this time was very severe on both sides, they suffering more than we, our rifles committing fearful havoc in their ranks. But they were led bravely on." Cobb determined to hold that position until Captain Wheeler could retire his guns, which had been firing canister into the Virginians ever since they reached the fence recently defended by the Wisconsin skirmishers. Having already sent his disabled piece to the rear, Wheeler waited until the Confederates were within 150 yards of his guns before sending back his left piece that "occupied heavy ground and from the position of the enemy was no longer effective."[22]

The orderly retirement of Wheeler's guns led McRae to doubt the Federals were truly routed, despite their apparent confusion after the 5th North Carolina opened fire at a 150-yard range. He hurriedly dispatched his adjutant, a Lieutenant McRae, to find Hill and voice his fears as well as beg him to "throw out the two regiments to support me." D. H. Hill, still with the delinquent regiments in the woods, turned to them after hearing the adjutant's message and shouted, "Boys, do you hear that? Let us go to Colonel McRae's relief." But instead of sending out the reinforcements, Hill, Sumner-like, changed his mind. "No," he instructed Lieutenant McRae, "go and tell him to draw off his men as he best can." Before the adjutant could convey this order to Colonel McRae, his horse took fright and dashed for the Federal line, and he had to spring off to escape being carried in.[23]

Meanwhile, the 24th Virginia and 5th North Carolina steadily advanced, though Wheeler's two remaining guns continued throwing canister at them until they were within twenty yards of a fence in front of his battery. His last piece limbered up just as the leading Confederates reached the fence. It then joined the other guns in their new position on a ridge to the left of Redoubt

21. *OR*, 11(1):539, 550, 553; McRae, "Williamsburg," 370.
22. *OR*, 11(1):531, 539, 555; Love, *Wisconsin in the War*, 271.
23. McRae, "Williamsburg," 370–1.

Eleven. Cowan had already succeeded in bringing off all his pieces and had come into battery again on the rise of ground to the fort's right. Hancock admitted some difficulty attended this maneuver, "owing partly to the bad state of the ground from the long-continued rain, and partly to the fact that in the gallop from their first position the cannoneers had generally been left behind."[24]

Also left behind was the 5th Wisconsin, which Hancock now imperatively ordered to "fall back in line of battle, fighting. The colonel had not thought of retiring until he received this order," Hancock commended in his report. Cobb's Wisconsin boys found, upon pulling out, that they lost the protection of the buildings. They were directly in front of the 5th North Carolina, supported on both flanks by the 24th Virginia, "all of whom advanced rapidly," Cobb observed, "concentrating upon me a rapid and heavy fire." One Wisconsin soldier noticed that "our men began to waver. Colonel Cobb seeing this, cried out, 'Will you leave me and the old flag?' 'No! Never!' was the hearty response; and around that old banner we made a rally, resolved to perish rather than run." Choosing not to enter this episode in the record, Cobb boasted instead, "My men fell back in good order, every man loading as he retreated, wheeling and returning the fire of the enemy with a rapidity and coolness worthy of veterans."[25]

Back at Redoubt Eleven, the other regiments were already formed and waiting for them. The 7th Maine anchored the extreme right behind the crest of the earthwork, its right against the woods to prevent more surprises. To its left stood three 33d New York companies with orders to support a section of Cowan's battery placed between them and the fortification. Four companies of the 6th Maine garrisoned the redoubt after reaching the crest on the left. "As my men faced about," wrote Colonel Burnham, "I read in their faces the stern determination to suffer death in any form rather than give up an inch of ground." Not a 6th Maine rifle had yet been fired, but farther to the left the 49th Pennsylvania was still shooting on a right oblique, except for two of its companies patrolling the woods on the extreme left. The arriving 5th Wisconsin advance companies filled in between the redoubt and the 6th Maine, while the remainder took their places behind the crest on the right.[26]

From this position, Hancock's troops watched as Early's stalwarts just kept coming. "Never have I witnessed such gallantry as was displayed by the enemy

24. *OR,* 11(1):531–2, 539.
25. Ibid., 539, 555; Love, *Wisconsin in the War,* 271–2.
26. *OR,* 11(1):539–40, 550–5.

in this advance," praised one Wisconsin soldier. "Every man at a shoulder arms, their officers in front, leading them bravely forward, while our fire was thinning and mowing them down like grass before the scythe; but forward they pressed, as if upon a drill, or parade." Nearly half of the 24th Virginia was down, including Colonel Terry, shot in the face, and his lieutenant colonel and several other officers. Major Maury, bareheaded and waving the Wisconsin captain's sword, now took command of the regiment. The 5th North Carolina was suffering too, and horses were falling as rapidly as men. Glancing at each other across the field, Maury and McRae realized with dismay that they were the only Confederate field officers still mounted.[27]

The Carolinians had now caught up to the Virginians at a rail fence, where the 24th paused "a moment to breathe and reform its scattered line, preparatory to a last dash." To the 24th's right, the 5th North Carolina also halted, directly under Hancock's guns and only about seventy-five yards from the redoubt. Both McRae and Maury noticed the Federals had stopped firing entirely. They were close enough to hear the ceasefire order "and voices calling to others to halt and stand steady." McRae suspected a feint to draw them on, but this did not stop the advance. As his men jumped the fence to continue the charge, McRae decided his force of two bleeding regiments was too small to storm a redoubt defended by five full regiments and ten guns and ordered his "command to fall off down to the cover of the fence." Just then his adjutant returned with General Hill's order to retreat. Maury's men were also clambering over the fence and the major was "seeking a gap where his horse could pass" when Adjutant McRae relayed the withdrawal order to him. Maury immediately pulled his Virginians out, but some of the Carolinians had already advanced underneath the crest of the redoubt within thirty paces of the waiting Federals.[28]

At that moment Hancock ordered his entire line forward to the crest. With a hearty cheer, the 49th Pennsylvania on the far left, "moved rapidly and steadily to the front, with their colors advanced and their line accurate." On the 49th's right, the 6th Maine had every man "in his place, and we poured a volley into them which thinned their ranks terribly." The 5th Wisconsin in the center also came "forward with alacrity, and delivered a few volleys in very close range." Simultaneously, the "well-directed fire" of the 33d New York

---

27. Love, *Wisconsin in the War*, 271; *OR*, 11(1):611; Maury, "Williamsburg, Va.," 116; Maury, *Williamsburg*, 14.

28. Maury, "Williamsburg, Va.," 117; Maury, *Williamsburg*, 15; McRae, "Williamsburg," 370–1; *OR*, 11(1):540, 611.

companies threw the Confederate "ranks into confusion." The 7th Maine on
the extreme right was still lying flat on the ground behind the crest when Hancock came "galloping toward us, bareheaded, alone, a magnificent figure," declared 7th Maine officer Thomas W. Hyde, "and with a voice hoarse with
shouting he gave us the order, 'Forward! charge!'" So emphatic was he, "the
air was blue all around him."[29]

One more tremendous cheer and Hancock's line of battle surged over the
crest and dashed down the slope as one man, bayonets at the ready. "A few of
the leading spirits of the enemy were bayoneted," Hancock reported, "three
resolute men who," a Wisconsin soldier asserted, "stood firm, and received
their death wounds without flinching." All others wearing the gray, in obedi-
ence to Hill's orders, were already in full retreat. The 24th Virginia instantly
melted into the woods on which its left flank had rested, thus escaping further
damage. But the 5th North Carolina was forced to retreat without cover down
the open field it had just traversed as Hancock's men halted at the base of the
slope and poured volley after volley into their ranks and Wheeler's guns raked
them with grape. "They run! they run!" was the Federal cry, "and a cheer arose
as hearty as was ever given."[30]

Indeed, as McRae put it, "the retreat was the signal for slaughter." Thomas
Hyde described the smoke-obscured view as "pitiful. They were falling everywhere; white handkerchiefs were held up in token of surrender." The 5th
North Carolina's Lieutenant Colonel Badham had managed to rally a group
of men and return fire from a small clump of trees in front of the 7th Maine's
left, but "the crack shot of Company D, ran forward a little and sent a bullet
crashing through his brain," effectively ending all opposition. Before the survivors could stumble out of range, they left on that fearful field their battle flag
and all but 75 of the regiment's 415 men. "The best blood of the Old North
State fed the fresh young wheat at their feet," lamented Maury. In Hancock's
words, "the plunging fire from the redoubt, the direct fire from the right, and
the oblique fire from the left were so destructive that after it had been ordered
to cease and the smoke arose it seemed that no man had left the ground unhurt who had advanced within 500 yards of our line." The entire assault, from

29. OR, 11(1):540, 550–4; Love, Wisconsin in the War, 270; Paul M. Angle and Earl Schenck
Miers, eds., Tragic Years, 1860–1865, 2 vols. (New York: Simon and Schuster, 1960), 1:278 (quoting Thomas W. Hyde, Following the Greek Cross or, Memories of the Sixth Army Corps [Boston,
1894], 50–3).

30. Angle and Miers, Tragic Years, 1:278 (quoting Hyde, Following the Greek Cross, 50–3);
OR, 11(1):540; Love, Wisconsin in the War, 270, 272; Maury, "Williamsburg, Va.," 117.

the moment the 24th Virginia broke out of the woods until the 5th North Carolina retreated to safety, had taken only twenty-three minutes.[31]

"The charge upon the battery was not attended by success." Such was McRae's understated assessment. "I have no doubt it would have been had the Twenty-third North Carolina and the Thirty-eighth Virginia, as originally designated, participated in the assault." What had those regiments been doing during these twenty-three minutes? D. H. Hill lost sight of the 23d North Carolina after he ordered it to advance from the creek. Maj. Daniel H. Christie reported that his regiment encountered "serious obstacles to rapid movement." One of these obstacles was an old rotten fence, at which Hill found the 23d "more or less jumbled" and sharply scolded "the men, now confused in ranks and each one commanding his comrades: 'Hush your infernal noise.'" The general then rode down the line inquiring for Colonel Hoke. Christie had advanced the line all the way to the edge of the woods, but Hill had other ideas than sending the 23d out to support the 24th Virginia and 5th North Carolina. Believing the woods "were full of Yankees," he ordered the regiment to make a ninety-degree turn by the left flank and sweep the forest for any blue uniforms. This "simple maneuver," as Hill termed it, to be executed at the double-quick while still among the trees, was impeded by "a fence, two ravines, and woods of thick undergrowth, with fallen timber intervening," according to Christie, now assigned to lead the 23d's left wing. Somehow Christie managed to form his companies upon the regiment's right wing under the immediate command of Hoke, but not quickly enough to suit his division commander.[32]

Hill had previously directed Hoke to form his regiment on the left of Whittle's 38th Virginia, which Hill had found "huddled up and in considerable confusion. The Yankee shells and balls were falling among them, and their crowded condition was such as to increase the mortality." Surprisingly, Whittle was the only member of the regiment wounded. The general then ordered the 38th into line of battle, which "was formed with considerable difficulty," and directed it, like the 23d North Carolina, "to move on through the woods and drive out the Yankees." As the two struggling regiments did their best to obey these orders, Hill rode out onto the field to push the 6th South Carolina forward "to gain the flank of the earthwork, while the troops in the

31. McRae, "Williamsburg," 371; Angle and Miers, *Tragic Years*, 1:279 (quoting Hyde, *Following the Greek Cross*, 50–3); Blacknall typescript, Oscar W. Blacknall Papers, North Carolina State Archives, Raleigh, 27; *OR*, 11(1):540–1; Maury, "Williamsburg, Va.," 117.

32. *OR*, 11(1):603–4, 611–2; H. C. Wall, "The Twenty-third North Carolina Infantry," *Southern Historical Society Papers* 25 (1897): 156.

woods should gain its rear." This, he concluded, was the "one possible chance of success." Unfortunately, the South Carolinians were also having trouble forming after Early had ordered them forward. Adding to Hill's frustration, the 38th Virginia "joined us, having emerged from the woods contrary to orders." The 38th formed in line of battle under fire and made about 250 yards at a double-quick through the field toward Hancock, reported Whittle, before Hill sent it back into the woods.[33]

The 23d North Carolina, meanwhile, had made some progress sweeping those woods, about six hundred yards by Christie's estimation. When it stopped to reform, the regiment was "fired upon by the enemy's pickets, in the woods on our left," Christie wrote, "covering a considerable force, which was returned with a loss to the enemy of 4 killed and several wounded, involving little injury to us." Just then the 24th and 38th Virginia broke over his lines on their way to the rear, and Hill ordered the 23d to cover their retreat. The 24th Virginia had already left a portion of its members in the hands of some 33d New York skirmishers still in the woods "in a favorable position to capture fugitives of the enemy when they made their disorderly retreat before our line," commented Hancock, "and they returned burdened with them." The 33d New York's Colonel Taylor asserted that they gathered over one hundred prisoners.[34]

Reluctant to pursue the fleeing foe without support in his rear, Hancock held his troops at the base of the slope and ordered the artillery to throw a few parting shots at the gray remnants seen retreating through the edge of the woods. At that moment Captain Aiken returned from his errand to the Whittaker House. Halfway back he had met Captain Currie, "riding at a furious rate," and paused only long enough for Currie to tell him Hancock had been attacked and "was severely suffering." Captain Hancock, a few minutes ahead of Currie, had already delivered these tidings to General Smith, who told him and then Currie that McClellan had just ordered up a division. Meanwhile, Aiken hastened back to Smith "with the welcome intelligence that the enemy had been repulsed," that Hancock "had full possession of the field, and that the enemy's dead were lying thickly on the ground in front of our lines." He met Smith already on his way with several regiments and "took occasion to correct a false impression prevailing among retreating stragglers that you had been defeated," Aiken reported to Hancock, "and also to assure General

33. *OR*, 11(1): 603–4, 613; G. Howard Gregory, *38th Virginia Infantry* (Lynchburg: H. E. Howard, 1988), 16.
34. *OR*, 11(1):540, 552, 609, 612.

Brooks, whom I met coming with re-enforcements, that we had won the day."[35]

It certainly looked that way from Hancock's perspective. "For 600 yards in front of our line the whole field was strewn with the enemy's dead and wounded," he observed. As soon as the fighting had subsided, he "sent out men to succor the wounded and collect the dead for burial." For want of shelter, the Confederate wounded had to be placed in his redoubt but "received the greatest care and attention from our men wherever they were found." Some three hundred prisoners were gathered before dark, according to Thomas Hyde. Custer boasted in a letter to his sister that he "captured a Captain and five men without any assistance." He also claimed to have captured the 5th North Carolina's battle flag, "a large white silk flag with a red cross in the center." More likely it was picked up by a 5th Wisconsin soldier and handed to Custer. Hancock relayed the trophy to General Smith, who but a short time later arrived on the field, followed closely by the 3d Vermont. Then came most of Naglee's brigade and two more of Smith's regiments, just as the last dim light faded into drizzly darkness.[36]

35. Ibid., 532, 540–1, 545–7.
36. *OR*, 11(1):540–1; George Armstrong Custer to Lydia Reed, 15 May 1862, Little Bighorn Battlefield National Monument, Crow Agency, Mont.

CHAPTER 9

Dismal Night

As the darkness intensified, so did the rain. Two hours after nightfall, Col. William Davis's 104th Pennsylvania finally reached Redoubt Eleven, having slogged eight hours through the infamous muck from one end of the battlefield to the other. "We had no guide," Davis complained, "and our course was directed by stragglers we met coming from the field." Joining their brigade, "the men sat down in their places in ranks in the mud, with their accoutrements on, and held their rifles between their knees. The horses of the mounted officers were kept saddled, and in some instances the riders passed the night in the saddle." Officers of the 7th Maine "spread a lot of fence rails in the mud and sat on cracker boxes in our rubber blankets most of the night," revealed Thomas Hyde. Between the rain and occasional shots fired by pickets, they had no desire for sleep and "reiterated to each other our experiences of the battle with an enthusiasm that could not be quenched." The men in the ranks engaged in hushed conversations around dim watch fires, shivering, damp, and hungry, having had no regular rations since Sunday morning in Yorktown. "The phosphorescent glow on the faces of the dead in the fields beyond became more weird as the night sped on," Hyde observed. Enhancing the eeriness, remarked Davis, were "the groans of the wounded enemy who lay near us, by no means a pleasant sound to waiting, expectant soldiers."[1]

Unpleasant sounds pervaded the entire battlefield that dreary night. On the Union left, a wounded James Burns of the 74th New York, waiting for help, could do nothing but listen. "My heart was moved with pity to hear the groans

1. *OR*, 11(1):540; Davis, *104th Pennsylvania*, 65; Angle and Miers, *Tragic Years*, 1:279 (quoting Thomas W. Hyde, *Following the Greek Cross or, Memories of the Sixth Army Corps* [Boston, 1894], 50–3).

of the dying and wounded, as they lay around, who were calling for their mothers—but no mother was there to aid or comfort them," he later wrote. The 2d Michigan's Lt. Charles Haydon, returning from the front that night, "found the woods & the road side strewed with dead & the moans & cries of the wounded could be heard on all sides. They were scattered around among the logs & brush so that it was almost impossible to get at them." That made it difficult for the diligent members of the Ambulance Corps, scurrying around the field with litters, picking up wounded, and carrying them to a large barn near the Whittaker House. "By nine o'clock the wounds of upwards of one hundred sufferers had been carefully dressed," counted a newspaper correspondent, "and after that hour few if any were brought in—the darkness, the storm, and condition of the fields and woods making it impracticable." Unhurt soldiers were of little help, as Haydon remarked in his diary, they "were so cold & used up that they would not attempt to care for any but themselves. Such as they ran onto they would cover up with blankets, give water to drink & leave as comfortable as possible but they would not turn out of their way to aid them unless they were acquaintances."[2]

With the rain now coming down in torrents, comfort was almost impossible to find, especially the warmth of a fire. Haydon fortunately stumbled upon a dozen men from his regiment able to maintain a fire and warmed and dried himself as best he could. The 40th New York, withdrawn from the front to a patch of woods in the rear, passed "the most dreary and uncomfortable night" Sgt. Fred C. Floyd ever experienced. "A few spread their rubber blankets on the wet ground, and with a woolen blanket covering them, they passed the night entirely oblivious of the falling rain or the condition of their clothing," Floyd wrote. "Nearly all of us remained awake to walk about and pass the desolate hours which seemed all the longer for the lack of fires, food and pastime." Their officers and even their division commander were in the same predicament. Phil Kearny's orderly lost the general's India rubber cape when he threw it off upon entering the battle, leaving him exposed to the cold and wet. Kearny wrote his wife that he "would have suffered, but for borrowing a dragoon overcoat from my guard."[3]

Later in the night, the regiments from Kearny's division that had participated in the aborted mission on the extreme left came in from Kingsmill and

2. Burns, *Battle of Williamsburgh*, 34; Sears, *For Country, Cause, and Leader*, 233; Frank Moore, ed., *The Rebellion Record: A Diary of American Events with Documents, Narratives, Illustrative Incidents, Poetry, Etc.*, 9 vols. (New York: G. P. Putnam, 1863), 5(2):22.

3. Sears, *For Country, Cause, and Leader*, 233; Floyd, *Fortieth (Mozart) Regiment New York*, 146; Kearny, *General Philip Kearny*, 241, 249.

relieved the 40th New York and Kearny's other regiments along Hampton Road. Joseph Hooker's division was also recuperating down Hampton Road, Major Wainwright bivouacking with his only two intact batteries about three-quarters of a mile to the rear in an open field. "Wet to the skin and very tired," he recorded in his journal, "I lay down at night with the officers of Osborn's battery under a paulin, but could not sleep much for the cold, and for thinking." Some of Hooker's infantry fell back as far as a mile and a half from the battlefield, but the 1st Massachusetts camped in the woods just one-half mile back. There, Pvt. Edwin Brown noted, "on the wet and spongy soil of the battle field we drop in painful weariness, surrounded by the wounded and dead, sleeping with arms by our side in readiness for the warning bugle that shall summon us to the pursuit."[4]

Not pursuit exactly, but defense against another expected attack was uppermost in the mind of Brown's corps chief, General Heintzelman. Exhausted from the day's exertions, Heintzelman built himself a fire back in the woods to rest awhile. He then hunted up one of the cavalry camps and composed dispatches to Generals Sumner and McClellan, the latter he assumed to be still in Yorktown, informing them what his command had been through that day. The communication he wrote to McClellan at 9:00 P.M. enclosed notes he had received from Colonel Averell estimating the Confederate strength at fifty thousand. "I think, however," predicted Heintzelman, "that they intend here to make a determined stand." He figured Hooker's loss to be at least five hundred men and feared his "division has suffered so severely that it will not be very reliable for to-morrow. I will try and hold the position, but it is necessary that I be strongly re-enforced."[5]

These reinforcements Heintzelman requested in a dispatch to Sumner as soon as he finished McClellan's note and sent it off by courier. Emphasizing Hooker's heavy loss and begging Sumner to send "at least a division before daylight," Heintzelman also asked him to "cut a road in front of the enemy's intrenchments" to bring reinforcements over to the left. "By cutting this road the troops can readily join me without having to make the large circuit by Cheesecake Church," he explained, recalling his two-hour journey by that route earlier in the day. At the close of his communication, Heintzelman offered Sumner one more plea. "Cannot you also attack him at daylight on his left and in your front? I fear greatly that unless he is strongly pressed I will not

---

4. *OR*, 11(1):474–5, 496–8; Nevins, *Diary of Battle*, 54–6; Edwin Y. Brown, "Battle of Williamsburg," EYB, MR-CWM.

5. Congress, *Report of the Joint Committee*, 1:349; *OR*, 11(1):453–5.

be able to maintain my position." In desperation he added, "May I rely upon your aid to sustain me?"[6]

After dispatching these notes near midnight, Heintzelman headed back to his bivouac and on the way met one of McClellan's aides sent to find him. McClellan had been searching for his Third Corps commander since arriving at the Whittaker House that evening. An infantry company he sent to the left to open communications with Heintzelman "returned after dark with the information that it was impracticable to get through the marsh." Another Mc-Clellan aide found Kearny between one and two o'clock that morning and received an oral report as well as a few strong opinions from the one-armed general. "We have possession of the field; but if the works are to be taken by force, this is not the place for it," Kearny lectured him. "I believe it to be in the flank and I guarantee to hold this place with any two of my Regiments against the whole Southern army."[7]

Kearny and Heintzelman were not the only northerners anticipating more action soon. Gen. Winfield Hancock allowed the Confederates to help clear their wounded and dead from the field in case they should choose to "renew the contest," while Hyde and his comrades "expected to attack Fort Magruder in the morning." In the center, General Peck withdrew his exhausted brigade and prepared "to resist a night attack" with six fresh regiments, including the 2d Rhode Island, forced to endure an artillery barrage from Fort Magruder. The men of Peck's withdrawn division huddling in groups "made big calculations to go into it early next morning," wrote the 62d New York's William Allcot.[8]

McClellan himself, after abandoning plans to attack soon after his arrival on the field, returned to the Whittaker House to issue orders and ponder his next move. "There people drink, smoke, dry themselves, and bustle about in the midst of a horrendous racket," as the Comte de Paris described the chaos. "The commanders do nothing and rest on their laurels. In the General's chamber people try to evaluate the day's results, prepare for tomorrow's attack, and expedite the flow of orders." The place was so crowded, McClellan could neither eat nor rest, but he managed to send orders back to Yorktown to push another division up the York River to West Point in an effort to cut off the

6. *OR*, 11(1):454–6.

7. Congress, *Report of the Joint Committee*, 1:349, 430; *OR*, 11(1):22–3; Kearny, *General Philip Kearny*, 243–4.

8. *OR*, 11(1):521, 540; Angle and Miers, *Tragic Years*, 1:279 (quoting Hyde, *Following the Greek Cross*, 50–3); Rhodes, *All for the Union*, 64; William P. Allcot to mother, 11 May 1862, William P. Allcot Papers, MR-CWM.

Confederate retreat. At 9:40 P.M. he thought "the enemy will evacuate during the night; if not, I can probably beat him." His tone was not so confident twenty minutes later in a telegram to Secretary of War Edwin M. Stanton, saying, "My entire force is undoubtedly considerably inferior to that of the Rebels, who still fight well, but I will do all I can with the force at my disposal." Hancock's "conduct was brilliant in the extreme," but Hooker, McClellan feared, "has lost considerably on our left."[9]

His fear was soon confirmed when Heintzelman's note reached him, emphasizing the Third Corps's need for heavy reinforcements. This caused the commanding general to reconsider. "I felt satisfied," he later testified, "from what I knew of Hancock's position, that the battle was won; that he had occupied the decisive point, and gained possession of a portion of the enemy's line; and that they must make a night retreat or we would have greatly the advantage of them in the morning." Besides, Smith's, Casey's, and Couch's divisions were still relatively unscathed and could be brought over from the right to sweep away any Confederates stubborn enough to remain in front of Kearny. "I could perfectly well hold my own and keep the enemy in position while the movement to West Point was being carried out," McClellan surmised. He therefore sent Heintzelman word "not to renew the attack in the morning." This message was placed in Heintzelman's hands about one o'clock in the morning of 6 May.[10]

By that time, totally unknown to the Federals, their adversaries were almost gone. The Confederates began pulling out soon after blue uniforms disappeared from their front. Late in the evening George Pickett's 19th Virginia marched off the field and bivouacked just southeast of Williamsburg. Realizing he had lost track of his 28th Virginia after he had pulled it back from the left, Pickett employed the services of the 19th's adjutant, Lt. Nat Wood, to find it. "Away I went alone in the direction of the enemy," wrote Wood, "leaving the battlefield to my left." He soon found himself on the wrong side of a deep gully going in the wrong direction, but when he tried to pass over the ditch on a rickety bridge, all four of his horse's legs slipped through the bridge, suspending him above the deep ravine. The horse finally extricated himself, and off Wood sped, coming "up with the Twenty-eighth in time to save them from capture, for they were going exactly in the wrong direction to find the brigade."[11]

9. McClellan, *Own Story*, 330–2; Grimsley and Glod, "'We Prepare to Receive the Enemy,'" 21; Sears, *Papers of George B. McClellan*, 256; *OR*, 11(3):143; *OR*, 11(1):448–9.

10. Congress, *Report of the Joint Committee*, 1:349, 430; McClellan, *Own Story*, 332–3.

11. Wood, *Reminiscences*, 15–6.

While Wood was off rescuing the 28th Virginia, another of Pickett's regiments on the right flank, the 8th Virginia, awaited orders. "As twilight settled down upon the battlefield," wrote Randolph Shotwell, "the men gathered in little groups and discussed the incidents of the day." They were uncertain as to the outcome of the battle, being isolated in the dense woods, and knew only that they were holding their own. To Shotwell, "the occasion was inexpressibly sombre and depressing. The twilight deepened into a solemn darkness, with nothing audible save the ceaseless patter of the rain, the moaning of the wounded in the thickets, the voices of the litter bearers hunting for comrades that had been left amid the heat of battle, the crackling of the underbrush as an officer came in from the out pickets—or the far-off cry of some poor wretch beseeching 'water, water, water!'"[12]

Joining the litter bearers were other soldiers prowling the battlefield that night. After his wounding, New Yorker James Burns had dragged himself between two trees, where a succession of passing graycoats stumbled upon him. One, "a big, burly rebel, asked why I fought against them" if he was fighting to free slaves, Burns related. "I answered: 'To preserve the Union, and for no other purpose have any of our men enlisted.' He immediately retorted with the answer: 'We'll preserve the Union for you.'" The next passing southerner shared his molasses with him, but about nightfall another came by and stole his pocket watch, promising to "send an ambulance to convey me to the hospital." Union litter bearers found him before the Confederates, however.[13]

Confederate litter bearers were also busy on their extreme left, as D. H. Hill withdrew Jubal Early's brigade back through the woods to its original position. He then advanced his brigade under Gabriel Rains into the woods to gather as many wounded as possible from the battlefield, with Hancock's permission. Hancock reported "a large number were thus carried off," though Colonel McRae lamented only forty wounded of the 5th North Carolina were among them. Darkness ended their efforts and forced them to abandon ten wounded officers, several of whom were found by Hancock's men and expired soon after being carried into the Federal-held redoubts. "The night was one of almost unparalleled suffering," according to Harvey Hill, because he placed his entire division in line of battle in the wheat field "all night, without fire, during a cold and wet rain." The troops, "wet and faint with hunger and fatigue," stamped their feet and crowded together in groups to keep warm. A major described his men huddling around his horse while he was still

12. Hamilton, *Papers of Randolph Abbott Shotwell*, 1:199.
13. Burns, *Battle of Williamsburgh*, iv–vi.

mounted, trying to absorb enough warmth to keep themselves alive. Contrary to orders, many sought shelter in whatever barns and outhouses they could find.[14]

One such exhausted lad desperate enough to defy orders was the 4th South Carolina's Cpl. Jesse Reid. After marching all night Saturday, pulling picket duty between the lines all night Sunday, and fighting in the cold rain all day Monday, Reid flatly refused to go back into one of the redoubts and stand guard. He "plainly but modestly" told this to his superior officer, who fortunately sympathized with his plight and allowed him to step out of ranks. "The darkness favored me in getting away unnoticed," Reid wrote home a few days later, "so I gave myself the word of command 'About face,' deployed off in single file and made my way to Williamsburg, about half a mile away." As tired as he was, Reid still did not feel at liberty to enter a vacant house without permission. The corporal "finally found an old negro in a kitchen cooking his supper" and was cordially invited in with the explanation that "de white folks is all gone up towards Richmond, an' da tole me dat if any o' de Infedret so'g-ers come here to give 'em anything they wanted, sah." Five more 4th South Carolina boys followed Reid into the kitchen and spent the night.[15]

Some detached members of the 1st Virginia, including Sgt. Charles Loehr, found similar lodging in Williamsburg that night. On the battlefield shortly before dark, having delivered instructions to a nearby North Carolina regiment, he started back to his command but blundered instead into Union lines. He turned around amid "a shower of balls" and continued his "solitary retreat among the dead and dying in the dark woods, not knowing where to go." The 2d Mississippi Battalion shot at Loehr next, mistaking him for a bluecoat in the darkness, then informed him "the First had passed through them for the rear some time previous." Starting toward Williamsburg, he came to the open field in front of Fort Magruder and had to lie down flat in the mud, for "our artillery was hard at work sending its iron messengers towards the Federal lines." At last in Williamsburg he found "every house was filled with wounded, and men who, like myself, were in quest of a dry spot." At the far western end of town, the weary sergeant heard voices belonging to some men in his com-

14. *OR*, 11(1):540, 604–5, 611; Janet B. Hewett, Noah Andre Trudeau, Bryce A. Suderow, eds., *Supplement to the Official Records of the Union and Confederate Armies* (Wilmington, N.C.: Broadfoot, 1994), ser. 1, 2:339–40; Robert E. Park, "The Twelfth Alabama Infantry, Confederate States Army," *Southern Historical Society Papers* 33 (1905): 217; Blacknall typescript, 32–3, Oscar W. Blacknall Papers, North Carolina State Archives, Raleigh.

15. Reid, *Fourth Regiment of S.C. Volunteers*, 81–3.

pany in a vacant building. "I was soon among them," Loehr wrote, "and by a rousing fire we spent the night after the battle."[16]

About nine o'clock the bulk of the 1st Virginia along with the rest of A. P. Hill's brigade moved silently from the edge of the woods back to the outskirts of town. There Hill's troops camped in the open field, sleeping on the saturated ground, with the exception of Pvt. James Petty of the 17th Virginia. His captain sent him into Williamsburg on a special errand. "I walked the streets until after midnight hunting up our wounded and stragglers," he recorded in his diary the next day. It was a difficult task, for nearly every home overflowed with sleeping officers and wounded soldiers. Dr. John Galt also wrote in his diary the next day that "large numbers slept at my house," and Sally later put the number at about one hundred "who came to our door in a cold & chilling rain wet wounded, bleeding & famishing from the battlefield." She "had a barrel of flour baked & that was not enough to feed the poor hungry soldiers." At the equally full Tucker House, Cynthia Coleman likewise struggled to feed the troops, as the proximity of the Union army was having an effect on servants who "had already begun to show their sense of freedom and prepared with reluctance any thing for those they had come to regard no longer as friends but as their bitterest foes." Among their guests were Cynthia's uncle, Capt. William Berkeley, and his three brothers, including Norborne Berkeley, all officers in the 8th Virginia. One of them "threw himself exhausted on the study floor under the piano I think," Cynthia later recollected, "asking me to wake him at a certain time, he was soaked with rain, the water literally running out of his boots."[17]

As acting head of the 8th Virginia, Lt. Col. Norborne Berkeley withdrew the regiment closely behind A. P. Hill's brigade. Shotwell remembered the whispered order came down the line about 10:50 P.M. "No one must speak—" he recounted, "no canteen be allowed to rattle, no sound be made: but stealthily file to the rear like Indian warriors approaching an enemy's camp." Although they were glad to get in motion and shake the dripping rain from their clothes, an all-night march through knee-deep mud and slush did not appeal to them. "The darkness was intense, rendering it guess work as to where one's foot would land when outstretched," Shotwell wrote. "Especially was this the case in the shadow of the woods. Sometimes I caught myself stumbling over

16. Loehr, "First Virginia Infantry," 108–9.
17. James Thomas Petty Diary No. 2, 6 May 1862, MC; John Minson Galt II Diary, 6 May 1862, GFP, MR-CWM; SMG to cousin, 15 Apr. 1863, GFP; CBT, "Peninsula Campaign," TCP, MR-CWM.

a dead horse, and sometimes upon a half living man." He stopped to give one of the latter a drink of water, losing his place in line, and trying to catch up he nearly plunged headlong into the flooded moat of one of the redoubts.[18]

Still shaking from this brush with death after surviving a day of battle, and now hopelessly separated from his regiment, Shotwell finally reached Williamsburg and found the streets jammed with soldiers. By that time he saw "no signs of inhabitants, no lights in the houses and everything as quiet and desolate as a country village at midnight." He suspected "the citizens were not asleep but had extinguished their lights as the best way to escape annoyance from stragglers, and men seeking places to leave wounded friends." Finding a place to deposit the body of a beloved commander was a problem for the little squad of 2d Florida soldiers carrying Col. George Ward from the battlefield in a blanket. They "were until ten o'clock trying to get his body into some friends house," David Maxwell informed his mother, "but I say with the utmost contempt for the people of that town that we *could not find* one house that would take his remains in. We finaly took him into one, laid him out & pinned a card on his breast telling who he was & asking them to bury him."[19]

In the darkness, these men probably could not tell they had left Ward in the Old Courthouse, which Shotwell passed as he continued through Williamsburg searching for a dry corner in which to sleep. At last he came to the college with "lights flashing at nearly every window." Entering the main building, he discovered why. Where, that very morning, peaceful halls had sheltered him from the rain, now "wounded, dying and dead—here, there, everywhere—halls, recitation rooms, dormitories—all were crowded with bloody bodies!" In one of the larger rooms, he encountered two or three surgeons "busy at low tables, sawing off, or binding up limbs of poor fellows who lay upon the tables in such a way that the ghastly hue of their distorted faces showed all the more horribly from the flickering glare of the tallow candle at each corner." Shotwell then tripped upon "a pile of legs and arms that had been amputated and thrown on the landing of the stairway, that being the only place unoccupied by the wounded." Out the door past several corpses, the sickened soldier fled into the storm to escape this "chamber of horrors."[20]

At the campus gate Shotwell met Norborne Berkeley, just leaving the com-

18. Hamilton, *Papers of Randolph Abbott Shotwell*, 1:199–200.

19. Ibid., 1:200–1; Maxwell to mother, 11 May 1862, David Elwell Maxwell Papers, VHS.

20. CBT, "May 5, 1862," TCP; Hamilton, *Papers of Randolph Abbott Shotwell*, 1:193, 201–2.

fort of the Tucker House after he and his brothers had been awakened by Cynthia Coleman with word that the army was falling back. Berkeley too was separated from the 8th Virginia, but while he was well mounted, Shotwell would have to run to catch up to the regiment. Deciding he had enough exercise for the day, Shotwell "at once resolved to spend the night at one of the camp fires near town." A large pile of blankets abandoned in a small apple orchard across Richmond Road from the college was just what he wanted. "I calmly spread a couple of dozen of them down on a dry spot where a fire had been smothered by the rain," he later reminisced, "and was soon stretched thereon, enjoying intensely the much needed rest and warmth." The tramp, tramp, tramp of a weary army on the road about forty feet away lulled Shotwell to sleep. "Wagons, ambulances and artillery were mingled with the troops, all plodding on together" through the endless mud, repeating their Saturday night march as Monday rolled into Tuesday.[21]

General Johnston was also resting briefly at the college. That evening he stopped with his staff to visit Longstreet, who had his headquarters there and was now preparing to move his division out of Williamsburg. With the roads almost impassable, Longstreet decided that the captured Federal guns would have to be abandoned. "I sent an ax to General A. P. Hill," he reported, "with orders to destroy the pieces that we could not remove from the field; but he had passed them so far, and night coming on, they could not be found." Of the four carried off, two fine 10-pounder Parrott guns Johnston presented "with a complimentary message" to Robertson Garrett's battery, which had remained in the redoubts until midnight before joining the retreat. The Confederates brought off eight Federal standards as well as four hundred prisoners, but they had to leave behind all wounded prisoners for lack of ambulances. Wounded Federal officers "were allowed the privilege of remaining on parole or following us on the march," Longstreet explained. "They preferred their parole."[22]

Noticing that only northern wounded were being carried into town from the field, Longstreet assumed that all the southern wounded had been brought in. Among them were Williamsburg natives Tommy Mercer of the 1st Virginia and his 11th Virginia cousin, Johnny Waller. Both were able to leave town, but generally, due to the transportation shortage, only walking wounded could follow the rest of the army up the Peninsula. General officers naturally

21. Hamilton, *Papers of Randolph Abbott Shotwell,* 1:202–3; CBT, "Peninsula Campaign."
22. Gallagher, *Fighting for the Confederacy,* 81; *OR,* 11(1):566; W. R. Garrett to CBT, 15 May 1890, TCP.

would be the exception. Jubal Early, his wound dressed at Williamsburg, took an ambulance out of town soon after midnight and eventually reached his home in the mountains to recuperate.[23]

Shortly before leaving Williamsburg at eleven o'clock that night, Longstreet's chief surgeon, Dr. John S. D. Cullen, reported that some four hundred bleeding Confederates were scattered among the college, church hospitals, and private homes. Maj. William Payne had been delivered to William Peachy's house, where Payne and Dr. Pendleton, still holding onto his artery, were lifted out of the ambulance together. "The doctor's fingers had to be prized apart, and it was feared for sometime that his hand had been paralyzed," Payne's wife later wrote. Dr. Cullen gave Payne little chance to live. The deserted houses on the Palace grounds were being used as hospitals as well, for Richard Bucktrout noted Monday night that a 9th Alabama lad "died palice Hospital" and was buried in the twenty-fourth grave in the City Cemetery's Alabama row. Bucktrout had been backlogged all day building coffins for Hampton Legion casualties from the Sunday skirmish. The 18th Virginia's chaplain, Rev. William Stoddert, on behalf of his absent brother Benjamin Ewell, scribbled coffin orders for two of them, to "guarantee you from loss in the absence of proper authority, consequent on the evacuation of this place," he assured the undertaker. Gen. Richard Anderson's brother, E. McHenry Anderson, "shot below town" and treated at Dr. Garrett's, was placed in the twelfth South Carolina plot, the sixth coffin built and burial recorded by Bucktrout on that busy Monday.[24]

Only about an hour was left in 5 May when Johnston started toward Richmond with Longstreet and their entourage of some twenty-five or thirty staff officers. By one o'clock in the morning, they had traveled nine miles from Williamsburg and arrived at the farmhouse belonging to Mary Anne Piggott, sister of Williamsburg's own "Virginia Yankee," Lemuel J. Bowden. All Monday morning Mrs. Piggott had been feeding the hungry Confederate soldiers passing by her home, keeping five or six cooks constantly employed, while Bowden sat on the front porch, becoming increasingly concerned lest their Union sentiments be discovered. An officer with Johnston's compliments rode up at one o'clock in the afternoon and requested refuge that night for his chief.

    23. OR, 11(1):566–7; Johnston, Narrative, 124; Wallace, 1st Virginia Infantry, 106; Robert T. Bell, 11th Virginia Infantry (Lynchburg: H. E. Howard, 1985), 97; Early, Memoirs, 73.
    24. Johnston, Narrative, 124; Payne to CBT, 21 Feb. 1891, TCP; Mrs. William H. Payne, "Search for My Wounded Husband," 1910, VHS, 1; Richard M. Bucktrout Day Book, 4–5 May 1862, MR-CWM; William Stoddert to R. M. Bucktrout, 5 May 1862, Bucktrout-Smith Papers, MR-CWM.

Bowden advised his sister "to send word to General Johnston that she would entertain him and his staff very willingly; but in order to make suitable preparations for him it would be necessary for her to have complete control of the house, and there should be a guard placed there to keep the soldiers away. The guard was accordingly placed there," Bowden related, "and we were not troubled with the soldiers any more."[25]

Before the arrival of the Confederate high command twelve hours later, Bowden prudently retired to his upstairs room as his sons lingered below to listen to the conversation. They heard Johnston say "that there had been a pretty severe skirmish at Williamsburg, and he had lost probably 500 men." Soon an aide came in with the news that McClellan was sending two divisions up to West Point to cut off the Confederate retreat. Johnston indicated he was not particularly concerned, as G. W. Smith's division had already reached Barhamsville eighteen miles from Williamsburg, Magruder's had made it to Diascund Bridge not far from the Chickahominy River, and the rest of Johnston's men—now battle-hardened veterans all—were at that moment trudging past his headquarters toward their next fight.[26]

Back in Williamsburg, only a few brigades still waited to depart. Wilcox's started up the road for Richmond about 2:00 A.M., with A. P. Hill's pulling out of its camp east of town an hour later. As they marched through Williamsburg, the men of the 11th Virginia gathered "up their knapsacks deposited along the street in the front yards the day before, and which the people had taken care of." Close behind Powell Hill, Harvey Hill's division also decamped about three o'clock, once again forming the army's rear guard as on Saturday night. Those who had sought shelter in barns and outhouses near the wheat field were first driven out "with the utmost difficulty," reported D. H. Hill. "Cold, tired, hungry, and jaded, many seemed indifferent alike to life or capture." Just as they got started, the rain at long last ceased.[27]

Quiet though the Confederate withdrawal may have been, it did not go entirely unnoticed across the lines. Thomas Hyde later reflected that "distant noises would have told older soldiers that the enemy was in retreat in the black darkness off toward Williamsburg." In front of Fort Magruder, Sgt. Elisha Rhodes of the 2d Rhode Island noted, "sometime after midnight we could hear the rumble of teams in the direction of Williamsburg." Brig. Gen. Wil-

---

25. Gallagher, *Fighting for the Confederacy,* 81; Johnston, *Narrative,* 124; Congress, *Report of the Joint Committee,* 1:583–4.

26. Congress, *Report of the Joint Committee,* 1:584; *OR,* 11(1):276.

27. *OR,* 11(1):593, 605; Petty Diary No. 2, 6 May 1862; Morgan, *Reminiscences,* 110; Blacknall typescript, 33.

liam Keim, spending the "rainy and unpleasant" night on the field with Generals Peck and Couch, reported hearing sounds "of cutting wood, and commands were given to 'Forward, march,' which induced a belief that the enemy were about evacuating." Even Averell's cavalry near the James River in Kingsmill could hear "the continuous rumble of wheels" all night. An hour and a half after midnight, some scouts from General Jameson's First Brigade of Kearny's division reported "that the rebel troops were moving from their works in front of the scene of action." This Jameson immediately communicated to Kearny, who neglected to pass it along to Heintzelman but suggested that Jameson send scouts out again to go closer to the redoubts and confirm their suspicions. These returned to Jameson at half past three "fully satisfied that the rebels were deserting their works."[28]

Jameson's skirmishers watched from the left as a self-appointed scouting party of two 2d Rhode Islanders appeared from the center. "Just as day began to break," wrote Rhodes, he and his major "crawled towards the fort. After approaching quite near and not seeing anyone we arose and walked up the glacis and looked into an embrasure. Behold, the fort was deserted." They then hurried around to the rear of Fort Magruder and, entering the gate, found the ground "covered with dead men and horses." At that moment a detachment of fifteen men from the 7th Massachusetts showed up, having crossed a ravine to the edge of the plain, and "charged across the open space and entered the fort. They were surprised to find two Rhode Island soldiers already in possession," commented Rhodes. The captain leading this Massachusetts party reported that as they drew near to Fort Magruder, a staff officer from Kearny's division rode up from the left, directing them to pass around to the left of the fort and into the barracks. These buildings too were empty, except for one gray straggler awaking to find himself a prisoner of war.[29]

Heintzelman also aroused himself about daylight and rode to the front, meeting Kearny at the edge of the woods. Instead of immediately informing his corps commander of the suspected Confederate withdrawal, Kearny tried to dissuade him from riding out into the field "for fear we should draw the fire of the enemy upon us," Heintzelman later expounded. "The cleared space was so small that we would be very much exposed the moment we showed ourselves on horseback outside of the woods." Willing to chance it anyway, Hein-

28. Angle and Miers, *Tragic Years,* 1:279 (quoting Hyde, *Following the Greek Cross,* 50–3); Rhodes, *All for the Union,* 64; Rawle et al., *Third Pennsylvania Cavalry,* 51; OR, 11(1):496, 562; Congress, *Report of the Joint Committee,* 1:350.

29. Rhodes, *All for the Union,* 64–5; OR, 11(1):525.

tzelman took Kearny and proceeded into the open field, where he found a company of the 85th Pennsylvania advancing toward Fort Magruder by order of General Keim. He also found Generals Jameson and Birney. "They thought the enemy were abandoning their works," Heintzelman wrote, "as they had heard them moving in the night." Birney had earlier ordered his 4th Maine under Col. Elijah Walker to form a picket line at the edge of the woods in front of the redoubts. Now Heintzelman told Walker to advance his pickets into Fort Magruder. While they came up from the center, Jameson with two companies of the 105th Pennsylvania approached from the left to reconnoiter the earthworks on that side. They found all of them deserted.[30]

The 4th Maine skirmishers, especially proud of their new possession, planted their colors on the ramparts of Fort Magruder. Besides five unburied bodies, "the only article of consequence discovered in the fort was a rebel banner," an elaborately embroidered South Carolina company flag declaring "Preserve Southern Institutions, or Perish with them." Heintzelman mentioned finding some ammunition as well, but at the moment his attention was on the Confederate troops still visible in front of Williamsburg. A large body of Stuart's cavalry, remaining in the field between Fort Magruder and town, covered the tail of D. H. Hill's infantry now disappearing through the streets. Then the cavalrymen also turned their backs to the breaking dawn and filed up Main Street past homes and churches bulging with wounded. Bruton Church held special significance for Stuart's young artillery chief, Capt. John Pelham, for there his grandfather Peter Pelham gained renown as the organist a century earlier. On the plain behind him were massing the blue hordes of Jameson's brigade, sent by Heintzelman in pursuit. Couch also directed one of his brigades to advance. His four regiments took the earthworks on their right and entered Fort Magruder "without opposition." Neither did Jameson's brigade meet any opposition, "the rebel cavalry retreating as we advanced," he reported. Stuart's rear exited the west end of town just as Jameson's advance entered the east. At that moment McClellan joined Heintzelman near Fort Magruder in time to watch through the dim gray light his Confederate quarry elude his grasp once again.[31]

30. Congress, *Report of the Joint Committee*, 1:349–50; *OR*, 11(1):496–7, 500, 562.

31. *OR*, 11(1):460–2, 496–7, 500, 517–20; Congress, *Report of the Joint Committee*, 1:349–50; Fred R. Martin, "Pelham of Alabama," *Confederate Veteran* 29 (1925): 9; Olmert, *Official Guide*, 61.

CHAPTER 10

Postmortem

The battle of Williamsburg, in the words of George McClellan, "was an accident, brought about by the rapid pursuit of our troops." Having no intention of fighting there, he blamed this "accident" on his corps commanders. Once engaged, their incompetence "very nearly resulted in a most disastrous defeat," he believed, averted only by his timely arrival. "Had I been one half hour later on the field on the fifth we would have been routed & would have lost everything," McClellan informed Secretary of War Stanton. The army's organization into corps caused the loss of "at least a thousand lives," which, McClellan boasted to his wife, he could have saved "had I reached the field three hours earlier."[1]

His own failure to reach the battlefield earlier McClellan also attempted to blame on his corps commanders. Despite positive orders to keep him informed, he charged, neither Sumner, Heintzelman, nor Keyes sent word to Yorktown throughout the day that would suggest he was needed. Major Wainwright later learned from an officer who had been with McClellan in Yorktown that Sumner sent him frequent reports, "and all described matters as progressing most favourably." That may explain why the commanding general remained fourteen miles in the rear ignoring the unmistakable sounds of a full battle, but Hooker would not accept this excuse. He bitterly maintained that McClellan was told as early as 10:00 A.M. that his presence was necessary at the front, but the commanding general "showed a great indisposition to go forward," thus sacrificing Hooker's division to the corps commanders' bumbling.[2]

1. McClellan, *Own Story*, 324; Sears, *Papers of George B. McClellan*, 258–60.
2. Sears, *Papers of George B. McClellan*, 258; Nevins, *Diary of Battle*, 68; Congress, *Report of the Joint Committee*, 1:577.

And a bloody sacrifice it was. Even a casual glance at the casualty list reveals how badly Hooker's division was mauled. Every regiment in his New York and New Jersey brigades lost at least 100 men, with the 70th New York suffering the highest regimental loss of the battle—330 killed, wounded, and missing out of about 700, including 22 of its 33 officers. The New Jersey brigade, counting 1,767 aggregate present Monday morning, finished the fight with 526 fewer men, 42 of whom were officers. Of the 8,000 men Wainwright estimated Hooker took into battle, a reported 1,551, or nearly 20 percent, were killed, wounded, or missing.[3]

Hooker, along with many of his men, firmly believed that "the killed of the enemy must have been double my own," but the numbers do not bear him out. The five Confederate brigades in Longstreet's division of approximately 9,000 reported a combined loss of 1,052, just two-thirds of Hooker's total. Of these, 326 were in A. P. Hill's brigade, and the 11th Virginia sustained the division's highest regimental loss of 134. Anderson's brigade, spending much of the day in Fort Magruder and the redoubts, suffered only 91 casualties, while Cadmus Wilcox's 1,154 men, in the thickest fighting the longest, were reduced by 231 at the battle's close. The prize for the highest percentage brigade loss in this division went to Roger Pryor's at 31 percent of its 700 muskets. Out of 1,529 men George Pickett reported entering the action from his brigade, 190 were left on the field and the hospitals in town. Although Raleigh Colston's brigade was "hotly engaged," according to Longstreet, it came last to the field and its unreported loss was probably relatively small.[4]

By the time Colston arrived, Longstreet was facing another Federal division, albeit a depleted one. Kearny asserted that he reached the field with no more than 1,900 effectives after their arduous mud march and their detachments to support Emory on the left. Fewer than 1,500 men remained after a couple of hours of sharp fighting, with the 5th Michigan posting the division's largest casualty list of 144. The 38th New York lost 88, including 9, or more than one-third, of its officers. This regiment "was badly cut up, being very badly managed," in the opinion of the 40th New York's J. H. B. Jenkins, "but we lost but 4 killed, 23 wounded, and 4 missing, owing to our leaders having the judgment to place their men where such as had serviceable pieces could do execution."[5]

3. *OR*, 11(1):450; Nevins, *Diary of Battle,* 55.

4. *OR*, 11(1):468, 566–9, 587–9.

5. Kearny, *General Philip Kearny,* 250; *OR*, 11(1):450, 501; J. H. B. Jenkins to Mary Benjamin, 17 May 1862, HCH, MR-CWM.

In contrast to the 38th New York's alleged mismanagement, "General Peck's admirable disposition of his forces" was the reason given by Keyes for Peck's comparatively light loss during his afternoon fighting in the center around Telegraph Road. His entire brigade of five regiments counted only 124 fallen from its ranks while holding off "the furious onslaught of the enemy." Colonel de Trobriand, after reporting 17 casualties in his 55th New York, was disappointed to find in the abatis in front of his regiment only 15 Confederate dead. "Three hours of firing and sixteen thousand cartridges expended to kill fifteen men and put perhaps a hundred and fifty *hors de combat!*" he lamented.[6]

Participating briefly in the Confederate "onslaught" against Peck were the 2d Florida and 2d Mississippi detached from Early's brigade of D. H. Hill's division. The Florida colonel and 80 of his men fell in the fight with Peck and Kearny, yet this detachment could have suffered more had it participated with the rest of Early's brigade in the fateful charge against Winfield Hancock. Though the 23d North Carolina and 38th Virginia lost only a few to stray shots, the 24th Virginia left half its complement, nearly 200 men and 14 officers, on the half-grown wheat field. No official casualty report survives from the 5th North Carolina, but Col. Duncan McRae later wrote it had suffered 290 killed and wounded out of 410 rank and file, with 10 commissioned officers killed and 10 others wounded out of 24 who entered the fight. Hancock mentioned his men picked up 120 Confederates killed on the field, 250 wounded, and 160 prisoners for a total of 530, or nearly one-third of the total southern casualties in the entire battle.[7]

Opposing Early's two regiments, which looked to Hancock like two full brigades of 5,000 infantry plus cavalry, were five regiments estimated at about 1,600 men. The 5th Wisconsin, taking the brunt of Early's attack, suffered more casualties (79) than the other four regiments combined. Even with the artillery's loss added, Hancock's total was a relatively light 126. That brought the overall Union killed to 468, wounded to 1,442, and captured or missing to 373, or an aggregate of 2,283 out of approximately 14,600 actually engaged. Against them the Confederates fielded probably some 12,500 men, of whom maybe 1,573 were killed or wounded and another 297 captured or missing for an aggregate of 1,870.[8]

What was gained in exchange for this terrible carnage? At the close of bat-

6. *OR*, 1(11):450, 513; Wheeler, *Sword over Richmond*, 160 (quoting Regis de Trobriand, *Four Years with the Army of the Potomac* [Boston: Ticknor, 1889]).

7. *OR*, 11(1):542, 569; Maury, "Williamsburg, Va.," 117; McRae, "Williamsburg," 360.

8. *OR*, 11(1):450, 541–3; Johnson and Buel, *Battles and Leaders*, 2:200–1.

tle both armies, with the exception of Hancock, occupied the same ground they had at the opening, neither side able to claim a clear advantage over the other. When the Confederates resumed their retreat toward Richmond, the Federals immediately took possession of the earthworks and proclaimed victory. A common opinion among the Union ranks and repeated in northern newspapers asserted the redoubts were the main objective of the battle, magnifying Hancock's accomplishment. The southern army's withdrawal therefore proved its defeat. As Jenkins put it, "The backing out may have been 'military strategy' of the first water, but we *don't see it.* I suppose they will tell their people that the place was of no importance, &c, as usual, but if they spend 6 or 8 months in fortifying such unimportant points, they must intend to have 'somebody hurt' at the first place that *is* of importance, 'in a strategic point of view.'" A more perceptive analysis came from Wainwright. "The rebs evidently meant at one time to hold this line, or they would not have expended so much labour on it," he surmised. "But it is now pretty certain that they would have passed right on had we not pressed them so close."[9]

Virtually everyone in the Confederate army, from privates up, understood that Richmond was the real prize of the contest and that Joe Johnston was even less inclined to fight at Williamsburg than McClellan. Once the York and James Rivers were open to Union gunboats, the redoubts had no more strategic value to the Confederates than did the town, merely providing a convenient line from which to defend the army's rear. "It was not our desire to make a decided stand so far from Richmond," James Petty of the 17th Virginia wrote in his diary the day after the battle. "We only meant to stop long enough to cover the retreat of our trains which we accomplished." This was later confirmed by Longstreet's memoirs, "The object of the battle was to gain time to haul our trains to places of safety," and echoed by Johnston's: "We fought for no other purpose than to hold the ground long enough to enable our baggage-trains to get out of the way of the troops. This object was accomplished without difficulty."[10]

The Federals were not convinced. Although the Confederates retreated as orderly as road conditions and fatigue would allow, the northern press characterized them as "a beaten and demoralized army in full flight from imaginary as well as real terrors." William Allcot of the 62d New York sent a letter home,

9. *New-York Daily Tribune,* 10 May 1862; Jenkins to Benjamin, 17 May 1862; Nevins, *Diary of Battle,* 59.

10. James Thomas Petty Diary No. 2, 6 May 1862, MC; Longstreet, *From Manassas to Appomattox,* 79; Johnston, *Narrative,* 124.

claiming the enemy "is compleatly demorerlized and it will take a long time to make them fight again." For evidence of this charge, Allcot cited his mistaken belief that the southerners tried to burn the town before leaving, abandoned their dead and wounded, and left broken-down equipment strewn along the road out of town. According to Jenkins, "cannon, caissons, forges, wagons of all descriptions and sizes, ambulances, ammunition for all sizes and kinds of ordnance, provisions (wet and spoiled), ragged clothing, (all of the meanest description, generally butternut jeans and 'nigger-cloth') were just about *paving* some parts of the road, and horses, dead, dying, lame, serviceable, and unserviceable, were in no way scarce." The Comte de Paris considered "these trophies" to be "the most substantial proof" of the northern army's success, and "although the battle had, in reality, been undecided, its effect upon the *morale* of the two armies was entirely to the advantage of the Federals."[11]

On the contrary, "our men are in fine spirits," wrote J. E. B. Stuart's aide, Chiswell Dabney, two days after the battle, "and confident that they will always defeat the enimy whereever they appear." Whatever equipment had been lost during their "advance to the rear" was not the direct result of the battle but of the bad roads and the Confederates' haste to reach Richmond in time to concentrate for its defense. Yet northerners, eager to take credit for having "demorerlized" the southern army, all but ignored any legitimate military objectives, perhaps because they had failed to destroy or even delay their adversaries long enough to cut them off before Richmond. Upon reflection, Hooker did recognize this failure, blaming it on a lack of energetic pursuit. "I think we could have moved right on, and got into Richmond by the second day after that battle without another gun being fired," he conjectured ten months later. With less hyperbole, Pvt. Edwin Brown too believed Williamsburg should have resulted in "the successful close of the campaign. For had Franklin's Corps been promptly pushed up the York river in the transports already in waiting, and the remaining troops about Yorktown sent forward to the support of the forces facing Johnston, it is hard to conceive how Johnston could have escaped across the Chickahominy with any considerable part of his army."[12]

Williamsburg was a lost opportunity in the minds of some Confederates as well. "I have always thought that Gen. Johnston erred in not throwing his

11. *New-York Daily Tribune,* 10 May 1862; Allcot to mother, 11 May 1862, William P. Allcot Papers, MR-CWM; Jenkins to Benjamin, 17 May 1862; Comte de Paris, *Civil War in America,* 2:25.
12. Dabney to father, 8 May 1862, Saunders Family Papers, VHS; Congress, *Report of the Joint Committee,* 1:578; Edwin Y. Brown, "Battle of Williamsburg," EYB, MR-CWM.

whole force on McClellan at Williamsburg," Robertson Garrett commented nearly three decades later. "I believe he could have inflicted on him a signal defeat." Benjamin Ewell concurred. Twenty years after the war, he expressed his opinion that Johnston should have fought "a pitched decisive battle with McClellan at Williamsburg," since his gray army of 55,000 was ample "to man the redoubts, to resist McClellan in front—to send a flanking force to attack both of his Flanks, to form a sufficient reserve, & to furnish a detachment to repel any threatened movement up York River." Johnston, however, indicated that he was entirely satisfied with his limited rear-guard action, delaying the northern army far longer than the southern, diverting it from its movement to West Point, and preserving all the Confederate trains not captured by the mud. Had the Federals won the battle, as they claimed, the Confederates "should have been pursued from Williamsburg and intercepted from West Point," Johnston asserted. Longstreet pointed out the overall effect of the battle "was to call two of the divisions from their flanking move to support the battle, and this so crippled that expedition that it gave us no serious trouble." Strategically, the battle of Williamsburg, if not an outright Confederate victory, was considered by the top southern generals to be a successful rear-guard action.[13]

Victory or defeat was more often related to battlefield honor, however. Here opinion ranged widely even within each army. Many based judgment on the number of enemy banners and guns captured, the number of foemen believed killed and captured compared to one's own losses, and who finally possessed the battlefield. On the night of 6 May, James Petty reviewed the previous day's events in his diary. "The general result of the battle I have not heard," he wrote. "I know this much, however, that we captured a field battery of 8 pieces, held our own ground at every point and drove the enemy from several positions which we occupied until after night when we evacuated the field." He heard rumors that over a thousand northerners had been captured. "We left most of our wounded in the hands of the enemy, but they took few if any prisoners on the field. So," he concluded, "we got the better of the fight."[14]

Captured flags were a special source of pride. Petty's regiment took the colors of two Union regiments, and his entire brigade seized an average of two flags per regiment. The 11th Virginia's Lawrence Meem also mentioned "a quantity of flags were taken some of their splendid ones" and "six or seven

13. W. R. Garrett to CBT, 15 May 1890, TCP, MR-CWM; BSE to T. T. Gantt, 17 Aug. 1885, EFP, MR-CWM; *OR*, 11(1):276; Longstreet, *From Manassas to Appomattox*, 79.
14. Petty Diary No. 2, 6 May 1862.

guns were taken from the field," which in his opinion, "we had so gallantly won." The 11th's Lieutenant Morgan concurred with most of Longstreet's men that "we had whipped them in a fair, stand-up fight with muskets at Williamsburg." After all, he reasoned, "we drove the enemy back, held the battlefield, and marched off the next morning at our leisure." The evacuation caused Shotwell to call it "a drawn battle," though he too believed "we had whipped in all the fighting of the day," and by the time the rear guard crossed the Chickahominy River, "every man regarded it as a complete victory for us." The 2d Florida's David Maxwell likewise had no doubts that "it was a complete victory for us, for they had possession of the field in the morning & at night after eight hours hard fighting we had undisputed possession of the field." Chiswell Dabney was disappointed that the Federal landing at West Point forced the Confederates "to leave the field so gloriously won in the hands of a defeated enemy."[15]

Glorious it was too in J. E. B. Stuart's official report. There he bubbled with characteristic enthusiasm about the battle, "which terminated so gloriously to our arms," and again in a letter to his wife. "The battle of Wmsburg was fought and won on the 5th," he announced to her on 9 May. "A glorious affair, brilliantly achieved by the rear portion (Longstreets) of our army." Both Col. Micah Jenkins and General Pickett saw it as a victory that encouraged the troops and redoubled "their confidence in their own ability and cause." General Anderson, though, was not so sanguine. "Victory seemed almost within our grasp," he reported, "when night came on and put an end to the conflict." Perhaps his perspective was dampened by the death of his brother, but before receiving the other brigade reports, Anderson cautiously judged "the evidences left upon the ground show that the advantage lay largely on our side in the numbers of killed and wounded."[16]

A. P. Hill plainly stated that the battle "ended victoriously for us on the right," and D. H. Hill added that "our right, aided by my two regiments, had been completely successful, not only checking, but driving the Yankees." Harvey Hill's analysis of the debacle on the left was typically more critical. "We unquestionably lost more men than the Yankees and failed to take their guns," he admitted. Johnston made no mention of this action in his report and dismissed it as unnecessary in his memoirs, but he declared overall success in

15. Ibid., 8, 19 May 1862; John Lawrence Meem to father, 10 May 1862, VHS; Morgan, *Reminiscences*, 110–1; Hamilton, *Papers of Randolph Abbott Shotwell*, 1:198, 208; Maxwell to mother, 20 May 1862, David Elwell Maxwell Papers, VHS; Dabney to father, 8 May 1862.

16. *OR*, 11(1):570, 581, 584–6; J. E. B. Stuart to Flora Stuart, 9 May 1862, VHS.

inflicting twice the casualties and sleeping on the battlefield. Longstreet in his report called the battle "a very handsome affair" and later commented in his memoirs, "the trophies of the battle were with the Confederates, and they claim the honor to inscribe Williamsburg upon their battle-flags."[17]

The 38th and 40th New York Regiments insisted they too had the right to that particular honor, as Kearny announced at the end of the day's fighting "the victory was ours." Yet few of his subordinates were so confident they had won, even fewer in Hooker's division. Unable to admit his troops had been repulsed, Hooker steadfastly maintained, "my men stood their ground with the bayonet," but he had to concede, "we failed to capture the rebel army on the plains of Williamsburg." A day or two after the battle, McClellan noticed that Hooker "was much depressed and thought that he had accomplished nothing." Not one of Hooker's brigadiers or colonels alluded to success in their official reports, with the exception of the 73d New York's Col. William Brewster, who believed "victory was within our grasp" just before the Federal line crumbled. Heintzelman acknowledged that "our troops were driven back, some in a panic," but the addition of Kearny's division "undoubtedly defeated the enemy's rear guard." If Kearny "had arrived on the ground ten minutes later, I think," Heintzelman admitted, "we should have been defeated, for my troops were exhausted and out of ammunition."[18]

Both Heintzelman and Keyes also gave Peck credit for preventing a rout by holding the center against "the enemy when he was flushed with his success in the repulse of a portion of Hooker's division." From William Allcot's point of view with the 62d New York of Peck's brigade, "We wiped the Enemy but we had know cowardly for to deal with and meny a man was made to bite the dust before they gave way." In Keyes's opinion, "the battle of Williamsburg was gained by our side, but at a very great loss in Hooker's division, and considerable loss in Hancock's and Peck's brigades." He considered the victory "nothing like as decisive as it should have been, nor gained so early in the day. In fact the victory was not what in military language is generally called a perfect victory, because we were not able to sleep in the enemy's camp except in part." Keyes concluded that had Hancock been reinforced as early as three o'clock, "the victory would have been one of the most brilliant of the war."[19]

17. *OR*, 11(1):566, 577, 604; Johnston, *Narrative*, 124–5; Longstreet, *From Manassas to Appomattox*, 79.

18. *OR*, 11(1):453, 468, 485, 492, 499; Congress, *Report of the Joint Committee*, 1:353–4, 577; McClellan, *Own Story*, 325.

19. *OR*, 11(1):459, 514–5; Allcot to mother, 11 May 1862; Congress, *Report of the Joint Committee*, 1:603.

Had disaster befallen Hancock, he would likely be facing a court-martial for his disobedience to Sumner's repeated direct order to retire. He was fortunate instead to end up the hero rather than the goat of the battle, and McClellan's praise further elevated his accomplishment. Newspapers published McClellan's telegram the morning after the battle hailing Hancock as "superb" and another to Stanton asserting "the effect of Hancock's brilliant engagement yesterday afternoon was to turn the left of their line of works." Thus, after a twenty-three-minute fight and a relatively small loss, Hancock was all but given credit for the Federal "victory."[20]

Hooker, after fighting all day with heavy casualties, was practically ignored in McClellan's initial dispatches. In a private letter to his wife, "Little Mac" did mention that "Hooker fought nearly all day without assistance," but he never once referred to the heroic contributions of Kearny's division. These slights did not go unnoticed among Hooker's and Kearny's men. Wainwright observed, "the division is feeling somewhat sore at all the glory going to Hancock, who did but very little fighting." In a 9 May letter, Kearny confided to a friend that "at present I feel discouraged, determined to resign at the first opportunity; and my soldiers I know must feel the same. It is overheard—; it is the subject of their bitter railing! Their byword in camp is 'Hancock'; 'Hancock this' and 'Hancock that'; and my men look sulky."[21]

Two days later McClellan attempted to make up for slighting Hooker and Kearny. In a telegram to Stanton, he praised "the splendid conduct" of their men. "Hooker's division for hours gallantly withstood the attack of greatly superior numbers, with very heavy loss. Kearny's arrived in time to restore the fortunes of the day, and came most gallantly into action." McClellan tried to explain that, on the night of the battle, he spoke of Hancock only because he was in communication with the right only. That failed to appease Kearny, who had given McClellan's aide a full oral report that night. Kearny contended *his* timely arrival on the field, not McClellan's, had won the battle and thus preserved McClellan's job. He surmised the commanding general was jealous of his success and wanted to divert attention "from the culpable facts that he, McClellan had allowed Hooker's single Division to fight unsupported from the morning until near 3 P.M."[22]

Hooker, Heintzelman, and Keyes all agreed with this "culpable fact" im-

20. Sears, *Papers of George B. McClellan,* 256–7; *New-York Daily Tribune,* 8 May 1862; *OR,* 11(1):449.
21. *OR,* 11(1):448–9; Sears, *Papers of George B. McClellan,* 257; Nevins, *Diary of Battle,* 60; Kearny, *General Philip Kearny,* 244.
22. *OR,* 11(3):164–5; Kearny, *General Philip Kearny,* 218, 248.

mediately after the battle but were more inclined to blame Sumner than Mc-
Clellan. Both corps commanders sharply criticized "Old Bull" for repeatedly
refusing to support Hooker, Heintzelman alluding in his report to "the dis-
heartening circumstance that our troops knew we had three divisions idle on
their right, within hearing of their musketry," yet Sumner never ordered them
to help. Hooker carefully preserved his 11:20 dispatch from the morning of
the battle, though rain had destroyed the envelope with Sumner's endorse-
ment, for it "will have much to do in history hereafter" as evidence of Sumner's
negligence. With a flair for the dramatic, Hooker added this scathing indict-
ment to his battle report: "History will not be believed when it is told that the
noble officers and men of my Division were permitted to carry on this unequal
struggle from morning until night, unaided! in the presence of more than
30,000 of their comrades with arms in their hands; Nevertheless it is true!"[23]

Within a few days, Sumner offered an equally scathing reply to these accusations. He insisted he could not reinforce Hooker "without endangering the
center. The maintenance of that point seemed to me of the utmost importance." Though Casey's and Couch's divisions were resting only a few miles
away at Cheesecake Church, he ordered up Kearny from nine miles in the
rear, "stupid," Kearny judged, "when he had reserve troops." Publicly, Mc-
Clellan stood by Sumner's decision, but Kearny heard through camp gossip
that McClellan had "quarrelled with Sumner, for sending me to come up to
support Hooker, instead of using nearer troops." Privately, McClellan confided to his wife the day after the battle, "Sumner had proved that he was even
a greater fool than I had supposed & had come within an ace of having us
defeated."[24]

Kearny had the same opinion of Heintzelman, calling him "an old fool"
and cautioning McClellan "never to trust him without minute written instructions." During his afternoon with Hooker, Heintzelman accomplished little
but gathering a band to inspire the troops and ordering Emory to attack the
Confederate right flank. Siphoning off three of Kearny's regiments to reinforce Emory proved a mistake, as Emory considered them inadequate for his
purpose and Kearny's attack was seriously weakened without them. Neither
was Keyes a more effective corps commander. His bustling about with Hancock in the morning and searching for his tardy divisions in the afternoon

23. *OR*, 11(1):459, 468–9, 515; Joseph Hooker, "Report to Capt. C[hauncey] McKeever,"
10 May 1862, John D. Rockefeller Jr. Library, CWF.

24. *OR*, 11(1): 452; P. Kearny to A. Kearny, 8, 15 May 1862, WCP, MR-CWM; McClellan, *Own Story*, 326; Sears, *Papers of George B. McClellan*, 257.

impressed the newspaper correspondents, but the Comte de Paris interpreted his activity differently. Keyes, he concluded, was more intelligent than the befuddled Sumner but seemed "dominated by a deep repugnance for danger and a profound desire to avoid it at all costs."[25]

Division chiefs received their share of criticism, as well, especially Hooker. "Though talented," Kearny considered him "no battle soldier." Immediately after the battle Kearny told McClellan's aide that "Hooker has been beaten because he did not know his mind; I have full evidence by the field over which he fought; that he wanted to take the enemy's works but did not even think that he could do it." Wainwright, standing near Hooker through much of the battle, judged him to be "as brave as brave could be beyond a doubt. But he seemed to know little of the ground where his infantry were fighting; and I must say did not impress me at all favourably as to his powers as a general." Observed the major, "His great idea was to go ahead quick until you ran against the enemy, and then fight him."[26]

Indeed, Williamsburg was "a battle fought without a plan, with inadequate numbers, and at a serious sacrifice without compensating result," in the words of Alexander S. Webb, present on the Peninsula as Federal artillery inspector. Hooker began his attack "on the strength of the orders he had received from McClellan the previous morning, before leaving Yorktown," but within a short time the three corps commanders "had adopted another plan of action, irrespective of Hooker," Webb wrote. "There was no concerted movement; hence failure." When Sumner wanted to "push Hancock forward, Hooker's somewhat alarming situation, which had not been counted on, suddenly baffled him," according to Webb. "In a word, neither Sumner nor any one else had the entire field under his eye and control. The battle was fought by piecemeal and ended in disappointment." Before the Joint Committee on the Conduct of the War—convened to investigate, among other things, this disappointment—Chief Engineer Gen. John Barnard summed up the fight concisely: "The battle of Williamsburg, fought as it was without reconnoitring the position, without concert of action among the different corps and division commanders, and almost without orders, was a blunder which ought not to have happened."[27]

25. Kearny, *General Philip Kearny*, 244; Moore, *Rebellion Record*, 5(2):21; Grimsley and Glod, "'We Prepare to Receive the Enemy,'" 20.
26. P. Kearny to A. Kearny, 15 May 1862; Kearny, *General Philip Kearny*, 244; Nevins, *Diary of Battle*, 56.
27. Alexander S. Webb, *The Peninsula: McClellan's Campaign of 1862* (New York: Charles Scribner's Sons, 1881), 73–4, 77, 80–1; Congress, *Report of the Joint Committee*, 1:391.

Almost the identical critique was applied in southern circles to Jubal Early's botched charge on the Confederate left, generating a lively postwar controversy among several participants and interested parties. In an 1880 monograph Richard Maury of the 24th Virginia characterized the assault as "a series of blunders by generals." A year earlier John Bratton of the 6th South Carolina ignited the war of words with an article elucidating his involvement in the battle, and the 5th North Carolina colonel, Duncan McRae, immediately countered with a reply to Bratton's insinuations against him. Johnston touched only briefly on the episode in his 1874 memoir, but when Jefferson Davis jumped into the fray in his 1881 *Rise and Fall of the Confederate Government*, Johnston retorted in an article he prepared for the *Battles and Leaders* series. Longstreet's memoir, published in 1896, covered the attack in more detail, as did Early's, which was not published until after his death. Others occasionally made known their views on the subject in the various periodicals.[28]

From all the accusations and counteraccusations came a vast array of "should haves." Johnston, Longstreet, and Anderson should have been better acquainted with the field and adequately garrisoned the far left redoubts to defend that flank. When D. H. Hill requested permission to retake these lost redoubts, Johnston and Longstreet should have adamantly refused. They all should have communicated with Colonel Bratton and consulted the Jeff Davis Legion. Early's brigade should have been farther to the left by nearly the full brigade front when it formed in the wheat field or, far better, been marched all the way down the field to the road leading to Redoubt Eleven, where Hancock could have been taken from the rear. Before the brigade advanced, Early and Hill should have surveyed the ground in front more thoroughly. During the advance through the woods, skirmishers should have been thrown out ahead and precautions taken to keep the regiments closed up in line. Upon emerging from the woods, Early should have waited for all four regiments to come out and form properly in line of battle facing the enemy. Hill's other two brigades should have been brought forward immediately in support. Both Maury and McRae agreed that Hill should not have ordered a retreat just as they reached the redoubt, and Maury thought McRae should not have sent his adjutant to Hill, furnishing him with a "ready messenger, by whom to order the troops to retire." Hill's timing was unfortunate; but when the battery

28. Maury, *Williamsburg*, 5; Johnston, *Narrative*, 122–4; Jefferson Davis, *The Rise and Fall of the Confederate Government*, 2 vols. (New York: D. Appleby, 1881), 2:94; Johnson and Buel, *Battles and Leaders*, 2:204–5; Longstreet, *From Manassas to Appomattox*, 77–8; Early, *Memoirs*, 68–72.

these two regiments thought they were assaulting proved instead to be a forti-
fied redoubt defended by five regiments and ten guns, he prudently changed
his plans. The irony of attacking their own unassailable earthwork, now occupied by a superior enemy force, apparently escaped all concerned.[29]

Not surprisingly, nobody wanted to accept responsibility for this costly fiasco. In his battle report, D. H. Hill pointed out that Early proposed the attack and that he led only one regiment into the open field before the others
could join it. Longstreet likewise noted that Early was wounded "while leading his brigade in an impetuous assault on the enemy's position." Though
Longstreet complimented Hill for arranging "his forces for the attack with
excellent judgment," Early ruined these arrangements when he, "not waiting
for orders or the brigade, rode to the front of the Twenty-fourth Virginia, and
with it made the attack." Why Longstreet allowed the attack in the first place
he never explained. Perhaps he wanted Harvey Hill, who "was anxious to take
an active part in the battle," to have his own chance for glory. Hill later admitted to Longstreet that he could not think of the charge "till this day, without
horror." Equally culpable was Johnston, standing by while Hill begged Longstreet for permission. Several years after the war, in conversation with a former
23d North Carolina private, Johnston "placed the responsibility for this charge
upon General D. H. Hill. He said he did not order it made, but permitted it
only, however, after repeated requests from General Hill."[30]

Such mistakes could be expected of generals, both southern and northern,
still learning how to handle large numbers of troops in battle. In many ways
Williamsburg was a "practice battle," a proving ground for officers and men
alike. It provided the first opportunity for Longstreet to demonstrate his capa-
bilities as field commander, though as he modestly asserted, his job was "comparatively simple and easy, that of placing the troops in proper positions at
proper times." He was promoted within five months to lieutenant general and
command of the army's First Corps, a position interrupted by his wounding
in the Wilderness two years and a day after Williamsburg. Longstreet's successor as First Corps commander had been his senior brigadier at Williamsburg.
Richard Anderson "displayed great ability and signal gallantry and coolness"
during the battle and gained a major generalcy and a division two months
later. Anderson's brigade went to the Palmetto Sharpshooters' Col. Micah

29. Maury, *Williamsburg*, 6–7, 10, 16; Longstreet, *From Manassas to Appomattox*, 72–3, 77–8;
Bratton, "Battle of Williamsburg," 299–302; Johnston, *Narrative*, 124; Early, *Memoirs*, 68–9, 72;
Maury, "Williamsburg, Va.," 113–4; *OR*, 11(1):603–4, 607–8; McRae, "Williamsburg," 371–2.

30. *OR*, 11(1):565–7, 603–5, 608; Early, *Memoirs*, 70; Longstreet, *From Manassas to Appomattox*, 78; Johnston, *Narrative*, 122; Wall, "Twenty-third North Carolina Infantry," 157.

Jenkins, highly praised by Stuart as a "gallant officer and heroic commander" at Fort Magruder. General Jenkins continued as brigade commander until he was killed at Longstreet's side in the Wilderness.[31]

Some Confederate promotions resulted directly from conduct at Williamsburg and its preceding skirmish. On Sunday afternoon, Lafayette McLaws "made his dispositions with prompt courage and skill, and quickly drove the Federal troops from the field, in spite of disparity of numbers," so impressing Johnston that he was elevated to major general and assigned a division of his own on 23 May. Three days later A. P. Hill was also awarded a division and promotion after his brigade drew high praise from the division commander. "Its organization was perfect throughout the battle," Longstreet commended, "and it was marched off the field in as good order as it entered it." The following May Hill became corps commander and fought in every battle with the army until his death at Petersburg the day before Richmond fell. Two of Hill's four colonels at Williamsburg also drew promotions within a month. James Kemper, "conspicuous throughout for his daring and energy," succeeded Hill as commander of the First Brigade, continued on to major general, and after the war became governor of Virginia. Also catching Hill's eye for refusing to leave the field despite his wound, Samuel Garland earned brigade command under D. H. Hill but died at South Mountain in September. Garland's adjutant, Lt. Lawrence Meem, cited by Hill as "indefatigable in his endeavors to secure the victory," was promoted to captain and raised to Garland's chief of staff before taking a bullet through the head at Seven Pines near the end of May.[32]

Williamsburg catapulted other Confederate officers into notable careers. Extolled by Longstreet for handling his Gamecock Brigade "with great effect, ability, and his usual gallantry" in its initial combat, George Pickett survived a severe wound in June to become a major general commanding a division destined for immortality at Gettysburg. J. E. B. Stuart "was exceedingly active and zealous in conducting the different columns to their proper destinations and in assisting them to get properly into action," noticed Longstreet. As Stuart wrote his wife reassuringly soon after the battle, "I was not out of fire the whole day." His outstanding ability elevated him to major general that July and command of the Cavalry Division, then of the Cavalry Corps until his

31. Douglas Southall Freeman, *Lee's Lieutenants: A Study in Command,* 3 vols. (New York: Charles Scribner's Sons, 1970), 1:191–2; *OR,* 11(1):566–7, 572; Warner, *Generals in Gray,* 9, 155, 192–3.

32. *OR,* 11(1):275, 567, 578; Warner, *Generals in Gray,* 98–9, 135, 169–70, 204; Morgan, *Reminiscences,* 126.

death while leading a charge at Yellow Tavern two years after Williamsburg. The legendary career of Stuart's boy captain, John Pelham, was born at Williamsburg, where he demonstrated both the agility and effectiveness of his horse artillery, only to perish at Kelly's Ford in March 1863.[33]

Of all the Federal brigade commanders at Williamsburg who rose to major general before the end of the war, only Winfield Hancock gained lasting fame. Forever "the Superb," Hancock stepped up six months afterward to command a division, then a corps. He sustained a wound at Gettysburg while repulsing another desperate Confederate assault, this time by Pickett's division. At Hancock's side during the Williamsburg action that first brought him into the public eye was George Armstrong Custer, who ended the war as a cavalry general and in 1876 made his own distinctive mark on American history at Little Big Horn. His personal papers found at that time included an unfinished chapter of his war memoirs, interrupted in the middle of his detailed account of the battle of Williamsburg.[34]

In the eyes of many Union soldiers, Phil Kearny was the real hero of Williamsburg. Like Stuart, he could not resist writing his wife "that I went into the worst fire, continually exposed, a clear mark for the enemy, exposed from being the only one mounted, & was in the advance to hundreds of marksmen, who coolly fired in my face." Kearny rose to major general in July, but lack of official recognition for his accomplishments at Williamsburg continued to frustrate him until his death at Chantilly in September 1862. Hooker, however, received his major generalcy immediately after Williamsburg and by January had ascended to command the Army of the Potomac. At Chancellorsville, one year almost to the day after Williamsburg, he again displayed the lack of self-confidence and generalship that Kearny and Major Wainwright had detected in him. Legend has it Hooker picked up the sobriquet "Fighting Joe" at Williamsburg when a careless typesetter dropped the hyphen between the words in a caption. His biographer, however, could find no newspaper immediately after the battle with that coupling.[35]

Newspapers were notoriously inaccurate, anyway, in the opinion of soldiers on both sides. After perusing a battle account in the 9 May edition of a captured *New York Herald*, James Petty was "perfectly astounded at the easy facil-

33. *OR*, 11(1):567–8; Warner, *Generals in Gray*, 239, 296–7; J. E. B. Stuart to F. Stuart, 9 May 1862; Freeman, *Lee's Lieutenants*, 1:192; Boatner, *Civil War Dictionary*, 630.

34. Ezra J. Warner, *Generals in Blue: Lives of the Union Commanders* (Baton Rouge: Louisiana State University Press, 1964), 203; Carroll, *Custer in the Civil War*, 68.

35. P. Kearny to A. Kearny, 8 May 1862, WCP; Kearny, *General Philip Kearny*, 330, 407–8; Warner, *Generals in Blue*, 234, 259; Hebert, *Fighting Joe Hooker*, 91.

ity with which they lie about it." Michigan's Lieutenant Haydon expressed similar amazement that not one name was correct in his regiment's published casualty list. "Nothing has surprised me more than the astonishing & incomprehensible stupidity or untruthfulness of newspaper reporters as shown by their accounts of the battle of Williamsburgh," he jotted in his journal eleven days after the battle. "I have seen several & among all hardly a single statement was true. Their unalloyed falsity surpasses what the human mind is supposed capable of, viz to tell a long story without ever accidentally relapsing into truth." Since Williamsburg was the first battle in the eastern theater that could be considered a victory, the northern press made the most of it. Splashy "Onward to Richmond!" headlines and half-page maps of the battlefield adorned front pages. Hailed by the *New York Herald* as "the most important victory of the war," Williamsburg "avenged Bull Run," the *New-York Daily Tribune* assured its readers, and "has opened to the troops of the North a pathway (if need be) to the Gulf of Mexico," presumably to connect with the Federal army occupying New Orleans. An optimistic editorial viewed Williamsburg as a major step toward "a reconstruction of the Union."[36]

The southern press, though, viewed "our brilliant victory of Monday" as an incentive for European nations to intervene on behalf of the South to ensure its independence. This opinion, printed in the *Daily Richmond Examiner*, was intended to hearten the Confederate capital still recovering from a panic caused by news of the army's retrograde movement from Yorktown. On 8 May Richmond citizens lined the streets to gawk at 350 dust-caked Federal prisoners arriving from Williamsburg. "They were Yankees of the genuine blue," reported the *Examiner*, "runts in statu[r]e, mean and vile in physiognomy, and, as a specimen of the material to be encountered in the Peninsula, were very encouraging to southern observers." Two days later the *Richmond Enquirer* threw in more inspiring words: "The Battle of Williamsburg may well give us courage and confidence and calls for the congratulations and gratitude of the Confederacy towards the gallant men who won it—may this victory be the harbinger of many to come!"[37]

Apart from reconstruction and foreign intervention, reasons for fighting at Williamsburg varied among the common soldiers who participated in the battle. "My heart sickens at the recollection of the scenes of carnage in which we were such bloody actors," Virginian James Petty reflected the day after the

36. Petty Diary No. 2, 19 May 1862; *New York Herald*, 8, 9 May 1862; Sears, *For Country, Cause, and Leader*, 239–40; *New-York Daily Tribune*, 10 May 1862.
37. *Richmond Enquirer*,10 May 1862; *Daily Richmond Examiner*, 9 May 1862.

battle, but despite the suffering, "it is for home and loved ones, and liberty, and I am glad to be able to make the sacrifice." New Englander Edwin Brown likewise strove to justify the killing. "Better a thousand times war with all its accompaning desolation and woe, than the servile surrender of one human right," he mused while surveying the battlefield. "Better that millions of homes be made desolate, than that liberty should languish one hour in chains. Better that the land be drenched again and again in blood than human progress be stayed, or selfish indifference or greed eat out the heart of virtuous patriotism."[38]

Thus, the battle of Williamsburg proved a mutually satisfying engagement, providing both sides with heightened confidence in their respective causes and in their superiority over the other. Soon, a protracted series of battles in front of Richmond would dwarf Williamsburg and relegate it to a footnote of the Peninsula campaign. Yet throughout the three years of bloody fratricide that lay ahead, soldiers in both gray and blue would never forget their grim introduction to the realities of war on the rain-soaked plains of Williamsburg.

38. Petty Diary No. 2, 6, 8 May 1862; Brown, "Battle of Williamsburg."

Benjamin S. Ewell, president of William and Mary College, colonel of the
32d Virginia Infantry, and post commander of Williamsburg.
Courtesy University Archives, Swem Library, College of William and Mary

William and Mary College in early 1862 as a Confederate hospital. This sketch by
David E. Henderson shows the Italianate main building flanked by the
Brafferton on the left and the President's House on the right.
Courtesy Virginia Historical Society

Williamsburg, Va. the main street, courthouse of two counties on either side, one on the right used a picket station, built of brick brought from England, and where Patrick Henry said, "Give me liberty, or give me death."

Though mistaken about the location of Patrick Henry's speech, New York soldier Thomas Place rendered an accurate view of Main Street looking west toward the college at the far end, showing telegraph poles down the center and mulberry trees lining the walks. The Old Courthouse stands in the right foreground with Bruton Church's spire beyond. Williamsburg's new courthouse is shown in the left foreground next to the Methodist Church.

Courtesy Virginia Historical Society

Confederate general Lafayette McLaws supervised construction of the Williamsburg
line and commanded his troops on it during the 4 May 1862 skirmish.
*Courtesy Massachusetts Commandery Military Order of the Loyal Legion
and the U.S. Army Military History Institute*

Union general Joseph Hooker, "Fighting Joe," whose division did most
of the fighting in the 5 May 1862 battle of Williamsburg.
*Courtesy Massachusetts Commandery Military Order of the Loyal Legion
and the U.S. Army Military History Institute*

One-armed general Philip Kearny, the true Federal hero of the battle of Williamsburg.
*Courtesy Massachusetts Commandery Military Order of the Loyal Legion
and the U.S. Army Military History Institute*

Union general Winfield Scott Hancock, praised as "The Superb" after a
twenty-three-minute fight at Williamsburg.
*Courtesy Massachusetts Commandery Military Order of the Loyal Legion
and the U.S. Army Military History Institute*

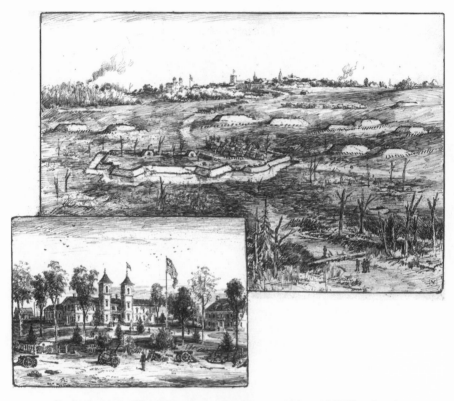

Postbattle sketch of Fort Magruder and the adjacent redoubts with Williamsburg in the background. The inset shows William and Mary under the Union flag.
Courtesy University Archives, Swem Library, College of William and Mary

A Union soldier's sketch of "Miss Bowden," probably Lemuel J. Bowden's
fifteen-year-old daughter, Mary, displaying the height of Williamsburg
fashion to welcome the northern army into town.
*Courtesy Civil War Collection, Manuscripts and Rare Books, Swem Library,
College of William and Mary*

Lithograph, circa 1860, of the Eastern Lunatic Asylum's Gothic Building with ninety-foot towers used during the battle and throughout the war for observation.

Courtesy Colonial Williamsburg Foundation

Built in 1851 on the site of the Capitol, the Female Academy was Williamsburg's first Confederate hospital in 1861 and later served as barracks for the Federal provost guard.

Courtesy Colonial Williamsburg Foundation

Williamsburg's 1856 Baptist Church, a Confederate hospital before and after the battle.
The Powder Horn, a Confederate ordnance depot, stands in the background.
Courtesy Tucker–Coleman Papers, Manuscripts and Rare Books, Swem Library,
College of William and Mary

Palace Green as depicted in an 1850s lithograph showing Robert Saunders's house,
the first Federal provost marshal's office, on the far left, with the Colemans' house
to its right rear and Letitia Semple's house on the far right.
Courtesy Colonial Williamsburg Foundation

The Vest House provided ample headquarters for Generals Johnston and McClellan in May 1862 and for the Federal provost marshal during the latter half of the war. *Courtesy Tucker-Coleman Papers, Manuscripts and Rare Books, Swem Library, College of William and Mary*

Early-twentieth-century photograph of the Tucker House with Nathaniel Beverley Tucker's office still standing in the front yard on the far left.

Courtesy Cynthia Barlowe

Lucy Anne Smith Tucker maintained her post defending the Tucker House until forced to relinquish it temporarily for refusing to take an oath of allegiance to the Federal government in the fall of 1864.

Courtesy Lucy Henry

Cynthia Beverley Tucker Washington Coleman remained in Williamsburg more
than two months after the battle, helping her mother defend the Tucker House
and verbally sparring with the Federal military governor, before "refugeeing"
into Dixie to join her husband, a Confederate surgeon.
Courtesy Cynthia Barlowe

Philip Montegu Thompson, the Tucker family's next-door neighbor and business manager, who fled Williamsburg during Wise's raid and left his sisters to guard their home.
Courtesy University Archives, Swem Library, College of William and Mary

Marble bust of Dr. John Minson Galt II, superintendent of the Eastern Lunatic Asylum from 1841 until his death May 1862, two weeks after the Federal takeover of Williamsburg.
Courtesy Eastern State Hospital

Sketch of Confederate general Henry A. Wise's 9 April 1863 raid on Williamsburg.
The artist, Provost Marshal David E. Cronin, depicted the action around the marble
statue of Lord Botetourt, with the charred ruins of the college as a backdrop.
Courtesy New–York Historical Society

Late-nineteenth-century view looking west on Main (Duke of Gloucester) Street, much as it appeared during the war. The two-story brick on the right was Virginia Slater's house, and Peggy Parsons's small frame shop immediately this side of it was the site of Capt. D. C. Hannahs's 9 September 1862 murder.

Courtesy Colonial Williamsburg Foundation

PART 3

Occupied Williamsburg

CHAPTER 11

Most Sorrowful Day

Tuesday morning, 6 May 1862, broke clear and calm in Williamsburg. "Not a soul is to be seen in the streets," remarked Cynthia Coleman, "all is quiet and still as though paralysis had stricken the City." With the Confederate army's departure, only women, children, and a few men, mostly old, remained, along with multitudes of wounded, whom Dr. Charles Coleman tended as long as possible. His mother and sister had fled their Palace home on Sunday, and before leaving at sunrise Tuesday, he begged his wife to come with him out of danger. Cynthia adamantly refused to leave her mother alone to defend the Tucker House, bravely sending Charles away with the army's rear guard. Now, however, sitting at the breakfast table with her mother, Lucy Tucker, and five-year-old daughter Sadie, the blinds closely drawn, Cynthia admitted having second thoughts. "We presented a rather scared picture notwithstanding our boasted courage when we insisted on staying behind," she later reminisced. Suddenly, Lucy's Mamy Patty burst into the room.[1]

"Oh! Lord Mistiss just look out of the window," she exclaimed. Taking care not to be seen, the ladies peaked through the blinds. "At our front gate stood a sentinel placed there by order of McClellan to protect us in our homes, though we did not understand that at the time," Cynthia vividly recalled. "I shall never forget his appearance or how I hated him." The guard was from Gen. Charles Jameson's Federal brigade, now sweeping through town and flushing out the last gray stragglers like game before dogs. Those who had slept at Sally Galt's house "at sunrise bade us good bye," she related, "& told me to make haste & efface every trace of Confederate Soldiers having been there for the enemy would be in in half an hour." Sgt. Charles Loehr and his

1. CBT, "May 5, 1862," TCP, MR-CWM; CBT, "Peninsula Campaign," TCP.

1st Virginia comrades, sleeping in a vacant building, awakened just as the last of the Confederate army left Williamsburg. Quickly gathering their baggage, these men "also turned our faces toward the West" and departed without delay. "The sun was beginning to peep above the vast forest that formed the eastern horizon" when Randolph Shotwell awoke to find the army completely gone. Off he scampered up Richmond Road, catching up to Stuart's cavalry in less than a mile. By the time Cpl. Jesse Reid walked out into the yard of his kitchen refuge after sunrise, Jameson's men were already overrunning the town, but to his relief, "none of them had quite gotten up to where we were." Reid called out the other 4th South Carolina stragglers, then they too "hastily evacuated Williamsburg. In passing the suburbs of the town we found a large quantity of clothing and blankets some of our men had left," wrote Reid. "I got as much as I wanted and went my way rejoicing."[2]

Close behind them followed Jameson's van, visible to Cynthia and her family soon after the sentinel appeared. The ladies first spied two sections of Federal artillery rumbling up Main Street. Since these guns had seen no action on Monday, Cynthia thought them "as fresh to all appearances and richly caparisoned as though no battle had been fought." Next in line came the infantry. Cynthia counted twenty-eight regiments led by Jameson's brigade and "bands of music playing Dixie, Yankee Doodle, Hail Columbia and John Brown's Body." Appropriately, the jaunty tune of "On to Richmond" also strained forth, remembered John Charles. He was only eleven at the time, but as long as he lived, he regarded this as "the most sorrowful day in Old Williamsburg's history." Cynthia too was filled with indignation at the "desecration" of the city. Despair overwhelmed her to "see for the first time the strength of the foe with whom the Southern Army must contend." How could a "little band of badly clothed badly fed patriots who foot-sore and hungry plough through mud and water on to Richmond" withstand this "great army with all its warlike appliances in gallant array"?[3]

Also admiring the invaders in spite of herself was Harriette Cary, sitting at her window near the eastern end of town. On Sunday night she had sadly watched brother Miles Cary and uncle John Henley of the Williamsburg Junior Guards march away with Magruder's troops. Now, living in her grandmother's two-story frame house on Main Street, Harriette had a front-row

2. CBT, "Peninsula Campaign"; *OR*, 11(1):497; SMG to cousin, 15 Apr. 1863, GFP, MRCWM; Loehr, "First Virginia Infantry," 109; Hamilton, *Papers of Randolph Abbott Shotwell*, 1:204; Reid, *Fourth Regiment of S. C. Volunteers*, 83.
3. CBT, "May 5, 1862"; John S. Charles, "Recollections of Williamsburg, Virginia, as It Was at the Beginning of the Civil War," 1928, John D. Rockefeller Jr. Library, CWF, 5, 55.

seat for the grand entry of the northern army. "It seems finely organized and most splendidly equipped—the men robust and well uniformed—especially the officers," she conceded in her diary, "yet the utter detestation with which I regard these vandals engenders a disgust which I would not feel for the vilest man on our Southern Soil." A friendlier reception greeted Jameson's men on the other end of town at Frog Pond Tavern across Richmond Road from the college. John Charles passed along the tradition that on this day the proprietor, Old Jucks, "highly excited and greatly alarmed, as every one else was, went out in front of his house, from the porch of which hung a white flag; and with hat in hand made a polite bow to the advance guard of McClellan's vast army, and exclaimed, 'Good morning Gentlemen—Come in, and have some hot biscuits and coffee.'"[4]

Frog Pond Tavern was as far as Jameson's brigade advanced before being put into camp around the college by order of McClellan, still at the Whittaker House. More relieved than disappointed that he would not be facing the Confederate army with his "considerably inferior" force that morning, McClellan had his staff saddle up about nine o'clock for a tour of the battlefield. They first headed to Hancock's position on the right, where "fifteen or twenty men are lying in the middle of a field of green wheat," wrote the Comte de Paris of his first encounter with the enemy. "They are dead, dead in strange positions which picture the fight in which they died. Their graves are already dug beside them, while all around us mounds of freshly-dug earth hide most of the victims from our sight and yet reveal their number to us." A *New York Evening Post* correspondent, signing his name "Mack," noticed that one of the dead "was in the act of raising his gun to fire, and had stiffened in the same position—another was opening his cartridge-box and had died in the attempt—a third was evidently retreating, and had fallen with his back to our advance—a fourth clasped his hands to his pistol and so received the fatal shot."[5]

Many bodies had already been carried into nearby redoubts. Ninety-six dead and wounded of the 5th North Carolina, "lying in the mud just as they had been carried in from the field," filled one redoubt in which the men of the 104th Pennsylvania awakened early and hungry after two days without rations. Close by, a burying party was collecting more of "the enemy's dead, and preparing to consign them to the narrow trench that shortly received their mortal

4. HC Diary, 6 May 1862, MR-CWM; Charles, "Recollections," 4–5.

5. *OR*, 11(1):448–9; Grimsley and Glod, "'We Prepare to Receive the Enemy,'" 24–5; Moore, *Rebellion Record*, 5(2):23.

remains." Col. William Davis was appalled by the "heart-rending groans, and pitiable condition" of the wounded as well as "the unsympathizing gaze of the lookers on." De Paris, however, marveled that "despite their own exhaustion the troops of Smith's division spent the night gathering the wounded, showing the same concern for the enemy as for their own comrades."[6]

Davis's Pennsylvanians formed the advance as the party marched the entire length of the field along the country road toward Fort Magruder. "Bodies were seen every few yards—in the road, along the sides of the road, in the grass and grain, in the ditches and along the fences," recounted Davis. McClellan and his staff followed behind, inspecting the numerous rifle pits and redoubts, "shrewdly located and admirably built," in the newspaperman's estimation. Continuing into Fort Magruder, "much damaged by our artillery fire," the party found one abandoned siege gun, several broken caissons, and some ammunition. From the fort's ramparts, "all spyglasses are turned toward Williamsburg," wrote de Paris. "Yellow hospital flags float above all the buildings but nothing else reveals the presence of the enemy."[7]

The inspection tour then passed out of Fort Magruder. Many nearby trees had been "splintered by our shells," Mack informed his readers, "and the barracks on the Williamsburgh side were more or less shattered. Our men were exploring them, finding bacon, flour, and hominy, garments, muskets, and filth." While examining the ground on the Federal left, the party picked up Heintzelman, then Hooker, "still covered with mud, very moved as a leader who has just lost some of his finest troops, but calm and determined," in the opinion of de Paris. "He says he has 2,000 men *hors de combat* but that he inflicted at least as many casualties on the enemy." Some of these they found in a cluster of barracks, where McClellan dismounted and entered. The buildings were filled with both Union and Confederate wounded "lying together in perfect amity who had met in mortal combat the day before." The first man McClellan approached was one of his own. "In reply to my question as to how they had been treated by the enemy he said: 'Just like their own men.'" The commanding general then remounted and continued westward.[8]

As McClellan and his entourage approached the first house on the eastern end of Williamsburg about 11:00 A.M., they came across "a fieldpiece sunk in

6. Davis, *104th Pennsylvania*, 69; Grimsley and Glod, "'We Prepare to Receive the Enemy,'" 25.

7. Davis, *104th Pennsylvania*, 69; Moore, *Rebellion Record*, 5(2):23; Grimsley and Glod, "'We Prepare to Receive the Enemy,'" 25.

8. Moore, *Rebellion Record*, 5(2):23–4; Grimsley and Glod, "'We Prepare to Receive the Enemy,'" 25; McClellan, *Own Story*, 337–8.

mud up to its hubs, its ammunition scattered over the ground." Upon reaching the town streets, "our horses floundered about as though in an extended quagmire, and the mud flew in every direction," grumbled Mack. "For much of the way, even in the best street, we were obliged to drive upon the side-walks, and their condition was far from inviting." De Paris took more interest in the structures they passed on Main Street. "Every house is situated in the middle of a garden at the end of which are sheds of rough-hewn wood, randomly built in all corners," he observed. "The larger ones are used for storage, the medium ones are inhabited by Negroes and the smaller ones by pigs and poultry." He thought the Powder Horn resembled a pigeon house and was surprised to see many inhabitants out on their verandas watching the procession from their rocking chairs. Mack, however, noticed few white persons on the street but many white flags hoisted on the houses "and the yellow bunting freely displayed, indicating what we soon found to be the fact, that the city was filled with the enemy's dead, wounded, and sick." He also commented that "the shops and stores were, with scarcely an exception, closed, and seemed to have been abandoned for some length of time. On several of them were notices to the effect that they had been closed for want of goods, probably a correct announcement."[9]

The black population, however, was well represented. "A large crowd of Negroes rushes toward us from all sides," recorded de Paris in his journal. Mack wrote: "Negroes of every shade and size gazed at us from the streets and yards, and carefully watched our advent. There was much bowing and scraping on the part of the dusky spectators, and an evident relief at our occupation of the town." Although the correspondent "entered into conversation with several of the intelligent, and found their knowledge of the war and its causes very clear and complete," the Frenchman had a different impression. "They are strange," he concluded; "even after spending nine months in slave states I cannot look upon them without laughing."[10]

Unwilling to make war on these helpless civilians, white and black, Jameson had already "placed guards at all the principal houses" in town and "protected all persons and property." The town also had to be searched for materiel of war as well as southern stragglers, sick, and wounded. Harriette Cary's diary tells how "a fine looking Officer with two men very respectfully announced

9. Grimsley and Glod, "'We Prepare to Receive the Enemy,'" 25; Moore, *Rebellion Record*, 5(2):24.

10. Grimsley and Glod, "'We Prepare to Receive the Enemy,'" 26; Moore, *Rebellion Record*, 5(2):24.

this morning their orders to search, which was but *nominal*—a glance at each room seemed only necessary—all houses were subjected to the same with more or less scrutiny." Sally Galt was also relieved to discover the dreaded search not so bad, for "so far from tearing the house to pieces as I had thought they would they were very polite & agreeable & some very elegant officers amongst them not withstanding our prejudice to them." At eight o'clock that morning, "the enemy came by the Asylum," reported Dr. Galt in his diary entry for 6 May, the last he would write. "I went out & addressed the Colonel, telling him that I was the Superintendent & I supposed that this house would be included in the protection. He simply smiled & observed that he would attend to this."[11]

Another young Federal presented himself at the door of widow Elizabeth Ware's house on Main Street, one block down from the college. As instructed, he politely inquired "if there were any sick or wounded soldiers there," whereupon Mrs. Ware ushered him into the parlor. There lay the body of a Confederate boy she and her daughter had attended during the battle. "Upon removing the sheet that covered the face of the corpse, the sorrowful fact was revealed that the live Union Soldier was the Brother of the dead Confederate lad," remembered John Charles, who lived nearby. The ladies stood around the room weeping "as the Soldier in 'Blue' knelt by the bier and implanted a kiss on the brow of his dead Brother, clad in 'Confederate Gray.' Soon an ambulance arrived, the corpse was placed therein and driven away—thus grimly demonstrating the truth of the expression so often heard, that this War was one of 'Father against son, Brother against Brother.'"[12]

Passing by this house, McClellan and his escort rode to the college, "from the roof of which the Stars and Stripes caught the breeze," wrote Mack, "and our signal corps had already established a station communicating with the several divisions of the army." De Paris described the college yard "filled with discarded small arms now broken or rusted by the rain," and Mack added, "the fences prostrate, the stone gate-posts overturned, the sod and trees destroyed, and even the marble statue of Baron de Botetourt disfigured and begrimed with mud." A group of Confederate wounded and prisoners "gathered on the steps beneath the arcade," some without uniforms, others in "ash-gray tunics stained by the dust, mud, and blood." De Paris was struck by their seeming

11. *OR*, 11(1):497; HC Diary, 6 May 1862; SMG to cousin, 15 Apr. 1863; John Minson Galt II Diary, 6 May 1862, GFP.
12. Charles, "Recollections," 11–2.

indifference "to everything and everyone. Their general expression has a savage quality, their rough and strange faces betray deep humiliation."[13]

In the main building "the spectacle of suffering" that met McClellan and his party almost overwhelmed them. Wounded lay everywhere amid blood and filth, some on straw, some on the stretchers that brought them in. Wounds festered undressed, "here and there the stiff bodies of those who had died in the night were lying in utter neglect," Mack recited. In one room he counted a half dozen dead and found "one poor fellow, whose skull was crushed, had slipped from his cot out on the floor, and was dying in dreadful agony." De Paris thought the conscious displayed "good spirits despite their suffering. In the midst of so much misery I do not hear any complaint."[14]

Making his way up the stairwells, choked with rubbish and filth, McClellan entered a room on the second floor filled with the wounded of the Excelsior Brigade, including the 70th New York's Col. William Dwight, stretched on a cot in the center. His leg wound had been only partially dressed, yet Dwight displayed "the good humor that won for him so many friends," wrote de Paris, delighted to see a familiar face among "these wretched scenes." In answer to McClellan's commendation for his conduct on the field, Dwight "stated that he would not have given up, but for the severity of his wound," Mack related, "and that the approbation of his commanding officer more than compensated for his suffering." McClellan ordered him moved into a nearby private home "and attended by a skilful surgeon."[15]

More doctors were needed to handle not only the wounded already there, but also the many from both sides now being carried into town from the field. Since few Confederate surgeons had remained behind, Jameson "sent a mediator to tell Johnston that any doctor would be received on parole and that our surgeons would do everything possible to help." McClellan assured the Confederate wounded that "although I was perhaps the most brutal among the Northern generals, I would treat them precisely as I did my own wounded," then directed his chief surgeon, Dr. Charles S. Tripler, to summon fifteen Federal doctors of the volunteer corps from Yorktown. After issuing "the necessary orders to organize the hospital," McClellan rode a little past

13. Moore, *Rebellion Record,* 5(2):25–6; Grimsley and Glod, "'We Prepare to Receive the Enemy,'" 26.

14. Grimsley and Glod, "'We Prepare to Receive the Enemy,'" 26; Moore, *Rebellion Record,* 5(2):25.

15. Moore, *Rebellion Record,* 5(2):26; Grimsley and Glod, "'We Prepare to Receive the Enemy,'" 26.

the college to await Col. William Averell's 3d Pennsylvania Cavalry, which he had ordered to the front earlier that morning.[16]

Before long the troopers trotted up, having traversed the battlefield "with all its horrors" from their bivouac in Kingsmill and splashed through the streets of Williamsburg. McClellan instructed them "to go forward until the rear guard of the enemy was found and then report the position it occupied." Upon leaving the hospital, about noon, McClellan's staff spotted a group of gray officers surrounded by an escort of blue cavalry returning down Richmond Road. A curious crowd formed around the eighteen Confederate surgeons Johnston sent "under a flag of truce, to offer their services in tending their own wounded." At first they appeared "worried and embarrassed," sitting on their horses and clutching their instrument cases, until their leader dismounted and introduced himself as Dr. John Cullen, Longstreet's chief surgeon. "He has a soldier's posture and a gentleman's manners," de Paris noted with approval. "After five minutes, like a true American, he is at ease with everyone." McClellan asked the doctor "for news about all the secesh generals, his classmates and comrades in the army." Others joined in, and soon they were "chatting with our officers as if they had all campaigned together."[17]

After giving these physicians permission to visit their wounded, McClellan took them back through town to the Vest House, where his headquarters flag and the Stars and Stripes now floated from the central upper window. There he entertained them "as well as could be done without baggage or supplies." Later that day McClellan wrote his wife that he had "taken possession of a very fine house which Jo Johnston occupied as his Hd Qts—it has a lovely flower garden & conservatory—if you were here I would be much inclined to spend some weeks here." With convenient stables below the garden, lavish furnishings, and two servants left behind by the Vests, the mansion was comfortable and well suited for a military headquarters. Stone steps led up from the sidewalk into a wide central hallway running through the house. A spacious drawing room occupied the front of the east wing and contained a long, broad mahogany table. To the rear of the drawing room, a chamber had been converted into a bedroom for the commanding officer, and the upstairs bedrooms could accommodate several of his large staff. Others were forced to seek

16. Grimsley and Glod, "'We Prepare to Receive the Enemy,'" 26; McClellan, *Own Story,* 338; "William and Mary College as a Hospital," *William and Mary Quarterly,* 2d ser., 19 (1939): 181; Rawle et al., *Third Pennsylvania Cavalry,* 48, 51.

17. Rawle et al., *Third Pennsylvania Cavalry,* 48, 51; Moore, *Rebellion Record,* 5(2):25; Grimsley and Glod, "'We Prepare to Receive the Enemy,'" 26; McClellan, *Own Story,* 333, 338.

shelter elsewhere. Harriette Cary mentioned in her diary that one staff member applied to her grandmother for rooms but was refused.[18]

Other generals were also settling into such accommodations as they could find. Heintzelman chose Dr. John Mercer's home on the eastern end of town, using the doctor's office in the front yard as convenient quarters for his staff. On the western end, in the front yard of the college, Jameson took over the brick building known as the Brafferton for his headquarters, since McClellan appointed him military governor. Across the lawn from the Brafferton, the President's House still contained Rebecca Ewell, who invited Phil Kearny, a prewar acquaintance of her brother Maj. Gen. Richard Ewell, to stay with her. Perhaps Mack the correspondent was referring to Rebecca when he commented that Williamsburg ladies "were disposed to treat our army with respect—refused to accept pay for such simple refreshments as they were able to provide, and opened their houses for our officers, but had nothing to say in favor of the old Government or the old flag."[19]

One matron who did not fit this description was the widow Mrs. Helen Anderson, a self-described "aged Female of this City." She addressed McClellan as "Illustrious Sir" in a note soon after his arrival at the Vest House, earnestly "soliciting your Protection for myself, Household and property under the present truly distressing circumstances." Another "old maiden lady in all the amplitude of excessive hoop skirts" decided to accost the commanding general personally. As Cynthia Coleman told the story, this lady found McClellan "at his headquarters surrounded by his staff, some of whom represented the flower of French nobility, and requested him to furnish her with a guard 'if there was such a thing as a gentleman in the Yankee army.'" She then mounted "an assault upon the unfortunate soldier deemed worthy to act as her protector," for his whistling on duty "greatly offended her as being an infringement upon her dignity and importance." When told his brother had been killed in battle, she relented and "offered him a cup of tea, which he declined, 'fearing it might be made of gunpowder.'" This episode, Cynthia concluded, demonstrated that "the milk of human kindness" could still be

18. Moore, *Rebellion Record*, 5(2):25; McClellan, *Own Story*, 338; HC Diary, 6 May 1862; David Edward Cronin, "The Vest Mansion," 1908–10, John D. Rockefeller Jr. Library, CWF, 2–3; Grimsley and Glod, "'We Prepare to Receive the Enemy,'" 26; Sears, *Papers of George B. McClellan*, 258.

19. Edward R. Crews, "The Battle of Williamsburg," *Colonial Williamsburg Journal* 18 (summer 1996): 18–9; P. Kearny to A. Kearny, 7, 8, May 1862, WCP; Moore, *Rebellion Record*, 5(2):25.

found among the proudest southerners and that "the Yankee in the midst of a great sorrow was not devoid of a sense of humor."[20]

Fear of poisoning was no laughing matter to another Federal, who happened into the yard of Williamsburg painter Thomas Whiting. To prevent her hired slaves from running away to the Union army, Mrs. Whiting told them "that the Yankees were devils, with horns on their heads, and that they would make us all pull the artillery guns," related Eliza Baker, one of her hired servants then in her late teens. Eliza told of a man who came up to her and asked "how I liked the Yankees. And I said, 'I don't know, Sir, I ain't seen none.'" When he informed Eliza he was one, she retorted, "'You can't be, 'cause Mrs. Whiting told us the Yankees have horns.'" The soldier had Eliza take him to Mrs. Whiting, "told her she shouldn't frighten us slaves about the Yankees," and requested a drink of water from her well. "He asked her did she have any strychnine in it?" Eliza continued the story. "She said she wouldn't think of such a thing. But he made her get a dipper and bucket and two glasses, and he made her drink two glasses of the water before he would taste it."[21]

Soon bluecoats blanketed Williamsburg, as each division spread its tents over its assigned campsite. Supply wagons appropriated spacious Courthouse Green, and the cavalry took over Palace Green, "covered with its golden shower of buttercups." There Averell's troopers encamped after going about four miles up Richmond Road and returning with five abandoned guns, "a large number of small arms," and, by Averell's count, twenty-one gray stragglers too exhausted and starved to keep up with the army. On Palace Green these blue horsemen had their first encounter with Williamsburg's formidable ladies. "As the day advanced," wrote Cynthia Coleman, "finding we were not molested we decided to go out and look after our dear soldiers who had been wounded in the Battle and had been carried to the Episcopal and Baptist Churches." Obliged to cross Palace Green on their way to Bruton Church, she and her neighbor Isabella Sully, "with baskets in hand and faces closely veiled," joined other groups of two or three ladies winding their way around the men and horses. "They took no notice of us nor we of them."[22]

The condition of the churchyard looked bad enough. "On the grounds amidst the monuments and tents, the wounded had all been placed, and every

20. Helen Maxwell Anderson to George B. McClellan, 6 May 1862, Helen M. Anderson Papers, John D. Rockefeller Jr. Library, CWF; CBT, "Occupancy," TCP.

21. Eliza Baker, "Memoirs of Williamsburg," 1933, John D. Rockefeller Jr. Library, CWF, 1–2.

22. *OR*, 11(1):436; Rawle et al., *Third Pennsylvania Cavalry*, 48, 52; CBT, "Peninsula Campaign"; CBT, "May 5, 1862."

spot was baptized with blood, and even on the white slabs were the traces of human suffering," a Union chaplain recorded. A far worse "scene of horror" met the ladies when they entered the church. Dead and dying lay all around; seats were torn up; "beds, cots, and stretchers extended over the whole building"; and streams of blood flowed in every direction. Cynthia approached the chancel. "One poor fellow the most splendid looking man I ever saw," Cynthia declared, "lay in so natural a position that I thought he still lived, but on bending over him I found him one of the Immortals." Beside him "a wounded comrade with quivering lip said, 'He is dead Madam.'"[23]

An even more heartrending spectacle awaited the ladies at the Baptist church. "In the vestibule lay a negro," Cynthia wrote. "How he came to be on the battle field I never could ascertain, but he was not fighting, notwithstanding he had been severely wounded in both feet and I was told the Federal Surgeon had '*sawed* them off.' Perhaps, it was the most merciful way to do the work, but it filled me with a sickening horror which I feel to this day." Hurrying out of there, Cynthia and Isabella entered the Old Courthouse, now a morgue containing twenty-five dead, among them Col. George Ward of the 2d Florida. His body lay extended upon the clerk's table with the note his men pinned on his coat giving his name and requesting decent interment. Florida soldier David Maxwell later heard that the people of Williamsburg buried his colonel in Bruton Churchyard, assisted by a West Point classmate of Ward from the Federal Horse Artillery and a file of his soldiers. Rev. Thomas Ambler read the service, and Ward was placed in the first grave dug near the north wall. A captain Isabella had known at her former home in Alexandria and found dead in the church was immediately laid to rest beside him. They wrapped the captain in his blanket, for no coffin could be procured.[24]

Nor did the colonel have the dignity of a coffin, according to Richard Bucktrout's ledger, which records Ward's burial. The undertaker kept busy on 6 May furnishing coffins and cases and packing up bodies of five Federal officers, "shot at the battle below Williamsburg by agreement with the Chaplin of the Regiment and also one of the Cols," scrawled Bucktrout. The agreement for twenty dollars covered Bucktrout's services and shipment of the coffins home to New Jersey. None of these accounts charged to the slain officers' estates was ever marked "Paid" in his ledger.[25]

23. Rev. J. J. Marks, *The Peninsular Campaign in Virginia, or Incidents and Scenes on the Battle-fields and in Richmond* (Philadelphia: J. B. Lippincott, 1864), 162; CBT, "May 5, 1862"; CBT, "Peninsula Campaign."

24. CBT, "Peninsula Campaign"; CBT, "May 5, 1862"; Isabella Sully to CBT, 30 Oct. 1890, TCP; Maxwell to mother, 20 May 1862, David Elwell Maxwell Papers, VHS.

25. Richard M. Bucktrout Day Book, 6 May 1862, MR-CWM.

To relieve some of the overcrowded hospitals, the townswomen made arrangements, with their captors' permission, to transfer moveable wounded into private homes where the people were willing and able to care for them. Lucy Tucker accepted four men whom Cynthia found in Bruton Church—the severely wounded Col. Lewis Williams, Lt. Edward P. Reeve, and Pvt. James Dooley, all of the 1st Virginia; and Pvt. Van Taliaferro of the 11th Virginia. The Southalls took in two wounded, and the Amblers sheltered the 19th Mississippi's hero, Capt. Jacob Macon, until he died of his thigh wounds, then accepted Lt. William M. Richardson of the 17th Virginia. William Peachy and his family had their hands full with Maj. William Payne. The ball that hit him had penetrated his jaw, breaking the bone and knocking out four teeth, all of which passed through his tongue and broke three more teeth on the other side before coming out near the jugular vein. Nobody expected Payne to live— the Richmond papers listing him as mortally wounded—but the Peachys did all they could to make him as comfortable as possible.[26]

Despite his suffering, Payne was relatively fortunate, for besides the four hundred or so Confederate wounded in town, at least another four hundred were still on or near the battlefield. One newspaper correspondent reported seeing eighty-two wounded gray soldiers on cornhusks in an old barn near Hancock's position. In another barn, housing both Union and Confederate casualties, Capt. John W. Lea of the 5th North Carolina, suffering with a wounded leg, lay in a stall moaning that "all he has left out of 89 men is 5 and they are wounded with himself." Before the war Lea had attended the U.S. Military Academy, where he was known as "Gimlet" to his classmates, one of whom was more than a little surprised to stumble upon him here. "When we first saw each other he shed tears and threw his arms around my neck," Lieutenant Custer wrote his sister, "we talked over old times and asked each other hundreds of questions concerning our classmates who were on opposite sides of the contest." Bystanders asked Custer if the two of them were brothers.[27]

Custer was just one of the many Federal officers and men wandering around the battlefield that day. Some explored the redoubts, while others, including the 40th New York's J. H. B. Jenkins, sought replacements for their

26. CBT, "Peninsula Campaign"; Wallace, *1st Virginia Infantry*, 29; H. T. Jones, "Wounded at Williamsburg, Va.," *Southern Historical Society Papers* 24 (1894): 172–5; Bucktrout Day Book, May 1862; Mrs. William H. Payne, "Search for My Wounded Husband," 1910, VHS, 1–2, 8–9.

27. *New-York Daily Tribune*, 10 May 1862; Allcot to mother, 11 May 1862, William P. Allcot Papers, MR-CWM; Morris Schaff, *The Spirit of Old West Point, 1858–1862* (Boston: Houghton, Mifflin, 1907), 180; George Armstrong Custer to Lydia Reed, 15 May 1862, Little Bighorn Battlefield National Monument, Crow Agency, Mont.

faulty Austrian rifles. "I succeeded in finding a U.S. Harper's Ferry rifled musket, which is a splendid weapon," he informed his lady friend. "Numbers of our boys secured those pieces, & Austrians are at a heavy discount." Most were looking for other men in their units who had scattered during the confusion of battle. Among them was Major Wainwright, upset over losing four cannons but overjoyed to discover Captain Bramhall and his lieutenant unharmed. "I had heard nothing of them, since the capture of their battery," Wainwright wrote, "and was more affected at finding them alive and safe than by all the casualties of the day before." Lt. Charles Haydon also spent the day searching for 2d Michigan comrades and collected about 450 by evening. The 55th New York's Col. Regis de Trobriand found many of his boys in a "farmhouse transformed into a hospital," where the "patients were laid on the ground on beds of straw." He was amazed how "all showed a remarkable courage and bore their sufferings with a tranquil resignation. The most boastful were even laughing, and spoke of soon retaking their places in the ranks." A more depressing atmosphere pervaded another house crowded with Confederate wounded being treated by a Federal surgeon. "A little stream of coagulated blood reddened the steps" de Trobriand noticed as he approached, and amputated limbs were piled behind the door. Inside, the "mutilated creatures turned their eyes, hollow with suffering, towards me, the greater part of them listless but a few with an air of having a shade of defiance."[28]

Soldiers wandering the battlefield were greeted by even more ghastly sights, especially for those experiencing a battle's aftermath for the first time. Shock mixed with morbid curiosity as they walked among the dead, "lying so thickly on the ground that, in some places, it was necessary either to pick your way or step on the body of some dead or wounded soldier half-buried in the mud." To the 62d New York's William Allcot, the sight was worse than the battle itself. "Dear Ma it is nothing to go into battle but after the battle it is orfull to look around and see so meney dead lying in all shapes ho a feiw houers before was full of life and as active as I am but such is War," he wrote a few days later. "I passed over the Battle field on the morning of the 6th. I volinteared to go and look up the dead and wounded if thear was eney and such a site met my eyes I hope and pray I may never see again." Many lay in grotesque, almost lifelike, positions. "In the fallen timber a reb was found who

28. Moore, *Rebellion Record*, 5(2):24; J. H. B. Jenkins to Mary Benjamin, 17 May 1862, HCH, MR-CWM; Nevins, *Diary of Battle*, 58–9; Sears, *For Country, Cause, and Leader*, 233; Wheeler, *Sword over Richmond*, 161–2 (quoting Regis de Trobriand, *Four Years with the Army of the Potomac* [Boston: Ticknor, 1889]).

had one hand in the pockets of a Union soldier and had been shot while lean-ing over a log and rifling the pockets of his enemy," wrote Alfred Bellard of the 5th New Jersey. A man "standing on his hands & knees with his head shot off" caught Haydon's attention, and nearby "a friend and foe were found, each tightly clutching his rifle, each having the other's bayonet in his body, and both dead on the ground." Another soldier came upon a comrade still aiming over the branch of a fallen tree, but he was dead, "shot through the brain; and so suddenly had the end come that his rigid hand grasped his musket, and he still preserved the attitude of watchfulness, literally occupying his post after death."[29]

Some observers were fascinated with the variety of facial expressions. "Over by yon little breast-work of rails a face of horror stares at me distorted with passion and hate, the cold lips still framed in an expiring curse," noticed Edwin Brown while touring the field. "Nearer by, in strong contrast is the fair face of youth whose mouth still parts in the expression of a cheer. Some are frightfully disfigured with wounds; but the most of them are faces of peace and repose, their eyes fixed and vacant, yet full of pathos." The 40th New York's Sergeant Floyd perceived a sectional difference in the countenances of the dead. "Our soldiers had generally died with pleasant expressions of face," he asserted, "but the rebel dead bore a more anxious look at the moment of death, and the skin was the pale hue of sulphur, instead of white like the faces of the Union victims."[30]

That morning the Mozarters had buried their comrade whose brains had been blown out, the first member of Floyd's company to be killed in battle. They placed him "near the roadside where he fell, and those who saw his man-gled head were awed by the sad spectacle." Most bodies were interred as quickly as possible. Fatigue parties spent the day digging large trenches fifty to one hundred feet long, six to eight feet wide, and two or three feet deep. Corpses, grouped by regiment, were placed in the trenches "side by side, with marble features, glassy eyes, and in their torn and bloody uniforms," de Trobri-and noted. The ditch was then filled and "covered over with a little hillock to provide for settling." For Union dead, the burial parties placed at the head of the deceased a piece of cracker box with the name, company, and regiment.

29. Burns, *Battle of Williamsburgh*, 51, 54; Allcot to mother, 11 May 1862; Sears, *For Coun-try, Cause, and Leader*, 234; Donald, *Gone for a Soldier*, 68; Johnson and Buel, *Battles and Leaders*, 2:199.

30. Edwin Y. Brown, "Battle of Williamsburg," EYB, MR-CWM; Floyd, *Fortieth (Mozart) Regiment New York*, 147.

Confederate dead they "decently buried" but necessarily without identification.[31]

Live Confederates occupied the attention of the 40th New York that afternoon. After moving their camp beyond the battlefield to the eastern edge of
town, the Mozarters watched with curiosity as stragglers captured by Averell's
cavalry paraded in. "These prisoners were clad in all sorts of uniforms, and
there were many strange specimens of humanity among them," commented
Sergeant Floyd. The southerners' odd accents and use of "you uns" and "we
uns" these New Yorkers interpreted as ignorance, and their "reckless, defiant
attitude" irritated their captors. Fingering a South Carolinian's uniform but-
ton bearing a palmetto tree and the motto *"Animis opibusque parati"* on the
face, Floyd asked the prisoner what it meant. "Give the d——n Yankees fits"
was the gray soldier's loose translation of "Prepared in mind and resources."[32]

Resources still presented a problem for McClellan, for with the roads so
muddy, he could not bring the supply trains up to feed his men, "many of
whom have had nothing to eat for 24 hours & more." His own baggage had
not yet arrived when, that afternoon, he complained in a letter to his wife, "I
had no dinner yesterday, no supper, a cracker for breakfast & no dinner yet."
The commanding general had not been able to change his clothes or boots
and "could not even wash my face & hands," he added. At the other end of
town, Kearny's baggage finally reached him later that night. As a guest of Rebecca Ewell, the general had plenty of food for body and ego. "She knew all
about me," Kearny later informed his wife. Rebecca's brother Richard Ewell
had told her, "in the secession army, that they all said, that I was bound to be
a good officer."[33]

As darkness closed Williamsburg's first day under the "degrading yoke" of
humiliating "Yankee despotism," wrote Harriette Cary, "all is quiet, and being
assured of protection by two sentinels placed at our door, I shall seek repose."
Her thoughts and prayers that night were with "my dear relatives and friends"
in Confederate gray just settling into camp near Burnt Ordinary, ten miles
west of Williamsburg. Although General Johnston and his staff, floundering
out of one mud hole and into another, passed Burnt Ordinary about sunrise
that morning, the rear guard dragged into camp some time after dark. The

31. Floyd, *Fortieth (Mozart) Regiment New York,* 147; Nevins, *Diary of Battle,* 57; Peterson,
"Battle of Williamsburg," 272; Wheeler, *Sword over Richmond,* 161 (quoting de Trobriand, *Four
Years*); Donald, *Gone for a Soldier,* 69; *OR,* 11(1):499.

32. Floyd, *Fortieth (Mozart) Regiment New York,* 147.

33. Sears, *Papers of George B. McClellan,* 257; P. Kearny to A. Kearny, 7, 8, 15 May 1862,
WCP.

men formed in line of battle and arrayed the artillery, anticipating attack, but fortunately the Federal soldiers had no more interest in renewing the fight than the Confederates and remained snug in their camps around Williamsburg. For the first time in four nights, both armies enjoyed an uninterrupted sleep.[34]

Wednesday, 7 May, was another lovely spring day on Virginia's Peninsula, opening with a clash at Eltham's Landing opposite West Point. There an infantry brigade and some cavalry of G. W. Smith's division drove Brig. Gen. William Franklin's division, which had finally ascended the York River, back to the shelter of its gunboats. In Williamsburg "the Federal army is still moving and seems exhaustless," Harriette remarked in her diary. All day she watched "artillery, infantry and cavalry going up and coming down incessantly. Yankee maneuvers—in double quick time. God grant us a retreat as double again!" The roads had improved enough for McClellan to send two infantry regiments and more cavalry in pursuit. After picking up some abandoned guns and stragglers, the cavalry advance met a section of John Pelham's Horse Artillery near Burnt Ordinary and retired with casualties. Before long, rumors started filtering back into Williamsburg. "Richmond is taken," was one Harriet caught from passing soldiers. "Magruder captured with 12,000 men, both of which I believe to be Yankee lies."[35]

Despite her low opinion of the Federals, Harriette did condescend "to chat a little with our sentinels, who seem rather hard cases, yet treat my sentiments with respect. They seem faithful to their trust, which we endeavored to encourage by a little attention, so completely do we feel at their mercy." Having a guard did not guarantee protection, however, as Cynthia Coleman discovered that same day while sitting at the window of her father's study. She had vowed to "keep his home and above all his Study, where he was wont to write on all the great themes that filled mens minds, sacred from the intrusion of the foe" and was dismayed to see "three Officers rapidly approaching the house" after pushing past the sentinel. Springing to the front door, Cynthia opened it and held "it in such a way that they could not enter without rushing over me and this they seemed well inclined to do." They boldly demanded food, and when she refused, "one of them swearing a wicked oath said 'This woman ought to be arrested.'" Cynthia feared her hour had come, but the

34. HC Diary, 6 May 1862; Gallagher, *Fighting for the Confederacy,* 81–2; Loehr, "First Virginia Infantry," 109; Barrett, *Yankee Rebel,* 23.

35. *OR,* 11(1):24, 276, 575, 11(3):149, 152–3; HC Diary, 7 May 1862; Johnston, *Narrative,* 126; Carter, *From Yorktown to Santiago,* 30.

intruders left and never returned. She later wrote, "the guard told me he had felt very sorry for me, 'but they were Officers Madam, and I could not stop them.'"[36]

Other bluecoat officers were too busy to harass townswomen. "Fighting a battle, I find, is the smallest part of a campaign," observed Major Wainwright in his diary entry for 7 May. "The repairing of damages, writing reports, and getting ready to go at it again is infinitely more fatiguing." That morning he "saw several hundred rebel prisoners in Williamsburg. They were a seedy-looking lot," he commented, "most of them in grey or butternut clothes, and all sorts of slouch hats; you could hardly call it a uniform at all." He spent the afternoon inspecting the redoubts and watching men still at work burying Confederates, since most Union dead had been interred by 3:00 P.M., Lieutenant Haydon believed. "Our men are becoming vindictive & revengeful very fast at the sight of their dead comrades & dislike even to help bury the enemies' dead," Haydon murmured in his journal. They were eager "to join the pursuit. We shall do so as soon as provisions arrive."[37]

Bringing up provisions continued to be a major task. Since wagons still could not negotiate the soggy roads, the Federals set up a temporary depot on Queens Creek. Observed de Paris, "In one day the wooded banks of Queen's Creek are cleared and rude wharves built, where transports come to deposit their cargoes of salt pork, biscuit, rice, and forage, which the army-wagons, lightened by several days' consumption, proceed to distribute among the various regiments." For the return trip to Fort Monroe, these steamboats were supplied with blankets and mattresses and loaded with both northern and southern wounded able to bear transportation. Cpl. James Burns was among those taken to the wharf by ambulance. He felt "highly honored" to be placed next to the 26th Pennsylvania's Col. William Small, who had suffered a severe thigh wound early in the battle. Small kindly shared his opium pills with Burns and conversed with him about the battle.[38]

Most amputees and seriously wounded soldiers were not being sent off right away but were held back in Williamsburg hospitals until they recovered enough to travel. By Wednesday, fifteen volunteer doctors from Massachusetts and New York ordered up by McClellan's chief surgeon, Dr. Tripler, had overcome "mud, swamps, ravines, and logs" between Yorktown and Williamsburg

36. HC Diary, 7 May 1862; CBT, "Peninsula Campaign"; CBT, "May 5, 1862."

37. Nevins, *Diary of Battle*, 59; Sears, *For Country, Cause, and Leader*, 234.

38. *OR*, 11(1):23; Comte de Paris, *Civil War in America*, 2:26; "William and Mary College as a Hospital," 182; Burns, *Battle of Williamsburgh*, 61.

to relieve the overworked brigade and regimental surgeons already in town. Another thirty special surgeons came along with them. All were immediately assigned to duty, the New York doctors placed in the four churches and various homes, and the Massachusetts physicians given the hospitals. Dr. Samuel Cabot already had charge of the Seminary Hospital, filled with Union wounded. The senior surgeon at the College Hospital, Dr. Alfred Hitchcock, had assistants Dr. J. R. Bronson and three Confederate surgeons, who "generally were equally attentive & kind to Confederate and Union men." During the next few days, they attended "every conceivable wound" and performed "almost every operation known to Military surgery" while treating numerous simpler fractures with materials found in the college. "I had no hesitation in appropriating the mahogany and white wood of those consecrated halls to extemporize a 'Desault' or 'Double inclined plane,'" admitted Dr. Hitchcock. "It was a great marvel to these poor deluded fellows that a Yankee surgeon could do them a kindness." Dr. Hitchcock also made house calls to tend Colonel Dwight, "a true soldier and a noble man." Added the doctor, "I trust his Country will not withhold the gratitude and honor due his valor."[39]

McClellan echoed these same sentiments that evening after riding out to Redoubt Eleven, where Hancock's brigade was on dress parade. He stopped before the colors of each regiment in turn and delivered "a graceful speech" thanking the men for their "gallant conduct the other day. You have gained honor for your country, your State, and the army to which you belong," McClellan proclaimed. "Through *you* we won the day, and WILLIAMSBURG shall be *inscribed on your banner.*" He concluded by assuring them, "Your country owes you its grateful thanks," and rode off as the soldiers "broke out into wild cheering."[40]

The commanding general had no graceful speeches of gratitude for Hooker's and Kearny's divisions, bivouacked from the battlefield to the college. That day Kearny wrote his wife about the battle and the loss of two staff members. "They both had displayed much gallantry," he assured her, "& fell in the last of the action." Kearny had them buried "in a sweet spot, in the old 'Grave Yard' of Williamsburgh." He thought it "a lovely sweet College town of charming villas & old mansions," which, "despite events, breathes peace & tranquility." So calm was the evening air that a regimental band at the college

39. "William and Mary College as a Hospital," 181–3; J. R. Bronson to William J. Dale, 12–14 May 1862, William and Mary College Papers, UA-CWM.

40. Angle and Miers, *Tragic Years,* 1:279 (quoting Thomas W. Hyde, *Following the Greek Cross or, Memories of the Sixth Army Corps* [Boston, 1894], 50–3); Love, *Wisconsin in the War,* 272–3.

playing "the familiar tune of Dixie" could be heard by Harriette nearly a mile away. Then, she recorded in her diary, "Perfect quiet—an occasional 'who comes there' alone interrupting the stillness of the night."[41]

This tranquility continued into the next morning, Thursday, 8 May, another beautiful, warm day, as four squadrons of the 3d Pennsylvania Cavalry left Palace Green for a leisurely reconnaissance up Richmond Road. The 2d Michigan's Lieutenant Haydon was assigned guard duty in town, giving him his first look at Williamsburg. It impressed him as "a very old but pleasant place containing many things of interest if one had an opportunity to look about." The college and asylum reminded him of Kalamazoo near his hometown. Since most business had been suspended, he was surprised that the "inhabitants have plenty of provisions for their prisoners & wounded." The only stores he noticed open belonged to the German Hofheimer family.[42]

Perceiving "very little commotion" in town that morning, Harriette mistakenly assumed that most of the army had passed through, "with the exception of some encamped in the neighborhood." She decided to venture out of her house for a walk up to the Methodist church, containing only Confederate wounded with Federal surgeons in attendance. There she "conversed with one or two patients, who appeared cheerful and hopeful." But Harriette was dismayed to discover "a few minutes after entering the Surgeons engaged in amputating a leg—a shocking operation—although the patient had been rendered insensible to suffering." A similar shock awaited Victoria King, carrying a pitcher of buttermilk to the wounded at the Baptist church. When she stepped through the basement door, "one of the most horrible sights I have ever seen met my eyes: in a corner of the basement room was a pile of human arms and legs." Her father, a Confederate surgeon, told her that the amputation rate was so high because the battle was fought in thick underbrush.[43]

Richard Bucktrout's daughter Delia too stumbled across "a pile of arms, legs and other parts of the human body, the pile higher than a man's head," when she passed by the Baptist church. Her post of duty as a nurse's aide, however, was at Bruton Church, full of mostly Confederate wounded and a few Federals. Of diminutive stature and cherubic face, Delia in her sixteenth year looked even younger. Yet in spirit she rivaled any Williamsburg denizen, man or woman, in her single-minded and intense devotion to the southern

41. P. Kearny to A. Kearny, 7, 8 May 1862; HC Diary, 7 May 1862.
42. HC Diary, 8 May 1862; Rawle et al., *Third Pennsylvania Cavalry*, 67; Sears, *For Country, Cause, and Leader*, 235.
43. HC Diary, 8 May 1862; Victoria King Lee, "Williamsburg in 1861," 1933, John D. Rockefeller Jr. Library, CWF, 17.

cause. Thus, an encounter with "a Yankee patient" groaning in great pain and begging for water left her torn between compassion and loyalty. Her solution to this dilemma was characteristic, as her daughter later related. "Delia, with compressed lips brought the water and helped him, but said, 'Remember, this is our land. We did not ask you to come here and fight. I give you the water, but if you were well I would gladly kill you.'" His interest piqued by these less-than-comforting words, the northern lad continued watching his little nurse and was no doubt relieved to be able to leave Williamsburg before his wounds were completely healed.[44]

This open disdain for blue uniforms was universally resented by its victims, who were at a loss to understand the reason for it. One Federal officer complained that Williamsburg ladies "took advantage of the uniform courtesy of the 'Yankees,' whom they despised and hated." The ladies "compressed their dresses whenever they met an officer or enlisted man," he complained, "so that the garment would not touch the persons they passed. They pulled their hats over their faces to preclude scrutiny." Cynthia Coleman experienced an example of the Union soldiers' "uniform courtesy" on Thursday while attempting to remove some furniture from her mother-in-law's home, now filled with Union soldiers. "The house was occupied by the lowest of the rank and file who seemed to try to provoke me by using the most violent oaths, abusing the Confederates whom in every instance they called rebels," she fumed.[45]

The sound of distant booming broke Thursday morning's quiet, and that afternoon brought news of a Confederate victory between Williamsburg and Richmond. Someone whispered to Harriette that "a neighbor caught a part of a conversation, in which one of the parties informed the other—the d——d Rebels have cut us to pieces again." More than likely the battle sounds and rumored victory were not related. The firing could have been the Federal bombardment of Norfolk or a James River fight between Federal gunboats and shore batteries, and Eltham's Landing the previous day was the only action that could qualify as a victory. The two Federal infantry regiments out for the second day had yet to make significant contact with the Confederate rear, but Union cavalry kept pushing ahead in an effort to communicate with Franklin's division before nightfall.[46]

McClellan was counting on this junction between his advance and Franklin

44. Minnie B. Jenkins, "When Delia Bucktrout Ran the Blockade to Richmond," Dorothy Ross Collection.
45. Wheeler, *Sword over Richmond*, 164 (quoting Henry N. Blake, *Three Years in the Army of the Potomac* [Boston: Lee and Shepard, 1865]); CBT, "Peninsula Campaign."
46. HC Diary, 8 May 1862; *OR*, 11(3):152–3.

to complete a supply line enabling the rest of the army to march to Richmond. The roads were still so bad that he had yet to see his own baggage, writing his wife Thursday afternoon, "I hope to get within a few miles of my tooth brush in a day or two." Nevertheless, he planned to send W. F. Smith's division up the Peninsula that afternoon, with the bulk of the army to follow early Friday. In preparation for the move, the 40th New York returned to Cheesecake Church to retrieve knapsacks deposited there the day of the battle. Marching back through the battlefield, the Mozarters noticed the felled timber had been "fired to purify it and prevent contagion," Sergeant Floyd assumed. De Paris, however, surmised the fire had started accidentally. A few wounded men, clinging to life after three days hiding in the tangled branches, were being removed when the dry wood, cut ten months earlier, ignited. "The conflagration spread rapidly," de Paris wrote, "and stifling the agonizing cries of those who were perhaps still waiting for the succor of their friends, swept away the last traces of the victims of the struggle."[47]

The Mozarters returned past the smoldering abatis and plodded through town to pitch their camp closer to the rest of Kearny's division around the college. Floyd remarked that the inhabitants "were mostly bitter secessionists and did not fear to disclose their sentiments." Their defiant spirit was dampened that evening upon hearing "great cheering" from the Federal soldiers. Harriette asked her sentinel the meaning of it. "The evacuation of Norfolk he tells me—poor deluded wretch." Joining in the Union celebration, "the Band gave forth its *cracked notes* this evening to the tune of 'Red, White & Blue,'" Harriette remarked. At last all was quiet. "'Tis a calm, still night and the moon in her splendor looks unconsciously down on a distressed people—bereft of all that's cheering, no familiar faces and indeed no social liberties from which at such a time we could derive some comfort." So ended Williamsburg's third day of captivity.[48]

47. *OR*, 11(3):150; Sears, *Papers of George B. McClellan*, 260; Floyd, *Fortieth (Mozart) Regiment New York*, 147–8, 150; Comte de Paris, *Civil War in America*, 2:25.

48. Floyd, *Fortieth (Mozart) Regiment New York*, 147–8; HC Diary, 8 May 1862.

CHAPTER 12

So Yankee-like

The northern army's grand exit from Williamsburg was even more spectacular than its *grand entree* had been three days earlier. Spellbound, Harriette Cary watched from her bedroom window as regiment after regiment, brigade after brigade, with banners gaily flapping, paraded past to the martial strains of nine full bands, the last band mounted on twenty-four white and iron gray horses. Victoria King, among the many grimfaced Williamsburg residents at their doors and windows, thought it "one of the most magnificent sights I have ever seen—countless thousands of blue-clad troops, all in new uniforms." It began at daybreak Friday morning, 9 May, with the departure of W. F. Smith's division, followed by Darius Couch's, then Silas Casey's, and finally Phil Kearny's division in the late morning. Enjoying this sight as he stood on a porch with his staff, General McClellan "received the salute of the army," wrote Col. William W. H. Davis, whose 104th Pennsylvania passed in review about 7:30 A.M. "My troops are in motion and in magnificent spirits. They have all the air and feelings of veterans," McClellan telegraphed the War Department about noon, then mounted his handsome steed and followed his army up Richmond Road.[1]

Sitting at her window, Harriette noticed that not all movement was toward Richmond that morning. Competing for road space with the "on to Richmond" crowd were ambulances coming from the direction of the capital and "discharging their burdens" into the Vest Store, across Main Street from her grandmother's house. By the end of the morning, Harriette estimated the

1. HC Diary, 9 May 1862, MR-CWM; Victoria King Lee, "Williamsburg in 1861," 1933, John D. Rockefeller Jr. Library, CWF, 14; McClellan, *Own Story,* 341; *OR,* 11(3):157–9; Davis, *104th Pennsylvania,* 74.

store was "very nearly filled" with northern boys struck down by malaria. Despite the departing multitudes, Williamsburg streets still thronged with Hooker's division, which stayed behind for another day of rest. Major Wainwright, taking the opportunity to tour the town, judged it "a queer old place; apparently has not grown any since the last century." At the college Wainwright found Hooker's First Brigade leader, Gen. Cuvier Grover, now residing in the Brafferton, vacated by Brig. Gen. Charles Jameson, and relishing the servants, who waited "on him just as they did on their old master. Many of our officers have picked up servants here."[2]

The next day, Saturday, 10 May, "the bustle continued" as Hooker's division and Averell's cavalry departed to rejoin the army. Many townspeople again turned out to see the show. "We marched through the city," wrote Pvt. Alfred Bellard of Hooker's New Jersey brigade, "with bands playing and colors flying much to the disgust of the secesh women, one of whom said that she wished we would never get back." Harriette, also glad to see them leave, exclaimed, "there seems no fag end to the Army, nothing infirm in the way of equipment—an imposing Host." The wagons were still rumbling through town after nine o'clock that night. For the second night in row, no sentinels stood at private houses.[3]

Williamsburg was not left totally unguarded, of course, for Hooker detailed one brigade to stay behind "to hold and protect the Town and torment the inhabitants," in Cynthia Coleman's view. This honor belonged to the First Brigade under Grover, appointed military governor. Under him, Lt. Col. George D. Wells of the 1st Massachusetts became provost marshal, whose duties included transferring prisoners and wounded to York River steamers and enforcing respect from the townspeople for the U.S. authorities. The latter no doubt continued to be his most difficult task. A Pennsylvania chaplain ministering to the wounded at the college asserted that "the secession ladies of Williamsburg treated our soldiers and officers with indecent rudeness, and yet there was no utterance on our part of violence or revenge."[4]

As far as the ladies were concerned, "indecent rudeness" constituted one of the few weapons at their disposal. Also in their arsenal were "instances of *courageous retort*, for which frequent opportunities have been given by these provoking villains, and every opportunity eagerly taken advantage of," Harriette

2. HC Diary, 9, 11 May 1862; Nevins, *Diary of Battle*, 60.

3. HC Diary, 10 May 1862; Rawle et al., *Third Pennsylvania Cavalry*, 67; Donald, *Gone for a Soldier*, 74.

4. CBT, "Peninsula Campaign," TCP, MR-CWM; Swem Notes, WCP, MR-CWM; Marks, *Peninsular Campaign*, 164.

listed. "Various remarks have been made I am told, as regards *our impudence* and the seclusion of the girls—moreover, their indifference to dress—all of which is intended." Their most potent defensive weapon, they believed, was prayer. On Sunday, 11 May, Harriette noted, "Our Church services have been suspended owing to the apprehension of interference, which an omission of the prayer for the President of the U.S. would most certainly occasion." Therefore, she and others remained in their homes Sunday morning to pray for deliverance and protection and for the welfare of their army.[5]

When they were not praying, many ladies braved the "intolerably dusty" streets "on errands of mercy," observed Harriette that same Sunday, and visited "their friends, to relieve the monotony of home-life." She again ventured out, calling on Lucy Tucker to inquire after the wounded Confederates recovering there and "found them much the same." The Federal sick in the Vest Store were not so fortunate. Harriette heard on Sunday that "numbers are dying at the Hospital opposite, and consigned to rude interment in the yard of the same." Southern boys, daily expiring in the Baptist church, were similarly buried immediately west of the sanctuary on Courthouse Green in big square graves. "A deep pit was dug on the open Common under the Hospital windows large enough to contain several bodies," Cynthia later wrote, "then when two or three were dead, wrapped in their coarse blankets, on which a woman would sometime place a flower, they were carefully interred." Isabella Sully, attending the wounded in the Baptist church, found them deeply distressed "to think of being buried out in unconsecrated ground." She promised them if she "lived to see the end of the war," she would "see their bones laid in the Church yard" at Bruton. Two Confederates dying on 11 May rated a decent burial, according to Bucktrout's ledger. He placed an artilleryman into grave number nineteen in the City Cemetery's Virginia row and a 28th Virginia captain into grave number twenty.[6]

Those still alive were being transferred rapidly to steamers at the Queens Creek Wharf for transport to Fort Monroe and from there northward. Harriette discovered this on Monday morning, 12 May, while visiting the College and Bruton Hospitals. "The agonized countenances of the poor creatures, as they were lifted from their cots, showed plainly their condition unequal to the fatigue they must undergo in the journey." She registered her protest by cast-

5. HC Diary, 11–12 May 1862.

6. Ibid., 11 May 1862; John S. Charles, "Recollections of Williamsburg, Virginia, as It Was at the Beginning of the Civil War," 1928, John D. Rockefeller Jr. Library, CWF, 40; CBT, "Peninsula Campaign," TCP; Isabella Sully to CBT, 30 Oct. 1890, TCP; Richard M. Bucktrout Day Book, 11 May 1862, MR-CWM.

ing "deprecating looks" at the Federal director, probably the senior surgeon of the College Hospital, Dr. Hitchcock, who the day before sent about half of his 355 patients, including 80 southerners, downriver. Despite Harriette's pleadings, he continued shipping most of the remainder that day, "leaving only a few 'stumps,'" as he put it, "and a few with mortal wounds."[7]

Filling the beds almost as fast as the wounded were vacating them were Union sick, some fifty admitted to the college Sunday night alone. The next day Harriette watched ambulances hauling patients out of the Vest Store until she suspected it was empty. These were distributed between the College and Seminary Hospitals, now left in charge of assistant surgeons while the chief surgeons accompanied their patients on a steamer to Fort Monroe. Dr. Hitchcock was among the latter, taking Col. William Dwight back to Massachusetts. Four Confederates died on the boat, one by suicide, and many worsened, "owing to the defective ventilation and crowded state of the ship," the doctor surmised. Or perhaps, as Harriette maintained, they were just too weak to travel.[8]

In Williamsburg on Monday, the Federals installed Lemuel Bowden as mayor, "in this 'Reign of Terror,'" Harriette murmured. Shortly after the Union takeover, Bowden and his sons returned to their home, where they furnished a *New York Herald* correspondent "the luxury of sleeping in a nice clean bed for the first time since leaving Washington." Bowden impressed the reporter as "a thoroughgoing Union man," for he voted against secession "at the imminent peril of his life" and has "suffered all manner of persecution in consequence" of his "fidelity to the old Union." This account, published in the 16 May *Herald,* amused Harriette, who remarked, "*truth,* however, Yankee-like, is not regarded."[9]

Despite the tension between captors and captives, some Federals were actually gaining an appreciation for their unwilling hosts. On 14 May Dr. J. R. Bronson took charge of the College Hospital's eighty Union sick and seven Confederate wounded as well as thirty-five Union sick at the Seminary Hospital. Also responsible for daily dressing the wounded officers in private homes, Dr. Bronson made the acquaintance of several townspeople. "The citizens here are becoming more familiar from day to day, but at heart are rank Secessionists," he wrote his surgeon general. "Williamsburg is a beautiful town and

7. HC Diary, 12 May 1862; Hitchcock to doctor, 12 May 1862, William and Mary College Papers, UA-CWM; "William and Mary College as a Hospital," 182.
8. Hitchcock to doctor, 12 May 1862; "William and Mary College as a Hospital," 183–6; HC Diary, 13 May 1862.
9. HC Diary, 12, 29 May 1862; *New York Herald,* 16 May 1862.

gives evidence of a growing feeling of familiarity & confidence. The ladies visit our hospital with little luxuries that the army ration list does not contain, and if ever men appreciate little kindnesses of this character it is when sick away from home."[10]

Not so cordial were the relations between Williamsburg ladies and the Federal surgeon overseeing the Baptist Church Hospital, filled only with Confederate wounded. Already earning the nickname "Head Devil," Dr. Rogers of New York seemed to the townspeople the epitome of the drunken incompetent foisted upon them by a heartless and insensitive administration. Cynthia avoided the Baptist church, not wishing "to witness suffering that I could not alleviate," but Isabella Sully daily attended patients there and had frequent skirmishes with the doctor. He accidentally poisoned one Confederate boy, and another's broken leg he broke "afresh, that drunken wretch lifted the leg and carelessly let it fall," Isabella recorded in her journal. Dr. Rogers once told her that he "was not a Commissioned Officer, but a Volunteer, receiving no pay for his services, that he was working for eternity and hoped to get his reward there." To this she boldly replied, "I trust you may get what you richly deserve, but it will not be in Heaven."[11]

On 14 May, the same day that Doctors Bronson and Rogers took over the hospitals, Williamsburg civilians discovered they were to have a change of guard as well. Grover's brigade, awaiting orders to advance toward an anticipated battle near Richmond, was scheduled to march on the morrow. In a farewell celebration that night, during a gentle and refreshing rain, Grover's brigade band serenaded Mayor Bowden at his house. "Loud cheering heard in conclusion," Harriette sneered. "Down with the Traitor!" No fond farewells to this brigade came from the inhabitants, daily deprived "secretly and openly of their stores, with which they had provided themselves for their own consumption," Harriette fumed. "Negroes, horses, mules, sheep, bacon and grain are the booty of these marauding parties, which scour the Country in every direction." Now, the people were told, this brigade was to be replaced by one "even more rapacious."[12]

Incessant rain continued the next day, 15 May, as Grover's men vacated their camps, soon swarming with Williamsburg boys collecting souvenirs. The 476 officers and men of the 5th Pennsylvania Cavalry immediately succeeded them. This regiment was recruited in Philadelphia, largely from Pennsylvania

10. Bronson to Dale, 12–14 May 1862, William and Mary College Papers.
11. Ibid.; CBT, "Peninsula Campaign"; CBT, "Occupancy," TCP.
12. HC Diary, 13–14 May 1862.

Dutch, and was first named the "Black Huzzars" after a famous Prussian regiment. It soon dropped this pretence to be known simply as the "Fifth." One member observed that "the rebs didn't care whether we were real black or only just common purple, as long as we were Yanks—and they always let drive at us, as soon as we hove in sight." The Pennsylvanians' commander, Col. David Campbell, a "dignified gentleman," took over as military governor and replaced Grover as resident of the Brafferton.[13]

The same day Campbell and the Fifth trotted into town, all Confederate wounded, except those in private homes, were concentrated in the Baptist church under Dr. Rogers. The following day, 16 May, as Isabella made her rounds, somebody shouted, "They are going to blow up the Hospital." Instant chaos ensued. "The poor bed-ridden wounded unable to move filled with alarm, the women flying about like crazy people, nobody seeming to know exactly what was the matter," Isabella described the wild scene. "I finally discovered that a train of powder had been laid along the passage to reach a keg of powder concealed in a closet by old clothing cut from the wounded, and thrown aside with the bloody rags used in dressing their wounds." When Isabella, "almost paralyzed with terror," reached the closet, she "had just sense enough left to drag" the bloody rags "upon the train of powder, at the other end of which the fuse was sputtering." The "dastardly wretch" guilty of attempting to blow up a hospital full of southern wounded and women was a northern private who immediately took to his heels but was evidently caught. Later that day Isabella told Harriette that "she reported the Conspirator and he was lodged in the guard-house." Both ladies concluded that the episode proved the "villainy" of the Federals, "for they are fiends in human form."[14]

The next day, Saturday, 17 May, remained mercifully quiet. "No excitement to-day," Harriette penned, but the strain of Federal occupation was already taking a toll on the less robust among them. Dr. John Galt, staggering under the responsibility of more than two hundred patients at the asylum and prohibited from taking his usual evening walk to College Landing, necessary for his health and sanity, was visibly sinking. Dyspeptic all his adult life, he had been ill for four days. On the evening of the seventeenth, his cousin Gabriella Galt, living a block up from the Superintendent's House, noticed Dr. Galt had "a tendency of blood to the head," and she "feared apoplexy for him." According to another cousin, he was suffering from "a fearful diarrhea. To

13. Ibid., 15 May 1862; *OR*, 11(3):184; David Edward Cronin, "The Vest Mansion," 1908–10, John D. Rockefeller Jr. Library, CWF, 19–20; *(Williamsburg) Cavalier*, 25 June 1862.
14. HC Diary, 16 May 1862; CBT, "Occupancy."

cure this he took a dose of laudanum that was too much for his weak condition." The Galts' mammy, Arena Baker, did not think Dr. Galt had taken the drug but suggested he had eaten "a good deal of cold pork," which "acted as a foreign substance in his stomach and he had a convulsion." A northern soldier on guard in the neighborhood heard his "death struggle," wrote Gabriella, "awoke my servants, and then scaled the Asylum walls" to summon Dr. Williamson. All treatment availed nothing. The attending doctor told Arena that if Dr. Galt had another convulsion he would die, and he did, early Sunday morning, 18 May. Arena believed "the fits caused his death."[15]

Sally Galt was devastated. The first letters she wrote after the tragedy begged her friends and relatives to "pity my wretchedness. My darling Brother was as you know all the world to me, & life is dark & dreary without him." Life also became considerably less comfortable, as she was forced to move out of the Superintendent's House and back to the Galt family home, already occupied by a renter. Pulling herself together within a couple of months, Sally composed John's obituary, stressing his contributions to the field of mental health and his benevolence and stating the cause of death as "an affection of the stomach, to which he had been subject for many years." Others, however, suspected laudanum overdose, which, if self-administered, spelled suicide to many. This suspicion followed him to the grave—his body conveyed in Bucktrout's "most elegant mahogany coffin"—and is still attached to his name.[16]

The passing of Dr. Galt not only marked the end of Galt family rule of the asylum but also plunged Williamsburg into deeper depression. That Sunday morning, as news of his death spread through town, some fifteen faithful gathered in Thomas Ambler's basement to avoid "everything that might create suspicion" and sang and prayed. "No interruption as yet," Harriette reported, "and we are thankful for the opportunities for uniting our supplications to the God of Victory." The next morning, 19 May, Harriette noticed, while walking to a friend's house, that "the streets are very bad—very muddy—indeed the whole Town begins to wear the garb of a mourner." It was appropriately dressed for the funeral that day of Capt. Jacob Macon of the 19th Mississippi, succumbing to his battle wounds and buried in the ninth grave of his state's row. Bucktrout interred two more the next day, 20 May, Alabamians who died at the Baptist church but avoided the trench graves. He put them in the

15. HC Diary, 17 May 1862; SMG to Peggy, 26 June 1865, GFP, MR-CWM; Gabriella Galt to Mary Jeffrey Galt, 25 May 1865, GFP; John M. Galt II Diary, footnotes in the hands of Mary J. Galt and William R. Galt, GFP.

16. SMG to friend, [July 1862], GFP; SMG to Peggy, 26 June 1865; SMG draft of obituary for John M. Galt II, GFP; Bucktrout Day Book, 18 June [May] 1862.

twenty-third Alabama plot and the second grave in the Tennessee row. "An air of neglect pervades this once happy little village," Harriette observed during her walk, and though the spring "flora has been quite lavish," she was distressed to find "the most favored spots have been despoiled by the ruthless hands of these Yankee invaders. Our once beautiful 'Greens' are cut up and their lovely sward destroyed—the side-walks preferred by equestrians, much to the annoyance of pedestrians."[17]

The invaders were destroying Williamsburg's age-old social structure as well. "Negroes are presuming very much under the present administration," Harriette complained on 21 May. "Campbell, the Military Governor, lends an ear to the statement of any grievance, which is promptly redressed." Campbell's provost marshal, Capt. T. Hennessey, extended this leniency so far as to practice a policy of practical emancipation. One day, Arena Baker's daughter Eliza Baker, still working for the Whiting family, called upon Hennessey at his office in the Saunders House to request a pass into the country for the next Sunday. When he asked why she wanted to wait until Sunday, she replied she had to work for Mrs. Whiting during the week. "You can go when you want to," he told Eliza. "You are just as free as she is!" With a pass for Tuesday in hand, Eliza went back to the Whitings' house, where the children had already told their mother about the foregoing conversation. "I went upstairs and got my dress (I only had two)," Eliza later related, "and that night I took out and went down home, and I ain't never been back to the Whitings since!"[18]

While many blacks were enjoying their first taste of freedom, Williamsburg had become for the white inhabitants a prison, cut off from all friends and family in the Confederacy. "We are inured, now, to *incarceration*," sighed Harriette, "and very naturally after supper retire to our apartments." She found, however, that "sociability very much alleviates our bondage." On the afternoon of the twentieth, Harriette alleviated her bondage at nearby Bassett Hall, socializing with Colonel Goodrich Durfey's family and the two "very interesting gentlemen" staying with them. One was Lt. John F. Hays of the 5th North Carolina, wounded in the arm. The other was none other than Custer's classmate, Capt. John "Gimlet" Lea. Shortly after the battle, Colonel and Mrs. Durfey packed their wagon full of food and drove out to the battlefield to succor wounded of both sides. Happening into the barn housing many of the 5th North Carolina, Mrs. Durfey brought Lea and Hays home to Bassett

17. HC Diary, 18–19 May 1862; Bucktrout Day Book, 19–20 May 1862.
18. HC Diary, 21 May 1862; Eliza Baker, "Memoirs of Williamsburg," 1933, John D. Rockefeller Jr. Library, CWF, 2.

Hall. Two weeks later Harriette found them "both doing quite well" and Lea "the happiest soul I ever saw," no doubt due to the attentions of the Durfeys' seventeen-year-old daughter, Margaret.[19]

Many wounded were happily recovering in Williamsburg homes. On 21 May Harriette commented, "Nearly every family has one or more of the wounded, whom it affords them great pleasure to nurse." With over twenty Confederate soldiers scattered about in private residences, Harriette wanted one of her own, and Col. William H. Forney of the 10th Alabama was almost well enough to be moved from the hospital. "Stricken down with a painful wound while leading his regiment," the then Major Forney earned commendation from Brig. Gen. Cadmus Wilcox for "displaying both coolness and skill" in the battle while "encouraging his men in the thickest of the fight." His shoulder wound was not as severe as first thought, but to Harriette's disappointment, on the twenty-second he could not yet be moved into her grandmother's home.[20]

Halfway up Main Street from Harriette's, the Peachys were barely hanging on to their wounded guest. Surprisingly, the "horribly mutilated" Major Payne was still alive, with a rubber support holding his face together. Payne could receive nourishment only through a rubber tube in his jaw, yet "I was crazy to get back to the army," he later confessed. One day he informed his doctor in writing, since he could not talk, that he "wished him to consider me as delivering myself up as a regular prisoner of war, owing no obligations whatever. I asked him if he understood my declaration, and he said he did. I noticed, however, that he was quite amused," Payne later reminisced. His friends prepared a detailed map of the James River for him, as he planned to cross at Jamestown and work his way up the south side to Richmond. To ascertain his strength before he made his escape, Payne "took an experimental walk to the College, fainted before I got there, was brought back in an ambulance to my cot, and discovered, in my discomfiture, the cause of the Doctor's amusement. I weighed 95 pounds at the time, and suppose, if I had started out on my expedition, I should have died before I got outside the corporate limits."[21]

When he was not trying to escape, Payne appreciated the company of concerned townspeople such as William Peachy, Montegu Thompson, and Talbot Sweeney, who congregated in his room perhaps out of "compassion at my ex-

19. HC Diary, 19–21 May 1862; Schaff, *Old West Point*, 180.

20. HC Diary, 21–22 May 1862; Jones, "Wounded at Williamsburg," 172–5; *OR*, 11(1):592, 11(3):94.

21. Payne to CBT, 21 Feb. 1891, TCP; Mrs. William H. Payne, "Search for My Wounded Husband," 1910, VHS, 9; William Henry Fitzhugh Payne, Map of James River, 1862, VHS.

ceptionally wretched condition." Many also continued to gather from house to house at well-attended prayers meetings. Rain on Saturday, 24 May, did not prevent the prayer meeting, but only eight people, including Harriette, assembled. At least one, the town's Presbyterian minister, Samuel Blain, was so bold as to kneel "at a front window, invoke the blessing of Heaven on our arms & cause, and pray that the Northern Army might be driven far from us," Cynthia Coleman revealed. Yet they were not molested by the soldiers. "Perhaps they thought us fighting with harmless weapons." Neither were they molested on Sunday the twenty-fifth, when for the first time since the occupation, parishioners were free to attend Bruton Church and "once more enjoyed unity of spirit and prayer."[22]

By that time, movements near Richmond had pulled all remaining surgeons out of town, leaving only the despised Dr. Rogers, who, Harriette feared, "will very much neglect *our wounded*—so heartless and relentless he seems." On 24 May she visited the Baptist church and found "the majority improving," though amputations seemed unnecessarily frequent. "Our wounded are being moved to private houses, which can very well accommodate them," Harriette related on Monday the twenty-sixth, "there being only 18 out of 61 left.—O the atrocity of these Yankee murderers." At the Amblers' parish house, Lt. William M. Richardson of the 17th Virginia was "in a dying condition, which may be justly attributed to neglect on the part of the Yankee Surgeon, Rogers," wrote Harriette on 28 May, "every attention possible given him by kind Mrs. Ambler." A small prayer meeting at Harriette's house that afternoon united fervently "in behalf of our Army and Country" and presumably of Lieutenant Richardson. Nevertheless, he died the following night and was buried "with much respect" during the afternoon of 30 May in Bruton Churchyard in the same mound as Colonel Ward.[23]

Asylum patients provided another worry for Williamsburg people as well as for the Federals. Since Dr. Galt's death, Harriette disclosed in her 25 May diary entry, "a Yankee has been appointed his successor, which was but the beginning of a complete revolution in the Asylum government." Federal military surgeon Dr. W. Clinton Thompson now headed the institution, and on the twenty-sixth Harriette learned from her friend Joan Douglas that her father, steward William Douglas, would be allowed to remain. "The officers at the Asylum have not as yet been suspended but have received orders, and are making preparations to leave." That day asylum clerk Charles Waller, a

22. Payne to CBT, 21 Feb. 1891; CBT, "Peninsula Campaign"; HC Diary, 23–25 May 1862.
23. HC Diary, 23–30 May 1862; Sully to CBT, 30 Oct. 1890.

nephew of Dr. Robert Waller, made the mistake of dashing home to look in
on his sick child, for when he returned to his office he discovered that he had
been removed and the mayor's brother, Henry Bowden, put in his place. Soon,
Henry's wife and Lemuel's son, Thomas Russell, were installed as well, confirming Harriette's statement, "the Bowdens are supreme, and will exercise
authority over the Institution hereafter." Charles Waller was not even allowed
to return to the asylum to visit his father, a residing inmate.[24]

The state government in Richmond had also been concerned about the asylum ever since it fell into Federal hands. On 17 May Governor Letcher was
authorized to appoint investigators to send to Williamsburg if the Union army
would allow it. Judge W. W. Crump, after obtaining McClellan's permission,
started out on horseback from Richmond on the evening of 26 May. Forced
to ride blindfolded through the Union camps, Crump arrived in Williamsburg
the night of 28 May, bearing "cheering news" to the inhabitants. The next
morning he reported his presence to Colonel Campbell and conducted his inspection of the asylum. According to a later account by his daughter, Crump
found "everything in good condition, they having command of much greater
means than our Governor; after going through and seeing everything in most
satisfactory condition he felt more than content to leave it in their hands."
Crump "felt the greatest anxiety to return" to Richmond, knowing a major
battle was imminent, but before he could leave Williamsburg, a violent thunderstorm, "or rather a succession of storms," wrote Harriette, struck the evening of 30 May. Campbell ordered Crump to remain in Williamsburg until
further notice. He therefore lodged with old friend Lucy Tucker and found
amiable company among the wounded Confederates recuperating there.[25]

"Sweet converse" with friends, as Harriette put it, helped pass the time as
the seemingly endless month of May drew to a close. On 30 May her grandmother's house became a social center with the arrival of Colonel Forney.
Much to her disgust, Dr. Rogers, "whose tarrying in W—— is unpleasant to
all," also came to attend the colonel. The next day the battle of Seven Pines
began at Fair Oaks outside of Richmond and just forty miles west of Williamsburg. It continued on Sunday, 1 June, the booming cannon audible from
morning, when Ambler held services in his basement, till night, when Williamsburg greeted yet another outside visitor.[26]

24. HC Diary, 25–26 May 1862; Flournoy, *Virginia State Papers*, 11:478, 492.

25. Dain, *Disordered Minds*, 171–2; Emmie [Crump] Lightfoot, "My Father's Second Expedition for the Confederate Government," 1–9, VHS; HC Diary, 29–30 May 1862.

26. HC Diary, 30–31 May, 1 June 1862.

This new arrival was Major Payne's wife, Mary. While a refugee in Danville, Virginia, she heard of his wounding, packed up her infant daughter, and despite her advancing pregnancy, took the next train to Richmond. McClellan, however, denied her passage through the lines. Undaunted, she headed up to Washington, crossed the lines, and sailed from Baltimore to Fort Monroe, stepping from boat to boat over the bodies of Seven Pines casualties to disembark. A pass brought her to Yorktown, and a two-wheel ambulance, "which almost shook out the little life remaining in me," conveyed her to Williamsburg. There Mary inquired her way up Main Street until she found the Peachy House. Years later she remembered, "My husband, who had been moved on to the porch for the first time, heard my voice and burst into tears."[27]

The major was no more shocked than his wife. "He was utterly changed," declared Mary, horrified to find his face trussed up in the rubber support. All escape plans were abandoned as Campbell promised Payne would be released soon in the daily exchange of prisoners. About a week later, the Paynes headed home by way of Yorktown to Fort Monroe, where they were detained two weeks before securing a pass from the new commandant of the district and Mary's old friend, Maj. Gen. John A. Dix. Soon after returning home in Warrenton, Virginia, Major Payne met J. E. B. Stuart passing through with his cavalry. Stuart "caught him around the waist, put him behind him on his horse, and although his wound was still bandaged and not healed, and he was unable to eat solid food, carried him away from his anxious wife, and to the front." Payne's future held a major generalcy, two more wounds, and two more imprisonments before the war ended and he could obtain proper treatment for his jaw.[28]

Judge Crump too received permission to leave Williamsburg on 6 June and begin a journey to Richmond via Fort Monroe that would take more than a week. The day before Crump's departure, Dr. Gillet F. Watson took over from Dr. Thompson as asylum superintendent. Watson had actually received the appointment soon after Dr. Galt's demise from Francis Pierpont, governor of the Unionist "Reorganized Government of Virginia," meeting in Wheeling in what would become West Virginia. But Campbell would not give him control without express orders from McClellan, obtained during the battle on 31 May. Finding "the Physicians and officers extreme Rebels," Dr. Watson apprised Pierpont in a letter, "I made a clear discharge of them all." Harriette men-

27. Ibid., 1 June 1862; Payne, "Search for My Wounded Husband," 2–8.
28. Payne, "Search for My Wounded Husband," 8–13; Payne to CBT, 21 Feb. 1891; Warner, *Generals in Gray*, 230–1.

tioned on 6 June that William Douglas "refuses to take the oath of allegiance, which is required of all officers retained." Of the nineteen officers tendered the oath, eight, including the three Bowdens, took it. Besides Douglas, Doctors Williamson and Robert Garrett declined. Henry Bowden became steward in place of Douglas, who had stocked the asylum with a year's supply of food and clothing. Nevertheless, Dr. Watson asserted he "found no clothing, medicines or provisions of any consequence."[29]

Williamsburg was finally rid of the "nuisance Dr. Rogers, [who] left this morning—his services required above," Harriette noted on 7 June. A Confederate surgeon named Goodman took charge of the remaining nine or ten soldiers in the hospital. Rogers's last "victim," as many saw it, was one of the Durfeys' guests, Lieutenant Hays, "a fine intelligent young man, who has won the esteem and even affection of all around him." An operation on 2 June attempting to reverse his worsening condition proved unsuccessful. On the third, Harriette "was called to the bed-side of Lieut. Hays who died shortly after—surrounded by weeping friends—he passed away quietly and unconsciously." Harriette missed his interment two mornings later, but it was well attended. As Cynthia Coleman wrote, "on such occasions every woman and child who could do so followed the remains to the grave."[30]

Another large funeral occurred on the evening of 9 June. William D. Davis of the 18th Virginia, "Little Davis," as he was affectionately called, died that morning, though he had been tenderly nursed by Emily Morrison in her mother's home, directly across Main Street from the Vest House. "The whole Confederate heart of the town is filled with pity for the poor lad who having lost one leg has now lost his life," mourned Isabella Sully. When Emily complained to Bucktrout that his grave, number twenty-three in the Virginia row, was too shallow, the undertaker "excused himself on the ground that after the War was over the body would probably be removed." He then assured Emily, "never do you mind for when you die, just send for me and you shall have a grave deep enough and I will put you away with pleasure," quoted Isabella with the remark, "A compliment of some ambiguity, but every body loves Miss Emily and wants to do something for her."[31]

Before the month was out, two more graves in the Virginia row would be occupied. Number twenty-four received the remains of a 17th Virginia infan-

29. HC Diary, 5–6 June 1862; Dain, *Disordered Minds*, 172–3; Flournoy, *Virginia State Papers*, 11:376–9.
30. HC Diary, 1–7 June 1862; CBT, "Peninsula Campaign."
31. HC Diary, 9 June 1862; Jones, "Wounded at Williamsburg," 173–4; CBT, "Occupancy"; Bucktrout Day Book, June 1862.

tryman. He expired under the Southalls' care at the President's House, where they now resided. Another Virginia lad, shuffling off his mortal coil at Catherine Maupin's boardinghouse, was buried the last day of June in grave number twenty-five, the final grave recorded for Virginia. The last body added to Colonel Ward's mound in Bruton Churchyard, a South Carolinian, died under the care of Charles Waller's family and, mourned by many, was buried that same day, 18 June.[32]

Those not dying were recovering and, under the terms of their paroles, freely moved about the community. On the morning of 12 June, Dr. Goodman departed with a few "recovered or convalescent wounded," including Captain Lea, "in a four horse waggon with an escort of ten" bound for Fort Monroe. Harriette wrote two letters for them to carry out. The next day more recovered soldiers left to be exchanged and to smuggle more letters into the Confederacy. Cynthia Coleman wrote one to her sister-in-law to tell her "that their house & lot were nearly destroyed, the furniture ruined, & every thing that had been left locked was broken open." But Benjamin Ewell in Richmond mentioned on the twenty-fifth that several persons had come up from Williamsburg recently and reported "the citizens are not unnecessarily molested." Even regular church services had been allowed to resume on 15 June, for, according to Harriette, "the Governor has said he had not the power to interrupt."[33]

Indeed, Campbell seemed to be going out of his way placate the citizens. When Cynthia solicited his aid in May, he assured her, "Any priveleges consistent with the duty of the Commandant of this Post, shall be freely accorded Mrs. Coleman." Twice more in May she wrote formal pleas for help with servant problems and with her mother-in-law's house, and each time he granted her wish but begged "that in the future she will not prefer requests under a 'Flag of Truce,' but directly *claim* what priveleges she may desire." In another written exchange dated 12 June in which Cynthia complained about the food given to hospitalized Confederates, she added that she "had come to regard him as one, who though ranking among her foes, might still be regarded as a man of magnanimity and justice." In reply Campbell requested "the honor of a personal interview at Head Quarters" to discuss the complexities of the hospital problem.[34]

32. Bucktrout Day Book, June 1862; HC Diary, 18 June 1862; Sully to CBT, 30 Oct. 1890.

33. HC Diary, 11–15 June 1862; R. Page Saunders to Elizabeth Ewell, 2 July [1862], EFP, MR-CWM; BSE to EE, 25 June 1862, EFP.

34. CBT to Campbell, rough draft, n.d., TCP; Campbell to CBT, 23, 28 May, 12 June [1862], TCP.

Whether Cynthia ever so honored the governor is not recorded, but on 16 June Harriette decided to call upon him to post a letter to a friend on the Eastern Shore. Her face closely veiled, Harriette strolled up Main Street to the college grounds and found Campbell standing in the Brafferton's doorway, reviewing a handful of troops. He promised to send the letter without charging her postage. She gave him a "distant bow," then hurried home to record "my first appearance in the presence of this Yankee ruler." Four days later she returned to the Brafferton with a friend to inquire about the mail. "We were ushered into his apartment neatly furnished," she noted, trying her best to appear dignified, "& were soon in his august presence—found rather easy in manner, and quite talkative."[35]

The next day, 21 June, Harriette took another walk with a friend and wrote, "the Ladies resume possession of the streets with much independence, Yankees treated as usual and deservedly—*not at all.*" That afternoon she hosted a prayer meeting at her home and the following morning, Sunday, went to church "services, which we now engage in without apprehension." On Monday morning, 23 June, came the distressing news that her Aunt Susan Coupland's baby had died. At the funeral on the twenty-fourth, Harriette heard tidings from the outside. Since only "Yankee women," officers' wives, now came to Williamsburg, residents were almost entirely dependent on local boys in the Confederate cavalry for any reliable information. These troopers, with their superior knowledge of the terrain, were able to elude Federal pickets on the roads and creep up unguarded ravines after dark. The night before the Coupland baby's funeral, one such native son made it through, and Harriette learned that her brother Miles was well but two other Williamsburg soldiers had died of disease.[36]

One day later, Wednesday, 25 June, Williamsburg was blessed with the advent of another source of news, albeit not of southern origin. After Mrs. Mary Lively surrendered the office keys to a Federal officer threatening to break down the door, her son's presses were impressed into service for the North's propaganda war. A five-cent weekly christened the *Cavalier* supplanted the *Gazette*, "to foster and defend loyalty to the Union," wrote the new editor, Lt. S. H. Yocum of the 5th Pennsylvania's Company A. From the masthead of this "little intruder" flew "The Union Forever, And Freedom To All," but, Editor Yocum carefully disclaimed, only "'white folks' are meant. We do not wish it even insinuated that we have any sympathy with abalition-

35. HC Diary, 16, 20 June 1862.
36. Ibid., 21–24 June 1862; CBT, "Occupancy."

ism." After perusing a copy, Harriette judged it "more thoroughly false than any collection or edition I have yet seen." Yocum included "a well selected page of romance and poetry" and "the latest and most authentic telegraphic news, an arrangement to that end having already been consummated." One of the paper's four pages he devoted to items of local interest. The first issue warned troopers to keep their horses off the footpaths. "It is no unusual thing to see equestrians passing along the side-walks with as much indifference as though they were made to be trampled up with horses' feet," the *Cavalier* scolded. "It is sometimes almost impossible to pass the street without danger of swamping, but this is no excuse for indiscriminate riding on the walks."[37]

For lack of war news, the *Cavalier* reported on local skirmishes between townspeople and soldiers. The Federals installed a brand new fifty-foot flag-pole in Williamsburg, and the Stars and Stripes waved tauntingly from every building they occupied, until some girls could tolerate it no longer. Yocum watched one "supercilious flirt" with "protruding tongue" approach the "place where our banner was proudly floating." Unwilling to tread beneath its folds, she "gently stepped off of the beautiful sidewalk, her fairy foot lightly pressing the mud six inches deep." Victoria King told of another episode in front of a Courthouse Green lodging house converted into a Federal commissary. "A large flag—a United States flag, of course—was placed on the front of this building, so that it hung out over the sidewalk," she later reminisced; "and the girls of Williamsburg, to avoid walking under it, used to walk out in the road. The United States troops, not to be out done, however, got a long flag and stretched it completely across the Main Street."[38]

The day the *Cavalier* first appeared in Williamsburg, the northern Army of the Potomac and the southern Army of Northern Virginia, now under General Lee since Joe Johnston's wounding at Seven Pines, commenced a titanic struggle for Richmond. The evening of 26 June, Yocum dropped his pen and buckled on his sword to lead a twelve-man squad up Richmond Road for "a pleasant '*scout*'" in McClellan's rear. During the next week McClellan executed a "change of base" from the York River to the James, fighting a series of battles that kept Williamsburg citizens on edge with every conflicting rumor. They did enjoy watching what appeared to be a Federal retreat all day Sunday the twenty-ninth. "Have seen a great many waggons and mules, cavalry and a few cannon guarded each by a body of cavalry—no infantry," Harriette recorded, "a jaded dirty set—very much subdued in spirit—quiet in their move-

37. *(Williamsburg) Cavalier*, 25 June 1862; HC Diary, 26 June 1862.
38. *(Williamsburg) Cavalier*, 25 June 1862; Lee, "Williamsburg in 1861," 16.

ment." These maneuvers excited hopes among townspeople that their own soldiers would soon arrive, and "great preparations were made in hot haste to receive them," the second issue of the *Cavalier* reported. "The house-hold machinery was put to work at cooking meats, baking bread, cakes, pies, &c., and in a short time large quantities of eatables were spread on extended tables, ready for hungry traitors."[39]

"We are anxiously waiting for a glimpse of our dear army," Harriette admitted on 29 June, but only blue uniforms continued to fill the landscape. "Our Town is yet in their possession," and worse, "we apprehend something *serious* in their exasperation—rumors of firing the Town &c. keep us quite uneasy." Adding to Harriette's frustration the next day, "the movement of the Yankees seems very mysterious—many of those we thought in Retreat seem encamped about Town." On 1 July, amid firing distinctly heard all day, some of the Federals actually turned back toward Richmond. The 2 July *Cavalier* could shed no more light on the situation but was certain McClellan was in Richmond. On 3 July the townspeople were equally certain he was there, as a prisoner.[40]

Both were mistaken. The all-day battle sounds of 1 July had emanated from Malvern Hill, the final major battle of the weeklong engagement. The loud firing, "very distinct but not quick," heard the evening of 2 July marked the parting shots as McClellan led his bleeding but intact army into camp on the James River at Harrison's Landing near Berkeley Plantation, some thirty miles from Williamsburg. The sound of more firing drifted downriver on 4 July, seemingly quite close but actually a "national salute" for Independence Day at Harrison's Landing. Federals in Williamsburg celebrated too. "A large dinner I hear was to-day enjoyed by the Yanks," wrote Harriette, "partaken of also by the contrabands, with whom there seems to be much congeniality." Other Williamsburg civilians gathered to pray for "humble hearts" and for Dr. John Williamson, who had been ill several weeks and was not expected to live through the night.[41]

The next morning, 5 July, Harriette found Dr. Williamson "a little better" and Colonel Forney well enough to walk about. Spirits further lifted by the return of Captain Lea from Fort Monroe. He "could not get an exchange which is not very much regretted though from the aspect of things," Harriette coyly commented, "he thinks *all will be right very soon*." She no doubt referred

39. *(Williamsburg) Cavalier,* 2 July 1862; HC Diary, 26–29 June 1862.
40. HC Diary, 29–30 June, 1 July 1862; *(Williamsburg) Cavalier,* 2 July 1862.
41. HC Diary, 1–2, 4 July 1862.

to his developing romance with Margaret Durfey. Throughout that day residents were serenaded by the sounds of bursting guns coming from the direction of Fort Magruder and by the arrival of the 11th Pennsylvania Cavalry's band, accompanying five companies of its regiment, now stationed in Williamsburg. During the evening of Sunday, 6 July, a number of friends filling Harriette's porch, "quite like 'old times,'" were entertained by Lea's stories of his stay at Fort Monroe and by the "Yankee band quite *vociferous—discordantly so*—in its performance this evening." Two evenings later these friends again congregated at Dr. Garrett's. "We forgot our bondage for the time, and enjoyed the Band, which was distinctly heard as we eat supper by moonlight," Harriette penned in her diary.[42]

Wednesday, 9 July, brought the third issue of the *Cavalier* with a harangue against Williamsburg ladies who had clamored "loud and long" to have their wounded placed under their care. Yet now the Baptist church patients were suffering from neglect, the hospital was "filthy beyond description," and the ladies more interested in insulting Union soldiers than caring for the afflicted. Campbell had already addressed the problem to Cynthia Coleman two days earlier and solicited her aid in procuring "a competent Surgeon and the necessary assistants to remedy the existing state of things at the Hospital." Most of the wounded were recovering and leaving town by the second week of July anyway. Campbell ordered Colonels Forney and Williams to Fort Monroe on the twelfth, though neither had well healed. Forney carried personal letters and a copy of the *Cavalier* to smuggle into the Confederacy. As sad as Harriette was to see him leave, she believed "it natural and advisable he should make some effort to be exchanged."[43]

Sadder still was the death of Dr. John Williamson only a few minutes after Harriette visited him the morning of 12 July. James Griffin commented in his commonplace book how soon he followed "our other highly esteemed & beloved fellow-citizen," Dr. John Galt. Sally Galt later revealed that Dr. Williamson "told me he could not survive John, & his words proved prophetic." The next day, in striking contrast to the town's somber mood, Harriette, "while preparing for Church was attracted by the whole body of Cavalry, numbering I hear 5-5-0, passing on its way to the battle field where they had dress-parade—their return was heralded by a considerable flourish of trumpets, band &c." That afternoon Griffin attended Rev. Thomas Ambler's fu-

42. Ibid., 5–6, 8 July 1862.

43. *(Williamsburg) Cavalier*, 9 July 1862; Campbell to CBT, 7 July [1862], TCP; Lewis Williams to CBT, 24 July 1862, TCP; HC Diary, 11–12 July 1862.

neral service at Bruton Church for Dr. Williamson, who was laid to rest in one of Bucktrout's more modest coffins next to his cousin John.[44]

Spirits continued to plunge throughout July as details of the Seven Days Battles began to dribble into town. Townspeople had known of the Confederate victory since Richmond newspapers had been smuggled in on 9 July, but on the sixteenth Harriette read of "Gen. Magruder's rashness in attacking a battery numbering probably three times his men which resulted in great loss" at Malvern Hill. Since the Junior Guards were still under Magruder's command, these reports caused "great anxiety in our Community—so many dear ones may now be numbered with the fallen patriots," Harriette worried on 17 July. They had to wait until the twenty-first to hear that the Guards were well, for the company had not participated in Magruder's attack.[45]

Greatly relieved, Harriette allowed herself a little flirtation with the Federal guards posted outside her home. "Constant complaints of the citizens have induced the posting of sentinels at various houses for the protection of property—they seem very unwilling," she indicated on 21 July and the next day took it upon herself to cheer them up. "Two of our sentinels have been quite pleasant to-day, and I have found myself laughing & talking with them several times—they took very . . . good humoredly all I could say in defence of 'Secesh,' and seemed more polite than any I have seen." One kindly brought Harriette the 16 July *Cavalier,* the fourth and last issue under Editor Yocum, for Company A was detached and deployed elsewhere.[46]

The next issue came out 23 July under its new editor, Company H's Lt. Samuel Williamson. He observed the gutters dug on each side of Main Street were "gradually drying away the long *mud hole* that met our eye upon arrival here," except in front of Bruton Church. "Will it be left for the '*cussed Yankees*' to at last become tired of the eye-sore and mend it," he asked, "or will some enterprizing citizen do his duty to his native city in seeing it remains there no longer." The band continued enlivening the town with "strains of soul-stirring music that float upon the air, day after day," usually when "the ladies were quite numerous *at promenade-hour*—after sun down," added Harriette. Dress parades provided more entertainment every evening at six on Palace Green, so the entire town could enjoy the display of "our brilliantly dashing arm of the service," Williamson boasted. Sighed Harriette, "things are all getting so Yankee-like."[47]

44. HC Diary, 12–13 July 1862; JLCG Commonplace Book, 12–13 July 1862, JLCG F/A, UA-CWM; SMG to friend, [July 1862]; Bucktrout Day Book, 13 July 1862.

45. HC Diary, 9, 16–17, 21 July 1862; Jensen, *32nd Virginia,* 79.

46. HC Diary, 21–22 July 1862; *(Williamsburg) Cavalier,* 16 July 1862.

47. *(Williamsburg) Cavalier,* 23 July 1862; HC Diary, 19–20 July 1862.

On the morning of 23 July, Harriette visited the two soldiers still recuperating at the Tucker House and learned that "all Confederates leave to-morrow—exchanges going on, which we hope may be true." She spent the afternoon writing a letter to her brother, possibly to send with Cynthia Coleman, who had secured a pass across the York River into the more loosely occupied Gloucester. There Cynthia hoped to "gather some tidings" of the army and loved ones in the Confederacy. Sally Galt also penned a note to Richmond friends to send via Gloucester, enclosing her brother's obituary and ten dollars to publish it in some Richmond newspaper.[48]

The next edition of Williamsburg's current newspaper came out 30 July. "The most difficult duty at the present time, is to keep cool," moaned Editor Williamson, suffering typical July weather of sultry one-hundred-degree days and swarms of mosquitoes in the evening. Discomfort increased over fears that Lee's army, location unknown, was poised to retake the Peninsula. Then fires began to break out around town. The first building found in flames early morning on 29 July was the old Clerk's Office on the south edge of Courthouse Green, which had housed the town's court records until most were removed at the evacuation. "Axes were obtained, the doors and windows broken open, the contents as far as possible, saved; but the building, being already too far gone, was allowed to burn," the *Cavalier* reported. Most assumed the fire to be "the work of an incendiary," and many believed contrabands were responsible, trying to destroy "papers respecting their ownership." The following night another fire broke out. This burning of a barn was insignificant, the paper asserted, except that "it gives us warning that incendiaries are in our midst." Three more barns ignited before midnight.[49]

August began more peacefully with the opening of a sutler's shop on Main Street, offering everything from sugar to shoes. On 7 August Bucktrout buried a Stuart cavalryman in grave forty-four in the Louisiana row, and one week later he interred an Alabamian in the fifty-seventh plot in the Georgia row. The next day, 15 August, James Griffin entered in his commonplace book, "Today, a large expedition went up the Richmond stage road. Perhaps this is but 'part & parcel' of 'skedaddling,' the troops going up to cover the retreat of Gen. McClellan's forces." Either Griffin was a good guesser or the rumor had already reached Williamsburg that McClellan received orders to break camp at Harrison's Landing and move his army north to unite with a new Union force near Washington. Since Lee lay between him and Washington, McClel-

48. HC Diary, 23 July 1862; CBT, "Peninsula Campaign"; SMG to friend, [July 1862].
49. *(Williamsburg) Cavalier*, 30 July 1862; Charles, "Recollections," 41; CBT, "Occupancy."

lan marched his men down the Peninsula to embark at Yorktown and Fort Monroe.[50]

About 8:00 A.M. Saturday, 16 August, McClellan's advance arrived in Williamsburg. "This morning *many* troops & a numerous train of wagons, with some considerable artillery pieces, have passed thro' this city," Griffin wrote. These belonged to the Fifth Corps under Maj. Gen. Fitz John Porter, who found "the whole community under high excitement—the Union people depressed and alarmed; the secessionists exultant." A *New York Herald* correspondent noticed the "secessionists of Williamsburg, as elsewhere along the route, were much rejoiced to see our army making a retrograde movement, anticipating that soon this part of the peninsula also would be surrendered to the rebel rule again." In contrast, the "colored population had taken the alarm and were very anxious to learn what the future had in store for them."[51]

"Portions of the Army of McClellan continue to arrive here. This looks like '*Skedaddling*'!!!" proclaimed Griffin on the seventeenth. Some townspeople, in Porter's opinion, were indiscrete in their celebration. After notifying Colonel Durfey and farmer Robert F. Cole that he was going to "hold them as hostages for the good behavior of their friends," Porter arrested them along with William Douglas on Saturday night and early Sunday morning. He released Douglas but sent Durfey and Cole under guard to Fort Monroe, charging Durfey with "having aided to stir up ill feeling toward those who had been friendly to our cause." Porter accused Cole of "having concealed arms in possession and having run bullets in large quantity within a few days, with the avowed purpose of using them against the 'damned Yankees,' and aiding the guerrillas, who they pretended were expected soon to attack the town." These arrests "produced the salutary effect of checking alarm and attempts to create it," crowed Porter in an accompanying letter to General Dix. Griffin, however, was incensed his neighbors "were made prisoners by the tyranny of *fraternal, Union* authority, exercising itself in a *brevity of strutting* on our soil!!!"[52]

More grumbling than strutting pervaded the ranks, however, as soldiers complained that they were "moving in the wrong direction." This was not the same army that had started off from Williamsburg more than three months earlier. As Victoria King commented, "it didn't look so splendid" as it did before, nor so large. Sally Galt believed more than half "'sleep' between here &

---

50. *(Williamsburg) Cavalier*, 30 July 1862; Bucktrout Day Book, 7, 14 Aug. 1862; JLCG Commonplace Book, 15–17 Aug. 1862.

51. JLCG Commonplace Book, 15 Aug. 1862; *OR*, 12(3):579, 595; *New York Herald*, 20 Aug. 1862.

52. JLCG Commonplace Book, 17–20 Aug. 1862; *OR*, 12(3):595–6.

Richmond," and Williamson in the 20 August *Cavalier* remarked: "Regiments, once so proud of their known strength, and ability to compete with the flower of the enemy, have been more than decimated by the ravages of fever and the power of outnumbering antagonistic forces. Companies numbering when enlisted a hundred men, now muster on an average scarcely, indeed, half that number."[53]

Though fewer in number, the men arrived, as they had arrived fifteen weeks before, hungry. They foraged all the way down the Peninsula, and in Williamsburg they stopped under Sally Galt's "huge apple tree covered with apples" growing in her garden and hanging over the street. "They would ask us for them, & tell us of the battles between here & Richmond," she later wrote. The "thieving propensities" of Capt. James S. Brisbin's 6th U.S. Cavalry kept him well furnished. "I sent my man into town this morning to see what he could buy and all he could get was six sad biscuit for which he paid a quarter," Brisbin wrote his wife on 18 August. His men also supplied him with peaches, apples, and pears, and one brought a chicken. "He said he tried to buy it from an old secessionist but he would not sell it so he 'borrowed the chicken from him until next time we came along.'"[54]

Along with this plague of blue locusts came another plague of fires. It began on the night of 19 August with a blaze that consumed some small buildings at the gristmill on College Mill Pond. The Old Steward's House at the college, former home of the late Professor Morrison, went up in flames the following night as did Dr. Garrett's barn, stable, and corn house. "The loss at this crisis is heavy," judged James Griffin, "as the Dr's wheat & corn were all destroyed, except *some* corn that he had stored in his *Library*." By the twenty-first, everybody in town was on edge. "Our fellow-citizens are in such apprehension about fires," Griffin related, "that there is no little watching among them at night. This is, truly, an afflictive state of things." The Federal authorities were also watching, asserted Griffin, "sending out at night, a large patrol, with a view to prevent fires—to arrest suspicious characters."[55]

During this crisis, some Williamsburg residents found comfort in unlikely houseguests. On the night the "fire was raging" at Dr. Garrett's, James and Dr. Griffin were entertaining in their parlor three 5th Pennsylvania officers from Philadelphia, where James had one time lived. The Durfeys too had been

53. Rhodes, *All for the Union*, 77; Lee, "Williamsburg in 1861," 14–5; SMG to cousin, 15 Apr. 1863, GFP; *(Williamsburg) Cavalier*, 20 Aug. 1862.

54. *New York Herald*, 20 Aug. 1862; SMG to cousin, 15 Apr. 1863; James S. Brisbin to wife, 18 Aug. 1862, MR-CWM.

55. JLCG Commonplace Book, 21 Aug. 1862.

sheltering a Federal officer. George Armstrong Custer, now a captain on Mc-Clellan's staff, arrived with his chief on Monday evening, 18 August, and immediately looked up his old classmate "Gimlet" Lea. At Bassett Hall Custer received a "cordial reception" from the Durfeys and was invited to spend the night. "After partaking of a good supper we withdrew to the parlor where we listened to some very fine music (secesh)," Custer wrote his sister. He then learned that Lea and Margaret Durfey were engaged to be married the following week. Lea invited him to stay for the wedding, but Custer feared he could not remain in town that long. "After consulting all the parties concerned, it was decided that the ceremony should be performed the next evening in order that I might be present." It was further decided that Margaret's visiting "Cousin Maggie" would be bridesmaid and Custer would "stand up" with her as the only guest outside the family.[56]

Custer spent the next day, Tuesday the nineteenth, with Lea and that night at nine o'clock arrived at Bassett Hall in his full uniform of blue, complementing Lea's fine new gray uniform trimmed with gold lace and ordered especially for the occasion. The bride and her attendant caught Custer's eye. "Both were dressed in pure white, with a simple wreath of flowers upon their heads," he informed his sister. "I never saw two prettier girls." Reverend Ambler performed the ceremony in the parlor, Lea "perfectly happy and *resigned to his fate*," and Margaret "evidently confused and excited," making "no response whatever except to the first question." Custer escorted "Cousin Maggie" to supper and again stayed the night. The next morning he discovered that Mc-Clellan had left town the day before, but upon sending him a telegram, "obtained permission to remain in Williamsburg as long as I chose." With card games every night and the girls singing and playing southern tunes on the piano, Custer was in no hurry to leave. "I never had so pleasant a visit among strangers," he wrote his sister after finally departing nearly two weeks later.[57]

The rest of McClellan's army had long since hit the dusty road out of town. Many paused while passing through the battlefield to reflect on the experience. "Every pine could show from 5 to 20 ball holes on either side low as a man's head to testify to the fierceness of the conflict," Lt. Charles Haydon recorded in his diary on 19 August. "The idea is abroad that it was a mere skirmish. There was no such battle in the Mexican War & those who were at Williamsburgh will all tell you that they have seen nothing like it in this," even

56. Ibid.; Frederick Whittaker, *A Complete Life of General George A. Custer*, 2 vols. (1876; reprint, Lincoln: University of Nebraska Press, 1993), 1:126–7.

57. Whittaker, *Custer*, 1:127–8.

those who had just survived the Seven Days Battles. As the army continued down Telegraph Road, retracing its 5 May advance, Haydon complained, "In places where infantry could scarce wade through then we were now nearly stifled with dust. Sometimes we could not see two rods ahead."[58]

Dust clouds billowed over local Union sympathizers as well, "those unworthy men who affiliated with the enemy," in the words of Talbot Sweeney. "As the deposed but rightful attorney" of the asylum, Sweeney had been keeping an eye on it while under Unionist rule and now watched as asylum officers and staff made hasty preparations to "stampede." To replace them, the superintendent Dr. Watson applied to McClellan, who told him to make his own arrangements. Watson then appealed to President Lincoln. According to clerk and steward Henry Bowden, Lincoln advised the doctor to leave. On his way out of town during the afternoon of 20 August, Watson loaded asylum provisions and furniture onto a chartered boat at College Landing and, accompanied by Henry Bowden and other staff members, sailed to Norfolk, Mayor Lemuel Bowden's destination as well. As Sweeney put it, they "buckled on their armour *(plunder)*, and, in the choice language of the Yankee nation, 'did everlastingly skedadle.'" The inmates had only enough supplies for dinner that day, not enough for supper.[59]

Left with the keys to the asylum and two hundred hungry inmates, Colonel Campbell asked the former officers to return to their posts, "without accompanying his invitation with the condition of the *hateful parole or oath*," added Sweeney. Out of a sense of duty, William Douglas accepted this invitation but found the year's supply of provisions he had laid up less than three months earlier "gone—nothing left to feed or clothe the patients with." Campbell instructed Douglas "to send down wagons to his quarters and supplies would be furnished for immediate wants, which was done." Subsequently, Campbell ordered regular supplies from Yorktown. For superintendent and physician, Campbell appointed on 21 August the 5th Pennsylvania's assistant surgeon, Dr. Peter Wager, who had been attending Confederate wounded in town.[60]

Williamsburg could not get out of August without a funeral. "Albert Gallatin Southall died in this city, last night," James Griffin recorded on the twenty-seventh. On Thursday evening, 28 August, Griffin "accompanied the Funeral train of the late A. G. Southall to the *New Cemetery* on the College Landing Rd.," where Reverend Ambler gave the funeral service. Southall left his wife,

58. Sears, *For Country, Cause, and Leader,* 273.
59. Flournoy, *Virginia Papers,* 11:228, 476, 480, 484, 493.
60. Ibid., 229, 476–7, 487–8.

Virginia, with four daughters and a two-year-old son, now living by themselves in the President's House. Rebecca Ewell had by this time moved to Baltimore.[61]

McClellan too was headed north. Before embarking at Fort Monroe 23 August, he ordered the two 5th Pennsylvania Cavalry detached companies to rejoin their regiment in Williamsburg and sent the five 11th Pennsylvania Cavalry companies in Williamsburg to Suffolk. Returns at the end of the month indicated that the Fifth, some reserve artillery, and a battalion of the 6th New York Cavalry, altogether just under fifteen hundred men, were then posted at Williamsburg and attached to Gen. Erasmus Keyes's Fourth Corps, headquartered in Yorktown. Now the Federal outpost closest to the Confederate capital, Williamsburg was just beginning its experience as an occupied town.[62]

61. JLCG Commonplace Book, 27–29 Aug. 1862; Hamlin, *Making of a Soldier,* 114–5; U.S. Bureau of the Census, Williamsburg and James City County Records, 1870.

62. *OR,* 11(3):381–2, 18:376–7.

CHAPTER 13

A Melancholy Condition

On Monday evening, 8 September 1862, "the cry of fire" once again echoed through Williamsburg. Not an old barn or abandoned shack this time, but the main building of William and Mary College, so recently rebuilt, was in flames. Mary Southall, at home in the President's House, quickly organized a bucket brigade from the crowd of bystanders, mostly women and children, gathering at the alarm. While carrying a bucket, Mary "met three United States soldiers," she later testified; "one of them told her if the College was not burned that day, it would be the next, or words to that effect." The flames were soon extinguished but not "before their light was seen in the surrounding country as a beacon inviting the approach of the avenger."[1]

The avenger was not long in coming. At dawn the next day, 9 September, Williamsburg's streets suddenly came alive with cavalrymen "riding helter-skelter pell-mell," followed closely by shouts, clashing sabers, and the sharp report of pistols. Townspeople dashed to their doors. Charles Waller, though sick in bed, managed to reach his window and there with his boots "beat a tatoo of welcome on the Dutch roof of his house, calling out 'kill 'em kill 'em.'" Running out onto the street "in the wild delirium of the moment," shouting civilians contributed their voices to the chorus. "Such a scene of the wildest tumult and joy can only be imagined by those who have felt the sudden uplifting of the oppressor's heel," wrote Cynthia Coleman. "Women laughed and wept, wrung the hands of strangers, imploring Heaven's blessing upon them and the Cause for which they fought." They were, in James Griffin's

1. Mary R. M. Goodwin, "Historical Notes on the College of William and Mary," 1954, UA-CWM, 591; Edward S. Joynes to R. G. H. Kean, 5 Nov. 1863, Edward S. Joynes F/A, UA-CWM; CBT, "Occupancy," TCP, MR-CWM.

words, "most cordially welcomed" on this day "illustrious to us Williamsbur-
gians."[2]

Their beloved Confederate cavalry—some five hundred strong, by Griffin's
estimate—had at last arrived. Virginians, South Carolinians, and Georgians
led by South Carolina planter and banker Lt. Col. William P. Shingler galloped down Richmond Road and swept past the Federal picket guard, killing
eight. They then swiftly overtook the 5th Pennsylvania's reserve of thirty-three
men, sleeping on the college lawn. A few bluecoats escaped with their commander, Maj. Jacob P. Wilson, and ran, in some cases, all the way to Yorktown, though many were captured and eighteen were wounded on the way.
Shingler's men charged down Main Street before splitting up in different directions. About half of them proceeded "down to Fort Magruder on the York
road, where they set fire to the tents the federal soldiers had been creating,
barracks, tents &c.," Griffin related. "There they burnt much of the provisions
of the enemy, & made the whole 'garrison' there surrender." To add to the
Federals' confusion, somebody cut the telegraph wire to Yorktown.[3]

A few raiders peeled off at Union headquarters to call upon Col. David
Campbell. Soon he along with about one hundred officers and men were
headed for prison in Richmond. Isabella Sully watched them take some twenty
blacks, "a quantity of commissary store, and wagons loaded with ammunition." By ten minutes after ten that morning, the last of Shingler's cavalry departed and the celebrating ceased. Already, two companies of the 6th New
York Cavalry were on their way from Yorktown, ordered by General Keyes to
collect the scattered Fifth and reform the picket line west of Williamsburg.
Chosen to lead these companies was a young Yale graduate, Capt. D. C. Hannahs. He accomplished the mission by midafternoon, establishing camp on
the college campus, but had trouble controlling some disgruntled Pennsylvanians who had found a case of liquor in an unguarded commissariat and were
taking out their anger on civilians. So many "drunk and boisterous" soldiers
crowded the college yard that the Southalls were advised to leave their premises, which they did.[4]

For cheering Shingler's cavalry through town, Charles Waller had made

2. CBT, "Occupancy"; JLCG Commonplace Book, 9 Sept. 1862, JLCG F/A, UA-CWM.

3. JLCG Commonplace Book, 9 Sept. 1862; David Edward Cronin, "The Vest Mansion,"
1908–10, John D. Rockefeller Jr. Library, CWF, 25–6.

4. Cronin, "Vest Mansion," 25; OR, 18:11; Anne S. Frobel, The Civil War Diary of Anne S.
Frobel (McLean, Va.: EPM, 1992), 119; E. P. M. McKinney to Lyon G. Tyler, 15 Dec. 1902,
William and Mary College Papers, UA-CWM; Goodwin, "Historical Notes," 591, UA-CWM.

himself particularly odious to the Federals. "As soon as it was safe for them to do so the Yankees swarmed into his house, broke up his furniture and destroyed every thing they could lay their hands on," wrote Cynthia, who was staying in Richmond at the time. "Mrs. W endeavored to prevent their going up stairs to the sick room of her husband was herself forced to jump with her infant in her arms over the banisters and flee she knew not whither." Only the arrival of an officer at this juncture prevented further destruction. He "commanded the Soldiers to depart, unfortunately he could not restore order in the dismantled wrecked house."[5]

Besides Charles Waller's house, other Williamsburg residences had their "windows and doors forced in, elegantly furnished apartments dashed into by savage ruffians, dismantled and every thing torn and broken to pieces," Isabella reported in a letter written shortly afterward. As she "ran to the house of a sick friend a soldier in the street fired at her but fortunately he was too drunk to take steady aim, and when he found he had missed such volleys of blasphemous oaths and imprecations never before fell upon her ears." Appealing to an officer to stop this madness did no good; he refused to interfere, he told Isabella, because "every one has his own path and must walk in it." Mrs. Maria Peyton, a sister of Col. Robert H. Armistead, told Lt. Col. S. E. Smith, assuming command after Campbell's capture, that she heard "a rumor the town was to be fired. He replied: 'No such orders had been or would be given.'"[6]

This "was truly an eventful day," wrote James Griffin. His father, Dr. Samuel Griffin, was threatened twice "with a presented pistol in the hands of 2 different 'fellows of the baser sort,' composing the *illustrious* Army of the *'Union'!!!*" he recorded in his commonplace book. Later that afternoon, while visiting merchant John Deneufville in his Main Street home just east of the Peachy's, Griffin happened to glance out the window. Directly across the street stood two structures: a two-story brick home belonging to City Sergeant Parkes Slater and, to the east of it, a small frame tailor shop, which its owner, ninety-year-old free black Peggy Parsons, had converted into an eating establishment. Griffin noticed Hannahs's horse by Peggy's gate. While the captain was buying something to eat inside, "a hideous, dark-looking, be-whiskered man" rode up to his horse. Parkes Slater's ten-year-old son, James, standing nearby, heard this man talk to the boy holding the horse. "The soldier, with an oath, ordered the boy to call the captain out," James Slater later wrote.

5. CBT, "Occupancy."
6. Frobel, *Civil War Diary*, 119; CBT, "Occupancy"; Goodwin, "Historical Notes," 591.

"The captain came out, and the soldier ordered him to mount." Hannahs refused this obviously drunken demand, and the moment Griffin turned his head away from the window, the soldier drew his pistol and shot the officer.[7]

"At first I thought he was dead," surmised Griffin, looking back on the street toward the sound of the gunshot; "but some soldiers coming to him raised him up & helped him into the house of Mrs. Virginia Slater, who kindly opened her doors to the wounded man, tho' an enemy, nationally speaking." James Slater remembered the unruly soldier, a private in the Fifth, coming into his mother's house and threatening Hannahs again with his pistol until some 6th New York cavalrymen threw him out. Later that afternoon the captain, badly wounded and in great pain, requested James to find his first lieutenant at the college. The boy got as far as the college gate "when I met one of the Fifth Pennsylvania Cavalry, who was cursing and saying, 'I burned that d——d College, and I intend to burn this d——d town.'"[8]

About five o'clock Mary Southall learned the college was on fire once more and returned for fear the President's House too would burn. This time she could do nothing to stop the destruction. "A cordon of drawn *sabers* surrounding the building" prevented any attempt to extinguish the blaze, according to eyewitnesses. Again Smith provided no help during the crisis, asserting "that it would be now impossible to save the Building for want of buckets. He said further, he had a set of drunken soldiers, and that it would take two sober men to control one drunken one." Before dark descended upon this momentous day in Williamsburg, the college building was reduced to charred walls.[9]

Around that time Lt. E. P. M. McKinney of the 6th New York Cavalry rode into town looking for Hannahs. Keyes sent him to Williamsburg "to ascertain the state of affairs" and report back to Yorktown as soon as possible. As he turned up Main Street, the smoking ruins of the college standing massively against the western twilight caught his eye. "Capt. Hannahs I found in a small house lying on a bed," McKinney later wrote. "He had been shot through the lungs." After reporting this to Keyes, McKinney returned to Williamsburg about midnight. Virginia Slater, who had a son in the Junior Guards, "was all kindness and sympathy," the lieutenant remembered, as he kept watch all night over his tent-mate and most intimate friend. Hannahs

7. JLCG Commonplace Book, 10 Sept. 1862; J. L. Slater, "Burning of the College in 1862," *William and Mary Quarterly*, 1st ser., 11 (1903): 179; McKinney to Tyler, 15 Dec. 1902; John S. Charles, "Recollections of Williamsburg, Virginia, as It Was at the Beginning of the Civil War," 1928, John D. Rockefeller Jr. Library, CWF, 43–4.
8. JLCG Commonplace Book, 10 Sept. 1862; Slater, "Burning of the College," 179.
9. Goodwin, "Historical Notes," 591–2; CBT, "Occupancy."

"proved himself to have possessed magnanimity," wrote Griffin, for "on his death-bed he was very particular in exonerating our citizens of all blame; assuring his friends that they were entirely innocent, & that he was shot by a member of the 5th Penn. Regt." About three o'clock that morning, Hannahs died in Virginia's arms.[10]

Those Williamsburg inhabitants able to sleep that night awoke on 10 September relieved to find their town unburned. McKinney spent all day procuring a coffin for Hannahs and interviewing people in an effort to gather evidence against the captain's murderer. Members of the Fifth threatened James Slater if he told on their comrade, but James Griffin was willing to talk and able to describe the man so accurately that he was identified, arrested, and confined in the Yorktown guardhouse pending a court-martial. The Fifth's Major Wilson and his men were also in trouble for running during the raid. "Order immediately a court-martial on the cowards of Williamsburg," demanded Union general in chief Henry Halleck after General Dix filled him in on the raid. "If no one has courage to have them shot report them here, so that we can ask the President to cashier them." Trial was set for the following Monday.[11]

As the dust and smoke from the raid and its aftermath slowly settled, both sides tallied their losses. Besides Campbell, the Federals counted six other officers and sixty men captured, with seven killed and thirteen wounded. Of the attackers, two were captured, and Griffin stated at least two were killed and several wounded. The townspeople were not allowed to nurse these Confederates, but all were "sent away by the enemy" within a day, along with the Presbyterian minister Samuel Blain. This fearless divine was accused of cutting the telegraph communication with Yorktown, arrested, and carried off to Fort Magruder. "Here in the darkness of the night he fell asleep on a bench," Cynthia later learned. "He was aroused from his heavy slumbers, by such execrations and oaths that for a moment he thought he had died and had gone to hell." After the raid two inmates were missing from the asylum; one had gone fishing and decided to remain in Confederate lines.[12]

Williamsburg's greatest loss by far was the college. For the third time in its 169-year history, the interior of the main building was entirely gutted, though much of its three-foot-thick walls still stood. Mary Southall had rescued "a

10. McKinney to Tyler, 15 Dec. 1902; JLCG Commonplace Book, 10 Sept. 1862.

11. McKinney to Tyler, 15 Dec. 1902; Slater, "Burning of the College," 179; *OR*, 18:11, 390.

12. *OR*, 18:11–3; JLCG Commonplace Book, 10–11 Sept. 1862; CBT, "Occupancy"; Eastern State Hospital, Report, 20 Aug.1862, Eastern State Hospital Papers, MR-CWM.

large portion of the valuable library of the College," probably during the 8 September fire. Many other books, along with the old college portraits and philosophical apparatus, had been placed in the asylum and private homes for safe keeping before the Confederate evacuation. But the remaining library books and all chemical apparatus and furniture were destroyed, totaling, Benjamin Ewell estimated after the war, more than $61,000. He was "credibly informed" that the damage came from unorganized bodies of the 5th Pennsylvania who, "under the excitement produced by their defeat and the use of a quantity of whiskey which they found, fired the College Building."[13]

By the evening of 10 September, about 430 of the 817 Federals supposed to be present in Williamsburg were reported to have returned to their posts. The next day their number had increased to 500, and Dix requested at least one more reinforcing regiment from Halleck, who pointedly inquired: "What is the object of holding Williamsburg? Why not withdraw the garrison to Yorktown?" Dix wired his explanation on the twelfth: "I have kept them there the last four days with the hope that they might do something to retrieve the character of the regiment." He also feared that "in abandoning Williamsburg we leave to the mercy of the insurgents some good Union men, whom we induced, by assurances of protection, to come out for us." Though he assured Halleck that he was planning to withdraw the Fifth to Yorktown, Dix wrote on 20 September that he still had a small cavalry force in Williamsburg. The town itself he considered "of no importance, except as an advance post for watching a movement of the enemy from the Chickahominy" and as a convenient point from which "to push our vedettes farther out." But to hold Williamsburg, Dix thought he now needed at least 800 more men.[14]

As far as the townspeople were concerned, Williamsburg already had more than enough men to plunder them. The old widow Helen Anderson complained to General Dix on 13 September, "My house was broken open this morning by an armed band of Soldiers, and a large quantity of very valuable old wine, which has been in my family for many years, taken away." Leading this band in person was the new provost marshal, Lt. W. John Simpson, a nephew of Colonel Campbell. Mrs. Anderson urged Dix to act immediately and telegraph his orders before the wine was totally consumed by the soldiers and the blacks accompanying them. That afternoon Lieutenant Colonel

13. "Henley T. Jones to the Editor," *William and Mary Quarterly*, 1st ser., 11 (1903): 178; Joynes to Kean, 5 Nov. 1863, Edward S. Joynes F/A, UA-CWM; CBT, "Occupancy"; BSE, "The College in the Years 1861–1865," 292–3.

14. *OR*, 18:11, 390–1, 396–7.

Smith promised her the wine would be returned, "but it must be kept at the Insane Asylum for safe keeping" and given to her as she needed it. On the eighteenth Smith placed the remaining stock under William Douglas's care and forbade him to issue it to anyone but Mrs. Anderson. Instead, the bottles continued to disappear into the hands of officers, drawn by order of Lieutenant Simpson until the twenty-sixth, and after that date by order of a new acting provost, Lt. S. H. Bayley. Between 20 September and 1 October, Cpl. H. M. Flanagan, guarding the supply at the asylum, delivered thirty-five bottles, including four to Dr. Wager. Mrs. Anderson finally appealed to Captain Hennessey as a gentleman "to redress the indignity & outrages that have been committed." After being reinstated as provost, Hennessey ordered the remnant of the wine removed to his own office on 2 October.[15]

Where Hennessey had been since the raid remains a mystery. If he was among the men captured by Shingler, his name was not listed with Colonel Campbell and six other 5th Pennsylvania officers included in a mass exchange of prisoners on 21 September. The regiment continued to reassemble its officers four days later when Major Wilson was found not guilty of the formal charges of "cowardice" and "misbehavior before the enemy" preferred against him at his court-martial. Though he was allowed to "resume his sword and return to duty," the stigma would hang over his head and that of the Fifth "until this stain on its character is effaced by worthier conduct in the face of the enemy." Within a month Campbell resigned his commission and went home to Philadelphia. Cynthia counted that another loss to Williamsburg, for she believed he had "observed as mild a policy towards the citizens as the nature of his position would permit."[16]

The last week of September brought news by northern newspapers of a series of engagements in Maryland culminating in the extraordinarily bloody battle at Antietam Creek near Sharpsburg on 17 September. Again, Williamsburg people trembled for their own, as the 32d Virginia participated, but no details of losses were available. The town's gloom further deepened on the night of 4 October at the outbreak of a particularly disturbing fire consuming Robert Cole's kitchen, barn, and stable behind his Main Street home. "Mr. C's dwelling narrowly escaped, while the Episcopal Parsonage—Rev. Mr. Ambler's & the intermediate house,—formerly our Post Office—were in no

15. Helen M. Anderson to John Dix, 13 Sept. 1862; S. E. Smith to H. M. Anderson, 13 Sept. 1862; "An Account of the Disposal of the Wine," 20 Sept. 1862; and H. M. Anderson to T. Hennessey, 3 Oct. 1862, Helen M. Anderson Papers, John D. Rockefeller Jr. Library, CWF.

16. *OR* II, 4:577, 581–4; *OR,* 18:12–3; Cronin, "Vest Mansion," 26; CBT, "Occupancy."

little danger," Griffin entered in his commonplace book the next day. The former post office caught fire but the blaze was extinguished, and "the Episcopal Church, too, shared the dangers. This fire was, beyond doubt, the work of an incendiary or of incendiaries!!" Though his stable burned, Cole's dark gray mare was spared, having been taken from him earlier that day by order of Lieutenant Colonel Smith. The mare "moves very sluggish and is some what disposed to stumble," Cole's receipt read, and "when used very hard has a swelling of the Vains under her belly," making her of questionable use to the blue cavalry. Nevertheless, Cole's mare was not the only local animal to enter Federal service, for on the seventh Major Wilson promised "to make a complete report of all the horses taken from citizens of Williamsburg tomorrow."[17]

The day after that tomorrow, 9 October, at Wilson's outpost on Richmond Road, Col. Benjamin Ewell presented himself "with a flagg of truce and communication" from Richmond requesting safe conduct for the purpose of "looking into the condition of the College & Asylum." Accompanying Ewell was Williamsburg farmer and asylum director James Custis and Maj. John Munford, who had also been an asylum director but was more interested in seeing his family. He had recently received a letter from Williamsburg describing his wife's declining health due to tuberculosis, and he planned to make some arrangements to remove her and his younger children still at Tazewell Hall. Unofficially, Ewell bore letters and messages to Williamsburg loved ones, including several that Cynthia Coleman had written and collected in Richmond. She hoped Ewell would bring back "some favorable news," but after a week of cooling their heels at the lines, the three men were denied entry into Williamsburg and marched back to Richmond. "No report can, therefore, be made of the condition of the Eastern Lunatic Asylum as to its inmates at the present time," Ewell wrote Governor Letcher upon his return.[18]

Information on the asylum came instead in a 24 October letter Talbot Sweeney addressed to Letcher. "The patients, I am told, have enough to eat, *such as it is*, the food being dealt out to them somewhat after the manner and kind of a soldier's rations," he expounded. "They suffer, however, greatly from want of clothing and attention of every kind." Attention, indeed, was lacking on all levels, from superintendent and physician Dr. Peter Wager—on leave

17. JLCG Commonplace Book, 25 Sept., 5 Oct. 1862; Jensen, *32nd Virginia Infantry,* 88–94; Robert F. Cole receipt, 4 Oct. 1862, WCP, MR-CWM; J. P. Wilson to G. C. Johnston, 7 Oct. 1862, WCP.

18. J. P. Wilson to C. D. Suydam, 9 Oct. 1862, Presidents' Papers–BSE, UA-CWM; Sally Munford to Elizabeth Ewell, 22 Oct. 1862, EFP, MR-CWM; CBT to BSE, [Sept. 1862], TCP; Flournoy, *Virginia State Papers,* 11:227–8.

in Philadelphia for the last ten days—to the hired servants, most of whom had "taken their *freedom*, and those that have remained to this time are under no restraint, it would seem, and are wholly indifferent to the wants of the inmates." Though the old asylum officers had returned "from what they considered a sense of duty to the patients," they were working only halfheartedly because their presence at the institution while under Federal control amounted to "a tacit acknowledgment of wrongful authority." For this reason they refused pay from the Federal government, and having received no salary from the Confederate government for six months, they were suffering materially almost as much as the unfortunate inmates. This predicament fueled rumors, then buzzing around town, that the Federals planned to carry the patients north and distribute them among northern hospitals. "I fear that if this should be done," Sweeney warned, "the finale of the whole would be the destruction of the Institution by fire."[19]

The best way to avoid this catastrophe, Sweeney advised the governor, was to give the officers his official permission to work at the asylum and authorize their salaries. Sweeney volunteered to arrange for them "such currency as they can spend while in the enemy's lines," for "Confederate money the enemy will not take, and Virginia money is now at a discount of fifty per cent. at 'Old Point.'" This would have to be done without the Federals' knowledge, or they would not allow the officers to work, "and the whole plan would be frustrated." Letcher would have to send his reply with "the utmost secrecy," directed to Sweeney in care of a James City County resident ten miles above town. How it would be delivered to Williamsburg Sweeney did not explain, but his letter contained details on the 5th Pennsylvania, which usually numbered about five hundred fit for duty encamped four and a half miles below Williamsburg on York Road near Whittaker's Mill. One company remained at Fort Magruder with eight pieces of artillery. Federal pickets extended a mile up Jamestown Road and two miles up Richmond Road. These would have to be eluded as Confederate scouts carried the mail into town during their nocturnal forays.[20]

The scouts apparently had a thriving business in outgoing mail in October. Dr. Robert Waller, suffering his usual anxiety about his property, family, and health in Lynchburg, mentioned in his diary receiving at least ten letters that month from Williamsburg. One came from Peggy Parsons and five or six "from my negroes in Wmsburg to their relations, that I brought from there

19. Flournoy, *Virginia State Papers*, 11:228–30.
20. Ibid., 229–32.

when I came away." Most were written on the seventh or eighth. Dr. Waller spent half of October trying to retrieve some slaves he had left on his Williamsburg farms after receiving word they wanted to come to him. He recovered a dozen, and one told him that out of his entire work force left behind, only two had run away.[21]

While they remained faithful, servants provided another outgoing mail route for Williamsburg inhabitants. On 29 October Lucy Tucker addressed a letter to Cynthia and sent it out by servants able to pass freely into Gloucester County and thence to Richmond. Though feeling "so desolate & stricken" without her family, Lucy was determined to remain in Williamsburg to protect her home from the vandalism and dismantling suffered by abandoned dwellings. The provost may have relocated after Shingler's raid "because the Confederates kept comin' up the ravines about the Saunders House and surrounded it, so they had to move," according to Eliza Baker. That left the invaluable Saunders library vulnerable to looting. "Yesterday I saw a Yankee with as many of Mr Saunders *books* as he could carry going down town to pack up or take to camp below Whittakers Mill," Lucy informed Cynthia. She and Isabella Sully watched the provost's wife taking her share of books in "an ambulance well loaded with them. Day by day I see them carried away by the armful," wrote Isabella. When Lucy begged the Saunders butler, Edmund Parsons, who had been left behind to guard the house, to "bring some thing to me to take care of," he refused. Isabella had received Captain Hennessey's permission to move the library to a safer place, and she too asked Edmund "to help me to save his Master's books, but he declined, was 'afraid to meddle'— all bosh, a good-for-nothing, ungrateful wretch."[22]

The absent Saunders family was fortunate that Edmund still held his post to save the house, at least. Lucy Tucker had Mamy Patty and a few other servants, but many "are going off rapidly," she told Cynthia. During this period, the slaves "did not immediately leave their homes or refuse the usual service, but went off by degrees as they made their arrangements," Cynthia later learned. "While they remained they were very different beings from the trusted and faithful friends they had been supposed to be." As with Helen Anderson's experience, they would betray hiding places of treasured old wine to northern soldiers, who "seized upon bottle after bottle snapped off the necks, and drank the nectar to the health of the justly irate owner." For some

---

21. Robert Page Waller Diary, 14, 23, 29 Oct., 8, 22, 24 Nov.1862, MR-CWM.
22. LAT to CBT, 29 Oct. 1862, TCP; CBT, "Occupancy"; Eliza Baker, "Memoirs of Williamsburg," 1933, John D. Rockefeller Jr. Library, CWF, 7.

time, the sight of "a Yankee, and a negro promenading" openly on Williams-burg streets had been common. "Negro women held high carnival with the soldiers of the United States Army, who thought it no debasement to associate with them on terms of perfect equality and to dance with them night after night," as Cynthia delicately phrased it. The vacant Coke House on South Back Street across from the Powder Horn was "selected for their entertainments."[23]

Worse than obnoxious, the "negroes are becoming more & more danger-ous," Benjamin Ewell wrote daughter Lizzie after returning to Richmond from a late October trip down the Peninsula to recover some furniture from his farm. He was referring to the murders of two white men and a boy on Jamestown Island by several former slaves. Another intended victim, a free black man, escaped to a nearby farm owned by Williamsburg planter John Coupland. The following month Richard Bucktrout entered a charge in his ledger for the coffin and burial of "the little boy that was murdered by the negroes" at Jamestown.[24]

The undertaker's business had been tapering off since summer. On 7 Octo-ber he buried the last recorded Confederate casualty from the May battle, an Alabamian placed in the fourth grave in the Florida row. This completed the military section of the City Cemetery, with the Georgia row, as near as can be determined, containing fifty-seven graves; the Louisiana row, forty-four; the Virginia row, twenty-four; the Florida row, four; the South Carolina row, twelve; the Mississippi row, nine; and the Tennessee row, two. No burials were recorded for a Texas row. Williamsburg citizens, however, feared more casual-ties might be on the way. "Various rumours reach us about our troops coming down," Lucy included in her 29 October letter. "I hope they will not think of it *unless they can hold* the place, which I presume they cannot do, as they might be flanked by a superior force. If they come for a short time our situation will be worse than before."[25]

Everyone knew that gray horsemen were coming uncomfortably close. On the night of 28 October, "800 finely mounted rebel cavalry, under Colonel Shingler, approached to within a short distance of the town," Keyes reported to Dix. This time the 5th Pennsylvania was "on the alert," capturing a picket and making "such dispositions that no attack was made." The next day Keyes

23. LAT to CBT, 29 Oct. 1862; CBT, "Occupancy"; *(Williamsburg) Cavalier*, 16 July 1862.
24. BSE to Elizabeth Ewell, 5 Nov. 1862, EFP, MR-CWM; David F. Riggs, *Embattled Shrine: Jamestown in the Civil War* (Shippensburg, Pa.: White Mane, 1997), 83–5; Flournoy, *Virginia State Papers*, 11:236; Richard M. Bucktrout Day Book, Nov. 1862, MR-CWM.
25. Bucktrout Day Book, June–Nov. 1862; LAT to CBT, 29 Oct. 1862.

reminded his garrison to "be vigilant and the men ready to turn out at a moment's notice." Four days later, on 2 November, a clash fourteen miles above Williamsburg resulted in one dead and one captured Virginia lieutenant, providing "evidence of improvement," Keyes assured Dix, that "there is in the Fifth Pennsylvania Cavalry the material for a very good regiment."[26]

Throughout October, Richmond newspapers smuggled into Williamsburg brought tidings of deaths occurring with disturbing frequency in "Secessia." Casualty lists for Sharpsburg included several local loved ones, and obituaries contained some surprises. A 16 October *Richmond Enquirer* announced the demise of Marianne Wilmer, wife of former 32d Virginia chaplain George Wilmer and eldest daughter of Robert Saunders, in Pittsylvania County, where the family was staying. On the last day of the month, James Griffin recorded, "Not many weeks ago, little Sarah—*Sady,* as she was familiarly called—departed this life." Five-year-old Sadie Washington died in Gloucester of typhoid fever on 1 October, plunging mother Cynthia Coleman into deep and prolonged mourning.[27]

In a 20 November condolence letter to Cynthia, the Tuckers' next-door neighbor Julia Thompson expressed the shock and dismay felt by the community over Sadie's death, which intensified the town's darkening mood. "Everything here is sad, as you can well imagine," sighed Julia. Her sister, Isabella Sully, was trying to obtain a pass to leave town with daughter Jennie, and their brother, Montegu Thompson, wanted Julia to go with them, "but it appears to me it would be best for me to remain here," she decided, "at least during the winter." Lucy Tucker worried about Julia staying all winter, for, Lucy had written 29 October, "Montegu has made no arrangements for poor Julia who is thin & worked to death & to do without fire will kill her." The shortage of firewood and coal caused more fear to grip the town, as Lucy confessed, "My greatest dread for the winter is that my fuel will give out."[28]

William Douglas, as asylum steward, was similarly concerned. On 1 November he penned a note to Governor Letcher bringing him up to date on his situation. Since the end of August, the U.S. government had enabled Douglas to secure "an abundant supply of Provisions," and he had "been promised goods for the winter clothing of the Patients." Yet they were still liable to freeze without fuel, which had not yet been ordered at that late date. An un-

26. *OR,* 51(1):900, 926–7.

27. JLCG Commonplace Book, 19, 31 Oct. 1862; *Richmond Enquirer,* 14 Oct. 1862; CBT to Lawrence and Sarah Washington, 23 Apr. 1863, Louis Malesherbes Goldsborough Papers, Special Collections Library, Duke University, Durham, N.C.

28. Julia Thompson to CBT, 20 Nov. 1862, TCP; LAT to CBT, 29 Oct. 1862.

usually heavy and early snowfall the night of 6 November, continuing through the next day, only aggravated the situation and prompted Douglas to write again on the ninth. "Indeed, the matter of *fuel* is made peculiarly urgent by the present inclement weather," he informed the governor, "and unless some arrangement be made, and that quickly, to supply the Asylum with it the Patients must suffer severely."[29]

The problem was not so much the scarcity of firewood as a lack of transportation. Lucy had "engaged wood at 4 dollars per cord," but all she had was a horse and cart to haul it. That was more than Margaret Munford had after Federal soldiers and runaway slaves stole her wagon, mules, and oxen. On 19 November Margaret wrote from Tazewell Hall to Brig. Gen. Henry Naglee, temporarily in command at Yorktown during Keyes's absence, that in the last few days she had also lost "one milch cow, two young cattle, an ox yoke, the wheels off of a wagon, and a considerable portion of my provender for wintering my cows." Since she now had enough wood for only two days, "with four helpless children, & no gentleman friends *to call* on for assistance," she requested the use of government wagons to haul some to her house. Runaways further contributed to "the melancholy condition of things in our little community" by "destroying for fuel many unoccupied houses, fences, and shade trees. It is my opinion," Margaret advised Naglee, "that unless there is some radical change made in the government of these people before the winter sets in, that the white inhabitants, particularly defenseless ladies like myself, will suffer severely."[30]

Williamsburg's black population contributed to the asylum's woes as well. Douglas's first missive to Letcher complained that "in the last few months many of the hirelings of this year have left the Institution, and all, or nearly all, I fear, will leave on or about the Xmas holidays." The steward was at a loss for a remedy. "White servants cannot be procured in this region of country, and it will be impossible, I suspect, to hire negroes for the ensuing year under existing circumstances." The matter had become "intensely embarrassing" by 9 November, for "the few that remain are in such a state of insubordination as to make it almost impossible to have anything done." Douglas closed with the plea, "my dear Sir, that you may be ready with a correction, and that you will apply it with the least possible delay."[31]

His government responded almost immediately. Douglas's letters, coupled

29. Flournoy, *Virginia State Papers*, 11:236–7; JLCG Commonplace Book, 7 Nov. 1862.
30. LAT to CBT, 29 Oct. 1862; M. N. Munford to H. Naglee, 19 Nov. 1862, WCP.
31. Flournoy, *Virginia State Papers*, 11:236–7.

with Sweeney's mentioning possible Federal plans to move asylum patients north and newspaper accounts of alleged mismanagement, induced inmates' families to pressure President Davis into investigating. On 27 November Brig. Gen. Henry Wise addressed a communication to Keyes on behalf of "the State of Virginia's children of affliction." In it Wise listed the rumored abuses and requested flag-of-truce passage for two of his officers to inspect the asylum. Keyes replied on 3 December that the inmates were attended by an army surgeon and issued full rations. "Coal is now being sent up, and nothing in my power has been omitted to render the unfortunate inmates of the Asylum as comfortable as circumstances will permit," Keyes assured Wise. The Confederate officers would not be allowed to inspect the institution but could talk to Douglas. Insulted by Wise's implication that the Federals would be cruel to these helpless "little ones," Keyes passionately concluded, "who knows which deserves the greater pity, the poor lunatics in the Asylum at Williamsburg, or the men who have made this war."[32]

Or perhaps the "defenseless ladies," as Margaret Munford reiterated in her next letter to Naglee, dated 10 December. She thanked him for his "prompt, and kind attention" to her last request and again stressed the growing problem of runaways. "Their depredations on my property, both by day and by night," Margaret asserted, "continue unabated until I stand appalled to think where I am to obtain additional supplies for my family." Meanwhile, "my woods are filled with stout negroe men cutting and hauling my wood to market." On 14 December James Griffin noticed the vacated Benjamin Waller House on Woodpecker Lane was filled with runaways, and on the night of the nineteenth, a small law office in front of the Coke House burned to the ground, "the result, probably, of carelessness or stupidity—*not of design*," for a change.[33]

As sad as Williamsburg was becoming, John Coupland decided to move into town from his farm near Jamestown. On 18 December Bucktrout charged Coupland $1.50 for forcing open the front door of the Vest House, repairing the damage, and furnishing a new lock and key. Four days later Mary Ann Lively was forced to surrender the complete printing press, including fonts of type, to Lt. Samuel Williamson "for the use of U.S. forces at Yorktown," according to his receipt. Fearing the near approach of the Confederates, no *Cavalier* had been printed since 20 August.[34]

32. JLCG Commonplace Book, Dec. 1862.

33. M. N. Munford to H. Naglee, 10 Dec. 1862, CWF; JLCG Commonplace Book, 14, 20 Dec. 1862.

34. Bucktrout Day Book, 18 Dec. 1862; S. Williamson to M. Lively, 22 Dec. 1862, *Williamsburg Gazette* microfilm, CWM.

Northern newspapers arriving in Williamsburg on 20 December brought "glorious tidings" of a Confederate victory at Fredericksburg on the thirteenth, but soon after came news that Tom Tucker had been "*slightly* wounded" in the battle. Donning her India rubber boots she used for gardening, Lucy Tucker eluded the pickets by walking out of town through the woods and three days later, with the help of Confederate scouts, reached Richmond. There she found Tom with a serious knee wound, barely alive, being nursed by his sisters, Bland Taliaferro and Cynthia, who had just given birth on 27 November to Charles Washington Coleman Jr.[35]

Back in Williamsburg, with little to bring joy but the victory at Fredericksburg, families and friends observed Christmas with traditional dinners. At last 1862 "departed amid clouds," as James Griffin meditated in his commonplace book. "Like last year, it has been a most momentous year indeed! Intestinal war, with all its miseries & vices, still bears away!" He was confident that posterity would admire the battle of Williamsburg and all other battles fought that year for "the patriotism & the valor, of a free people in defense of their liberties—of their homes & firesides!"[36]

Eighteen sixty-three opened with "bright and glorious sunshine" that could not dispel the gloom of "hard times." Poor Dr. Griffin was compelled to celebrate his eighty-first birthday without his traditional mince pie. James could not attend his father's party anyway, for he was called to Yorktown, as he had been in December, to testify at the trial of Hannahs's murderer. A week later, on 12 January, he returned to Yorktown for the last time, but the accused soldier was "discharged for want of sufficient evidence." Traveling to and from the trial, Griffin observed the condition of the intervening country, most of it in ruins. Yet Cheesecake Church appeared "to be pretty well preserved, being used by 'the Yankees,' as a Hospital."[37]

This hospital was not far from the 5th Pennsylvania's main Whittaker's Mill camp about two miles below Fort Magruder. One company of the Fifth, armed with six or seven guns, garrisoned the fort. Expecting "a raid by the Southrons, in force" any day, Keyes on 6 January ordered Lively's "entire printing establishment," stored at Fort Magruder since its confiscation, removed to Yorktown for safekeeping. The fort's present commander, Lt. Col. William Lewis, feared an imminent attack in mid-January and begged Keyes

35. JLCG Commonplace Book, 20 Dec. 1862; CBT to Lawrence and Sarah Washington, 23 Apr. 1863.
36. JLCG Commonplace Book, 26 Dec. 1862, 1 Jan. 1863.
37. Ibid., 14 Dec. 1862, 1, 7, 13 Jan. 1863; McKinney to Tyler, 15 Dec. 1902.

for an infantry regiment "at once," but Dix refused. "You must do the best you can," Dix encouraged Keyes. "If your force is not sufficient to hold Fort Magruder it should be abandoned when the proper time comes."[38]

To gauge the proper time, Lewis needed information about local Confederate strength. Thus, on the morning of 19 January, 120 Pennsylvania troopers trotted out of Williamsburg up Richmond Road. They split up to scout in three directions between the rivers and, from Mrs. Piggott's gate to Burnt Ordinary, skirmished with a small body of Confederates. From four scouts they captured, the Federals learned that one gray infantry regiment and 500 cavalry were stationed at Diascund Bridge about twelve miles above Williamsburg. An attack by Confederate scouts on Federal pickets west of town on the morning of 27 January elicited another plea from Keyes to Dix for reinforcements, again in vain, but the generals were gratified that the Fifth showed marked improvement in conduct, "activity and energy" since September.[39]

When not firing on blue pickets, the Confederate scouts, along with the rest of Wise's brigade of four regiments with attached artillery and cavalry, had the duty of patrolling the Peninsula between Williamsburg and Richmond, intercepting southern deserters attempting to reach Federal lines, watching for espionage activities among Union sympathizers, and "keeping the miserable 5th Pennsylvania Cavalry timidly at bay," in Wise's words. They were also responsible for the clandestine mail system now assisted by the hoop skirts worn by Williamsburg ladies. Delia Bucktrout later indicated that outgoing mail would be collected at her father's house. She would sew the letters into her petticoats and smuggle them through the picket lines above town, or "run the blockade" as townspeople generally termed it, to drop them with scouts who relayed them to Richmond and exchanged them for incoming mail to Williamsburg. On 2 February James Griffin received a letter from his wife in Mississippi written two months earlier. Overjoyed to hear from her, he replied three days later with instructions to direct her next letter to Richmond to be conducted "to me by the *underground* R. R. I understand that a mail of that character reaches our City once a week; but the matter has to be managed in the most cautious & secret manner."[40]

Caution and secrecy did not always guarantee success in smuggling operations, as two ladies of the Hofheimer family learned about this time. While

38. C. C. Suydam receipt, 6 Jan. 1863, *Williamsburg Gazette* microfilm, CWM; *OR*, 18:517. 39. *OR*, 18:130–1, 529.
40. Wise, "Wise's Brigade," 3–4; A. D. West affidavit, 19 Aug. 1912; and Minnie B. Jenkins, "When Delia Bucktrout Ran the Blockade to Richmond," Dorothy Ross Collection; JLCG Commonplace Book, 2, 5 Feb. 1862.

their husbands were serving in the Confederate army, they had been carrying on the merchant business, until one day they drove two wagons out of town under pretext of taking a load of corn to the gristmill. The picket, "being somewhat curious to know if the entire load consisted of corn, thereupon turned one of the bags over, and immediately there appeared to view boxes, boots, etc.," according to a story in the *Richmond Dispatch*. "Upon further examination it was ascertained that the ladies had on their persons under their hoop skirts, arranged in fantastic order boots, shoes, bags of coffee, sugar, tea, etc., one of the ladies having on her as many as eight hoop skirts." They were brought back to Williamsburg to await adjudication and forced "to sit upon the wagons for half a day in the cold," the article continued. Further investigation uncovered the truth that, with the assistance of the provost Hennessey, "who had been bribed very largely," the Hofheimers had been smuggling "through the lines quite $5,000 worth of goods a week for fellow extortioners in Richmond." The ladies were taken to Baltimore and Hennessey was replaced by Maj. Christopher Kleinz.[41]

On the morning of 5 February, Kleinz led another scouting party up the Peninsula from Williamsburg, almost a repeat of the 19 January expedition. This time, however, about 180 troopers went along, including former *Cavalier* editor Samuel Williamson, and they captured only one Confederate scout. Two days later three southern deserters surrendered to the Federal pickets at Williamsburg with the story "that several more were outside who desired to come in," Kleinz reported. Two more deserters, arriving shortly afterward, confirmed their story, prompting Kleinz to order the Fifth's Capt. Andrew Faith to take 84 men and search toward the York River and up Richmond Road. Again, Williamson accompanied the scouting party, but it ran into an ambush, and only about half its number returned. Faith sustained a wound in the face, and among the seven Federals killed was nineteen-year-old Williamson. That evening under flag of truce, his body came into the lines strapped to his horse, with a note pinned to his uniform: "I regret the necessity that compelled me to shoot such a brave young officer: but found it absolutely necessary to do so to save the lives of my own men. He positively refused to surrender when ordered to do so and still kept firing his revolver at my men after he had been twice wounded." It was signed "A Lieut. of the C.S.A." Bucktrout furnished Williamson a coffin and case, packing, and shrouding and sent him home to Philadelphia a few days later.[42]

41. *Richmond Dispatch*, 10 Mar. 1863.
42. *OR*, 18:148–53; Cronin, "Vest Mansion," 34; Bucktrout Day Book, 14 Feb. 1863.

Several members of the Fifth, separated from their command during the confusion of ambush, straggled in over the next day or two, along with five more Confederate deserters, now looked upon with more suspicion. For allowing himself to be deceived by the deserters and sending Faith out, Kleinz received sharp criticism from Keyes. As provost, Kleinz also managed to provoke the townspeople, endeavoring "to suppress the secretly active co-operation of the citizens with their friends outside, by many summary arrests." He further "excited deep resentment among all classes of the population" by suspending serviced at Bruton Church about the first of February "on account of disloyal utterances from the pulpit." Rev. Thomas Ambler, however, continued to hold regular Sunday services in his home.[43]

More resentment among white inhabitants came from Federal recruiting officers arming and drilling contrabands in the area. A 15 February letter to the *Richmond Dispatch* mentioned that over "four hundred negroes are at Kings Mill." When visiting Williamsburg "they appear very pompous and superior among their color, but supremely ridiculous to others, in their uniform of red pants and black jackets. The ladies in the town say they know not what the God-forsaken Yankees are going to do with them, unless it be to turn them loose upon the women and children."[44]

Tensions continued to mount in March as Keyes, recently promoted to major general dating from the battle of Williamsburg, was in Washington testifying on that battle before the Congressional Joint Committee on the Conduct of the War. In his absence, New York lawyer and politician Richard Busteed commanded at Yorktown. On the morning of 26 March, Busteed telegraphed Dix "that our pickets at Williamsburg were fired on by a number of the enemy's infantry. A continual warfare of this character is kept up against us at and about the town." He decided the only way to stop it was "the destruction of Williamsburg, and if you will approve it I would give the inhabitants notice that upon a repetition of these attacks the place should be destroyed." In case Dix was not already aware, "the town is a stronghold of rank traitors." The general immediately advised Busteed that "our troops at Williamsburg must defend themselves as long as they can and drive off assailants. We must not destroy towns unless they are actually taken possession of by the enemy, and then not unless absolutely necessary for our own safety."[45]

<hr>

43. *OR*, 18:150–2; Cronin, "Vest Mansion," 29; Rev. W. A. R. Goodwin, *Historical Sketch of Bruton Church, Williamsburg, Virginia* (n.p., 1903), 61.

44. *Richmond Dispatch*, 15 Feb. 1863.

45. *(Yorktown) Cavalier*, 17 Mar. 1863; Congress, *Report of the Joint Committee*, 1:597; Cronin, "Vest Mansion," 37; *OR*, 18:568–9.

Palm Sunday came three days later on 29 March. Early in the morning Col. William B. Tabb brought his 59th Virginia Infantry, the 46th Virginia Infantry, a battery, and some cavalry to a point three or four miles above Williamsburg on Richmond Road. At 2:00 A.M. he detached two companies of the 59th and one company of the 46th, just over one hundred muskets, and sent them with two local guides all under Capt. G. A. Wallace. Tabb ordered them to circle around left or north of Williamsburg and surprise Fort Magruder before daybreak. "Through ploughed fields, over fences, deep and wide ditches, through a swamp that took the men over knee-deep, and through some timber with very thick undergrowth," the guides led Wallace's troops in the darkness. In two hours they did not quite cover four miles, but by then dawn was breaking and two of the three companies were lost. The remaining company finally emerged from the timber into the open field a mile or two from the fort. Wallace "sent back one of the guides to find the two lost companies and when he returned with them it was so light that we could be seen, and were undoubtedly seen from Williamsburg." Nevertheless, they pushed on to a point northeast of town near Capitol Landing Road, where about five o'clock they found three mounted Federal pickets approaching them from town. Upon spotting Wallace's column, the bluecoats turned tail and took a volley at their backs while galloping into Williamsburg.[46]

Another volley Wallace's men fired a few minutes later signaled Tabb that Wallace had abandoned the plan to capture Fort Magruder. His new objective, as he headed into town, was to form a juncture with Tabb's main body, which had advanced to within a mile and a half of Williamsburg and rode rapidly down Richmond Road after hearing Wallace's shots. The 5th Pennsylvania's pickets stood their ground and allowed Tabb to approach within five hundred yards before prudently retiring on horseback. By then, Wallace had started up Main Street. He could see the Fifth's pickets, trapped between him and Tabb, forming at the college and quickly deployed his men along the north side of Main Street just as the pickets boldly charged. "We held our fire until they were close to us," Wallace reported. "Our fire broke and confused them." It also killed two or three, wounded another three, and unhorsed seven, who were promptly captured along with their horses and arms. Wallace then continued up to the college but turned and made another stand when cavalry from Fort Magruder began to follow him up the street. The sight of Tabb's overwhelming force and battery "planted at the College ready for action" behind

46. *OR*, 18:207–8.

Wallace caused the blue cavalry to reconsider, then retreat back to Fort Magruder, where the regiment formed in line of battle.[47]

All this commotion naturally awakened the townspeople. John Coupland's ten-year-old daughter, Leonora, spotting gray uniforms outside the Vest House, "rised the window and waved a nice clean towel, and like gentlemen took off thir caps," she wrote two weeks later. "We went to the door and offered them some water which they accepted, but just as I got it they were gone." For a better view of the action, William Douglas climbed to the observation platform on the asylum's Tower Building and saw smoke billowing from Fort Magruder and Whittaker's Mill. To Tabb he "reported that the enemy were burning their stores." Both Tutters Neck and Kingsmill dams had been cut by the bluecoats to prevent cavalry from capturing Kingsmill, another of Tabb's objectives, and "nothing could be gained by going there; the negroes have all been removed." Disappointed that no sorely needed commissary stores could be captured, Tabb was not about to leave town empty handed. His men began loading wagons and packhorses with Federal goods from Williamsburg shops thrown open by merchants. The Confederates could not resist pulling boots off fallen Pennsylvanians before they swiftly departed, carrying their plunder and eleven prisoners, as Fort Magruder's artillery tossed about a dozen rounds at their heels. By 11:00 A.M., all was quiet once again.[48]

This time Lieutenant Colonel Lewis was the one eager to burn the town, prevented only by Busteed reminding him of Dix's directive just three days earlier. Although Williamsburg could not be burned, perhaps it could be punished. Worse than stealing boots off of "murdered" Union troopers, in Busteed's opinion, was the collaboration of civilians with these murderers and marauders. "Conclusive evidence has been furnished to the commanding general that the attack was aided, if not planned, by citizens of Williamsburg," he declared the day of the raid, "and carried to a successful end by them and their abettors outside the lines." He accused inhabitants of leading the attackers into the city, allowing them "to occupy the most advantageous points for attack and defense," and assisting "their attack upon our forces, who were fired upon from the houses lining the streets." Nor was Busteed happy about shopkeepers giving away Federal goods.[49]

47. Ibid., 205–9.
48. Leonora Coupland to [Juliana Dorsey], 13 Apr. [1863], DCP, MR-CWM; *OR*, 18:205–8.
49. *OR*, 18:203–4.

Determined this would never happen again, Busteed issued an order revoking buying and selling privileges from all Williamsburg merchants and requiring citizens to take the oath of allegiance to the U.S. government by 1 April. All citizens not willing to take the oath, except servants and asylum employees, "will prepare themselves and their families to be placed beyond the lines now occupied by the armed forces of the said Government by the 2d day of April, 1863," the order read. Dix rescinded this order the next day on the grounds that it should not have been issued without his authority, pointing out that the government preferred "to leave the people unmolested if they continue in the quiet pursuit of their customary occupations and give no aid or comfort to the enemy." Of course, if it "be found that any house in Williamsburg was occupied by the enemy with the consent of the owner for the purpose of firing upon our troops it will be razed to the ground." Upon receiving this communication, Busteed resigned his commission and retired from the service.[50]

To replace Busteed's order, Dix issued a proclamation on 31 March requiring the oath of allegiance for anyone entering or leaving town from the east or for anyone wanting to trade in Williamsburg. He also cut off all supplies to the inhabitants, except from the neighboring farms, and ordered an investigation into the alleged complicity of the citizens. Town guards would not allow any lights to burn at night, "for fear it should be a signal to our people, who had Guerillas surrounding the town," Sally Galt informed a cousin. "Just as Mrs. Sherwell Annie & myself would get to reading & sewing at night, we would hear the clanking of swords & tap at the window, & the Yankee soldier saying 'put your light out,' which we would most obediently & submissively do, & as soon as they were out of sight, light the lamp again."[51]

Confederates surrounding the town so worried the Federals that an infantry regiment, the 139th New York, recently organized in Brooklyn, was at last assigned to Fort Magruder, now commanded by the 1st Pennsylvania Artillery's Col. Robert M. West. On 3 April, "the morning of Good Friday we had a whole company of Infantry, from New York City, to search the house for rebels, arms & contraband goods; they supposed some of the rebels had remained from the raid the previous week," Sally revealed. "I think the Capt must have been one of the New York detectives he conducted the search in such a through & scientific manner. One of our keys was tyed with a blue ribbon, & a federal soldier said, 'I did not think your soldiers would let you

50. *OR,* 18:204–5; Cronin, "Vest Mansion," 37–8.
51. *OR,* 18:205; SMG to cousin, 15 Apr. 1863, GFP, MR-CWM.

have anything blue.'" Despite augmented guards, the town was not sleeping any sounder, for, Sally added, "the sharp sound of rifles" could be heard "any time you waked at night."[52]

And the sound of digging could be heard all day. "Since the raid Col. Tabb made they have been strengthening the fort and digging rifle pits," Mattie Pierce wrote her cousin Harriette Cary, who had gone to Richmond a short time earlier. Contrabands were excavating two new redoubts along a road northwest of Fort Magruder to defend the Federals' right flank from attack from the west. These works would be needed soon, for during the past three weeks, Longstreet's corps had been massing in Suffolk, south of Norfolk, to find forage and supplies while General Lee watched the main Federal army, now under Joe Hooker, on the Rappahannock River. To prevent Keyes at Yorktown from moving against him and perhaps even to draw off some Union troops now in Norfolk, Longstreet needed a diversion down the Peninsula from Richmond. Maj. Gen. Arnold Elzey, commanding the Department of Richmond, agreed with him in a 6 April dispatch and chose Henry Wise's brigade. "Wise had been chafing for a chance and I am glad he has got it," Elzey confided to Longstreet. "He knows the country thoroughly and no doubt will do well." Longstreet warned Elzey that Wise must not pass Yorktown "unless he finds that he will by doing so draw out the force at Yorktown."[53]

On 7 April Wise received his orders. By nine o'clock the next morning, he had gathered his force and began moving down the Peninsula. At Colonel Tabb's headquarters near Diascund Bridge, he rested his men and collected more infantry, cavalry, and artillery for a total of 1,773 of all arms. "I will certainly attack them Saturday morning as early as my men can take aim," he assured Elzey on Thursday the ninth. During Friday night, Wise sent Tabb with a detachment of 218 men of the 59th Virginia to circle through the woods south of town to Tutters Neck, while Wise took the remaining 1,555 to Williamsburg's western edge just beyond the Federal pickets. Through the peaceful night, Williamsburg inhabitants slumbered, blissfully unaware their "people" were at the gates.[54]

52. *OR*, 18:677; *(Yorktown) Cavalier*, 17 Mar. 1863; Cronin, "Vest Mansion," 57, CWF; SMG to cousin, 15 Apr. 1863.
53. Mattie Pierce to HC, 15 Apr. 1863, DCP; *OR*, 18:556–71, 965–8.
54. *OR*, 18:975–6; Wise, "Wise's Brigade," 4.

CHAPTER 14

Temporary Relief

Saturday, 11 April 1863, promised to be a beautiful spring day in Williamsburg. John Coupland in the Vest House rose early that morning, before his
wife and four children, to begin another day of struggle to survive. Both his
own family and that of his mother-in-law, Harriette "Ma" Henley, three doors
up Main Street from the Vest House were "dependent entirely on my exertions
to scrape a little something together to keep us all from starving," Coupland
wrote his mother, "for the Yankees had forbidden the citizens even to pass to
the Mill for some weeks." To compound these problems, his wife, Susan, after
losing their baby just the previous June, was expecting another any day.[1]

This peaceful dawn exploded about six o'clock, when Wise's men suddenly
materialized near the college and began driving Union pickets back through
Williamsburg and into Fort Magruder. Startled residents were thrilled to find
themselves surrounded by "the *dear Confederates,*" Mattie Pierce wrote Harriette Cary a few days later, "they were under our window before we knew any
thing about it." Within moments "the Yankees commenced shelling very fast,"
as Colonel West ordered Fort Magruder's two Parrot guns to open on southern troops now forming along Williamsburg streets from the Henley House
east down Woodpecker. The booming instantly awakened the rest of the
Coupland family. "In a great hurry and confusion did we put on a few clothes
and thrust a few more as a change for us into a bag," John depicted the wild
scene. Sue and the three younger children he first sent up to her mother's, then
he and fourteen-year-old-son George dashed to the stables for their horse and
cart. "While hitching the horse a shell burst directly over our heads, but doing
no damage; two fell in the garden and 3 within a few feet of the house under

1. JRC to Juliana Dorsey, 26 Apr. 1863, DCP, MR-CWM.

our chamber window," John enumerated. "One burst in front of the door in the street killing a horse & wounding two men."[2]

His own horse hitched, John stopped at Ma Henley's and "took all hands up to the Asylum for protection," he continued. "I feared the excitement would prove injurious to Sue but she stood it like a hero." Many joined this rush to the asylum, creating "such confusion you never saw not even at the evacuation," declared Mattie. Yet others adamantly refused to leave their homes. "While the shelling was at the height," Sally Galt calmly sat in the library, writing a letter to her cousin, "& I am sure you will never as long as you live, have another letter written under such circumstances." A shell fragment that lodged itself under Sally's library windowsill did no damage, but across Main Street from the Vest House, "Mrs. Morrison's kitchen was penetrated by a ball and her porch steps torn up by a shell," Coupland noted. "She & Miss Emily were in the house. Many other houses were struck and portions of them torn to pieces, but strange to say none took fire. All that portion of the town from the Episcopal church down embracing much the larger part was pretty well peppered."[3]

Shells even reached the Tucker House front fence and landed in the yard. Lucy had left her two youngest children there with Mamy Patty when she went to Richmond to care for Tom. At the first roar of the cannon, young Monty Tucker hitched up the buggy and tried to talk his sister, Zettie, into going with him to Richmond, but she refused to leave the family home entrusted to her care. Monty then saddled his horse and galloped up Richmond Road. Servants unwilling to live under Confederate domination fled in the opposite direction. The Thompson's last two servants "took themselves off at sunrise," Isabella Sully informed Cynthia, who had recently joined Dr. Charles Coleman, now practicing privately in North Carolina. Both Isabella and her sister, Julia, hoped to weather the barrage at home, but when the shells started reaching the Tucker yard, "Montegu became so uneasy that we consented to go up to the Asylum." Zettie and Mamy Patty decided to go with them. There Dr. Peter Wager kindly offered protection and "welcomed them with a feast of Coffee which was very agreeable as most of them had not eaten or drunk anything that morning."[4]

2. SMG to cousin, 15 Apr. 1863, GFP, MR-CWM; Pierce to HC, 15–18 Apr. 1863, DCP; JRC to Juliana Dorsey, 26 Apr. 1863; OR, 18:262; (Yorktown) Cavalier, 14 Apr. 1863.

3. JRC to Juliana Dorsey, 26 Apr. 1863; Pierce to HC, 15–18 Apr. 1863; SMG to cousin, 15 Apr. 1863.

4. Thomas S. B. Tucker to CBT, 16, 20 Apr. 1863, TCP, MR-CWM; Isabella Sully to CBT, 14 Apr. 1863, TCP.

Meanwhile, at Fort Magruder, West hurriedly summoned the remainder of the 5th Pennsylvania from its Whittaker's Mill camp and telegraphed Brig. Gen. Rufus King, temporarily in command at Yorktown, that an unknown Confederate force had appeared at Williamsburg that morning. "Our pickets fell back in good order to Fort Magruder," King relayed at 7:45 A.M. to General Keyes, filling in for Dix at Fort Monroe. "Colonel West has opened fire on the town and is now firing." Keyes's instant response directed King to order West "to cease firing on Williamsburg unless he knows the enemy are present there in arms." Not only did Keyes fear West would waste his ammunition but also insisted "that town must be held as a shield, and it must not be destroyed except in accordance with my orders."[5]

Before King could pass this order to West, the telegraph wire went dead, severed soon after the Pennsylvania cavalrymen left their camp to come to West's aid. According to the *Cavalier*, resuscitated in Yorktown the previous month, this dastardly deed was perpetrated by "a body of rebel infantry that had skulked through the woods on the James River side, unperceived by our pickets, entered the camp and destroyed the greater part of it, together with some commissary stores." Colonel Tabb's men also captured the camp guard, burned the hospital, and paroled the patients. They then vanished as swiftly as they had appeared, but not before they had uncovered "pretty plenty of the 'O be joyful,'" recorded the *Cavalier*, "and, after imbibing freely, they were very good natured and accommodating. Mrs. Kleintz and some other ladies who were in camp, were treated with the greatest consideration. They were suffered to retain nearly all the personal effects of the field officers."[6]

That explains Tabb's delay in returning to Williamsburg, where the Confederates were becoming "very uneasy for fear he had been captured," wrote Mattie Pierce. His arrival brought Wise's force up to its full 1,700-man strength to face the Fifth, the 139th New York, and one section of Battery E, 1st Pennsylvania Artillery, altogether estimated at less than 1,600. Keyes believed that as long as he had provisions and ammunition, West should be able to defend Fort Magruder against 10,000. The *Cavalier* reported that the colonel was able to hold his own in the artillery duel, such as it was, on the eastern edge of town. After the "rebels got their battery in position behind a hill and threw two shells into the fort," the lieutenant of Battery E ordered his best marksman to dislodge it. His second shot passed over the Confederate battery, killing four horses and two men and damaging a gun carriage. "This was a

5. *OR*, 18:262–4.
6. *(Yorktown) Cavalier*, 14 Apr. 1863.

little too warm a reception," surmised the *Cavalier,* "and they promptly ske-daddled to a point out of range of our guns." Wise moved back a short dis-tance, not to save his troops, he later insisted, but to protect Williamsburg from further shelling and "to preserve the Asylum its quiet."[7]

With gray targets out of range, Federal fire slackened around half past noon, and the asylum's quiet was temporarily restored, allowing Isabella Sully and others to return home "to pack up in case it should be necessary to leave," she wrote Cynthia. "Just as the contents of all the drawers and trunks were emptied out preparatory to a repacking, a message came from Dr Wager that the shelling was about to recommence and we must hasten up to the Asylum as quickly as possible. Nothing would do but go we must, and accordingly we started, but by the time we reached your corner our Artillery received orders to retire. It came back and so did we, utterly broken down."[8]

Wise pulled his entire force back through Williamsburg, giving exuberant people a chance to greet their boys properly. Tabb was an instant hero for his destructive strike on Whittaker's Mill. "I had the honor of shaking hands with him, also had an introduction to Col. Shingler," swooned Mattie. "Harriette I was so happy I scarcely knew where I was." While this welcoming celebra-tion was going on, at 2:30 King wired Keyes that the telegraph to Fort Ma-gruder had been restored and "the enemy are retreating, but still occupy Williamsburg." Keyes passed this information up to General Halleck in Washington, adding "I have ordered Colonel West to hold the strong line of defense below the city at all hazards. It would be very injurious to give it up." So determined was Keyes to hold Williamsburg that he alerted Maj. Gen. John Peck, commanding in Suffolk, to the possibility he may have to send West reinforcements from his force, precisely what Longstreet had hoped. Be-fore Keyes could make this decision, however, Peck announced in a 5:00 P.M. telegram that Longstreet was now moving upon him in large numbers.[9]

Fortunately for West, reinforcements were already on their way to him from Yorktown, the 178th Pennsylvania Infantry, which arrived at Fort Ma-gruder that evening. At 8:00 P.M. Keyes assured Halleck that "the enemy was fairly repulsed at Williamsburg to-day. Our pickets are in the edge of the city, and the line of Fort Magruder, strengthened by another regiment, is now guarded from York River to James River." Lest the general-in-chief mistak-

7. Pierce to HC, 15–18 Apr. 1863; *OR,* 18:263; *(Yorktown) Cavalier,* 14 Apr. 1863; Henry A. Wise to J. D. Munford et al., 18 Apr. 1863, Governor (1860–1863: Letcher), Executive papers, 1859–1863 (ser. 1: Chronological Files), The Library of Virginia, Richmond.

8. Sully to CBT, 14 Apr. 1863.

9. Pierce to HC, 15–18 Apr. 1863; *OR,* 18:262, 598, 600.

enly think this crisis was over, however, "the telegraph operator reports enemy are hanging around Williamsburg."[10]

Wise and his men were mostly hanging around the western end of town, well out of range. That evening Dr. Wager "inquired what my intentions were in respect to the Asylum," Wise wrote a week later. "I distinctly informed him that I did not intend to interfere with it at all, and I stated that I expected him, of course, to go on with its conduct & superintendence at present at least as he had been doing heretofore." Unwilling to reveal whether he intended to hold the town permanently, Wise did tell the doctor that "every protection should be extended to him and all the enemy officers & men in the Asylum, and that they would be required *only to give their parole of honor not to divulge to the enemy any of our operations which might come to their knowledge.*" With that, Dr. Wager's personal interview with Wise abruptly terminated.[11]

The asylum came up as a topic in the Union camp the next day, Sunday, 12 April, during a strategy discussion between King and Keyes. King asked if he should continue supplying the patients after mentioning that West was all for abandoning Williamsburg and establishing his pickets along a shorter line, perhaps back at Cheesecake Church. Ten Confederates had been captured on Saturday, and deserters came into Federal lines carrying information that Wise's force consisted of "4,000 infantry, 500 or 600 cavalry, and 6 or 8 pieces of artillery." They also corroborated yesterday's rumor that Wise had made a dramatic speech to his men, "telling them he had orders to take the fort and it must be done." Keyes was not impressed. Though he gave King permission to withdraw the pickets from Williamsburg, he wanted to make sure that West will "cause Wise to repent his rashness if he assails those forts."[12]

Attacking the redoubts was not in Wise's battle plan for Sunday, however. Since the general actually had no orders to take the forts, he was evidently waging a war of nerves, trying to draw as many troops away from Peck as possible. His oratory and the grossly exaggerated reports of his strength did not seem to be working. He therefore tried a midafternoon feint toward Fort Magruder and more rumors of reinforcements. Stories that "Gov. Wise has commenced entrenching the other side of Williamsburg" were then reaching Yorktown, but also without effect. Keyes authorized King to send another infantry regiment to Williamsburg at his discretion but wanted no artillery sent up or anything brought over from Gloucester, after gray prisoners helpfully

10. *OR*, 18:262, 596.
11. Wise to Munford et al., 18 Apr. 1863.
12. *OR*, 18:264–5, 601; *(Yorktown) Cavalier*, 14 Apr. 1863.

leaked southern plans to attack Williamsburg, Suffolk, and Gloucester simultaneously. "The line of defense at Fort Magruder ought not to be given up lightly," Keyes sternly warned King. It would not be, King reassured Keyes Sunday night, for he was keeping a gunboat off Queens Creek to cover that side of the line. At 10:00 P.M. West telegraphed King that he expected an assault on the redoubts in the morning and could also use a gunboat off College Creek in the James River. Otherwise, all was quiet.[13]

While the Federals nervously prepared for Wise's next attack, Williamsburg inhabitants spent Sunday adjusting to their new situation. "The people in the county and town are wild with delight at the idea of being able to go and come at will," Mattie remarked to Harriette. "Freedom is certainly sweet." Sally Galt found it "so strange not to be a prisoner, you know we have not been allowed to go out of the confines of the town for nearly a year." With the loss of so many servants, they also had "such a strange state of things here. Gentlemen make all the biscuits sweep out the house & do all the work servants used to do." In the Thompson household, now devoid of slaves, Isabella admitted that she "volunteered as cook Julia and Jenny acted as house servant and chamber maid and Montegu cleaned the knives."[14]

By Sunday evening, Monty Tucker had arrived in Richmond, bearing tidings of Wise's raid. His mother, who had been waiting for an opportunity to return home now that Tom was recovering, determined to leave as soon as she was packed. First she sent Monty back to Williamsburg on Monday, 13 April, "with directions to take care of the house." During his return trip, Monty ran into heavy traffic heading up to Richmond, as many townspeople were taking advantage of the open lines to escape into Dixie. Federal pickets within five hundred yards of Wise's line on Monday reported "wagons loaded with furniture have been moving out of Williamsburg all day." Among the refugees was the town's last civilian physician, Dr. Robert Garrett, taking his two teenage sons to Lexington to enroll them in the Virginia Military Institute, which young Bob Saunders presently attended. Rev. Thomas Ambler also took his family and the Bruton communion silver to Richmond. Charles Waller decided to go in the opposite direction and convey his family to his wife's home in Gloucester. On Monday morning Montegu Thompson planned to leave Williamsburg too, giving his sisters only a half-hour notice. After Julia packed his trunks, off he went, leaving the ladies alone, though why Isabella declined

13. *OR*, 18:264–6; *(Yorktown) Cavalier,* 14 Apr. 1863.
14. Pierce to HC, 15–18 Apr. 1863; SMG to cousin, 15 Apr. 1863; Sully to CBT, 14 Apr. 1863.

to go after applying so long for a pass Mattie Pierce could not understand. Mattie herself removed to upper James City County Monday at the invitation of a friend.[15]

Indeed, Sally Galt feared that "there will not be a dozen people after a while, as everybody is glad to get in the southern lines once more." Several others like Sally preferred the uncertainties of living on a battleground to the near certainty of losing their homes if abandoned. "Ma Henley says she will stay at her house until forced to leave," Mattie wrote Harriette. Ma's daughter Sue Coupland, in no condition to travel, moved with her family into the relative safety of the Ambler's parish house across Main Street from Bruton Church. Since Bassett Hall's yard was the main skirmishing ground and "rifle balls are perforrating the house a dozen times a day," the Durfeys took refuge in the Galt House. A few slaves had elected to remain loyal, most notably the Tuckers' Mamy Patty and Sally's Arena Baker and Oliver, who felt, according to Sally, "that 'nobody cares anything for him at old Point & it is no use for him to go.'"[16]

Others did not seem to know what to do. "Numbers & numbers of our poor people are camping out in the woods, fearful of the rifle balls, which are flying about in the streets, & of another shelling, which may be inflicted on us at any moment." But even the dense woods could be little cover when, on Monday morning, a gunboat on the York River opened fire to shell blindly what it supposed was the Confederate position. West, apparently so unwell from the stress "as to be confined to his quarters," sent another plea for a gunboat in the James River to shell Williamsburg as well. As he told King, "the asylum tower is plainly visible from the James, and fire could be directed by the tower to the town; and the enemy's camp is north of town." A gunboat placed there would also prevent Wise from being supplied by water.[17]

West's scheme to use the asylum tower was questionable as long as the Confederates lingered nearby. They would not likely allow Dr. Wager or any of his cavalrymen acting as nurses to signal directions from the tower to Union gunboats. That Monday Wager was more concerned about his patients, addressing a letter of complaint to Wise that his provisions were running low. Food he could provide for a few days with the help of such townspeople as

15. Thomas S. B. Tucker to CBT, 16 Apr. 1863; Sully to CBT, 14 Apr. 1863; *OR*, 18:607; JRC to Juliana Dorsey, 26 Apr. 1863; Pierce to HC, 15–18 Apr. 1863; Goodwin, *Bruton Church*, 61.

16. SMG to cousin, 15 Apr. 1863; Pierce to HC, 15–18 Apr. 1863; JRC to Juliana Dorsey, 26 Apr. 1863; Sully to CBT, 14 Apr. 1863.

17. SMG to cousin, 15 Apr. 1863; *(Yorktown) Cavalier*, 14 Apr. 1863; *OR*, 18:604–6.

Sally Galt, "but without your assistance the patients must necessarily suffer for fuel—as I have no means at my command to furnish it." Wise reminded Wager that he, the doctor, was in charge of the institution and responsible "to make the best provision in his power," though Wise promised to assist him with transportation. "In case wagons are sent to haul fuel for the Asylum, Surgeon Wager will be expected to insure them complete protection."[18]

The next day, Tuesday, 14 April, Wise allowed a wagon sent from Dr. Wager under a yellow flag to pass through his lines to the mill. Upon inspection of the asylum, "it was found that several of the servants & nurses were fugitive slaves, belonging to masters who claimed their private property," Wise later explained, "and they were allowed to take them away." He also discovered that John Coupland had not yet reached forty years old, making him subject to conscription into the southern army. Thus, despite a wife approaching her confinement and two families depending on him for food, Coupland was compelled to leave Williamsburg and report to Richmond for duty. Accompanying him were William Douglas and his daughter Joan, along with William Peachy's daughter Betty.[19]

For those remaining in Williamsburg, the southern occupation provided a pleasant diversion. Isabella Sully, for one, did not object to the interruption of her Tuesday chores. "A continuous stream of Confederates pour in all the time," she wrote Cynthia that day, "and we are too happy and too anxious to see and talk to them to be hindered with the vulgar considerations, of pots, pans kettles, brooms, dust, dishabelle or anything else." The next day Sally Galt and Mrs. Mary Sherwell were similarly happy to cook for some South Carolina cavalry in battle array in front of the Galt House. Though no skirmishing disturbed the streets that day, some blue infantry had advanced to the foot of Woodpecker Lane in the morning and retreated at the sight of gray cavalry near the college. This proximity of the enemy made Margaret Munford nervous when her husband slipped into town to visit his family for a couple of hours. He hoped to remove them, but Margaret unfortunately was too unwell to leave and "was so much afraid the enemy might come in at any moment, that she was anxious for him to hurry off," Sally confided Wednesday afternoon, the fifteenth.[20]

By that time, rumors were circulating that the Federals had decided to sur-

18. Peter Wager to Henry A. Wise, with Wise's reply, 13 Apr. 1863, Governor (1860–1863: Letcher), Executive papers, 1859–1863 (ser. 1: Chronological Files); SMG to cousin, 15 Apr. 1863.

19. Wise to Munford et al., 18 Apr. 1863; JRC to Juliana Dorsey, 26 Apr. 1863.

20. Sully to CBT, 14 Apr. 1863; SMG to cousin, 15 Apr. 1863.

render the town and Wise had taken charge of the asylum. Neither was true, but when Keyes learned that Wise had paroled Dr. Wager and his two cavalry-man nurses, he assumed they had been taken prisoner. Furious that Wise would interfere with the hospital after his November 1862 letter professing great sympathy for the patients, Keyes ordered the doctor and his men "to withdraw from the asylum." Talbot Sweeney accepted the asylum keys from Dr. Wager, then consulted Wise, supposing him to be in military command of it. But Wise had no intention of taking responsibility for the institution and instructed Sweeney to provide for and manage it as best he could.[21]

Neither did Wise respond to the couriers in blue bringing a copy of Wager's withdrawal order to his headquarters under flag of truce on Thursday after-noon, 16 April. Their comment "that Fort Magruder is impregnable to any force short of 20,000 men" Wise interpreted as "they are very desirous to get rid of our presence in their front." He had been planning to depart that after-noon anyway, having completed all he could do in the area. "This is the fifth day after our attack upon the enemy, and they have shown no disposition to advance," he reported to General Elzey Thursday morning. Wise had not been able to draw them out of their entrenchments, but he had gathered all the forage and provisions in the area and had assisted "the citizens of Wil-liamsburg in removing their persons and effects from the reach of the enemy." One detail Wise had neglected. When Mary Southall in the President's House heard of his departure on Thursday, she wrote, "Please, *please* Gen'l Wise, don't leave us (if it is possible for you to stay) in the hands of the Yankees, and remember if you do return to Williamsburg, that our house is at your entire disposal for headquarters, or anything else you choose." She had sent him "word several times, that we have in our charge, the college library," compris-ing "about three wagon loads of books, many valuable ones." Mary begged him to take the books, for the "Yankees talk of selling them for the benefit of the E. L. Asylum."[22]

With or without the books, Wise's brigade decamped at 3:30 Thursday afternoon and headed up Richmond Road as a gunboat on the York River tossed a few shells in their direction. "You can't immagine how we feel when our people leave us after a raid," Sally Galt moaned to her cousin. "We always hope they have come to stay & when we see them leaving us we feel like . . . 'They have left me here to die!'" Worse, Mattie Pierce feared the "Yankees will certainly fire the town when our men leave." To afford some protection,

21. SMG to cousin, 15 Apr. 1863; *OR*, 18:622, 995; Flournoy, *Virginia State Papers*, 11:482.
22. *OR*, 18:994–5, 1006; *(Williamsburg) Virginia Gazette*, 3 June 1893.

Wise left his cavalry near town, taking his infantry and artillery to Six Mile Ordinary that evening. While there he contacted Dr. William Martin, "a resident practicing physician of this county," and sent him to the asylum "to superintend its hygeia."[23]

Colonel West learned of Dr. Martin's appointment the next morning, Friday, 17 April. At an early hour Sweeney, along with Capt. John Coke, Major Munford, and James Custis, applied to Wise for a flag of truce into Williamsburg. Wise issued a special order at 5:30 that morning, authorizing them to meet with West and inform him that since the Confederate military forces were unable to manage the asylum, "it is desirable that the civil authorities of the State should be allowed to make such temporary provisions for them as are absolutely necessary." The delegation was also to request protection for Dr. Martin, for provisioning wagons traveling into the county, and for the asylum staff members who were "not to be regarded in any event as prisoners of war."[24]

During their meeting at the Federal picket line east of Williamsburg, West told the delegation that he had stored at Fort Magruder five days supplies intended for the asylum. "He offers them to me," Sweeney informed Wise immediately after the interview, "as he assures me from a sincere motive to promote the comfort of the afflicted." Sweeney worried that accepting the supplies might compromise the Confederate position, but Wise assured him that he "may properly not only accept but actually as legal advisor of the Institution, *claim* the supplies already there or nearby, intended for it." At their next meeting at 7:30 that evening, the delegation accepted the supplies from West, who "declared that 'in this matter he would not be outdone by any person in generosity.'" Sweeney requested that West "reduce his assurances to writing and give them to us, that we might furnish each officer of the Asylum with a copy" to avoid all further misunderstanding upon the subject. Before parting, West agreed to meet the delegation the next morning at ten o'clock to hand them his written assurances.[25]

Before the colonel could deliver on this promise, Keyes decided that West had exceeded his authority in entering into an agreement with Sweeney. A promise of protection meant to Keyes the surrender of Williamsburg, which

23. *OR*, 18:995; SMG to cousin, 15 Apr. 1863.
24. Wise to Munford et al., 18 Apr. 1863; "Special Orders No. 57," 17 Apr. 1863, Governor (1860–1863: Letcher), Executive papers, 1859–1863 (ser. 1: Chronological Files).
25. Talbot Sweeney to Henry A. Wise, 17, 18 Apr. 1863; and Wise to Sweeney, 18 Apr. 1863, Governor (1860–1863: Letcher), Executive papers, 1859–1863 (ser. 1: Chronological Files).

he was not ready to do. But since the 250 asylum inmates were "on the borders of absolute starvation," Keyes ordered ten days' rations sent up. In the supply requisition Keyes blamed Wise for this sad situation, accusing him of "inhumanity and want of civilization," and directed West to furnish Sweeney a copy of the order so "General Wise may learn in what estimation he is held." Sweeney would also have to "make an official written application for the protection asked for the asylum, stating on what it is based" before Keyes would consider it. Thus, at their meeting the next morning, 18 April, West handed Sweeney an envelope and requested that he not open it until after they separated. Sweeney, disappointed to find Keyes's order and instructions instead of the needed assurance of protection, promptly cut off negotiations. Custis advised Dr. Martin not to accept the superintendency for fear he would not be safe, but Wise quickly reassured him. "You will be safe," the general insisted, "and I am anxious that the enemy shall not have it to say that we abandoned the cure and care of our own patients. I therefore beg you to go into the Hospital and take charge. Force them to turn you out."[26]

Wise expected the Federals would do just that as soon as they reoccupied the town, but on Sunday, 19 April, the Confederates had been out of Williamsburg three days and West had not yet moved in. Lucy Tucker had returned, however, probably on Saturday, having left Richmond on the York River Railroad on Thursday morning. After detraining, she likely found transport to Williamsburg by Wise's men and along the way ran into the general himself, who promised to deliver packages and letters to Richmond for her. Lucy arrived home in time to hear cannon booming distinctly from the direction of Suffolk all day Sunday and part of Monday. In a 22 April letter to Tom Tucker she announced that "our own home received *no* injury from the shelling & that much less injury was sustained in the Village than we had any reason to expect." Lucy sadly found Mamy Patty "not well, looks miserable & unhappy it makes my heart ache to see her." So few servants remained in town that Lucy had no one to tend her garden, and Zettie "had neglected to procure" tea and coffee when she had an opportunity. They now had nothing in the house to eat but bacon and some beef.[27]

Even worse than low provisions was the unnatural silence. "The loneliness & quiet is to me dreadful & unfits me for any thing," Lucy complained

26. *OR*, 18:628–9; Sweeney to Robert West, 18 Apr. 1863; Sweeney to Wise, 18 Apr. 1863; West to Sweeney, 18 Apr. 1863; and Wise to William Martin, 19 Apr. 1863, Governor (1860–1863: Letcher), Executive papers, 1859–1863 (ser. 1: Chronological Files).

27. Thomas S. B. Tucker to CBT, 16, 20 Apr. 1863, TCP; LAT to Thomas S. B. Tucker, 22–24, 25 Apr. 1863, TCP.

on the twenty-second. The Federals had not yet reentered the asylum; "there certainly are no Yankees there," she wrote, "but I have seen two or three ride up [the] street this morning so we will be liable to be trespassed upon at any time." Two days later, on the twenty-fourth, she continued her letter. "The Yankees have not again taken possession of our Village & we trust they will not at any time," she apprised her son of the situation. "I sometimes almost feel that it would be a relief to see even our enemies, the perfect stillness, & appearance of desertion is so depressing." Later that day seven Federals came into Williamsburg with a flag of truce, but Lucy did not know for what purpose. With their pickets still on the eastern edge of town, "they are very near, & may come at any time," she wrote in her next letter, dated 25 April.[28]

She would not have much longer to wait. Three days later, on 28 April, Dix addressed a letter to Wise, informing him that he had directed Keyes to reoccupy Williamsburg. Included was a stern warning to Wise that if he conducted any more raids, Keyes would send the asylum inmates to Richmond to relieve the U.S. government "of the burden of their support." Furthermore, he would raze "any house which may be taken possession of for the purpose of firing upon the troops stationed there" and would execute any citizen "not belonging to a regularly organized corps who shall be found co-operating in these attacks." Only if Wise left them alone could the army resume caring for the patients and the inhabitants continue "quietly pursuing their domestic avocations."[29]

One family truly suffering from Wise's incursion was the Couplands. On 28 April twelve-year-old Juliana Coupland composed a letter to her father, describing how all the children were pitching in to assist their mother. Big brother George "cuts all our wood and brings all our water," and even little Johnnie at six years "says that he is trying to help mother" by making "a bully fire." Confirming the Federal reoccupation, she informed him that "the Yankees are in town" and "wont let us go out without taken the oath of allegiance one way or the other." Nevertheless, Juliana, despite the disappointment of "these demons coming back," was elated to learn that her father might come back soon. William Douglas had just returned to town with the news that John had been given the clerkship of the asylum if the Virginia government regained permanent control. At least the office exempted Coupland from military service until the matter of control was resolved.[30]

28. LAT to Thomas S. B. Tucker, 22–24, 25 Apr. 1863.
29. *OR*, 18:664–5.
30. Juliana Coupland to JRC, 28 Apr. 1863, DCP; JRC to Juliana Dorsey, 26 Apr. 1863.

That very topic was under discussion between Generals Dix and Keyes on 30 April. Douglas had been appointed by asylum president Robert Saunders in Richmond to return to Williamsburg to "take charge of the institution & provide for its inmates," if permitted, but the Federal commanders were hesitant. If the Confederates took control, "they would be sending in and going out for supplies and it seems to me it would be a means of communications with the rebels," Dix suggested. "Douglass can come back as steward, if you think proper, under our superintendence." Keyes agreed, "the case of the insane asylum is a difficult matter in our hands or with the Confederates," but he did not wish Douglas to return, for the general regarded him "as a pretty bad rebel."[31]

While Douglas waited around Williamsburg for their decision, on the night of 1 May, Susan Coupland gave birth to "our darling little Stranger," Juliana announced in a postscript to her father; "oh he is so sweet how I wish that you could see him." Nearly two weeks later, John still had not received the happy word, but he had learned by 13 May that the Federals decided to retake the asylum and planned to retain Dr. Martin and the present staff Sweeney had assembled, at least for the time being. The 5 May *Cavalier* issue indicated that peace had returned to Williamsburg, though the previous Monday evening, the fourth, West telegraphed Keyes from Fort Magruder that he had intelligence "that cannot be disregarded that the enemy will attack at daylight or before." By Tuesday morning, the nine hundred blue cavalrymen now stationed at Williamsburg were no doubt at their posts.[32]

No Confederates showed up for the party, however, allowing Union soldiers not otherwise engaged to observe unmolested the first anniversary of the battle of Williamsburg. On 5 May the 178th Pennsylvania gathered on "the battle-field still bearing evidence of the fearful conflict," chronicled the *Cavalier*. With speeches and resolutions justifying the battle and glorifying the northern heroes buried here, the soldiers celebrated, unaware their main army, now under Williamsburg's "Fighting Joe" Hooker, had just suffered another defeat at Chancellorsville. Two days later Colonel West, leading a cavalry expedition up the Peninsula, found that all Confederate scouts had withdrawn from Diascund Bridge and crossed the Chickahominy. This opened the way for Keyes to take a force up the York River and threaten Richmond as a futile diversion in Hooker's favor. On the first of June, when Keyes's cavalry column

31. *OR*, 18:673.
32. Juliana Coupland to JRC, 28 Apr. 1863; JRC to Susan Coupland, 13 May 1863, DCP; Flournoy, *Virginia State Papers*, 11:695–7; *(Yorktown) Cavalier*, 5 May 1863; *OR*, 18:689, 693.

marched back down the Peninsula through Williamsburg, "some of the inhabitants were rude enough to stand out on the side-walks and silently stare into the faces of the dust covered troopers, with an expression which seemed to mean, 'we shall soon see the last of you fellows, and the sooner the better.'"[33]

Nevertheless, according to future provost marshal David Cronin, relations between the townspeople and the occupying force were improving since West became Fort Magruder's post commander and Williamsburg's military governor. Though "strict and often stern in discipline and precise in details," the colonel "was especially considerate of the condition of the people." His policy was to visit town often, "inspecting the picket lines but not interfering except by suggestion, with the regular duties of the Provost Marshal." This coincided with a noticeable decrease in Confederate attacks on his picket lines and a corresponding change in Williamsburg. "Shutters were thrown open," Cronin wrote, "children began to play in the door-yards; ladies with faces unconcealed by the customary veil, appeared upon the streets and exchanged social calls with their neighbors; old gentlemen sat together in groups on shaded front porticos and heedless of the proximity of provost guards boldly discussed the recent defeat of the Union Army at Chancellorsville." Now that the weather was warmer, flower gardens were again cultivated and "ladies, often young and pretty," could be found on their porches in the evening. They "chatted gaily and sometimes laughed demonstratively when some spruced young Yankee officer, passing within view, gave them opportunity to exhibit in this manner ridicule for the cause he represented."[34]

One Williamsburg lady feeling more sociable was Lucy Tucker, whose mid-April depression had been dispelled by the attentions of Sgt. John O. Fisher of the 5th Pennsylvania. "Soon after my return home, I felt very friendless & forlorn, had no one to offer me assistance, this Yankee aided me in time," Lucy later wrote Cynthia about the sergeant. "I first asked him to procure for me things, he then offered to do so, & I cant help feeling kindly toward him." Fisher was tall and handsome, sported a long, full brown beard, and became a favorite of the entire town, revealed Cronin, "popular with all classes, old and young—more particularly with the young ladies" because of the many favors he did for them.[35]

During the first week of June, Margaret Munford was finally well enough

33. *(Yorktown) Cavalier,* 12 May 1863; *OR,* 18:705–6, 1055, 27(3):6; David Edward Cronin, "The Vest Mansion," 1908–10, John D. Rockefeller Jr. Library, CWF, 51.

34. Cronin, "Vest Mansion," 51, 57.

35. LAT to CBT, 28 Oct. 1863, TCP; Cronin, "Vest Mansion," 64, 66.

to leave Williamsburg. She obtained the necessary permission and arrived in Richmond with her younger children on the sixth to be reunited with her husband and older daughters, only to die two months later. Also in June, Williamsburg welcomed a visitor from the North, Miss Dorothea Dix, superintendent of Union women nurses. She came to inspect the asylum and, as a prewar acquaintance of the Galts, stayed with Sally. While there, Dorothea insisted on taking Sally to visit the patients, "which I dreaded doing," Sally admitted to her in a letter written that month, "because of the tide of sad, (though they ought to be proud,) remembrances, which would overwhelm me, but their exceeding joy on seeing me again, made me very thankful that I went." The inmates likewise "were made very happy by your visit, & speak thankfully of your kindness," Sally assured Dorothea.[36]

Though far from the main theater of war, Williamsburg again had a front row seat for related troop movements. Lee spent the month of June leading his army north into Pennsylvania. To distract Lee from this course, Hooker, still commanding the Army of the Potomac, suggested that General Dix make a feint upon Richmond, much like his May expedition, only larger. On 11 June the movement up the Peninsula began from Williamsburg and included most of Fort Magruder's garrison. A week later Dix began shipping his troops up the York River from Suffolk. By the twenty-ninth, he had about twenty thousand concentrated at the White House on the Pamunkey River, ready to execute his plan of attack. While the main body was to destroy railroad bridges, disrupting Lee's communication with Richmond, Keyes was assigned a detachment of six thousand men to keep Wise's force around Bottom's Bridge too busy to attack the main body. On 1 July West, commanding Keyes's advance of infantry, artillery, and a contingent of the Fifth, scuffled with some Confederate skirmishers but never became fully engaged. For three days, during the time of the titanic battle at Gettysburg, Keyes repeatedly refused to attack the few gray troops in front of him, and Dix could do little damage against part of D. H. Hill's division, Wise's brigade, and Richmond's Home Guard.[37]

Back in Williamsburg, the skeleton garrison of 150 celebrated Independence Day with the new asylum surgeon, Dr. Watson of the 139th New York. They hoisted an American flag over the hospital and another doctor delivered "an able oration on the occasion." Up in Pennsylvania, Lee decided to fall

36. Robert Saunders to R. Page Saunders, 10 June 1863, PSP, MR-CWM; Dain, *Disordered Minds*, 187; SMG to Dorothea Dix, June 1863, GFP.
37. *OR*, 27(2):820–5, 855–7, 27(3):6–7, 66, 111, 207, 885.

back, having lost many of his best troops the day before in Pickett's Charge. Outside of Richmond, Dix issued one last attack order to Keyes, who again hesitated. The next day Dix called off the operation, withdrawing his force, derisively dubbed "The Grand Army of the Pamunkey" by Richmond papers. A week after this bungled operation, Keyes relinquished his command of Yorktown and Fort Magruder to Brig. Gen. Isaac J. Wistar, and on 18 July Maj. Gen. John G. Foster assumed command of the Department of Virginia in place of Dix.[38]

Still in command in Williamsburg, Colonel West about this time instituted market days, also called "Line Days," in an effort to relieve the inhabitants' destitution. These market days were held once or twice a week at fixed boundaries on Jamestown and Richmond Roads. People living outside Williamsburg could bring produce from their farms to trade with townspeople under the watchful eyes of provost guards, who formally opened and closed the markets at certain hours and were "ordered to prohibit the exchange of letters and articles contraband." Isabella Sully boasted that she was able to smuggle letters out anyway "while buying meat and meal at their lines. Even while the Yanks were watching me and I knew it, I have slipped off news of any increase of their numbers, the condition of Fort Magruder and many other items." Cronin commented that some people came a long way to attend these occasions, mostly women wearing huge sunbonnets to protect them from the "polite or rude gaze of the guards." Often accompanied by half-grown children and aged blacks, "they came in creaking carts drawn by infirm horses or mules of an age too great to tempt the confiscating propensities of the soldiers," wrote Cronin. He noticed "that most of these marketwomen were, in fact, ladies. Some of them owned plantations of hundreds of acres, naturally fertile," and yielding corn, fruit, vegetables, poultry, eggs, butter, and sweet potatoes in abundance.[39]

The Couplands' overseer, named Spear, left on their farm near Jamestown, also came to these line days, John Coupland learned in Richmond, where he now worked in a government office. Though in mid-July he had not yet received a single letter from Sue or any of Ma Henley's family, some Williamsburg friends with him in the capital had received several, and William Douglas, returning from Williamsburg in late May, brought news of his newborn. "I understand that Mr Spear has been allowed to go to the lines with

38. *OR*, 27(2):831–4, 27(3):723, 975; *(Yorktown) Cavalier*, 14 July 1863; *Daily Richmond Examiner*, 9 July 1863.
39. Cronin, "Vest Mansion," 57–8; CBT, "Occupancy," TCP.

provisions," John wrote Sue on 26 July, "if so I suppose you have made him bring in butter fowls, vegetables, and in fact every thing which that place afforded for sale, over and above what you all may need." That would give them some spending money for items not available at the lines. John also heard that the Federals had "appointed a man a sort of furnisher to the almost naked populace to purchase for them at Fortress Monroe whatever articles they have the money to buy, who, if he does not steal more than one third the sum confided to his keeping, is a real benefit to that pitiable people." Apparently, the new departmental administration had softened Federal policy on allowing communication between Williamsburg and the Confederacy, for on 26 July John wrote Sue that he thought she would be permitted by the authorities to send out "a plain, cold business-like letter," which would be better than nothing.[40]

Yet July turned into August, and still no letter from Sue. Other refugees heard "that a much better condition of things prevailed in Williamsburg than at any time previous." On 10 August, Montegu Thompson in Richmond passed this along to Cynthia Coleman, now living in Clarksville, Virginia: "Very few Yankees were there, only a picket guard who never intruded upon the premises of any one." West had drastically reduced the provost guard, believing that "the fewer soldiers stationed in town the better for the inhabitants as well as for his command," Cronin related. On 9 August West appointed a guard of seven cavalry privates, one from the Fifth and the rest from the 139th New York, with the popular Sergeant Fisher in charge. West evidently placed "great reliance upon his intelligence, fidelity and general efficiency, since he gave him authority usually bestowed only upon commissioned officers of high rank." These guards were constituted "for the purpose of enforcing a proper observance of the orders" issued from West's headquarters "concerning the intercourse between the inhabitants of the town and others," their instructions read. "The members of the Guard, will wear as a distinguishing mark, a red cross of worsted material fastened to the left breast."[41]

Other Federals, specifically recruiting officers, had managed to clear the community of able-bodied black men. "The woods all around Town are filled with negroes who have run off from the Yankees to escape the draft," Montegu informed Cynthia. His sister, Julia, was having a problem with one runaway. "A servant woman, Martha, who ran off from me, had returned,"

40. JRC to Susan Coupland, 19, 26 July 1863, DCP.
41. P. M. Thompson to CBT, 10 Aug. 1863, TCP; Cronin, "Vest Mansion," 63–4; General Orders No. 33, 9 Aug. 1863, Will Molineux Collection.

Montegu wrote, "but Miss Julia would not permit her to stay upon the Lot, where upon she became very insolent and threatened to bring the Yankees to avenge her wrongs." Julia courageously stood her ground and "was perfectly right not to permit her to come on the Lot, as she no doubt would have stolen whatever she could lay hands on and gone off again to the Yankees."[42]

The end of August at last brought Coupland his long-desired missive from Sue. "I am in receipt of your *first* letter since the horrid hour of our separation, and oh! how welcome to my anxious heart, and how dear dear the familiar hand writing," John exclaimed in his 27 August reply. Grieved to hear that she had been ill, John was furious to learn that his overseer Spear had so neglected the family that they "had neither flour nor bacon in the house for weeks." Sue received only one lamb and eleven chickens from him all season, and they had been living on nothing but a few vegetables and corn bread for some time. Even worse, Spear "has been trading at the lines with the Yankees," John found out. "His peculations of and trade in commodities at the *lines* has no doubt put hundreds into his pocket. I could stand this, but to think of his faithlessness to you and my little ones, after my special directions and charges to him at the farm, makes me feel like using a stick on his old grey pate." John's one ambition was to bring his family out of Williamsburg as soon as possible, for "I fear the people of that doomed place will suffer awfully this winter. What with Yankee restrictions and scarcity of fuel, cold and starvation stares them in the face."[43]

Williamsburg inhabitants were also facing an increased occupation force during the final week of August with the arrival of another full cavalry regiment. This was the 1st New York Mounted Rifles under Col. Benjamin F. Onderdonk, comprising "twelve companies, with ranks well filled, splendidly equipped and armed with Sharp's carbines the best cavalry weapon then known. About three fourths of its number had been recruited in the city of New York, the rest in different counties in the State," Capt. David Cronin of Troop C detailed. Most of "the rank and file were native born Americans with a sprinkling of foreign born in every troop, many of whom had received military training abroad." Cronin, one of the older members of the regiment at twenty-five, wrote, "when they rode into Williamsburg, their appearance was that of seasoned veterans, due to a years extremely active service" around Suffolk, including battles against Longstreet.[44]

42. P. M. Thompson to CBT, 10 Aug. 1863.
43. JRC to Susan Coupland, 27 Aug. 1863, DCP; JRC to Carter Coupland, 7 Sept. 1863, DCP.
44. Cronin, "Vest Mansion," 58–9.

Soon after their arrival, on the afternoon of 26 August, the Mounted Rifles headed out of Williamsburg on a familiarization tour of the Peninsula, escorted by members of the Fifth. Before returning home three days later, they skirmished several times with Wise and his scouts and encountered black and white civilians of varying loyalties. This turned out to be the Fifth's last scout in the area. On 9 September, one year to the day since Shingler so unceremoniously chased them out of Williamsburg, the 5th Pennsylvania Cavalry departed peacefully for Portsmouth, completing a trade of posts with the Mounted Rifles. "All were glad to leave the Peninsula, where sixteen months of arduous duty, whilst it had won them an enviable reputation for valor and daring, had lost them many a brave soldier in their numerous skirmishes," the *Cavalier* asserted. The paper's Williamsburg correspondent insisted that "there was considerable regret expressed by the inhabitants of this place at their leaving, for their gentlemanly and soldierly conduct had endeared them to the citizens of Williamsburg." Whether they were truly fond of the Pennsylvanians, who "had remained there so long that almost every member of the regiment had become personally acquainted with the inhabitants," or they preferred the known enemy to the uncertainties of an unknown New York regiment is debatable. But with no choice in the matter, Williamsburg denizens once again prepared to make the best of whatever came their way.[45]

45. *OR*, 29(1):86–8; Cronin, "Vest Mansion," 60–2; *(Yorktown) Cavalier*, 21 Sept. 1863.

CHAPTER 15

Up the Peninsula

The same issue of the *Cavalier* that announced the 5th Pennsylvania's departure from Williamsburg also mentioned an increase of Confederate deserters showing up at Federal lines "giving a horrid picture of things in Dixie." The paper hastened to add, however, that "deserters' stories are so common now that anything coming from them excites but little interest." One deserter on 18 September 1863 did excite some interest with the story that General Wise had received marching orders for South Carolina. Wise's replacement, Brig. Gen. Eppa Hunton, had already moved into his headquarters below Richmond at Chaffin's Bluff on the twelfth, bringing with him his brigade from Pickett's Division. Wise left behind both Lt. Col. William Shingler's Holcombe Legion and Maj. John Robertson's 32d Virginia Cavalry Battalion to give Hunton added strength and troops experienced with the territory. After spending a pleasant summer on provost duty in Petersburg, the 32d Virginia Infantry also joined Hunton's brigade on 1 October. Several Junior Guards from Williamsburg and James City County were soon detailed as Peninsula Scouts under the Holcombe Legion's Lt. Charles Hume, and many in the company availed themselves of the opportunity to visit their homes on a regular basis.[1]

The Federals were ready for them. "To strengthen the circular picket lines, a daily detail of 150 men from the Mounted Rifles, was required," wrote David Cronin. Colonel West "posted the outer pickets more closely together and at night required that every passable ravine should be regularly patrolled to prevent the stealthy entrance of scouts." As further protection for the town,

1. *(Yorktown) Cavalier*, 21 Sept. 1863; *OR*, 29(2):713, 783; Hamilton, *Papers of Randolph Abbott Shotwell*, 2:48; Jensen, *32nd Virginia Infantry*, 112–3.

West issued an order that no soldier or officer except pickets on duty could enter Williamsburg without written permission from himself. "To enforce this order, infantry guards were stationed at the entrance to the town, east of the Vest House," probably vacant since the Couplands moved uptown during Wise's raid. West may have used the mansion as an executive office when he visited Williamsburg but retained his headquarters at Fort Magruder, where he usually slept. Sgt. John Fisher, detached from the Fifth and still in charge of the provost guard in Williamsburg, saw no reason to waste the use of all these elegant furnishings and thus moved his men from their regular quarters into the Vest House. He allowed them "to occupy the upper bed-rooms at night and indulge in soothing siestas on the back porch in the afternoons," Cronin revealed, "so long as they behaved themselves, were not noisy and kept ever on the alert in case the Post Commander, who had not been informed of the new arrangements so far as the guards generally were concerned, should call at unexpected times and possibly explore the premises." Dubbed "feather-bed soldiers" by their envious comrades on regular duty, these guards hired "one of the colored hostelers" as cook and lived well on provisions bought at the lines.[2]

The less fortunate New Yorkers also envied these troopers because of "their opportunities for social acquaintances and flirtation with such small proportion of the fair sex as might condescend to notice a Yankee," admitted Cronin. The regiment's previous post near Dismal Swamp afforded little contact with civilians, "especially with real Southern ladies," rendering the blue cavalrymen more susceptible to the charms of Williamsburg belles. One of the younger "feather-bedders," when first playfully called a Yankee, parried with a grave denial, asserting "that he was a New Yorker, born and reared in the Empire State," and should be called a "'York Shilling' or even 'Albany Dutch,'" as Cronin told the story in detail. "He explained further that Yankees were a species of New Englanders, something like gypsies." With that the lady cut him short. "Well, I would reckon you were a Yankee from your long palaver, though you may have a gypsy blend," she told him. "Hereafter, to save your feelings, I will call you 'Gyp.'" And "Gyp" he remained throughout his Williamsburg tour of duty.[3]

Also doing his share of flirting, Sergeant Fisher, as the acting provost marshal during West's long and frequent absences, "was at liberty to call officially

2. David Edward Cronin, "The Vest Mansion," 1908–10, John D. Rockefeller Jr. Library, CWF, 63–4.
3. Ibid., 65–6.

at any door, and if he chose, ingratiate himself with the members of the household." Cronin noted that he "became speedily popular with all classes, old and young—more particularly with the young ladies. His moderately brilliant social qualities shone at many a porch and open window before which he posed prancingly on a handsome captured thoroughbred." Since most Williamsburg shops remained closed, Fisher could dispatch his trusted orderly, a Private Williams detailed from Cronin's company, to Yorktown, where an extensive sutler's establishment "carried a tolerable stock of dress material, ladies shoes and gloves and other like gear." These Fisher distributed freely in Williamsburg and in James City County during his occasional scouts beyond the lines. "With the people outside, he seemed to be as familiar and welcome as with those in town," remarked Cronin, "and if the heels of a new pair of shoes sometimes showed at the mouth of his well packed saddle bags, what of it? Wasn't he the acting Marshal and didn't he know his business? Perhaps he received valuable information in return for such trifles."[4]

Or perhaps he was laying siege to the heart of a particular Williamsburg belle, as all the guards were well aware, "and success might be dependent in a measure, upon securing the good will of all the other ladies," Cronin suggested. Mary Southall, known as "The Sunbeam" for her cheerful personality, had captured Fisher's heart, and "despite his Yankee uniform, she appeared as much captivated by him as he with her." Unfortunately, her home in the President's House was a little too public for a private courtship. On warmer evenings the picket reserve bivouacking at the college "would gather about the steps to listen to the dulcet strains of 'My Maryland' or livelier airs like the 'Bonnie Blue Flag,' which came through the open windows of the drawing room." Not to be outdone, the pickets countered with "songs obnoxious to Southern feelings, such as 'Old John Brown' and 'Rally round the flag,'" until the Southalls complained to Fisher. He reported to West that the guards littered "up the porch with their equipments, often emptying their haversacks there for luncheon," and "regularly disturbed the sleep of the family at night with the jingle and clatter of their arms when aroused to take their turns in relief." Consequently, West ordered the reserve to move across the lawn and remain at the Brafferton.[5]

That solved one problem, but a more serious obstacle to Fisher's courtship lurked on Williamsburg's outskirts. One of the Peninsula Scouts named Cpl. A. G. Tradewell was another "devoted admirer" of Mary Southall and "went

4. Ibid., 66–8.
5. Ibid., 68–70.

so far as to openly presume to be her chivalrous protector against the insidious arts of 'a common mudsill, no-account Yankee.'" Cronin described Tradewell as "a mere youth" but "fearless, ruthless and vindictive." After the young scout sent Mary letters threatening to shoot Fisher on sight, she wrote Major Robertson, in command at Charles City Court House, urging him to relieve Tradewell from duty on the Peninsula. She then advised Fisher to "discontinue his calls and not stir outside the lines."[6]

Wisely adhering to this advice, Fisher employed Orderly Williams as a go-between to deliver love letters and romantic poetry composed at the long mahogany table in the Vest House. But Tradewell was not put off easily. One evening shortly after another written threat came from the woods outside town, Fisher was riding alone on Main Street past the long brick wall enclosing Bruton Churchyard when he "was fired upon twice from behind the wall," Cronin narrated. "The shots, from a revolver, missed him," but they alerted nearby guards, who immediately appeared on the scene. Fisher curiously "denied that he had been fired upon and declared that he himself, had fired at a Confederate scout climbing over the wall, probably had hit him." A thorough search of the old, gray tombstones and neglected shrubbery in the churchyard, however, "found no one either wounded, dead, or alive."[7]

Meanwhile, relations between townspeople and occupiers began to deteriorate again. Early in September, trading for commodities at the lines was no longer allowed on market days, still held twice a week on Mondays and Thursdays, and only cash could now be used for buying produce. "There used to be quite a number at the lines on these days," according to a 13 September letter printed in the *Cavalier,* but "since the order forbidding exchanging has been issued, the number of persons who come down with their produce to our lines has considerably diminished." With money so scarce, especially U.S. currency, it was not surprising that "the people are very much dissatisfied with this late order."[8]

One result of the new policy was an increasing food shortage in Williamsburg. "A great many of the families of this town are dependent upon the bounty of our government for their support, and were it not for the fact that rations are issued to them every ten days regularly, there would be considerable suffering amongst them," the *Cavalier* asserted. "Many persons who, previous to the rebellion, were considered wealthy, are now compelled to be recipients

6. Ibid., 70–2.
7. Ibid., 72–3.
8. *(Yorktown) Cavalier,* 21 Sept. 1863.

of the charity which our Government so liberally bestows upon them." John Coupland was appalled to hear this. "The people in WmsBurg are for the most part living upon the charities of our vile enemies—what a condition," he lamented on 7 September and immediately began implementing a plan to rescue his family from such an intolerable situation.[9]

"I desire that you shall make application to the Federal authorities to be allowed to come out and bring whatever furniture and baggage it may be in your power to remove," John instructed Sue on 15 September. "I have no doubt if the application be properly made it will be allowed." Col. Goodrich Durfey, permitted by the Federals to travel between Richmond and Williamsburg once a week, delivered this letter to Sue and also helped her by making application on behalf of the Coupland family until John could get a furlough to come down for them. Hoping to be there before the last week of September, John optimistically advised his wife, "between now and that time (Sept 25) you could, at your leisure, by hiring Ma's servants, be enabled to get all the bedding, house linen, clothing, glass and crockery packed up."[10]

Before John was able to leave for Williamsburg, Durfey returned to Richmond, bringing word from Sue that she had not yet decided whether to leave town but preferred to wait until her husband came down. She would have to make her decision soon, as winter was approaching and she had no way to obtain wood. "George is the only one on whom you can rely, and it would be subjecting him to great hardship to haul through all weather a sufficient supply," John reminded her in his next letter, dated 1 October. If she decided to leave Williamsburg, "Col. D. will make the application for you and assist you in getting some one in town to help you pack up." Sue finally made up her mind to leave and hired Bucktrout for five dollars to pack "up your things for Mrs Copeland when she went out of the Yankey lines," according to the undertaker's ledger, which had but few entries lately.[11]

Within a week of his 1 October letter, John journeyed to Williamsburg to bring out his family. He and Sue were still packing by the latter part of the month and sent their daughters, Juliana and Nora, to Lucy Tucker's for the day. Lucy enjoyed their company in place of her youngest, who recently passed into "Secessia." "Mrs. Tucker being anxious to send her son Montegu to

9. Ibid.; JRC to Carter Coupland, 7 Sept. 1863, DCP, MR-CWM.
10. JRC to Susan Coupland, 15 Sept. 1863, DCP.
11. JRC to Susan Coupland, 1 Oct. 1863, DCP; Richard M. Bucktrout Day Book, 8 Dec. 1863, MR-CWM.

school, will be much obliged if Col. West will give him a Passport to go be-yond the lines," she penned on 5 October. West approved her request, adding as he forwarded it the next day to Brig. Gen. Isaac Wistar in Yorktown, "The son is a sickly youth of fifteen, who can do us no harm." With this endorse-ment, Wistar granted permission for Monty to leave by flag of truce from Fort Monroe on the fifteenth.[12]

During October, the Federals liberally distributed passes out of Williams-burg, apparently purging the district of the more obnoxious residents. Family stories indicate that they allowed the "little rebel" Delia Bucktrout passage to her grandmother's in New Kent County about this time. From there she con-tinued on to Richmond to live out the war. Another permitted to pass out of the lines "with caution 'never to return'" was a Mrs. Lee. This may have been Susan Lee, who had two sons serving in the Junior Guards. On 22 October she departed Williamsburg in her "buggy and cart driven by two negroes" with a cavalry escort of fifty men and an officer. West sent such a large force, he explained to Wistar, because the Peninsula Scouts had threatened to attack the next expedition. "They said of us that we were too cowardly to come out upon any other occasion than when ladies accompany us." Despite the pres-ence of Mrs. Lee, the scouts took the opportunity to attack the party both on the way up and on the way back, and even stretched telegraph wire "across the road to trip their horses as they returned," West reported the next day. Strange to say, no one was hurt.[13]

Either unable or unwilling to obtain a pass, Mary Southall also determined to leave Williamsburg before Tradewell took aim once more at Fisher. In Cro-nin's version of the tale, she attended line day around the first of October, dressed in faded attire and telescopic bonnet like the "outside women" with whom Fisher, in charge of line days, allowed her to mingle. "When the Mar-ket was declared closed, she clambered into a cart only partly occupied by two other ladies, and disappeared with the rest into the gloom of the forest," Cro-nin related. "Williams, who had keenly observed this infraction of the rules, called Fisher's attention to it, and was roughly reprimanded for not minding his own business." After riding up to Charles City County to consult with the

12. Juliana Dorsey to JRC, DCP; LAT to CBT, 28 Oct. 1863, TCP, MR-CWM; LAT to Robert M. West, 5 Oct. 1863, TCP; West to Isaac Wistar, 6 Oct. 1863, TCP; Wistar to West, 9 Oct. 1863, TCP.

13. Minnie B. Jenkins, "When Delia Bucktrout Ran the Blockade to Richmond," Dorothy Ross Collection; *OR*, 29(2):374–5; U.S. Bureau of the Census, Williamsburg and James City County Records, 1860; Jensen, *32nd Virginia Infantry*, 191.

commander, Mary, bearing intelligence to the War Department, continued on to Richmond.[14]

A few days after "The Sunbeam" slipped away, West rode into town and stopped as usual at the Vest House. Fisher happened to be absent, but Williams was in attendance at the door and later conveyed the following details to Cronin. After making a thorough inspection of the mansion, West "passed out with an unusually stern expression of countenance, mounted and rode to the College." There he found the picket reserves under Lt. William W. Disoway, a "neat and orderly" nineteen-year-old "growing his first slender mustache" on his "intelligent, handsome, boyish face." The lieutenant and colonel had a brief interview, then West rode back to headquarters, "where he stopped long enough to write out an order which he folded and addressed to the Lieutenant, dispatching a guard to deliver it." That evening at dress parade, General Orders No. 47, dated 5 October, were read: "1st Lieut W. W. Disoway, 1st New York Mounted Rifles, is hereby detailed and announced, as Acting Provost Marshall of this Command to be stationed in the City of Williamsburg. He will be obeyed and respected accordingly." Also displacing Fisher in charge of the provost guard, Disoway took possession of the Vest House the next day, while Fisher and the guards "retired to their regular quarters or barracks" at the old Female Academy.[15]

Like Fisher, the genteel Disoway quickly became a favorite among the ladies, but his career proved tragically short. On the morning of 13 October, only a week after he assumed the office of provost, Disoway called upon Isabella Sully. "He told me he had heard I wished to go into the Confederacy," Isabella wrote in her journal, "and that he had called to offer his services to procure a passport for me, as he was that day going to York Town." She was most grateful, and "as he seemed a gentleman," she engaged the youthful officer in conversation, asking him why he, an only son, left his mother for this war. "He made some foolish reply about the flag—as they all do," Isabella recorded. "Lieut. Disoway had only been gone about an hour when I heard a pistol shot." Lucy Tucker soon rushed in with the news that he had been killed by one of his own men.[16]

As Cronin told it, Disoway was seated in the doorway of the Vest House, reading a newspaper, when a provost guard named Pvt. William Boyle was

14. Cronin, "Vest Mansion," 73; Joynes to Kean, 5 Nov. 1863, Edward S. Joynes F/A File, UA-CWM.

15. Cronin, "Vest Mansion," 74–5; General Orders No. 47, 5 Oct. 1863, Will Molineux Collection.

16. CBT, "Occupancy," TCP, MR-CWM.

brought to him in custody. The previous day Boyle had been sent back to his company camp for being intoxicated at his post, "an extremely rare offense," and seeking revenge on Disoway, he had just tried to force his way past the guard east of town. "In arresting him the Corporal of the infantry guards had neglected to take away his only weapon—a revolver worn at the belt," Cronin continued. Looking down from the doorway, Disoway realized Boyle was drunk and ordered him back to camp. At that point, Boyle "drew his weapon and flourishing it toward Disoway, with a curse, threatened to shoot him. The guards instantly levelled their guns pushing Boyle's weapon aside and trying to secure it. Failing in this, they aimed their pieces to shoot him down. The Lieutenant sprang up and ordered them not to shoot, saying he would disarm him, himself, and descending the steps advanced toward Boyle, who, at that moment, fired, the ball entering Disoway's mouth, killing him instantly." Before he could shoot anyone else, Boyle was disarmed and taken to the guardhouse.[17]

The next day, 14 October, at Fort Magruder, "most impressive funeral services were held in the presence of the entire command turned out in lines forming a square," Cronin recounted. Isabella Sully, grieving for Disoway's stricken mother, wrote in her journal that she and Lucy Tucker "got some beautiful flowers which were sent with our cards to be put in his coffin." Four officers of the Mounted Rifles escorted his remains to his home in New York. Boyle was promptly tried, convicted, and sentenced to death, but when his case was sent to Washington for approval, Lincoln postponed signing the necessary papers authorizing his execution. "Pending the return of the death warrant," Cronin wrote, "Boyle was manacled and confined in the guard-house at Fort Magruder."[18]

Succeeding Disoway as provost marshal was Maj. James N. Wheelan of the 1st New York Mounted Rifles, "dignified but suave and engaging in manner, gallant where ladies were concerned but not inordinately susceptible to their charms," Cronin remarked. Wheelan kindly granted Isabella and Jennie Sully the passes out of Williamsburg they had so long desired, but on the day they were to leave, Isabella was not well enough to travel, and they missed their chance. Later, as Lucy wrote Cynthia on 28 October, "at night, the order came for all persons leaving the lines to go by Flag of truce, of course, she would not go that way, with all her goods & chattels. She renewed her application & is now waiting, all packed to start at once." Without servants, Isabel-

17. Cronin, "Vest Mansion," 77–8.
18. Ibid., 78; CBT, "Occupancy."

la's hard housework "has broken her down, & she thinks a winter would put a finishing touch to her earthly career," Lucy elucidated. "She looks very badly, & is in bad spirits." Jennie likewise expressed her eagerness to leave, saying she "would rather *die* than remain here." Lucy was "sorry they can't be satisfied to remain, for they may have difficulties to encounter in Dixie."[19]

Not that life was easy in Williamsburg. For one thing, mail was unreliable at best, and Lucy had not heard from Cynthia since the first of May. This 28 October letter she hoped to send through the lines "by some hocus pocus," as nothing else seemed to work. Servants were among her other problems. After Isabella left, Julia Thompson planned to take her meals with the Tuckers, "& I think we can get on very well, if dear good Patsy holds out," Lucy wrote. "I have now a *wild* stupid negro (just sense enough to do what I tell her) to assist her." And for that kind of "help," she had to pay $4.00 a month. Some other prices Lucy quoted for Cynthia's information included ground coffee, forty cents; tea, $2.00; candles, twenty-eight cents per box; boots, $3.25; oysters, fifteen cents per quart ("I seldom aspire to such a luxury"); beef, ten cents; and flour $10.00, "all yankee money."[20]

Yankee money was one of the few things Lucy had in abundance. Her brother in Union-held Missouri recently sent her a substantial sum, "& we were thereby much relieved & comforted," Lucy confided to Cynthia. With a portion of it, Lucy bought "a little of various things" for her children but was limited in what she could send, "as the articles have to be distributed among the clothes of a friend" to be smuggled out of Williamsburg. Going through legal channels to obtain Cynthia a bombazine (black silk twill) dress from Philadelphia was frustrating, for Lucy had to make applications to Generals Wistar and Foster as well as to Colonel West. "I almost begin to doubt my *loyalty*," sighed Lucy, who confessed to Cynthia that she had entertained the colonel "in the *Study,* I thought of you, but there was no help for it." West said he would mail a letter for her, but by the time Lucy reached the end of her epistle, she intimated that other arrangements had been made: "This letter is to go out as a *great favour* (a *secret*)."[21]

Exactly who was going to do this great favor Lucy hinted in another cryptic passage earlier in her 28 October missive. "I have received many little acts of kindness from a Sergeant, J. O. Fisher, & hope if he should ever be in Confederate hands, he may be treated with great consideration," she wrote. "He is

19. Cronin, "Vest Mansion," 79; LAT to CBT, 28 Oct. 1863.
20. LAT to CBT, 28 Oct., 6 Nov. 1863, TCP.
21. LAT to CBT, 28 Oct. 1863.

sent up the county occasionally, & I should not be surprised, if he is taken when he least expects it." Certainly, Major Wheelan had no idea what to expect only a few mornings later when "Sergeant Fisher smilingly presented himself at Headquarters, as usual, to make his morning report and receive orders," began Cronin, placing the date as 5 November. "He informed the Major that he had learned from a market-woman at the lines that several valuable horses belonging to an absentee planter were concealed in a piece of woods near Green Spring—about seven miles away." Proposing to circle around and capture the horses with a small squad, Fisher immediately secured permission with additional instructions "to be cautious against ambuscade by Hume's men" and "to gather all the general information he could."[22]

Fisher quickly selected his men, about a half dozen, including Orderly Williams, and started up Richmond Road. Williams later told Cronin that Fisher called a halt near Burnt Ordinary to rest the horses. First he suggested his men loosen the saddle girths, and when they hesitated, loudly ordered them to. "At the moment when they were stooping to unbuckle the girths and thrown completely off their guard, the little squad was suddenly and closely surrounded by Hume and his men, who with leveled pieces and fierce oaths used on such occasions demanded their instant surrender—and all were taken." While the squad marched to Richmond on foot, Fisher rode ahead of them with Hume, and that was the last any of them saw of Fisher.[23]

Before long, Fisher's men, now incarcerated in Libby Prison in Richmond, "reached the conclusion that they had been deliberately and most treacherously betrayed by their trusted commander and comrade." More than likely, Fisher had in his possession Lucy Tucker's 28 October letter to Cynthia, along with a message she sent the Richmond authorities "to have him treated with consideration for his kindness to the citizens here." In another letter, dated 6 November, Lucy fretted, "I am quite at a loss who to call upon, now my obliging Yankee *Friend* went up the county with scout a few days since, & has not returned, so we suppose, by this time is in Richmond having met the Confederates." With endorsements from Lucy as well as Mary Southall, Fisher was indeed treated well, being promoted to lieutenant when he exchanged his blue uniform for gray. Cronin later learned that he was installed as commander of prison guards at Castle Thunder in Richmond. Mary Southall also applied for a job in Richmond and was recommended for a position by former William and Mary College professor Edward Joynes, a civilian administrative officer in

22. Ibid.; Cronin, "Vest Mansion," 79–80.
23. Cronin, "Vest Mansion," 80–1.

the War Department. He cited her "meritorious character and patriotic services" in caring for sick and wounded Confederate soldiers and for saving part
of the college library when the building burned. During the last week of December, Mary became Mrs. John O. Fisher in a quiet ceremony southwest of
Richmond.[24]

About the same time Fisher left Williamsburg, a letter Cynthia had written
more than a month before, on 1 October, finally found its way into Lucy's
hands on 5 November. In her reply written the next day, Lucy mentioned that
she was trying to send Cynthia "some necessaries from home, but that is almost impossible as nothing is *allowed* to go out of the lines." Sue Coupland,
still in Williamsburg, "promised to take as hers, a carpet to be left with some
friends in the country, who will await your direction," Lucy instructed
Cynthia. Now that Isabella was also leaving, Lucy sent some things by her,
including calico for baby Charley, dresses, gloves, boots, coffee, sugar, and
candles—enough to fill a trunk.[25]

Judging from Lucy's 6 November letter, the Sullys probably departed that
morning. "I could hardly believe that I had left Williamsburg and the Yankees
behind me when I arrived at my friends, Mr. and Mrs. George Hankins' about
thirteen miles above Town," Isabella entered in her journal; "here I stopped
for the night." Before she was able to continue on her way, "Yankee raiders
arrived and began to destroy every thing right and left. I asked to see the Officer in command, who either recognizing me or hearing my name, inquired
if I were the lady who sent flowers to the mother of Lieut. Disoway?" To her
answer in the affirmative, the officer replied, "Then Madam, this whole thing
shall be stopped at your request." He then called off his men and rode away.
Isabella closed her journal, gratified that an earlier act of kindness helped relieve her friends in their distress.[26]

Unfortunately, the Hankins family was not spared long, for in a day or two,
they and several of their neighbors became targets of a large force "sent from
Williamsburg to spread out over the cultivated fields of the Peninsula to har-
vest the ripened crops before they could be secured to sustain the forces of the
enemy," Cronin revealed. Starting out on 8 November, the expedition included forty wagons and a new regiment, the 6th U.S. Colored Infantry,
which had arrived on the Peninsula in mid-October and had gone into camp

24. Ibid., 81–2; LAT to CBT, 6 Nov. 1863; Carrie [Hodges?] to CBT, 9 Jan. 1864, TCP;
Joynes to Kean, 5 Nov. 1863.
25. LAT to CBT, 6 Nov. 1863; CBT to CWC, 29 Nov. 1863, TCP.
26. CBT, "Occupancy."

around Yorktown. As they marched through Williamsburg on their way up-county, they were the first blacks in blue uniforms seen by the townspeople. "Besides over a thousand bushels of corn, almost everything else in the nature of provender was carried away, as a 'war measure,'" Cronin enumerated, "producing almost a famine in the markets at the lines, and increasing the number of people in town who were obliged to accept government rations or starve." At least John Coupland managed to bring off stock from his farm as he departed Williamsburg with his family around this time.[27]

A secondary purpose for this sizeable expedition was to lay a trap for Lt. Charles Hume and his Peninsula Scouts, comprising "men selected from various regular commands, on account of their experience and craft as woodsmen their skill as marksmen and general intrepidity," explained Cronin. A stocky South Carolinian, Hume had been on the Peninsula at least since the previous February. Cronin believed he was the Confederate lieutenant who pinned the note to Lt. Samuel Williamson's body and sent it back to Williamsburg after the skirmish. He had eluded capture ever since, though tangling at several points with the crop-stealing expedition. On the evening of 10 November, Hume addressed a dispatch to the Holcombe Legion's adjutant with an ominous warning: "This they promise will not be their last visit, but they intend robbing every farm on the Peninsula before stopping."[28]

Hume's communication never reached its intended destination, for he entrusted it to a chubby young scout from the Holcombe Legion named John Donnell, who delivered it instead to Major Wheelan in Williamsburg. Donnell's reason for changing flags Cronin credited to a personal quarrel with Hume. Accompanying Donnell was another scout, Sgt. F. George Wilson, also nursing a grudge against Hume. Through a lady friend suspected of being a Union sympathizer, Wilson had sent word to Wheelan that he was willing "to come in and take the oath." She accompanied him and Donnell to the Vest House, where West interviewed them and was apparently convinced of their sincerity to defect and become Union scouts. He immediately administered the oath of allegiance to both men as well as to the lady. "Then to bind the bargain," Cronin divulged, West "decided that the evidently infatuated couple should be married on the spot and dispatched a messenger to the Fort to fetch a chaplain—a duly ordained parson. 'And so they were married.'"[29]

27. *OR*, 29(1):637; Cronin, "Vest Mansion," 85; Horace Montgomery, "A Union Officer's Recollections of the Negro as a Soldier," *Pennsylvania History* 28 (Apr. 1961): 160.

28. Cronin, "Vest Mansion," 28, 34, 86; *OR*, 29(1):637–8.

29. Cronin, "Vest Mansion," 89–91; Janet B. Hewett, ed., *The Roster of Confederate Soldiers, 1861–1865,* 16 vols. (Wilmington, N.C.: Broadfoot, 1995–96), 5:84.

The diversion of Hume's scouts during the forage operation not only gave Wilson and Donnell the opportunity to desert but also allowed two "ragged, starved, woe-begone" Union officers just escaped from Libby Prison in Richmond to get all the way to Williamsburg. "There was scarcely a vestige of visible uniform on them," Cronin observed. They and other prisoners who, like them, had successfully eluded Hume's scouts and arrived in Williamsburg brought tales of suffering in Confederate prisons. For more than a year, West had been devising a plan to raid Richmond and release Federal prisoners, but now that two former Peninsula Scouts had fallen into his lap, he believed "the present to be an auspicious time to strike for the relief of our suffering soldiers in Richmond prisons." The Confederate capital, he learned, had the smallest defending force around it since the beginning of the war, and Wilson and Donnell told him only three scouts presently patrolled between the Chickahominy River and Williamsburg. The colonel saw no reason why all Federal cavalry in the department could not be brought to Fort Magruder secretly at night, "encamped on an adjacent farm out of sight of the main road," and organized "into a column for a rapid movement" against Richmond.[30]

All these ideas West submitted to General Wistar in a 24 November letter. Wistar in turn passed it along to Maj. Gen. Benjamin Butler, now known as "Beast" for his "Woman Order" declaring the ladies of New Orleans, where he formerly commanded, prostitutes for treating Union soldiers with even more disrespect than Williamsburg ladies showed them. On 11 November Butler had returned to Fort Monroe and relieved Foster from command of the Department of Virginia and North Carolina. In a cover letter Wistar added his ideas to West's plan, but before such an ambitious raid could be undertaken, some preliminary scouting would be necessary, penetrating into Richmond itself.[31]

For such missions the Union employed special agents. According to Cronin, they would show up at the Vest House as fully uniformed "staff officers" direct from Washington, carrying bulky valises that "contained an extra suit of clothes or properties useful in assuming the various disguises of a professional spy." These agents would be taken through the lines on routine scouting expeditions up the Peninsula and dropped off to make their way into Richmond. One of the most noted and daring of these operatives was called "Major Howard, the Paymaster," for his disguise in both the northern and southern armies. Another spy, Sgt. James Plunkett, Cronin characterized as "home talent,"

30. Cronin, "Vest Mansion," 91; *OR,* 51(1):1282–3.
31. *OR,* 51(1):1282–3, 29(2):446–7.

being a member of the Mounted Rifles. In November, on his way to Richmond, Plunkett stopped at a plantation belonging to a lady known to the Federals as a Union sympathizer. Cronin referred to her as "Mrs. Tentrees." Her husband, a clerk in the Confederate State Department, provided Plunkett upon his arrival in Richmond with decoy letters designed to identify the carrier who was transporting official correspondence from the Confederate government to the outside world. Under the Union blockade, the most reliable route for Richmond's overseas mail was through Williamsburg to the Federal post office in Yorktown.[32]

On his way back to Williamsburg with the decoy letters, Plunkett stopped at Charles City Court House and reported to Major Robertson, commanding the Richmond City Battalion of a little over one hundred men belonging to many prominent Richmond families. He briefly explained his errand "to deliver important foreign correspondence to Lieutenant Hume; and he wished to know where that officer could be immediately found," wrote Cronin. "Without the least mistrust the Major gave him all the particulars he needed." Plunkett found Hume at a nearby plantation, handed him the letters, and hastened on his way. Hume immediately suspected the letters were decoys and the carrier a spy, but Plunkett returned safely to Williamsburg with detailed information on both the Confederate picket placement and Hume's headquarters.[33]

West now had all he needed to implement his plan to capture the Richmond City Battalion and with any luck Hume, to pave the way for a raid on Richmond. On the morning of 12 December, a detachment of two hundred men from the 139th New York Infantry, guided by Donnell, marched out of Williamsburg toward Charles City County. West followed twelve hours later, "under lowering clouds, and an atmosphere that presaged storm," with Wilson by his side, leading six companies of Mounted Rifles. Throughout the night "the storm increased in violence and, added to the darkness, greatly hindered our progress," related Cronin, one of the expedition's members. In the morning, as the storm let up, the horsemen continued on to Charles City Court House, totally surprising the Confederates and easily capturing ninety prisoners. Neither Robertson nor Hume was among those captured, however. On the way back to Williamsburg, Hume "leaped from the woods a few paces in front of the advance guard and raising his rifle took deliberate aim at Wilson," fired a bullet into his arm, "and then sprang back into the woods and disap-

32. Cronin, "Vest Mansion," 53, 83.
33. Ibid., 111–3.

peared." By the afternoon of 14 December, the columns of blue and gray reached the safety of Williamsburg.[34]

"Williamsburg witnessed a pathetic scene when the prisoners arrived and were marched through the main street, surrounded by silent vigilant guards, on their way north via Yorktown," wrote Cronin, commander of the guard. All eighty enlisted men paraded in on foot, with the officers mounted in advance. "As the captives passed along, women and children at the windows wept and wailed, waving hands and handkerchiefs with fervent good-byes. In many instances half smothered greetings of mutual recognition and acquaintance were exchanged." The Federal surgeon saved Wilson's severely wounded arm, and the sergeant settled down to recover in his wife's Main Street residence, already rigged with an escape ladder out an upper window in case of a surprise visit from any of his former comrades in gray.[35]

For their faithful and efficient service as guides, both Wilson and Donnell were mentioned in West's report. Wistar too was pleased with their conduct and with the entire operation, highly praising it to Butler, who in turn boasted to Halleck of "the brilliancy of the achievement." He was especially impressed "that it had been accomplished during a terrible storm." Cronin learned long after the war that it had been accomplished precisely because of the storm. Usually, townspeople living near the eastern edge of Williamsburg could hear and understand the meaning of the various bugle calls at Fort Magruder and could tell when the Federal cavalry was preparing to march. Since an hour or more would pass between the first notes and the passing of troopers westward through town, the inhabitants had time to notify the Peninsula Scouts "by a continuous chain of signals that reached the western end of town," Cronin delineated. "These signals at night, varied according to the distance between neighbors' houses, and the sounds made were designed to appear as natural as possible so as not to attract the attention of the guards." Neighbors established their own signal systems, including clattering pots and pans and coughing children, "who were apt to overdo their parts," one lady informed him. "In the daytime, when people nearest the Fort could see an approaching column in the distance, a favorite signal was neighbor after neighbor loudly 'shooing' hens from their back yards, whether they had any hens left, or not."[36]

Waiting beyond the western edge of Williamsburg were Peninsula Scouts

---

34. *OR*, 29(1):974–6; Seth Eyland [David Edward Cronin], *Evolution of a Life* (New York: S. W. Green's Son, 1884), 188–92; Moore, *Rebellion Record*, 8:287–8.

35. Cronin, "Vest Mansion," 91, 119; Eyland, *Evolution of a Life*, 192.

36. *OR*, 29(1):974–6; Cronin, "Vest Mansion," 295–6.

posted behind trees and in some cases in the tops of trees, two or three of the tallest pines having been converted into observation platforms "by placing boards tied with ropes across their upper branches. From these elevations a leisurely espionage was almost constantly maintained." Because the racket signals could not reach that far, citizens communicated with these scouts by illuminating their west windows at night. Provost guards caught onto the purpose of the lights, however, and started firing into those windows, "but of course at such an angle as not to injure any of the inmates, 'unless they happened to be on the ceiling,' as one of the guards, more considerate than the rest remarked."[37]

Before long, Williamsburg residents grew tired of risking bullets through their windows and entrusted the night signals "to two persons who probably would never be suspected," Cronin disclosed. A free black couple named Til and Jake, known also as "Old Jucks," owned Frog Pond Tavern on the western edge of town, ideally situated to be a signal station. Naive northerners assumed that they, being black, supported the Union cause. "At night, an ordinary lambent lamp in Til's upper windows which could be seen plainly from some points in our front, would not have excited suspicion if noted at any hour by the reserves." Jake could also signal the Peninsula Scouts in the daytime by approaching the edge of the ravine near his cottage and making some gesture visible to their lookouts. "For example, he might wave his big basket wildly, to drive an invisible stray hen in the grass back to the coop." One of the few times such a system might fail would be during a deafening and blinding thunderstorm, and such a storm allowed the Mounted Rifles to make their one successful raid on Charles City Court House.[38]

Shortly after this operation, Butler visited Williamsburg and toured the town from the Vest House to the college ruins, accompanied by West. "It was said that when Col. West met him at Fort Magruder, an escort of a regiment of infantry was offered and declined, the General preferring only half a dozen Mounted Riflemen as being far more appropriate and fashionable at that time," wrote Cronin. Another notorious northern character showed up in Williamsburg about this time. "Whilst I was in command at Williamsburg an Official of the U.S. Treasury Department styled at the time 'Treasury Agent' came to my Head Quarters at Fort Magruder," West later related, "and stated to my Adjutant General (for I was not at home at the time) that he knew of a quantity of valuables belonging to Rebels which valuables were concealed in

37. Cronin, "Vest Mansion," 22, 71, 296.
38. Ibid., 297–9.

Williamsburg, and demanded facilities for making search for them." Being referred to Wheelan, "the Agent proceeded to Williamsburg, made his search, found, I presume, what he wanted, and went away before I returned to Fort Magruder." What he found were a pair of old waiters and some heirlooms belonging to Benjamin Ewell but kept by Gabriella Galt for safekeeping while he was away. "These Treasury Agents roamed the Conquered Districts at will with authority in their pockets which no officer of my calibre dared to question," West explained to Ewell, who complained to him of the loss after the war.[39]

As 1863 turned into 1864, an increased number of escaped Federal prisoners, Confederate deserters, and civilian refugees coming down the Peninsula convinced Butler and Wistar it was time to put West's plan to raid Richmond into effect. Despite the Federals' efforts to keep the operation secret, Richmond authorities were already aware of the threat by the second week of January. They had even been notified thirty-six hours in advance of a 19 January scouting expedition undertaken by one company of Mounted Rifles led by Maj. Edgar A. Hamilton and guided by Wilson. "Lieutenant Hume, the commander of the scouts, had received his information in letter direct from Williamsburg," Hamilton included in his report upon his return. Nevertheless, he managed to capture four Confederates and two fresh furlough passes carried by two Williamsburg boys of the 1st Virginia Battery overtaken while "trudging along the highway en route to their homes." Cronin commented that they "had expected to see their families before nightfall, having no doubt of their ability to creep between the pickets and get into town."[40]

Within forty-eight hours of his return, Hamilton was on the road again, setting up an ambush for Hume and putting these passes to good use. This expedition dropped off the two spies, "Paymaster Howard" and Plunkett, who would use the furlough passes to enter Richmond. While there they planned to assist the Federal raiding forces, which would temporarily occupy the city. These troops had already begun to assemble on the Peninsula under the watchful eyes of Confederate spies. Wistar was probably doing a better job of keeping his own side from learning about the gathering troops, for he scattered the units "in secluded encampments in the well wooded neighborhood between Fort Magruder and Yorktown," Cronin wrote.[41]

39. Ibid., 121; Robert M. West to BSE, 8 Apr. 1866, WCP, MR-CWM.
40. Eyland, *Evolution of a Life*, 194; *OR*, 33:20–1, 398, 1074; Cronin, "Vest Mansion," 122–4.
41. *OR*, 33:21–2, 1125; Cronin, "Vest Mansion," 130–1.

In another useless effort to prevent rumors of Federal intentions from spreading, Wistar issued an order in late January that all Williamsburg citizens must take the oath of allegiance on the third or fourth day of February or be sent away. This caused great consternation among many, particularly Sally Galt, who instantly began a letter-writing campaign. In a note to her old friend Dorothea Dix, Sally entreated her help to avoid the oath. "It would almost make me crazy to take any oath to any government even General Washington's government if he was living I could not promise to support," Sally reasoned. "You know slavery I have always said I did not like, but I can't take an oath." If she were banished from her home, Sally worried about her late brother's valuable medical books and collection of rare shells and "curiosities," but her greatest concern was for the welfare of her servants. Old "Unkle" Aleck Preston was "almost as helpless as an infant & says if I go away he shall die & that parting from me will be the cause of it," Sally confided to Dorothea. In an open letter she implored that Preston "may be protected & kindly treated by the Federals, for I know they know how to do a kind action. He is seventy-three years of age, & has lived for three generations in my family, & given to them, & received from them the deepest love & affection; & the bitterest anguish torturs my heart, at parting with him & his wife." A similar letter Sally composed on behalf of Arena Baker, her children, and her grandchildren: "From youth to my mature age Arena's life has been altogether lovely blameless & pure & I know that Heaven will bless those who are kind to her."[42]

Sally also addressed Colonel West directly on her own behalf and begged for an extension to give Dorothea time to intercede. "I have never said an unkind word to, or of any of the Federals," Sally asserted. "General Grover said in May 1862 when he was Governor of Williamsburg that I should be protected & have every kindness extended to me, because I was so kind to his people." On 2 February she added an appeal to a higher authority, General Wistar, assuring him that "we cannot, without bitterest, deepest anguish, leave the homes of our childhood, the scenes of our youth, those grassy mounds—& Oh! Holy Dust, we can not give Thee up, all that is left to some bereaved hearts of what made life precious."[43]

Knowing that others were as panicked as she about the oath, Sally penned another copy of the latter letter with the notation: "If it be not presumtuous

42. *OR*, 33:1148; SMG to Dorothea Dix, [Feb. 1864], GFP, MR-CWM; SMG open letters, Jan. 1864, GFP.

43. SMG to Robert M. West, [Feb. 1864], GFP; SMG to I. J. Wistar, 2 Feb. 1864, GFP.

to say so, perhaps the above may suggest some idea to the ladies, should they send their petition." They must have taken her advice, for several more drafts were made, some signed "The Ladies of Williamsburg." No names were listed, but Lucy Tucker may have been among them. She later wrote Cynthia that rather than submit to the oath she had "packed up everything that could be taken & . . . was looking at one spot, then another, calling up old associations, pleasurable & sad & asking myself, if it could be possible that I was to be *driven* from the dear old home." Like Sally, Lucy "shrank from the idea of being in my old days, a homeless wanderer; but *that* would have been far, *very far* preforable to doing aught to dishonour the name or make me lose my own self respect." But then, "to my amazement, I was called upon, by one high in authority, & *permission granted* to me to remain at my home, & enjoy all the privileges before accorded to me," Lucy declared. "I was so taken by surprise, that I am afraid I did not express my thanks as cordially as I ought to have done."[44]

Because the petitions had taken Wistar by surprise, Sally and the other ladies were spared. On 3 February West commended Sally's petition "to the favorable consideration of the Commanding General" when he sent it to Wistar. "She does not object to taking the oath upon any political ground," West concluded. "Her character is rather that of a religious recluse. Moreover she lives in a part of town which makes it almost impossible for her to hold Communication with the Enemy were she so disposed. I will be surety for her loyal deportment if she is permitted to remain." Wistar had already been so besieged by other petitions from Sally and the ladies that he felt compelled to surrender. He endorsed Sally's letter with "Let Mrs. Galt be undisturbed & all others like her" and sent it back to West. Lucy later revealed that the order requiring the oath "was not carried out in any case." For the time being, at least, Williamsburg ladies were safe.[45]

Despite all of Wistar's precautions, a security breach occurred from a totally unexpected source. Union soldiers around Williamsburg had already guessed the reason for the troop buildup. Excitement over the impending expedition reached Fort Magruder's guardhouse, where Disoway's murderer, Boyle, was still manacled awaiting Lincoln's signature on his execution order. One of his sentinels, Pvt. Thomas Abrahams of the 139th New York, became overly sympathetic and, in the wee hours of the morning of 2 February, filed off his man-

44. SMG to Wistar, 2 Feb. 1864; LAT to CBT, 14 Apr. 1864, TCP.
45. SMG to West, with 3 Feb. 1864 endorsements by West and Wistar, [Feb. 1864], GFP; LAT to CBT, 14 Apr. 1864.

acles and aided his escape. "A general search was instituted to discover the whereabouts of Boyle," wrote Cronin, "and although some trace of him was supposed to have been found in the direction of Norfolk, he was not recaptured." Apparently, Boyle's pursuers never expected him to run in the opposite direction, to Confederate lines, where he "delivered himself up to the enemy's scouts lying in the grass and woods in front of the town." He was immediately whisked off to Richmond, and, after telling the authorities everything he knew, was promptly confined in prison. His information merely confirmed intelligence long since known in Richmond.[46]

Unaware of Boyle's defection, the Federals continued with their preparations. On the evening of 4 February, Butler learned that all Union prisoners in Richmond were about to be moved to Georgia. "Now, or never, is the time to strike," Butler informed the secretary of war the next day. By then, the spies "Howard" and Plunkett in the Confederate capital had noticed that "unusual measures were being taken to increase the defenses of Richmond and that re-inforcements were hourly arriving," narrated Cronin. Not knowing when the expedition was set to depart, they decided to leave the city that night, 5 February. At the same time, Wistar was heading up to Williamsburg from Yorktown, "map in hand," to go "over every detail" of the raid with his subordinates. The troops involved had already assembled in Williamsburg, the largest force the town had seen since McClellan's retreat. The mass comprised about 4,000 infantry, consisting of the 118th and 139th New York and parts of the 11th Connecticut and 25th Massachusetts, under West, and the 4th, 5th, and 6th U.S. Colored Troops. The 2,200 cavalry included the 5th and 11th Pennsylvania, the 1st District of Columbia, the 3d New York, and the 1st New York Mounted Rifles, all to be commanded by the 11th Pennsylvania's Col. Samuel Spear. Two light batteries of about twelve pieces supported them. The plan called for the infantry and artillery to hold the Confederate pickets along the Chickahominy as the cavalry passed into Richmond, not only to rescue Union prisoners but also to destroy public buildings, factories, and storehouses, even to capture Jefferson Davis.[47]

After a "stirring general order by General Wistar was read to the command, hinting at the objects of the expedition and the important results that would follow success," Cronin related, the infantry started with "great enthusiasm" from Williamsburg at nine o'clock the morning of 6 February. Two hours later the cavalry followed, accompanied by Wistar. Throughout the day, they met

46. Cronin, "Vest Mansion," 139–41; Eyland, *Evolution of a Life*, 195.
47. Cronin, "Vest Mansion," 141–2; *OR*, 33:146, 519–22, 51(1):1285–6.

neither unusual opposition nor "Howard" and Plunkett, who were traveling along the south bank of the York River to avoid detection and arrived in Williamsburg at 10:00 P.M., about twelve hours too late to warn of impending danger. At dawn the next morning, while attempting to cross the Chickahominy at Bottom's Bridge, Spear's troopers ran into Confederates waiting for them in such numbers that the Federals could go no farther. Throughout the morning, all attempts to force a crossing for miles up and down the river failed. On the way back to Williamsburg over the next two days, the columns skirmished with Shingler and Hume and found out from "women, children, and negroes" in the vicinity that the Confederates "had received notice some sixteen hours previously" of the raid and had "been vigorously making preparations." Upon his return to Fort Magruder, Wistar heard about Boyle's defection and immediately wired General Butler, who had already read about it in the *Richmond Examiner,* brought by the flag-of-truce boat that evening.[48]

Furious over this betrayal by a soldier who should have been hung long ago, Butler shot off a telegram to Lincoln Monday night, all but accusing the administration's policies of ruining his operation. The *Examiner* stated the Confederates "were prepared for us from information received from a Yankee deserter," Butler wrote, after briefing Lincoln on the aborted raid and enclosing Wistar's telegram. "I send it to you that you may see how your clemency has been misplaced. I desire that you will revoke your order suspending executions in this department." Lincoln suspended the order in time to hang the hapless Abrahams, who "was speedily tried, condemned, and executed," wrote Cronin. "Boyle escaped to unknown parts."[49]

Boyle was not the only escapee. What the raid could not accomplish, the prisoners did for themselves, for on the evening of 9 February, over one hundred Union officers broke out of Libby Prison through a tunnel they had dug. Some were soon recaptured, but many found their way out of Richmond, evaded Confederate pickets, and headed down the Peninsula. As soon as the first two of them showed up at Federal lines outside Williamsburg on the morning of 14 February, battalions of the Mounted Rifles began scouting up the Peninsula. That afternoon they brought in eleven more escapees, and a total of twenty-six arrived in Williamsburg by nightfall. Over the next day or two, another two dozen men came in despite the Peninsula Scouts' best efforts to intercept them.[50]

48. *OR,* 33:143–8; Cronin, "Vest Mansion," 142; Eyland, *Evolution of a Life,* 196.
49. *OR,* 33:144; Cronin, "Vest Mansion," 140.
50. Cronin, "Vest Mansion," 146–51; *OR,* 33:560–6.

As the excitement of the raid and escaped officers died down, life in Williamsburg returned to its wartime version of normal. Dr. Peter Wager had already been reinstated as physician as the U.S. government prepared to take permanent control of the Eastern Lunatic Asylum. On 6 February he penned a gracious note to Sally Galt, offering "his sincere thanks for her kind offer of a book on Surgery from the library of the late Dr. Galt." Having weathered the battle of the oath, Sally admitted "some of the Federal people in power, treated me most kindly, in interceding for me, & would not let me do anything to return their kindness. As an esponent of my grateful feelings, I then said, any Surgeon on the Peninsula might select & take any of the Medical Works,—thus gave away many valuable books which I hope did much good."[51]

The medical books that remained Dorothea Dix saw as a potential therapeutic source for Sally. Upon receiving Sally's plea for help on 6 February, Dix could not believe she would be "required to abandon the old home" but promised to look into the matter during her next trip to Fort Monroe. By the nineteenth, she had learned the crisis was over and sent Sally sewing supplies, a twenty-dollar check, and the suggestion that she "at once set about cleaning & cataloguing, the Books—now is the time—and you owe it to yr Brother's memory, as well as to yr self to do this." Above all, Dorothea insisted "*earnestly* that you would let me know if I can be useful to you at any time in any way." Sally would have several months' reprieve before she would again need to turn to her generous friend.[52]

51. Flournoy, *Virginia State Papers*, 11:495; Peter Wager to SMG, 6 Feb. 1864, GFP; SMG to J. M. Jones, 11 Dec. 1866, GFP.
52. Dorothea Dix to SMG, 6, 19 Feb. 1864, GFP.

CHAPTER 16

A Polite Provost

Throughout the night of 1 March 1864, the tramp of infantry and clatter of cavalry once again disturbed Williamsburg streets. Col. Samuel Spear had formed his brigade, consisting of the 11th Pennsylvania Cavalry and 1st New York Mounted Rifles, about eight hundred effectives, in front of Fort Magruder at eleven o'clock. Finding their place in the column of some two thousand infantry and one battery, all under the command of Col. Robert West, Spear and his men proceeded through Williamsburg and up the Peninsula during a heavy rainstorm. Throughout the next day they entertained themselves by destroying the York River Railroad and a sawmill while they waited to rendezvous with a raiding party then sweeping down from the north upon Richmond. Like Wistar's raid, this expedition, under Brig. Gen. Judson Kilpatrick, intended to liberate Union prisoners and disrupt Confederate communications. And, like Wistar's raid, it was intercepted before Richmond and repulsed with casualties. Instead of bouncing back the way they came, however, Kilpatrick's raiders headed down the Peninsula, where their support met them on the third.[1]

The greeting Kilpatrick received from the Mounted Rifles was "effusively cheerful," according to David Cronin. "Two Companies of the regiment had been raised by him when he was a Captain, early in 1861, and several of our officers, including Col. Onderdonk and Major Wheelan, had then served under him." The riflemen "were much astonished, when they observed the rollicking, devil-may-care appearance of the retiring raiders covered with dust and mud." Though Kilpatrick's troopers had failed to liberate any prisoners, they had obviously liberated a great deal of "civilian apparel" along the way,

1. *OR*, 33:172–4, 186, 193, 198–9.

"spoils taken not for their value, but in the spirit of wanton mischief. One had adorned his horse with net armor made out of a hoop skirt; another wore a lady's 'skoop-bonnet' with a huge bow. A large number wore stove pipe beaver hats of antique model, piling them up one upon another." They continued down to Williamsburg, arriving the evening of 3 March. Cronin thought the town "had never witnessed anything quite so gay and flaunting, or so wholly ignored by the inhabitants, as the long column of Kilpatrick's raiders, riding by fours and retaining their regalia." Kilpatrick stopped at the Vest House for refreshments, then proceeded to Fort Magruder, where at 9:00 P.M. he reported his command "in good order." After covering the rear, Spear also returned to the fort on 4 March.[2]

All this activity made little impression on the people of Williamsburg as they went about their daily business. Gabriella Galt tried "making a support at keeping a school," Sally Galt informed a Norfolk cousin in March. On the fourteenth Sally wrote Dorothea Dix, thanking her for her last letter and the package that never arrived, but her gifts sent in February to the asylum patients had come. "You cannot immagine how grateful they are to you for your (to them) charming present namely tobacco &c," Sally assured her. "I was at the Asylum yesterday & heard preaching in the lady's parlour: they seemed to like it exceedingly & all looked very bright & happy." Sally too sounded brighter and happier in her letter, but she longed for some companionship besides her servants and implored Dorothea to "please come & see me soon, your room is always kept ready for you."[3]

Lucy Tucker had no hope for a visit from loved ones, with all in the Confederacy except Zettie. Since no news had come from her family since October 1863, Lucy decided to write Cynthia on 14 April. "It seems to be thought a 'military necessity' to cut off all communication between the Confederates within the lines, & their friends in Dixie if *possible*," Lucy complained in her opening, "be that as it may, I hope this will reach you, as I am well assured that you often feel anxious about us, & will be glad to know, that we are still in existence." To remain in existence, Lucy had been forced to acquire new skills. She wrote this letter while seated near her chamber fire, "by my side a tin bucket by the stove, containing *rolls* which *I* made up this eve, & will bake in the morning with my skillet on the stove hearth. I am quite proud of my

2. David Edward Cronin, "The Vest Mansion," 1908–10, John D. Rockefeller Jr. Library, CWF, 143–4; *OR*, 33:182, 193.

3. William R. Galt to SMG, 2 Apr. 1864, GFP, MR-CWM; SMG to Dorothea Dix, 14 Mar. 1864, GFP.

achievement, & wish I had begun earlier in life. Your mammys health is deli-
cate, & I do all I can to relieve her."[4]

Besides baking, Lucy occupied her time sewing, gardening, and watching
the movements of the Union army in her neighborhood. Unable to write
plainly in case her letter was intercepted and she be accused of spying, Lucy
attempted to inform Cynthia of recent developments. "I am in an agony now,
lest another army is sent through this place which I suppose will *certainly* be
the case (not by any means, that I am in the confidence of the 'Doodles')," she
cautiously hinted, "& in proportion to my suffering, so will be my joy when I
see them return worn out & troubled." Cynthia could get an idea of the Federal troop numbers by such obscure references as "she has a large family of
chickens & expects many more." But Lucy was confident that "'Marse Bobbie'
is prepared at *all points* to meet our well wishers."[5]

Lucy had obviously noticed the sudden tremendous Union troop buildup
in the area. Their reason for coming to the Peninsula was inspired partly by
Wistar's aborted February raid upon Richmond, after which the old battle of
Williamsburg veteran Maj. Gen. Samuel Heintzelman, now commanding the
Northern Department in Ohio, dropped Benjamin Butler a line. "Having seen
in the newspapers some account of an expedition to Bottom's Bridge for the
purpose of a raid into Richmond to release our prisoners, I have reflected upon
the matter," he wrote. His idea involved organizing a major expedition to ascend the James River and land just below Richmond to destroy the railroads,
using a demonstration up the York River and an advance upon the Chickahominy as diversions. Whether Butler ever acknowledged Heintzelman's sug-
gestions, he too developed a similar plan. Thus, when Lt. Gen. Ulysses S.
Grant succeeded Halleck as general in chief on 12 March 1864 and asked him
for his thoughts on such an operation, Butler was ready. Grant approved his
idea, only requesting that Butler begin his movement the same day Grant
planned a push on Richmond from the Rapidan River.[6]

By the middle of April, when Lucy composed her letter, many of the regiments Butler needed for his new Army of the James had arrived. Lucy was
right—it was "a large family of chickens," finally numbering some 36,000
gathered from Butler's own department and the Department of the South.
And Lucy was not the only one watching them. On 14 April the Confederate

4. LAT to CBT, 14 Apr. 1864, TCP, MR-CWM.
5. Ibid.
6. *OR*, 51(1):1287–8; William Glenn Robertson, *Back Door to Richmond: The Bermuda Hundred Campaign, April–June 1864* (Baton Rouge: Louisiana State University Press, 1987), 13, 21–2.

high command received intelligence that Union deserters coming into southern lines below Richmond "report that the enemy is concentrating at Williamsburg," poised "for an advance up the Peninsula." By 23 April all signs indicated "that a force will be sent up the Peninsula."[7]

Four days later the Mounted Rifles, scouting up the Peninsula, discovered that all fords on the Chickahominy were already heavily guarded and being reinforced to welcome this impending expedition. So as not to disappoint them, a large force of black soldiers landed at Old Point on 30 April and marched up to Yorktown and Williamsburg, where on 1 May Colonel West assumed command of the 1st and 2d U.S. Colored Cavalry Regiments. On the morning of 4 May, West led these eighteen hundred troopers out of Williamsburg for a demonstration to mask the embarkation of Butler's two army corps from Yorktown and Gloucester Point. The fleet of boats, jammed to the gunwales with blue uniforms, steamed down to Fort Monroe, picked up Butler, and headed up the James River. Soldiers watching the bank could occasionally spot West's black horsemen moving along the shore toward the Chickahominy.[8]

On the same day, 4 May, Grant opened his spring campaign, crossing the Rapidan with 122,000 troops to meet Lee's 60,000. As Grant pushed south toward Richmond and Butler bungled his approach from the southeast, Williamsburg enjoyed relative peace. A Quaker schoolteacher visiting the town in mid-May commented that the "streets are wide, the houses old, and picturesque, with sharp roofs & dormer windows. Radiant now with rose-draped porches." Passing Fort Magruder, "a formidable fort, with seven large redoubts, some of which are garrissoned," she noted a "large negro village is near, and many houses have sprung up to meet the various needs of the large force, until recently quartered there." Now, however, the fort was held by little more than a few battalions of the 16th New York Heavy Artillery and the battery of field guns still there over a year after their April 1863 duel with Wise. Williamsburg itself was occupied only by Troops C and K of the Mounted Rifles, for the rest of the regiment, along with Wistar and West and his black cavalry brigade, had joined the Army of the James. Col. William H. P. Steere of the 4th Rhode Island took over West's job as post commander. A participant in the battle of Williamsburg, Steere suffered a serious leg wound at Antietam and was still disabled from active field service. One of the first things he did was appoint Captain Cronin as provost marshal of Wil-

7. Robertson, *Back Door to Richmond*, 23, 28, 59; *OR*, 51(2):861, 873.
8. *OR*, 33:313–4, 36(2):327, 430; Robertson, *Back Door to Richmond*, 57–9.

liamsburg, replacing the 16th New York Heavy Artillery's Lt. James Matthews, who had temporarily relieved Maj. James Wheelan.[9]

Cronin's was a heavy "responsibility not usually placed upon one with the rank of Captain," Steere reminded him during their first interview. The post commander then spelled out what he expected of the young provost. "The whole army has left us, and I am placed here with a handful of men to defend this isolated post, and obtain all the information possible that may be useful to the General Commanders," he began. To that end, Steere instructed Cronin to "give me timely notice of the approach of any large body of the enemy," requiring his "constant energy and vigilance" and frequent mounted and dismounted scouts up the Peninsula. Furthermore, Steere informed Cronin that he was to pursue the Peninsula Scouts "into their retreats and arrest them" without provoking attacks from superior forces. Though he would back Cronin with an infantry battalion if necessary, heavier reinforcements must come from a long distance. "But above everything gather all the information you can of the movements of the enemy above New Kent or about Richmond," Steere concluded. Cronin was to question all contrabands coming from the capital and try to obtain copies of Richmond newspapers, for "these are worth taking almost any risk to secure."[10]

Since Steere's injured leg prevented him "from personally superintending the government of the town," he left all that to his new provost. Cronin recalled the "stern and inflexible administrations of Colonel Campbell and Major Kleinz," contrasted these with the "moderate and tactful course of Major Wheelan," and decided to follow the latter example. His background and easygoing personality facilitated his task. For two years before the war, Cronin had been studying in Europe and missed the vitriolic 1860 presidential campaign. "Perhaps, chiefly for this reason," he surmised, "the new Provost Marshal did not altogether share the intense hatred toward the people of the South, that animated most of his comrades." He did come home in time to vote for Abraham Lincoln, however, and he supported the president's slavery views. Cronin admitted that he was unacquainted with "the peculiar traits of the Southern negro," having known only one family of blacks at his home in upper New York.[11]

Soon after becoming comfortably ensconced in the Vest House, Cronin in-

9. Henry L. Swint, ed., *Dear Ones at Home: Letters from Contraband Camps* (Nashville: Vanderbilt University Press, 1966), 108; Cronin, "Vest Mansion," 155, 160–1.

10. Cronin, "Vest Mansion," 160–1.

11. Ibid., 156–7, 160.

creased his provost guard to twenty-nine selected infantrymen to patrol the streets regularly. Their commander, Sgt. E. Fellows Jenkins of the 16th New York Heavy Artillery, Cronin judged "a most intelligent and trustworthy young soldier." These guards, like their predecessors, were mystified by the "unusual number of curious noises" accompanying nocturnal Federal scouting parties leaving town. "Some times the guards would wonder at the amount of cooking done at night and the carelessness shown by the colored kitchen maids in accidentally dropping so many tin pans, resounding one after the other, like the roll of cracked drums," Cronin noted. Sudden outbreaks of "galloping consumption" among Williamsburg children defied investigation, one particularly sharp-tongued matron blaming it on the "rusty, poisonous government rations" townspeople were forced to eat.[12]

Among the new provost's first acts was placing part of Jenkins's guard around the brick Wythe House on Palace Green next to Bruton Church. This historically important edifice had belonged to George Wythe, a signer of the Declaration of Independence, William and Mary's first law professor, and Thomas Jefferson's mentor, and had served as George Washington's head-quarters before the siege of Yorktown. The occupants renting the house during the first year of the war were at dinner when word came of McClellan's approach in May 1862. "In their haste to get away, they left the house without even a servant to take charge of the premises," Cronin was told, "and a portion of costly dinner-plate remained upon the table."[13]

With nobody left to protect it, the house immediately became a magnet for Union soldiers, who ransacked it "from cellar to roof." Cronin conducted a thorough inspection of it one Sunday morning with Steere's chief of staff, Capt. E. V. Brown. "Through age and neglect the building had become quite dilapidated," and the interior they found "in a state of complete wreck, empty of furniture except in broken pieces: the walls stained by streams of rain falling through leaks in the decayed roof and the floors covered with litter indescrible; the former library in the most deplorable condition of disorder and ravage. In heaps on every side, were spread half destroyed books, vellum-bound volumes, some of them with ornate toolings; letters and documents of all sorts, ragged files of precious colonial newspapers: torn folios of rare old engravings." Cronin and Brown discovered many more "dusty manuscripts, letters and packets of papers" in the garret, some of them written by Thomas Jefferson, George

12. Ibid., 165, 178–80.
13. Eyland, *Evolution of a Life,* 206; Cronin, "Vest Mansion," 219; Olmert, *Official Guide,* 69–70.

Washington, Richard Henry Lee, and other founding fathers. "It was nightfall, before we left the house with our bundles of treasure," Cronin later recalled. "Stopping at my quarters, we sought to make an equitable division of
letters and autographs." The next day Brown sent a wagon and some infantrymen with shovels to the house to bring the library and garret contents, mil-
dewed from rain filtering through the roof, to Fort Magruder. There ladies
in the officers' families sorted through them, finding more treasures. Though
Cronin believed they ended up in the Rhode Island Historical Society, few if
any are known to have survived.[14]

Cronin's duties kept him too busy to take more than a passing interest in
such papers, but he did take time to listen to Williamsburg's living links to
the nation's birth. Dr. Samuel Griffin he considered "one of the most interesting," with his personal knowledge of the Revolutionary War generation. The
old doctor had been suffering with asthma since the previous Christmas but
was able to explain to the young provost the significance of such historical
landmarks as the Powder Horn, Wythe House, Bruton Church, and Old
Courthouse, which Cronin, a trained artist, drew with pen and ink. Cronin
also sketched portraits of a few select locals, particularly those of color, noting
that most northern officers made no distinction between the classes of southern blacks. He, however, observed wide behavior differences between field
hands, generally seeking their freedom, and household domestics, who "preferred the abundant dainties of a Virginia kitchen" to emancipation. At the
time he was unaware that Confederates in his front depended upon this "always well treated and favorite class" to provide "timely information of our
movements or any other intelligence having military significance or value."[15]

One member of this elite class was "a young, active but unobtrusive mu-
latto" named Yellow Jim, owned by a lady living near the Vest House. Cronin
told how he "hung about the headquarters stables, often helping the other
hostlers in a sociable way." Unknown to all the marshals, Yellow Jim "was a
shrewd spy in our very citadel." He was normally shy of encountering officers
but would "pump" the provost's personal servant in the stables when he came
with orders to saddle and prepare rations for an imminent scout. Since Cronin
had a new body servant "too dumb to be pumped," Jim would bring the captain bouquets of garden flowers, with his mistress's compliments, "for purposes of observation." Cronin was only a little suspicious when he detected a

14. Cronin, "Vest Mansion," 219–23; Eyland, *Evolution of a Life*, 206–9.
15. Cronin, "Vest Mansion," 157, 290–2; Eyland, *Evolution of a Life*, 219; JLCG Commonplace Book, 19 Dec. 1866, JLCG F/A, UA-CWM.

common weed or two in the bouquets. Enlightened to these tactics by Jim's former owner after the war, Cronin conjectured he might have been responsible for alerting the Confederates to several Federal scouts, including Major Hamilton's first expedition back in January.[16]

What Yellow Jim may have missed at the Vest House, Til and Jake could pick up at their Frog Pond Tavern. "Her little dining establishment was regarded as a sort of annes to Headquarters," Cronin related. "The horse of the Provost Marshal, hitched to one of the posts in front, was conspicuous at regular or irregular intervals, day and night, according to the nature of his duties." Cronin ate there often, frequently accompanied by Fort Magruder officers, now allowed to come into town since he withdrew the interior pickets between Williamsburg and the fort. While dining, the officers sometimes discussed military matters, unaware their words could be heard all the way to Richmond.[17]

To provide such meals, as well as catered luncheons at the Vest House and basket lunches for the picket reserves, Til was accorded special privileges at the lines on market day, "even allowed by the guards to pass beyond the rusty remnants of telegraph wire stretched breast high in two parallel lines across the Jamestown and Richmond roads, during market hours." Beyond these wires, "Til could select, without competition, the choicest fruits and vegetables or the plumpest live fowls to add to her stock in the coop." Out of earshot of the guards, she could also pass on any information she and Jake had gathered, to be relayed to Richmond. The Federals never discovered her espionage operation, and to enhance the deception, white townspeople pretended envy and disdain, calling her "Yankee trash" to her face. "She was not supposed to have any friends among them," Cronin noted.[18]

Williamsburg residents depended upon Til and Jake for more than gathering and passing information. Fat and seemingly lazy, Jake shuffled about carrying "a large basket filled with specimens of his wife's dainty cooking." Secreted in the bottom of the basket were Confederate mails, usually deposited by Peninsula Scouts in a ravine near Jake's cottage where he could pick them up and drop off outgoing mail in exchange. Provost guards exploring the area discovered several of these mails while Cronin was marshal. Letters were usually concealed in old salt or seed bags enclosed in dingy wrapping paper to camouflage them in the dried grass or among the stones and bushes. One incoming

16. Cronin, "Vest Mansion," 292–5.
17. Ibid., 166, 298.
18. Ibid., 166–7.

mail was found in the college chapel vaults when "an inquisitive Yankee youth" fell through a "thin crust of brick and mortar and landed in the midst of a number of colonial coffins." As his comrades were pulling him out, they noticed a cavity in the wall with a piece of cord dangling out attached to a mailbag. Cronin thought at the time that ladies attending market day collected these mails but later decided Jake, roaming the college grounds at will, was the culprit. "As he often applied for passes to Yorktown to make purchases at the sutler's for Til, probably he mailed letters there," Cronin assumed.[19]

Other ingenious methods of smuggling mail came to the guards' attention over the summer. A town woman and county lady attempted to exchange letters by inconspicuously trading sunbonnets while discussing a bargain on market day. Mail also traveled "in jars of butter and jam and inside dressed poultry, all it is presumed daintily protected." Plugged melons served as containers both for Confederate information coming into town and for Richmond newspapers brought to Cronin by the Union sympathizer "Mrs. Tentrees." Captured outgoing mail was "thrown into the fire place and destroyed," revealed Cronin, but incoming letters "were always minutely examined and in a few instances cipher communications were detected."[20]

About the middle of May, soon after entering his duties as provost, Cronin opened communications with "Mrs. Tentrees" during a scout up the Peninsula. For these forays, he usually selected twelve or fifteen men from his own company of Mounted Rifles, "chosen on account of their physical hardihood more than for other good qualities." They generally left town secretly at night to avoid the "tin pan telegraph" and kept within the woods as much as possible until they arrived at their destination. "With our breech loading Sharp's Rifles and a sprinkling of Colt's revolvers carried by a few," Cronin detailed, "we always felt ourselves a match for double our number of the Confederate scouts whose rifles mostly were ineffective." They were rarely outnumbered, for, with the renewed fighting around Richmond, Hume's force had been reduced to a widely scattered eighteen or twenty men. Furthermore, Cronin decided to conduct his expeditions on foot. One such dismounted scout departed 29 May with the double objective of locating Hume and reconnoitering the left flank of Grant's army, then fighting its way into the Richmond vicinity. Setting a pattern for the rest of the summer, Cronin and his party made no contact with the Peninsula Scouts.[21]

19. Ibid., 167, 212–3, 298–9.
20. Ibid., 187–9, 214–5.
21. Cronin, "Vest Mansion," 169, 180–2; Eyland, *Evolution of a Life*, 215–6.

Shortly after returning to Williamsburg from this mission, Cronin had his first lengthy interview with William Peachy, a "most outspoken and candid" man, who "had been engaged in many legal combats with the redoubtable Henry A. Wise." On 3 June, a "serenely beautiful morning," Cronin later reminisced, "we were seated on camp chairs on the east side of Court House Green, near the tents of Troop C," then encamped "nearly opposite Mr. Peachy's residence and at that time useless law-office." The two were discussing events that led up to the war when, "suddenly from the far Northwest burst an uproar of deep and prolonged cannonading." Although centered nearly forty miles away northeast of Richmond, the battle sounded as near as the York River, for the roar "seemed to float down the surface of its broad and deep waters. At times there would occur incessant peals of artillery, subsiding gradually in a dull muttering, like the retreating roll of thunder, and again booming rapidly into a violent din." The two men listened for several minutes before Peachy launched into a diatribe against Governor Wise and his unwise handling of John Brown's trial, which he believed contributed to the war. "At length Mr. Peachy arose to go," wrote Cronin. "'I cannot stand this any longer,' he said with some appearance of emotion. 'It's murder! I must go home.'"[22]

In this second battle of Cold Harbor, where some seven thousand Union soldiers fell, most within a half hour, Cronin lost more friends and acquaintances than in any other action of the war. The rumbling of cannon could be heard distinctly all the way down to Williamsburg for the next week as the Federals moved by the left flank from Cold Harbor to the James River. Again, Cronin led an expedition to the banks of the Chickahominy, eighteen miles in rear of the Union battle lines, to watch for any stragglers or scouts heading down the Peninsula. After dark on 4 June, he sent twenty picked men in squads out of town while he acted the decoy, riding halfway to Fort Magruder. He left his horse with an orderly, then made his way on foot to rendezvous with his men near a group of tall trees up Richmond Road. Over the next two days they found no stragglers. Nor did they succeed in capturing Hume and his men during a nighttime raid on a plantation dance party. Even a Richmond newspaper given to them by the plantation's mistress turned out to be a disappointing two weeks old, Cronin realized on his return to Williamsburg the morning of 7 June.[23]

The captain's next attempt to capture Hume occurred only one week later.

22. Cronin, "Vest Mansion," 158–9.
23. Ibid., 160, 191, 194–202.

Having received reliable information that the wily lieutenant slept at the Marston plantation near Burnt Ordinary, Cronin departed on the night of 14 June with fifteen dismounted cavalrymen and raided the farm at dawn the next morning. A thorough search of the houses and premises revealed no Confederates. The occupant of one bed in a slave cabin Cronin failed to check when the "aged 'auntie'" seated in the doorway identified him as her "drefful sick" old man. A short time later in Williamsburg, the provost learned his mistake. A lady near headquarters called him over as he rode by and told him "with a polite smile, 'Lieutenant Hume was in town the other evening and passed you on the street. He said he had a good look at you, and told me to tell you he would know you the next time he saw you. When he last saw you he was indisposed and could'nt see well.'" After the war Cronin found out that Hume's gun had been under the bed when he appeared at the cabin door. "It was the first time, he said, that he had slept with his gun out of reach and he resolved it would be the last."[24]

Returning from Marston's on the afternoon of 15 June, Cronin noticed "the peculiar actions of the vedette on the Jamestown road" near the college. He had spotted someone moving in the underbrush and pointed to a brown spot, which he believed was a Confederate uniform. "Shouting at the prowler several times to come in and surrender" brought no response until one of Cronin's men, an expert shot, opened fire with a six-shooter. "At the sixth shot, a fellow in butternut brown, jumped up and yelled with a strong German accent, 'Me surrender! Me surrender!'" The captive, sporting six fresh minor flesh wounds, spoke little English, but Cronin was convinced he was a bounty jumper recently arrived from Germany and run away from Grant's army. Another half dozen stragglers deserted during the heavy fighting around Richmond and managed to make it all the way to Williamsburg. One not so fortunate deserter was captured by a Peninsula Scout near the Bush plantation between Burnt Ordinary and Green Spring and shot. Cronin was assigned the task of learning the name of the homicidal scout.[25]

A clue to his identity soon came from an unexpected source. The turncoat Sergeant Wilson, now a paid "government guide," had reported to the Vest House shortly after Cronin became provost but "was received very formally and told that he would be sent for when his services were in demand." Thereafter, he "invariably attended the markets, meeting the looks of hatred in the faces of the townspeople with cool effrontery," strutting about in "a freakish

24. Ibid., 205–8.
25. Ibid., 223–6, 235–6.

non-descript uniform and posing as one in high authority." He would even go outside the lines to trade with market women, a privilege accorded only to Til. After "Mrs. Tentrees" mentioned that Corporal Tradewell planned to come to the lines disguised as a market woman and knife Wilson, Cronin had all the ladies at the next line day remove their sunbonnets for identification. He then ordered Wilson to report to him and bluntly inquired "if he had no apprehension at the lines, that there might be carried out some plot against his life." Wilson replied that Tradewell had been threatening him for a long time, and to show he was not afraid, he deliberately went outside the lines. He also volunteered his belief that Tradewell was the one who shot the Union straggler.[26]

Before Cronin could get an investigation underway, Williamsburg experienced another change of command. Grant had crossed the James during mid-June and begun a lengthy siege operation around Petersburg south of Richmond, putting him in desperate need of more troops. On the twenty-seventh Butler wired Brig. Gen. Joseph Carr, now commanding Yorktown, to send all Williamsburg troops not required there, including a light battery, to him. Carr was to leave only enough cavalry, not more than one hundred men, "to hold the telegraph line and assist in the defense, of the post station" in Williamsburg. Yorktown's guns were to be brought up to Williamsburg as replacements. Colonel Steere, his wound not yet properly healed, also received orders to rejoin his regiment in front of Petersburg and was replaced as post commander by Col. Joseph J. Morrison of the 16th New York Heavy Artillery on 29 June.[27]

Morrison busied himself confiscating horses from free black farmers in York County and wisely continued his predecessor's policy of giving Cronin free rein in the town. When it came time to go out to the Bush plantation and investigate the straggler's murder, Morrison instructed Cronin to burn the dwelling if he discovered any occupants were involved but left this to his discretion. The provost and his dozen dismounted troopers arrived at the plantation about midnight, impolitely rousted an old man and four or five young ladies out of bed, and held an intimidating but informal inquiry over which Cronin, trained in the law, presided. One of the ladies confirmed that "a tall boy named Tradewell" committed the crime. Before leaving, they also discovered the Bushes were harboring a Lieutenant Ware, possibly Williamsburg native Edward M. Ware of the James City Cavalry, "the most shockingly wounded man I had ever seen up to that time," Cronin admitted. "A bullet

26. Ibid., 162, 227–30.
27. *OR*, 40(2):474–5; Cronin, "Vest Mansion," 226.

had passed through his jaws which had fallen apart and could not be closed on account of the largely swollen and protruding tongue. Another bullet had passed through his shoulders, another had shattered his arm." More than a month earlier, Ware had been brought from the Cold Harbor battlefield "in a rude conveyance the jolts of which would have killed an ordinary man in his condition." Cronin left "an abundance of lint and linen bandages" with the ladies nursing him and returned to Williamsburg.[28]

A few days later, hearing that Ware was still alive, Cronin requested an ambulance and surgeon from Fort Magruder be sent out to fetch him. Some Williamsburg ladies who knew Ware "volunteered to nurse him if he were brought into our lines." Morrison approved, ordering Wilson to go along, and on 21 July Cronin led a three-hundred-man "demonstration in force" up the Peninsula to the Bush plantation. "Lieut. Ware bore the journey bravely" and, arriving safely in Williamsburg, was taken to the home of Virginia Bucktrout Smith, lawyer Sydney Smith's wife, on Palace Green. He eventually healed "under the skillful surgical care of Dr. Garrett assisted by a corps of Nurses from the most irreconcilable Secession families in Williamsburg." Cronin became acquainted with the doctor during his almost daily visits "to inquire after the Lieutenant's state of recovery." Several women would be present, including Mrs. Cornelia Jones, who lived across the Green and made herself obnoxious by insisting "upon discussing the issues of the war under such circumstances." Cronin finally threatened to send Ware to Fort Monroe for exchange, and at this she flew out in a fit of "hysteria" as the captain and doctor exchanged glances of "great satisfaction."[29]

Cornelia was an exception to Cronin's usual good relations with the townspeople, for he explained, "I made it a rule never to visit their dwellings or interfere with them in any way, except in the performance of duty—granting any reasonable favor within my power." His leniency even extended to the asylum. To about twenty patients, deemed harmless by Dr. Wager, he gave "the liberty of the streets," and some called socially at the marshal's quarters for friendly chats. Cronin in turn would visit the asylum. Dr. Wager "had made insanity the subject of long and close study and he imparted to me some of his theories concerning the causes of certain kinds of dementia, and illus-

28. Cases of William Scott and Mary Ashby, 1872, Box 404, Southern Claims Commission Papers, National Archives; Cronin, "Vest Mansion," 226, 235–8; Nanzig, *3rd Virginia Cavalry*, 132.

29. Cronin, "Vest Mansion," 238–9, 243; David E. Cronin to Lottie C. Garrett, 20 Dec. 1910, Garrett Family Papers, MR-CWM.

trated them by pointing out and describing various cases." One patient in particular fascinated the captain, a gentleman who believed himself a Revolutionary War general. Cronin would let him go outside the lines to pick chickapins, like a hazelnut, until one evening he failed to return and a few days later turned up in Richmond giving "a very intelligent account of military affairs in the town and also details of the management of the Lunatic Asylum."[30]

The provost's policies brought a degree of contentment to Williamsburg's relatively sane inhabitants as well, attested by a 15 July letter sent by Elizabeth Southall, still living in the President's House with her family, to her sister, Mary Southall Fisher, in Richmond. The "two companies of Yankees" committed "no depredations," she confirmed, "and do not interfere with the citizens." All were well and actually "getting on very comfortably." Even Julia Thompson "is looking better than for years past" and, "having a fine garden filled with fruit, vegetables &c," was apparently in "no danger of starvation." Indeed, Elizabeth had recently "enjoyed a feast of Raspberries and ice cream" while spending a pleasant evening with Lucy and Zettie Tucker.[31]

Also on July's social calendar was a wedding unique in Williamsburg annals, according to an account in Cronin's chronicles. The ceremony took place one hot, sultry morning, a little beyond the Richmond Road lines, on a grassy slope under the shade of an isolated group of tall trees. This unusual location was chosen because no pastors remained in Williamsburg and Fort Magruder's chaplain did not belong to the couple's denomination. "Therefore, permission was given to a minister of their own sect, who lived somewhere above New Kent, to come to the lines" and unite a "good looking, rosy and plump" bride of about twenty with a tall, thin, stooped widower over fifty. "Neither was identified with the more aristocratic families of the town," Cronin remarked, "yet the wide differences in their ages and the novelty of the circumstances under which the marriage was to be solemnized, aroused the greatest interest and curiosity among all classes of the inhabitants, eighty percent of whom were women and well grown children." When the marshal announced that "all might come to the lines without restriction, the same as on market days, members of the most exclusive families turned out with the rest. Several venerable ladies," attended by devoted servants, "managed to walk so far under a July sun and found seats along the grassy slopes, fanning themselves under the

30. Eyland, *Evolution of a Life,* 218, 222–4.
31. P. M. Thompson to CBT, 26 July 1864, TCP.

trees." Spruced young New York cavalrymen and Fort Magruder officers in full array joined the festivities and "surveyed the ladies on the grassy bank with attentive interest."[32]

The pastor, "a little dignified, rather austere looking man," arrived before the appointed time of eight o'clock, escorted in by Lieutenant Hume and the Peninsula Scouts, who hung around out of sight to witness the nuptials. The groom too showed up early, but when the bride long delayed, the groom "anxiously requested that a messenger might be sent into town" to tell her "'to hurry up, everybody is waiting.' The courier galloped back with this answer, 'Tell the old man if he don't stop hurring me, I won't come at all!'" At that, the groom borrowed a cavalry horse with the stirrups too short for him and rode awkwardly into town with a lieutenant. They soon returned and reported to Cronin that she "positively declined to come to the altar," whereupon the groom "implored me in a whisper, to go to town and 'order' her to come!" This the captain refused to do, "but not wishing to see so select an assemblage disappointed," he rode back with the groom to investigate the problem.[33]

In Williamsburg, Cronin "found the bride fully and tastefully arrayed, sitting on the porch between two bridesmaids, all languidly fanning themselves," he recalled. "She declared that she was not going to make a show of herself: that she had received no intimation that there were to be so many people on hand—all without invitation on her part: and finally she announced that she would never, never walk to the lines: that unless a carriage or some kind of conveyance were provided for her and her maids, she would not budge an inch." The groom knew where to find an old doctor's gig, and Cronin provided a horse, then returned to the lines to wait. "At length the bridal transport, moving slowly, came into view turning the bend of the road near the college grounds," and finally "the couple stood together in the shade before the officiating parson. The seated people rose to their feet, craning necks to obtain a better view." Cronin later heard that "some of the ladies present, praised the conduct of the bride, in being so exacting, declaring she stood upon her rights in demanding the observance of proper formalities, as a sensible woman should. It is said, despite predictions to the contrary, that the couple lived quite as happily together as most married people do, and survived for many years."[34]

No doubt Lucy and Zettie Tucker were among the "venerable ladies" and

32. Cronin, "Vest Mansion," 208–9.
33. Ibid., 209–10.
34. Ibid., 210–2.

"well grown children" present at this wedding, though no mention of it survives in the extant remnant of a letter Lucy addressed to Cynthia on 12 August in reply to one of two letters Cynthia had written her in mid-July. With the hope that at least one would make it through the lines, Cynthia had sent one by flag of truce and the other by the Peninsula Scouts. About a month later one arrived in Williamsburg, the first Lucy had heard from her eldest daughter in ten months. It probably brought news of Lucy's third grandson, born in July to Bland and Maj. Edwin Taliaferro, now commanding the arsenal at Macon, Georgia. Though relatively comfortable, life in Williamsburg remained somewhat precarious. Lucy indicated to Cynthia that the inhabitants were well supplied with what they deemed prudent to keep, not knowing how soon all would be taken from them. Lucy related a recent episode when two provost guards appeared at the Tucker House asking for Zettie. She came to the door and inquired, "'What do you want?'" Lucy told the story: "'I called to see Miss T——' 'Miss T does not receive visits from the enemies of her country' & attempted to shut the door which he prevented by placing his foot in the way, & after a few minutes, made a profound bow, & bade her 'good afternoon.'"[35]

Zettie may not have been impressed by the provost guards, but Lucy was willing to give Captain Cronin a chance. "I understand that the present Provost is very polite to Ladies & I will try to do something for my children," she assured Cynthia; "nothing shall be left untried. I am getting ready to begin the *shirts*," evidently planning to smuggle them out to her sons. After more than two years of fending for herself without Cynthia's help, Lucy insisted that she "never felt so self reliant as I now do." Yet she was unsure how much longer she would be able to stay in her home and asked her daughter "to look *out* for a place for me, some position for which I can earn my board."[36]

On 15 August, three days after Lucy penned this missive, another that Cynthia sent in June found its way to the Tucker House. "Your letter written by Flag of truce was received on yesterday it having taken two months to reach here," Zettie began her reply the next day. "If the authorities will permit me to send this letter across the line I shall do so as I think it will reach you sooner than by Flag of truce." She asked Cynthia to pass along tidings to Lynchburg from one of Dr. Waller's grandsons who had been captured and was languishing in a northern prison, but "he is quite well, and has every thing that is nec-

35. LAT to [CBT, 12 Aug. 1864], TCP; Thompson to CBT, 26 July 1864, TCP: CBT to CWC, 9, 22 Sept. 1864, TCP.

36. LAT to [CBT, 12 Aug. 1864].

essary." No need to worry about family in Williamsburg, for "we are very comfortably fixed at present, and are as cheerful and happy as it is possible for us to be, separated from all nearest and dearest to us."[37]

One who could never be content under this occupying force was Cornelia Jones. Early in August, Cynthia had heard that "Mrs. Corney Jones was ordered to quit Williamsburg after 48 hours notice. I know not for what reason." Cronin provided the details. As "one of the most irreconcilable ladies in the city," she "took especial pains to show her contempt for 'Yankees,' by insultingly taunting our men in the street, and twice she stopped me on the sidewalk and gave me a severe scolding for not permitting supplies to come in from her plantation, several miles beyond our lines, except on 'Line Day,'" he asserted. "Some of the men were so incensed by her stinging remarks that once, during my absence at Fortress Monroe, they attempted to burn her house." At last, "for her own safety as well as an example to others," Cronin determined to send Cornelia outside the lines. He formally notified her of the order and provided her with an escort and wagons "for the removal of her household effects." These were drawn up in front of her residence on the appointed day, along with an assemblage of Williamsburg society. "They gave me disdainful glances as I dismounted and entered the hall, where her trunks were all packed, and many followed and crowded about to watch a display of tyranny," wrote Cronin. "I raised the lid of one of her trunks and inquired if she would give me her word of honor, as a lady, that there was nothing contraband in it. She declared, solemnly, there was not, and I dropped the lid, locked it, and gave her the key. I did the same with the other trunks and boxes and then ordered their removal." The marshal felt he had disappointed many of the onlookers with the "mildness of my behavior," but at last he was rid of a major thorn in his side.[38]

Another continued to elude him, however, as one more attempt to capture Hume and his men in a morning raid on a Chickahominy plantation ended in the usual failure. Strangely enough, during all these forays into Hume's territory throughout the summer, Cronin lost no men; they were not even fired upon. Long after the war, when Cronin revisited Williamsburg, he learned from one of Hume's former scouts that despite all the secrecy of his movements, the scouts could have shot him fifty times. They only restrained themselves from the pleasure because the townspeople "were satisfied with you and claimed that if you were removed they might have a worse Yankee than you

37. Henrietta E. Tucker to CBT, 16 Aug. 1864, TCP.
38. CBT to CWC, 10 Aug. 1864, TCP; Eyland, *Evolution of a Life*, 220–1.

for governor: perhaps like one or two of the earlier ones who terrified them," the ex-scout explained. Several prominent friends Cronin had made in town protected him. Yet Hume's men were often tempted "to draw a bead" on him, and the scout claimed he twice put down Tradewell's gun, leveled at Cronin from short range.[39]

Neither were many attacks made on Cronin's pickets at the lines just outside Williamsburg, though an occasional false alarm kept the guards on their toes. "Late one afternoon, an able bodied contraband, just arrived at the lines, was brought to headquarters without delay because he had a wonderful story to tell," Cronin recounted. The contraband swore he saw at Six Mile Ordinary more than one hundred Richmond cavalry headed toward Williamsburg, but "on cross examination" the provost found "that his story was a pure fabrication." Nevertheless, upon riding up to the college that evening, Cronin found the newly transferred recruits at the lines "considerably excited" and preparing their weapons "in expectation of an attack." The lieutenant in command "asked what I thought of his using some of the rusty old telegraph wire lying around in the grass, to stretch across the Richmond road, to upset and entangle the cavalry if they should come." Cronin approved the plan, thinking it would keep the men occupied for a while. The lieutenant promised to string the wire "so that it would 'just take the Johnnies under the chins and dismount them before they knew what they were about,'" a better strategy, Cronin thought, "than entangling the horses' legs."[40]

All was peaceful until about midnight, when the two vedettes stationed beyond the wires, "mistaking something in the profound darkness for an approaching foe, discharged their carbines." Instantly the alert lieutenant "sprang on his horse and dashed out toward the vedettes, over estimating the distance to the wire which caught him neatly under the chin and dismounted him before he knew what he was about." Shaken but not seriously hurt, the plucky officer managed to remount and confirm the false alarm. "Then wrapping his handkerchief about his neck, he rode to Headquarters" and explained what had happened with some difficulty, as "he could not speak coherently." Cronin could barely contain his laughter, despite the poor lieutenant's nasty "red flowing abrasion." When "he expressed a most fervent desire to lay hands on 'that miserable contraband,' I pointed out the 'medicine case' in the corner, that is—'Magruder's demijohn,' and advised him to bathe his throat internally and externally." Cronin then rode out to order the wire removed.[41]

39. Cronin, "Vest Mansion," 243–4, 274–6.
40. Ibid., 215–7.
41. Ibid., 217–8.

Whether the headquarters liquor supply or Cronin's genial personality attracted more company, he welcomed "several aged citizens who had been ac-
customed all their lives to a morning dram" to Vest House hospitality "in the
shape of 'Commissary.'" Such scholarly old gentlemen as Dr. Griffin, Dr.
Robert Garrett, and Williamsburg sheriff Moses Harrell would gather there
mornings to partake and indulge in "free discussion of national politics,"
which the marshal considered "as good as attending a course of lectures on
the Constitution; though their talk was apt to be strongly tinged with party
prejudice." Cronin was busy in the drawing room and half listening to one
such discourse on an early September morning while a group of men sat at the
other end of the room discussing current events. He suddenly realized that
"one had made a remark indicating knowledge of a political item of recent
date, which I must have overlooked in reading the northern newspapers sent
daily from the Fort, but which were always a few days old." General McClellan had been nominated as the Democratic presidential candidate a short time
before, on 31 August, and Harrell's conversation suggested to Cronin that he
had seen a Richmond newspaper within a day or two.[42]

As the sheriff rose to leave, Cronin "followed him into the hall and when
out of sight of the others I stopped him with a gentle touch and in a confiden-
tial whisper said, 'Let me have that Richmond newspaper in your pocket that
came in last night.'" Harrell was struck dumb. "His jaw fell as he reached in a
breast pocket and drew the paper forth," wrote Cronin, who was just as surprised, having made the request on a mere venture. The paper was dated the
previous day and had been delivered that night by Harrell's son in the James
City Cavalry. "Continuing to whisper and thanking him, I told him I had no
objections to his receiving the Richmond papers provided he would bring
them to me as soon as he had read them. He assured me that there after he
would do so." The marshal regretted that from then on their "cordial greetings
of each other lacked the element of sincerity."[43]

Cronin was not around Williamsburg much longer anyway, for in August
a company of a newly recruited regiment, the 20th New York Cavalry, arrived
to relieve the two companies of the 1st New York Mounted Rifles. "Also came
a full regiment of negro cavalry to be regularly stationed at Fort Magruder as
part of the defensive force." According to Cronin, the presence of the 1st U.S.
Colored Cavalry "created intense excitement among the townspeople and

42. Eyland, *Evolution of a Life*, 219; Cronin, "Vest Mansion," 201–4; Cronin to Garrett, 20
Dec. 1910.
43. Cronin, "Vest Mansion," 204–5.

caused dismal forebodings as to the future outcome of the war." Thus in September, Cronin and his troopers "left the narrow field of partisan warfare without regret and afterward saw war on a grand scale" with the rest of their regiment southeast of Richmond. Once again, Williamsburg faced the uncertainties of a new regime.[44]

44. Ibid., 247; *OR*, 42(2):623.

CHAPTER 17

Swept and Garnered

Perhaps, as Captain Cronin suggested, "the presence of a regiment of colored cavalry" camped on the hallowed grounds of the college during the first days of September 1864 excited the Confederates' ire. Or perhaps the Peninsula Scouts were merely waiting for Cronin's departure so they could resume their favorite sport. In any event, no sooner had the next provost marshal, Capt. A. M. C. Smith of the 16th New York Heavy Artillery, commenced his new duties, than "his lines were attacked by a superior cavalry force which made a brief dash into town after midnight killing two and wounding several pickets near the college." The Confederates then charged across campus from Richmond Road to Jamestown Road to cut off the pickets before they could reach their reserve. The Jamestown Road outpost consisted of only one private, mortally wounded, and a corporal named Lucky, whose horse stumbled when shot, throwing the corporal over its head.[1]

"In falling, I naturally threw out my hands and my forehead struck on the back of my hands," Lucky later informed Cronin. "Something told me: You keep mum: don't breathe heavy. By this time, two dismounted rebs were at me and had unclasped my belt and pulled it from under me expecting, I suppose, to find a pistol which we did not carry as we had carbines." The disappointed raiders began to walk away until one realized Lucky was still alive and turned back. "He came close up, put his revolver against my side and fired at a slant, for I heard or felt the ball strike the ground under me," the fortunate corporal continued. "Though I was sure that I had not been seriously hurt, I thought it worth while to remain in the same position, playing possum, until

1. David Edward Cronin, "The Vest Mansion," 1908–10, John D. Rockefeller Jr. Library, CWF, 248, 250.

sunlight showed that all the rebs were gone." Lucky found that the "ball had gone through my overcoat, blouse, pants and outside shirt: my undershirt too was torn but not shot through, merely nicked." Luckily, his body was untouched.[2]

Another attack occurred on 3 September, when three troopers of the 20th New York Cavalry, escorting an ambulance to Jamestown Island, were ambushed en route. Col. Joseph Morrison at Fort Magruder ordered Lt. John D. Lee of Company H to search for the attackers. Lee could scrape up only twenty-one men for this detail, and these were either sick or just off twenty-four-hour picket duty. Nevertheless, they searched all night, scouring "the country within ten miles of the place of attack, but could discover none of the enemy," Lee reported. He was convinced the ambushers were neighborhood civilians, for during his search he found many away from home, "and in some cases their families were unable to tell where they were."[3]

Equally deplorable, in Lee's opinion, not enough men were "left in camp to relieve the picket guard, and they have been forced to remain on duty forty-eight hours." He therefore requested "more cavalry be furnished this post, that in case of another attack of this kind sufficient men may be on hand to send a force out, and leave enough in camp to do the regular picket duty required." Morrison passed this request on to Brig. Gen. George F. Shepley, now commanding the District of Eastern Virginia. "The two companies I have lost were invaluable," Morrison asserted, sorely missing Cronin and his Mounted Rifles, since they were "intimately acquainted with the country, having been here for more than a year." Many blue cavalrymen were sick, and Morrison lacked "half the command to perform the guard duty required," forcing his men to stand picket duty every other day. To the beleaguered colonel's urgent plea for just one more cavalry company, Shepley flatly replied, "I have none to send."[4]

Williamsburg citizens soon found that even this small occupying force could inflict major damage. On 20 September a circular emanated from Gen. Benjamin Butler's headquarters of the Department of Virginia and North Carolina addressed to all provost marshals administering the oath of allegiance in accordance with Lincoln's amnesty proclamation. It directed marshals to determine the sincerity of people taking the oath, "to ascertain for yourselves, with reasonable certainty that each party who takes the Oath of Allegiance

2. Ibid., 248–9.
3. *OR,* 42(2):696–7.
4. Ibid.

does it from a conscientious desire that peace shall be restored and the national authority established over all, and for no other reason." All others were to be sent across the lines. As before, at the first threat to her home, Sally Galt unsheathed her pen, requesting the provost on 30 September to send her an official copy of General Wistar's February order allowing her to remain in Williamsburg. She also sent another distress call to Dorothea Dix, who received it in Washington on 11 October and "immediately addressed Genl. Butler in the Field," Dorothea informed Sally on the fourteenth, "and if he gets the letter in time I have no reason to doubt the result in yr favor."[5]

On 15 October Sally sent her own plea to Butler, while Dorothea, finally realizing the gravity of the situation, personally accosted Butler near "Petersburg when the battle raged the fiercest, to ask him to stay proceedings as regards confiscating my goods & chattles," Sally later revealed. Dorothea had also sent "numerous letters & telegraphic dispatches on the same subject to the same person." An agonizing week went by with no reply, but on 23 October the acting provost of Williamsburg, Capt. Horace W. Fowler, took pity on Sally and granted her permission "to remain within these lines until action can be taken on her case by proper authority." The next day a dispatch from Butler's headquarters, "In the field," dated 22 October arrived, tersely informing Sally that the commanding general "can see no reason why you should be made an exception of the general order issued. Therefore you will have to take the oath as prescribed for general order or be sent across the lines." He advised her, however, that she was "at full liberty to donate your property to the Lunatic Asylum." Sally took the blow with characteristic grace and dignity. "Now is it not kind in General Butler, (letter rec yesterday), to allow me to give all my property here, to the Lunatic Asylum," she wrote Dorothea on 25 October. "I am so grateful to him. The thought will be comforting to me, that the flowers will bloom, & the fruit will ripen in the dear 'Old Garden' for the Patients."[6]

Expecting banishment any day, Sally's main concern now was for her family home, and for that she also solicited Dorothea's assistance. "I am anxious for my dear old Servant Arena to continue to occupy the room in the house which has been hers ever since I have been left alone, as she is thoroughly to be trusted & will take the best care of the place for the Asylum, it is desirable

5. "Department of Virginia and North Carolina Circular," 20 Sept. 1864, GFP, MR-CWM; SMG to Provost, 30 Sept. 1864, GFP; Dorothea Dix to SMG, 14 Oct. 1864, GFP.

6. A. P. Puffer to SMG, 22 Oct. 1864, GFP; Horace W. Fowler to SMG, 23 Oct. 1864, GFP; SMG to ?, undated fragment, GFP; SMG to Dorothea Dix, 25 Oct. 1864, GFP.

that some one should live here as a protection," she wrote in her 25 October letter. "She loves the old Homestead as much as I do from all the hallowed associations connected with it." Furthermore, Sally pointed out, "The Patients know her well, she having nursed the sick at the Asylum, & it will be pleasant for them to see her when they come down." Sally also addressed Morrison about the same time, requesting his permission for Arena to live in the house. "In these agitated times, it is almost impossible to get a good or permanent servant for a house," she insisted, "& I know of no one in the world who would take such good care of the place as Arena, for it is endeared to her, as it is to myself." Even worse than separation from her home, Sally assured the colonel, was separation from her people. "The severing of no tie, fills my heart with such bitter anguish, as leaving the dear & faithful old servants, who in these trying times have been to me the most generous & kindest of friends."[7]

Unfortunately, Lucy Tucker could no longer say the same for her Patty. "Mamy has deserted Mother," Cynthia Coleman wrote on 3 November to her husband, Charles, who had been serving as president of the South Carolina conscript board for the past year. "She made a visit to Norfolk which caused Mother to tremble, she afterwards directed her things should be sent her to Hampton." By that time, all of Patty's children had deserted her, even her eight-year-old son, and though Lucy promised her freedom if she would stay until the war was over, Patty and her husband, Jim, could not wait. "I cannot blame her, tho' I grieve she was not true to the last," Cynthia lamented. "Could she have known how short the time was, she might have remained faithful to the end. With her past services & duty in view it's impossible to regard her with any feelings akin to harshness. God bless and shield her from suffering."[8]

This news came to Cynthia in a letter she had received on 2 November from Isabella Sully in Richmond "stating that the night before, Mrs Maupin, Mrs Sweeney, Mrs Peyton had reached Richmond, driven from their homes because they would not take the Oath of allegiance to the Yankee Government. Nor was this all, Mrs Sully was hourly expecting my poor Mother & Sister, Julia, William Peachy, and the Garretts by 'Flag of Truce.'" Cynthia added she was glad to hear William Peachy was coming out, for "Mother wrote me sometime since that he said his troubles had brought him to Jesus and had been the means of his salvation." Virginia Southall and her family had already left Williamsburg before the trouble started, bringing out "a handsome

---

7. SMG to Dorothea Dix, 25 Oct. 1864; SMG to J. J. Morrison, [Oct. 1864], GFP.
8. CBT to CWC, 3 Nov. 1864, TCP, MR-CWM; CBT, "Peninsula Campaign," TCP.

bombazine dress and trimmings and many other things" that Lucy Tucker had been able to procure for Cynthia. "I see in the paper of this morning that a 'Flag of Truce boat' had arrived on the 1st," she informed Charles. "I presume, to-morrow or next day will bring me a letter from my Mother."[9]

Cynthia had already taken the initiative and composed one herself to her mother and another to Julia Thompson the day she received Isabella's letter, inviting them both to stay with her in Clarksville. She sent the letters to Richmond, where she expected Lucy and Julia to be by that time, but they had not arrived. In Williamsburg they joined a band of about sixteen who, upon the issuance of Butler's order, "decided promptly to give up all the sacred associations of home and to go forth stripped of the accumulation of years into the barren Confederacy." Not all were able to go, as Cynthia later learned, "and when the hated option was offered them with reluctance and protest took the fatal oath. Among those whose narrow means bound them to the spot was Miss Emily Morrison." Because of her "aged and ill mother there was no alternative, stay she must. When the Officer arrived to put the test she was in an agony of distress. In vain was the pen placed in her trembling fingers, they had no power to hold it." Her mother "exhorted her not to perjure herself" by signing an oath against her conscience. "The Officer was melted by this scene and left these two noble women in peace."[10]

While the officer administered the oath from door to door, "the Yankees placed a guard at each house to prevent persons from removing their property to any place of safety," according to Isabella's letter to Cynthia. This guard effectually preserved the property for looters, who started work even before the owners left town. "They moved off Julia's piano before Mrs Maupin left," Cynthia relayed to Charles on 3 November, "and, I presume, before Julia's face." Cynthia later learned that Julia made the mistake of leaving her house for a short time. "Walking along the street she saw a piano borne by soldiers, that she thought very like her own, she soon found this to be the case, and rushing after the robbers, for they were nothing else, implored them to restore her piano which was an unusually fine instrument. She never saw it again."[11]

Talbot Sweeney arrived in Richmond shortly after the first contingent of Williamsburg exiles, bearing the next installment of their saga. The Tuckers and others were taken to Norfolk, "detained several days, saw many friends,

9. CBT to CWC, 3 Nov. 1864.

10. CBT to LAT, 2 Nov. 1864, TCP; CBT to CWC, 3 Nov. 1864; CBT, "Occupancy," TCP.

11. CBT to CWC, 3 Nov. 1864; CBT, "Peninsula Campaign.".

had a pleasant little trip at the expense of the United States government," and were left to make their own way to Richmond. "Against this they protested and the Yankees then brought them back to Williamsburg, where Mother found her house 'swept and garnered,'" Cynthia quoted Sweeney in a 10 November letter to Charles, "and I presume the others shared the same fate." Sally Galt confirmed Cynthia's presumption, preferring "the confiscation of all possessions, to taking the oath of allegiance." She was allowed to keep only some manuscripts and family pictures. According to Eliza Baker, now working as an asylum attendant, "the Yankees came and carried out all the furniture and things they wanted. Then the plain people helped themselves to what was left. The plain people took the carpets off the floors, and they took the bureaus and everything else they wanted that was left behind."[12]

Zettie Tucker offered her version to Talbot Sweeney when she saw him at the lines and "told him everything both great and small had been taken from the house," Cynthia continued her 10 November letter. "She was at the lines trying to find some means of reaching Richmond." Cynthia instructed her brother, Tom, still an invalid unfit for duty and staying with friends and relatives around Richmond, to procure a flag of truce to go down and bring the family out. On the morning of the tenth, she received a letter from Tom, dated the seventh, saying the Tuckers were still in Williamsburg and he expected to go down in a day or two if he could get a flag of truce. "He is too uncertain to be depended on for anything," Cynthia concluded, but the "continued stay of our friends in W—— makes me hope that Talbot Sweeney's story about the house being 'swept and garnered' is an exaggeration, and things tho' doubtless bad enough, are not so desperate as he represented them to be."[13]

A letter Lucy wrote the next day, 11 November, gave a more accurate picture of Williamsburg at that time. She told Cynthia that "when she got home, she found much of the furniture had been taken, some of it was returned, dining tables, dicanters & some chairs. She was so delighted to get back home that she hardly minded the loss of the furniture, as she had enough left to be very comfortable." Lucy further assured Cynthia that the "Yankee Provost was very kind and considerate of them at the time of their banishment," allowing her "when she was sure of coming to Dixie to send out by Mr Sweeney a number of valuable articles, blankets, carpets some supplies &c." These arti-

12. CBT to CWC, 10 Nov. 1864, TCP; CBT, "Occupancy"; SMG to Dr. Thurman, n.d., GFP; SMG to Dr. Jones, 29 July 1867, GFP; Eliza Baker, "Memoirs of Williamsburg," 1933, John D. Rockefeller Jr. Library, CWF, 13; "Muster and Payroll of E. S. H.," 30 Nov. 1864, Eastern State Hospital Papers, MR-CWM.

13. CBT to CWC, 10 Nov. 1864.

cles, intended for Lucy's children, Sweeney had not yet transported to Richmond.[14]

Undertaker Richard Bucktrout was also trying to ship much-needed items to his destitute "Dear Daughter Delia," eking out a living as a seamstress in Richmond. On 23 November he wrote her a letter, as well as two more to Talbot Sweeney and Sydney Smith, telling Delia that he had sent her various things "at different times by ladies going up." Apparently, Harriette Cary had returned to Williamsburg, for when she left again, she took with her a pair of shoes and twenty dollars for Delia. Another lady carried out more shoes and a hoop skirt. Virginia Southall brought her one more pair of shoes along with another hoop skirt, a dress, and calico to make a sunbonnet. When Cornelia Jones departed in the summer, she smuggled out nothing for Delia but transported fifteen hundred Confederate dollars belonging to Bucktrout, intended to pay board for his young slave boy in Richmond and buy bonds with the balance.[15]

Nevertheless, at the moment money "is very scarce with me," Bucktrout confessed to Delia after scraping up as much as he could to send her yet another dress and pair of shoes. To his nephew and lawyer Sydney Smith, he confided, "every thing is very high keep and it is as mutch as i can doe to live as i am a doeing nothing for the Federal Army as they doe all their burying them selves, and what little i doe for the Citizens i get nothing for it as they have no money, or pay me any at any rates." His ledger confirms this paucity of business, with not a single entry dated 1864. The situation was worsening, for "i have not drawn any provisions as yet, but i am afraid i cat hold out mutch longer as we have had no meat for a week at a time and no coffee nor tea." Bucktrout now owed more board for his slave in Richmond, and Cornelia had written that she received only twenty dollars for each hundred-dollar note he had entrusted to her. Though he had appointed Smith in July to tend to his business matters in Richmond, he requested Sweeney to "let me know what you think about my account against the Confederate States for coffins."[16]

Cynthia Coleman also consulted Sweeney during a mid-December trip to Richmond. He assured her that her mother was "getting on well so far."

14. CBT to CWC, 8 Dec. 1864, TCP.

15. R. M. Bucktrout to Delia Bucktrout, 23 Nov. 1864, Bucktrout-Braithwaite Foundation Papers, MR-CWM.

16. R. M. Bucktrout to Delia Bucktrout, 23 Nov. 1864; R. M. Bucktrout to Sydney Smith, 23 Nov. 1864; and R. M. Bucktrout to Talbot Sweeney, 23 Nov. 1864, Bucktrout-Braithwaite Foundation, MR-CWM; Richard M. Bucktrout Day Book, 1863–65, MR-CWM; R. M. Bucktrout Power of Attorney, 26 July 1864, Bucktrout-Smith Papers, MR-CWM.

Rather than take his word for it, Cynthia decided to go down to Williamsburg to see for herself. She found a covered freight wagon heading down the Peninsula, due to depart the next night. Within a few days she arrived at a friend's home on Mill Hill above the college about a mile out of town on Jamestown Road. "Once there I sent in to acquaint the Provost-Marshal with my vicinity and requested permission to visit my Mother," Cynthia later related in a narrative about her adventures. The present provost, identified by Cronin as Capt. Henry A. Vezin, detached from the 5th Pennsylvania Cavalry, refused her request. "I was denied the privilege of entering my own Town, but I was told my Mother and my friends might meet me at 'The Lines.'"[17]

On the next market day, Cynthia went to the lines, where across the roads "just above the College a thick wire was thrown and a Sentinel posted to prevent passage to and fro." Before long she "saw my Mother, lovely young Sister and a host of friends approaching from the old City. Imagine their sensations in hearing once more news direct from the Confederacy, in feeling even for a few moments the uplifting of the heavy chains that galled them," she continued. "We really felt the Yankees to be very kind in giving us this much pleasure, not at the time considering that they were usurpers and assumed an authority which might alone had given them."[18]

While exchanging news, Cynthia learned about the recent death of Dr. Samuel Griffin on 19 December after a year of grappling with asthma. Toward the last he was confined to his room and forced to sit up because the "recumbent position aggravated the distressing symptoms from which he suffered," James Griffin later detailed. "He was a great sufferer but patient in an exemplary degree. He died sitting in his chair." Dr. Griffin, just weeks short of his eighty-third birthday, was buried in Bruton Churchyard beside his mother and his wife. "There is as yet no monumental inscription but, 'His memory will ever be embalmed in the *hearts* of his relatives & friends'!" James eulogized. Obviously not one of his admirers, Cynthia commented, "Old Dr. G—— has at last ended a life of sin and was true to himself up to the time of his illness."[19]

Cynthia also first heard about "the burning and pulling down of houses" that occurred soon after her mother and other exiles returned from Norfolk. "The last remnant of the circumstance and pomp of Colonial days passed

17. CBT to CWC, 8, 15 Dec. 1864, TCP; CBT, "Peninsula Campaign"; Cronin, "Vest Mansion," 250, CWF.

18. CBT, "Peninsula Campaign."

19. CBT to CWC, 11 Jan. 1865, TCP; JLCG Commonplace Book, 19 Dec. 1866, JLCG F/A, UA-CWM.

away with the total destruction of the Palace buildings," despite Dr. Wager's best efforts to save them. Colonel Morrison even promised "to let them stand, but in less than two hours his emissaries were at work and soon there was 'not one stone left upon another.' The houses were torn to pieces and the bricks carried away," probably to build structures at Fort Magruder. As Cynthia reported to Charles, "Not a vestige of your Mother's old house was left save a heap of rubbish." Only a "large stone ball that surmounted one of the pillars of the Palace gate, was saved through the instrumentality of a faithful negro."[20]

More than news passed between the Tuckers, for Zettie, "with a dexterity truly marvelous transferred to my keeping silver forks &c. that I had left behind me," Cynthia disclosed. "We met repeatedly at these Lines and each time some valuable article found its way to me." She was especially ecstatic when her mother smuggled into her hands a whole box of ninety candles, an item particularly scarce in the Confederacy. "I nearly betrayed it in my delight," Cynthia admitted. For some reason the Tucker ladies were never caught. "We could not help thinking the solitary sentinel did not watch us very closely, having some spark of human feeling lingering in his breast."[21]

One Federal picket's kindness allowed Cynthia to celebrate a memorable Christmas with her mother and sister, their first together in at least four years. "At these Lines there was a long row of roofless houses, the clouds of Heaven flitting over looked in, and dreary desolation sat at the vacant windows," she vividly described the scene. "In one of these cheerless places we determined to keep our Christmas in the year 1864. The snow was falling fast, but we put up our umbrellas, kindled a fire," and made themselves as comfortable as possible "on such logs as we could find." There the three ladies ate "our cake and drank toasts to our Confederate heroes in the hearing of the Sentinel whose forbearance we rewarded by giving him a glass of our wine, and then it was that he expressed his sympathy for us in a manly frank manner that touched us. Prisoners and Lunatics are grateful for very small favors."[22]

Cynthia remained on Mill Hill another week. One evening, as the family she was staying with prepared to sit down to dinner, three or four "Yankees appeared at the door. The supper table was spread, one of the girls quickly secured the spoons while the mistress of the house slipped out to put on a bustle made of letters confided to her to be sent into the Confederacy," Cyn-

20. CBT to CWC, 20–22 Jan. 1865, TCP; CBT, "Peninsula Campaign"; CBT, "Occupancy."
21. CBT, "Peninsula Campaign"; CBT to CWC, 11 Jan. 1865.
22. CBT, "Peninsula Campaign."

thia wrote. "She acted as a sort of secret post-mistress and our Scouts were her carriers. She was a very clever, bright, little woman and did many a good turn to the Confederates. The Yankees only stayed a short time, but before leaving they requested the loan of an overcoat, which was, of course, refused. I wonder they did not take it."[23]

Throughout the last week of December, Cynthia met her mother and sister at the lines as frequently as possible and collected, among other things, a dozen gold pieces, a pound of tea, soup plates, and a home-cooked ham for a feast for her January 1865 birthday. "I would have gotten more but that on the last two days we were too closely watched, & my return was hastened by a message from a friendly foe of warning," she explained in a letter to Charles. "I made a bold strike for your books and Mama's carpet, but without success, they would have given 'aid and comfort to the enemy.'" Besides her mother-in-law's carpet, only three Coleman slaves, two women and a child, remained in Williamsburg, and one man was at Fort Magruder, probably serving the officers. Market day fell on New Years Eve "and proved to be my last interview with my Mother. A great many Soldiers came to the Lines that day," she re-called in her narrative, and it "was agreed that I should retreat at once while I could do so in good order." On the final day of 1864, Cynthia sadly bid her family adieu and once again departed from her beloved Williamsburg.[24]

The next day, 1 January 1865, Cynthia started back to Richmond. She called on some friends that day while working her way from house to house until she found the carpet her mother had sent out with Susan Coupland. "I did my Country and her cause one piece of service on this trip," Cynthia later reminisced, by warning Confederate scouts that a plan they had laid "to drive in or capture the Yankee Pickets on the different points above Williamsburg on a certain night" had been betrayed by some woman. The Williamsburg "guard was at once doubled and every arrangement made to repel or capture the Scouts," she had learned at the lines. "Before the appointed time I was able to convey to them a warning of danger, and their proposed attack was not made." Perhaps realizing that Cynthia had carried this warning to the scouts, the Federals sent a body of cavalry up the county a few days after her departure "to 'overhaul' me, doubtless I should have been arrested and carried back." She escaped, however, and by 7 January was safely back in the Confederate capital.[25]

23. Ibid.
24. Ibid., CBT to CWC, 11, 17 Jan. 1865, TCP.
25. CBT to CWC, 11 Jan. 1865; CBT, "Peninsula Campaign."

As 1865 commenced, General Grant removed the bumbling Butler from the Army of the James and the Department of Virginia and North Carolina on 8 January. Soon after assuming command of the department, Maj. Gen. E. O. C. Ord ordered a survey and inventory of all fortifications under his jurisdiction, and on 21 January Colonel Morrison, still post commander at Williamsburg, submitted his report. He described Fort Magruder as "oblong in shape, with bastions on the west, south, and east sides, inclosed on the north, west, south, and part of east side, with abatis, ditch about fifteen feet wide and twelve feet deep, sally-port on the north side, with draw-bridge." Now containing seven magazines, "one of them lately built," Fort Magruder boasted a garrison of four hundred men composing four companies of Morrison's own 16th New York Heavy Artillery under Maj. Julius C. Hicks; five detached cavalry companies from the 20th New York, 1st New York Mounted Rifles, 4th Massachusetts, and 1st U.S. Colored; and a detachment of the 100th New York Infantry. Though the fort mounted nineteen guns of various models, only seven were considered in good order, eight were in "poor order," one had no ammunition, and three were listed as "useless" despite having over two thousand rounds of ammunition.[26]

The other thirteen earthworks in Williamsburg's line lay abandoned, containing neither garrison nor guns, but the Federals had completed two fortifications of their own, begun the previous spring before Wise's raid. About a quarter mile down the country road northwest of Fort Magruder sat a new Redoubt Five. "This redoubt is square, containing about 22,500 square feet, and occupied by 200 men, and surrounded on all sides by a wide ditch and abatis; sally-port on east side, with gates," Morrison stated. It mounted two iron guns, both of the old pattern and in poor condition. Federal Redoubt Six stood another quarter mile down the same road and a half mile from Fort Magruder, according to Morrison, about the same size and manned by the same number of troops as its companion, but mounting three more guns of the old pattern.[27]

Ord reviewed not only the military but also the civilian situation in his department and noticed a small problem in Williamsburg. Under Butler's administration, a fund accrued from fines, penalties, and taxes supported the Eastern Lunatic Asylum, but Ord found no appropriation "for such places" in the department budget. "As I presume I shall have no authority to collect such fund some other mode must be taken to meet the bills or the insane people

26. *OR*, 46(2):70–1, 195–6, 42(3):1129.
27. Ibid., 46(2):195–6.

should be sent somewhere else," he pointed out to Secretary of War Edwin Stanton on 9 February. Ord recommended that the inmates be transferred to a northern institution, "for it will not do to let them starve, and they can be supported much easier at the North than where they are now." Stanton disagreed, referring Ord's problem to Grant "to cause the rebel authorities to be informed that these insane people will not be supported by the United States, but must be provided for by them; and to propose that a part of the fund lately raised for the relief of rebel prisoners by the sale of cotton in New York be appropriated to this purpose."[28]

Before Stanton could send this reply to Ord, a brief clash once again enlivened Williamsburg's picket lines. About three o'clock on the morning of 11 February, "a party of rebel cavalry, numbering from twenty to twenty-five men," allegedly wearing Union uniforms, surprised the picket on Richmond Road and deceived them at first. "The vedette on the Richmond road challenged them, and, receiving no reply, attempted to discharge his carbine, but the cap snapped," reported Officer of the Day Lt. Ira L. Dudley. "He then retreated on the reserve, but was wounded in two places." The Confederates "advanced as far as the reserve, evidently with the design of capturing the horses there stationed." An exchange of shots resulted in one Union private killed, four wounded, and one missing. As soon as the alarm sounded in the garrison camp, two companies "lost not a moment in turning out," Dudley insisted, but by the time they reached the reserve, firing had ceased and the Confederate scouts had retreated, carrying off their wounded and four Federal horses.[29]

When the dust cleared, Major Hicks, now bearing the title of post commander, wired the news to district headquarters but characterized the assault as "only a dash." Nevertheless, he immediately reinforced his picket lines and strengthened his reserves. Later that day, after Dudley prepared his official report, Hicks mailed it to headquarters with the promise to give the attackers "a warm reception if they call again." They may have been the "detachment of Mosby's command" that Benjamin Ewell was told raided Williamsburg in the spring of 1865. Though Col. John S. Mosby operated primarily in northern Virginia, Monty Tucker had recently joined his battalion and may have assisted this effort. Either Mosby's crew or the Peninsula Scouts, possibly a combination of both, avoided Hicks's "warm reception" at the lines by continuing their horse-stealing raids on small bodies of troopers, from Burnt Ordinary to

28. Ibid., 503.
29. Ibid., 46(1):458–9.

Jamestown Island. On 18 February Hicks informed department headquarters that he would send scouting parties to chase these Confederates if he had any troopers to spare. Out of his 115 cavalrymen, however, 33 were daily detailed for guard duty. More worrisome than the loss of horses was the possibility that the gray scouts "may destroy or injure the telegraph wire between Fort Monroe and the front." He was no doubt elated to receive a telegram later that day from headquarters saying, "One company colored cavalry mounted and a detachment dismounted have been ordered to report to you at once." They were all Ord could spare.[30]

As Hicks anticipated, three days later on 21 February, "bushwhackers" cut the telegraph line between Fort Magruder and Jamestown Island. He reported the depredation that evening and asked if he had authority "to burn all the houses in the vicinity, say within one mile?" Instead of permission to burn Jamestown Island homes, which supposedly served "as shelter for rebel scouts," Hicks received orders relieving him of his duties as Fort Magruder post commander. On the twenty-fourth, Bvt. Brig. Gen. Benjamin C. Ludlow, formerly a major on Butler's staff, replaced him. Ludlow was to "take command of the line of posts between the James and York Rivers, including Jamestown Island and Yorktown, and the troops on that line." The monthly return dated 28 February named him as the commander of the ten companies stationed at Fort Magruder, and his jurisdiction embraced the entire line of Williamsburg defenses, "of which Fort Magruder is a post, and of which Colonel Morrison will retain command under you." Ord further instructed Ludlow to mount as many of the dismounted cavalry at Fort Magruder as possible and "endeavor to keep the country between the Chickahominy and York Rivers free from guerrillas and the inhabitants in his rear covered from attack and protected from interference."[31]

To implement the latter part of these orders, Ludlow instituted a new defensive system for Williamsburg. A 6 March letter by Lucy Tucker mentioned that "gentlemen are now made to work on fortifications," probably the line of works described by Ewell a few months later. These works, "thrown across the College yard," utilized the remaining walls of the main building, the nearby brick kitchens, the Brafferton, and the President's House, bricking up the doors and windows and drilling loopholes in them to accommodate small arms. "Deep ditches were dug from North, East, and the South East corners

30. Ibid., 46(2):538, 582–3, 589–90; BSE, "The College in the Years 1861–1865," 292; Hewett, ed., *Roster*, 15:342.

31. *OR*, 46(2):583, 618–9, 682–3, 792.

of the College, extending some distance beyond" Richmond and Jamestown Roads, John Charles later imparted. "In these ditches were placed vertically big logs ten feet long, and three feet in the ground. These logs were fitted with port holes so as to guard against Cavalry raids down the two roads." Farther out these roads, and forming in a curved line far beyond them, "was constructed an abatis consisting of tops of big oak and beech trees with sharpened limbs set in the ground, standing westward and all entangled with wire." If the gray raiders managed to penetrate these lines, they would be greeted by a big black cannon planted in the middle of Main Street, "ostensibly to sweep the street with 'grape and canister.'" This piece sat in front of the City Hotel Coach House, serving as barracks for the gun's squad of artillerymen. It provided more entertainment for Williamsburg boys than protection, however, for as far a Charles knew, "this old gun was never fired."[32]

The campus gained new fortifications and lost its lone figure, which had witnessed the Confederate banner rise nearly four years earlier; had stood watch over the first southern units to camp on campus and perish from disease; had on 5 May 1862 beheld the retreating gray tide and advancing blue as blood mingled with rain at its feet; had seen the main building again in flames; and for two and a half years had been caught in the crossfire of numerous raids and skirmishes. "Lord Bottetourt was carried to the Asylum yesterday, though not indicted for lunacy," jested Gabriella Galt in a 25 March letter to her cousin. Along with many of the college's books and its "Philosophical Apparatus," the old marble statue of Lord Botetourt went into storage at the asylum under the care of Dr. Wager. "Bottetourt is *the* topic of conversation at this time," wrote Miss Gibbie, and provided Williamsburg a welcome diversion to its unsurpassed dullness.[33]

That too was about to change. While Williamsburg was "adorned with the bright garments of spring, & carpeted with wild violets & blue periwinkles" as well as "charming hyacinths of every hue," the Confederacy commenced its death throes. On 1 April, the 32d Virginia Infantry, as part of Pickett's Division, participated in a battle at Five Forks west of Petersburg. Pickett's defeat broke the Confederate line, and the following night Richmond was evacuated. On 4 April Ludlow received orders to report to Richmond for duty with his Williamsburg garrison as General Lee led his dwindling army west toward

32. BSE, "The College in the Years 1861–1865," 292; CBT to CWC, 5 Apr. 1865, TCP; John S. Charles, "Recollections of Williamsburg, Virginia, as It Was at the Beginning of the Civil War," 1928, John D. Rockefeller Jr. Library, CWF, 2–3, 31.

33. Gabriella Galt to Mary Jeffrey Galt, 25 Mar. 1865, GFP; BSE, "The College in the Years 1861–1865," 293.

Appomattox Court House. There on the afternoon of the ninth, Lee surrendered. Among the Williamsburg boys paroled were Dr. Waller's grandson, Lt. Tommy Mercer, in the artillery; Harriette Cary's brother, Miles, now a commissary sergeant in the 32d Virginia; and Pvt. Robert T. Armistead of the 3d Virginia Cavalry. Before long they would join the many southern men and women heading home.[34]

34. Gabriella Galt to Mary Jeffrey Galt, 25 Mar. 1865; Jensen, *32nd Virginia Infantry,* 136–41; *OR,* 46(3):567; Wallace, *1st Virginia Infantry,* 106; R. T. Armistead to M. H. Barnes, 7 Dec. 1897, Armistead Papers, MR-CWM.

Epilogue: Plucked Chicken

On 13 April 1865, four years to the day after Union forces surrendered at Fort Sumter, Williamsburg officially became part of the Federal District of the Peninsula, commanded by General Ludlow. Two weeks later the title changed to the Subdistrict of the Peninsula, and Ludlow was instructed to "establish his headquarters at Williamsburg." There by the end of the month, he commanded eleven companies from the 4th Massachusetts Cavalry, 1st and 2d U.S. Colored Cavalry, and 20th New York Cavalry. The latter regiment provided Williamsburg its next provost marshal, Lt. John D. Lee, who on 1 May issued the *Gazette*'s prewar editor, Edward Lively, the oath "for loyal Citizens of the United States."[1]

Lively was part of an influx of Williamsburg soldiers who started for home immediately after Appomattox. On 16 May, Sallie Munford, in residence at Tazewell Hall with her family, wrote Lizzie Ewell that "nearly all of the *town boys* and one or two stranger soldiers have come back so you see we are not entirely destitute of the society of the *dear Confederates*." Williamsburg "will soon be full of returned refugees" as well, Sallie maintained. A few besides the Munfords had already returned, including Bland Taliaferro and husband, Edwin, who set to work surveying the college's damage to report to Benjamin Ewell. Others had sent family members ahead to scout out the situation in Williamsburg. Merchant W. W. Vest's son George "came down a day or two ago and took formal possession of his father's house," chronicled Sallie. The Saunders family dispatched a faithful servant with a letter to Sally Galt asking "her to find out if they could get possession of their house and Genl Ludlow

1. *OR*, 46(3):739, 985–6, 1035; E. H. Lively oath certification, 1 May 1865, *Williamsburg Gazette* microfilm, CWM.

said certainly they could." She also inspected the premises for them. "Found the house not much injured, & the garden was as sweet & pretty, as when they left it," she later wrote; "the servants are very faithful to them, & greatly wish for their return."[2]

The Munfords' home had also escaped relatively unscathed. "Tazewell Hall looks as natural and sweet as possible, nothing having been disturbed except the barn & outhouses, & their removal I think, is rather an improvement to the looks of the place than otherwise," Sallie Munford informed Lizzie on the sixteenth. Concerning Williamsburg in general, "I really was pleasantly disappointed on my arrival here, to find every thing looking so much better than I expected; though I expect the trees and flowers, hide a multitude of sins." They could not hide every sin, however. "The main st. does present rather a more dilapidated appearance than usual, owing to the hotel having been pulled down & several other *public edifices* the Ct. houses etc being minus doors & windows," she imparted. As John Charles later explained, "every vacant frame house in the city, with very few exceptions, were torn down by the 'Yanks,' or fell a prey to the axe of citizens who had no other way of securing dry kindling wood; but in justice to those destructionists who were mostly boys, both white and colored, the buildings which they 'finished up' had already been dismantled by the soldiers."[3]

Though definitely the worse for wear, Williamsburg churches managed to survive the war intact. "I know you will be glad to hear that the old church has been nicely fixed up and we have service there every Sunday morning," Sallie added to her 16 May epistle, hoping to entice Lizzie to come home soon. With no sign of her friend by the end of the month, Sallie addressed another letter to her on the thirtieth and boasted, "We are daily becoming more civilized, have *church*, a *telegraph*, a *tri-weekly boat* and a *daily mail*— picture it my dear!" Williamsburg society too was improving. "Confeds to be sure are sufficiently plenty," and the Peachys hosted "a treat, a few nights ago, at which fiddles, pound cake and Confederates predominated. 'There's life in the old burgh yet!' don't you think so?"[4]

One factor delaying Lizzie's return and affecting several refugees was the

2. Sallie Munford to Elizabeth Ewell, 16 May 1865, EFP, MR-CWM; Edwin Taliaferro to BSE, 13 June 1865, Presidents' Papers–BSE, UA-CWM; SMG to Peggy, 26 June 1865, GFP, MR-CWM.

3. Munford to Ewell, 16 May 1865; John S. Charles, "Recollections of Williamsburg, Virginia, as It Was at the Beginning of the Civil War," 1928, John D. Rockefeller Jr. Library, CWF, 7.

4. Sallie Munford to Elizabeth Ewell, 16, 30 May 1865, EFP.

amnesty oath ordered by President Andrew Johnson, who succeeded the assassinated Lincoln. This proclamation required all high-ranking Confederate officers and owners of property worth more than twenty thousand dollars to apply in person to the president for a pardon. As a colonel, Benjamin Ewell was subject to this order and would be unable to reassume his position as college president without a pardon. By August, the army had taken over the William and Mary campus, anyway, and General Ludlow was using the President's House for his headquarters, though he promised "to put the Faculty in possession of the Buildings and grounds in the event the College is reopened." In the meantime, Ewell confided to a cousin later that month, "I am in the condition some what as to means of living that a plucked chicken is as to feathers—with health weakened." His assets too were considerably diminished, for his house had been stripped of furniture and all his silver and other valuables had been confiscated by a treasury agent during the war.[5]

Also casting about for a way to make a living, Robert Saunders visited Williamsburg in early August to check on his house and was relieved to find it in better shape than he expected. "Under these circumstances I shall merely have such repairs done to the house as are *absolutely* necessary, & this is very little— and have it cleaned & whitewashed," he wrote on the tenth to his family waiting for him in Pittsylvania County. Yet he assumed he would have to go to Washington for the required pardon to reoccupy his property, even his house, for the "General here is kind enough" but has "not the power to put me in full possession himself." Nor would that solve his problems. "All here are as kind as possible, but there is a general condition of things here that makes me and every one else feel uncomfortably," he related. "In the first place there is nothing for any one to do."[6]

What to do with his extensive farmland even if he could get it back posed a difficult problem for both Saunders and Dr. Waller. Incensed to learn that his land had been declared abandoned, seized by the government, and rented to freedmen, Dr. Waller, still in Lynchburg and unable to travel to Washington for his pardon, feared he would never regain possession. Nevertheless, his son, Mercer Waller, who had returned to Williamsburg, and his son-in-law, Dr. William Morris, devised a plan to provide him with some income. They proposed a timbering operation on his property using a steam sawmill, which Dr. Morris traveled to Washington in August to procure. Before Dr. Morris

5. BSE, "The College in the Years 1861–1865," 296–7; BSE to T. T. Gantt, 6 Aug. 1865, Presidents' Papers–BSE; BSE to Rebecca Ewell, 20 June 1865, EFP.

6. Robert Saunders to Lelia Saunders, 10 Aug. 1865, PSP, MR-CWM.

could return to Washington to secure a pardon for himself and Dr. Waller, news arrived that Tommy Mercer had succumbed to pneumonia in Williamsburg on 7 September. "Oh! his death is a sad blow, after his Escape from all the Great Battles he participated in," mourned Dr. Waller. Richard Bucktrout provided Tommy a cherry wood coffin for forty-five dollars, including case and burial expenses. It was probably the best Dr. Mercer, who had just returned to Williamsburg, could afford.[7]

At last, on 21 October, Dr. Waller took "the Oath required by terms of Pardon by the President" and three days later boarded a train for Richmond on the first leg of his journey home. Coincidentally, Cynthia Coleman and two-year-old Charley were riding the same train. Dr. Coleman had made a brief trip to Williamsburg that summer to look over the opportunities but decided instead to open a practice in Boydton, Virginia, a few miles from Clarksville. Cynthia, however, was determined to return home. While Dr. Waller tarried in Richmond a few days, Cynthia continued by James River steamer to Williamsburg, where she found her mother "in very feeble health, looking wretchedly, and in very poor spirits." Suffering with severe jaundice, Lucy had almost despaired of ever seeing her eldest daughter.[8]

Lucy's attending physician was Dr. Wager, considered a friend by many for his kindness "in the time of trouble" and his efforts to save the town's historic buildings. For a month he had been wrangling with a new state-appointed board of directors over control of the Eastern Lunatic Asylum. Lemuel G. Bowden, younger son of Lemuel J. Bowden, who had died in Washington as a Unionist Virginia senator in 1864, presently served as board president and insisted that Dr. Wager turn over the asylum. This the doctor refused to do without instructions from Federal authorities. When orders finally arrived for Dr. Wager to relinquish control on 1 November, Dr. Leonard Henley became superintendent, but only briefly. Decades would pass before that institution had a stable administration. "Dr Wager has been made Post Surgeon tho' there are *at present* no troops in the place," Cynthia wrote Charles on 2 November. A week later she reported that "Dr Wager has hung out his shingle, but he might just as well take it in," for his intemperate habits drove away all patients and ultimately brought him to an early grave three years later. Besides him, only Dr. Mercer and one other physician were "occupying the ground"

7. Robert Page Waller Diary, 3 June, 8 Aug., 9–11, 14, 22 Sept., 10 Oct. 1865, MR-CWM; Richard M. Bucktrout Day Book, 1865, MR-CWM.

8. Waller Diary, 21, 24 Oct. 1865; CBT to CWC, 25 Oct., 2, 9 Nov. 1865, TCP, MR-CWM; P. M. Thompson to CBT, 21 Aug. 1865, TCP.

in November 1865. For Dr. Coleman's consideration, she passed along the tidings that "*all* the old Citizens are returning, and that there is a reasonable prospect of being remunerated in a measure for your services. *That if you intend coming now is the time.*"[9]

William and Mary now provided employment as well. "The College opened very well considering all things," Cynthia wrote on 2 November. Starting a week later than usual in October, due to the military's delayed departure, and forced to hold classes in the torn-up but still-standing Brafferton, the college registered sixty-two students. Thirty-nine attended a new grammar school taught by Robertson Garrett, former captain of a battalion of Tennessee cavalry under Nathan Bedford Forrest. Taliaferro headed the Latin Department, containing such Williamsburg veterans as young Bob Saunders and Monty Tucker. Tom Tucker enrolled in the Mathematics Department under Prof. Thomas Snead, who had served as engineer under Gen. Thomas "Stonewall" Jackson, then as adjutant to the chief engineer in Richmond. Reoccupying his place as college president was Benjamin Ewell.[10]

Several students at the college were grandsons of and supported by Dr. Waller, returning at last to Williamsburg on 8 November. "Arrived at home & found the Desolation much more complete than my worst fears had pictured to me, & the change so complete & radical that it must hasten my end before many days," he groaned. His outbuildings had been burned, his yard trampled, the front porch was crumbling, and the house was devoid of servants and stripped of all furniture and decoration. Eventually, "three Pictures stolen by Yankees out of the Parlour during the war" turned up at the asylum and were returned to him. Five days after his arrival, he began inspecting his farmland. "Disgusted with the entire desolation of the scene, the houses are the only thing of any value left, fences, all gone, & every thing swept as if by Besom of destruction." Only his new sawmill under construction presented "a very busy scene. Many houses erected, & building."[11]

Robert Saunders also brought his family home in November. Both he and

9. CBT to CWC, 2, 9 Nov. 1865; Flournoy, *Virginia State Papers*, 11:457, 485, 489; Dain, *Disordered Minds*, 190–4; Lemuel J. Bowden F/A, UA-CWM; Bruton Church Register, Bruton Parish Records, MR-CWM, vol. 1.

10. CBT to CWC, 2 Nov. 1865; Susan H. Godson, Ludwell H. Johnson, Richard B. Sherman, Thad W. Tate, Helen C. Walker, *The College of William and Mary: A History*, 2 vols. (Williamsburg: King and Queen Press, 1993), 1:338; *1860–1861, 1865–1866 Catalogue of The College of William and Mary, in Virginia* (Richmond: Gary and Clemmitt, 1866); "Capt. W. R. Garrett," *Confederate Veteran* 12 (1904): 129; *OR*, 12(2):185; *OR* IV, 3:1139.

11. Waller Diary, 8, 12–14 Nov., 15 Dec. 1865.

Dr. Waller, in a fruitless effort to make their land productive again, rented portions of their farms to freedmen but had to wrestle with government bureau agents for approval of all contracts with their tenants. The following month John Coupland returned to Williamsburg with his family. Finding no prospects in town, he decided "there was but one thing left for me to do—go on the farm and with my own hands make meat & bread enough to support us." Just before Christmas 1865 he wrote his mother, "There is no labor to be employed here as yet, & if there were I have no money."[12]

Indeed, poverty was now the common condition of all classes in Williamsburg. Nothing illustrates this sad situation more eloquently than a glance at Bucktrout's ledger from 1862 to 1866, with "insolvent" scribbled beside the names of the once-wealthy Saunders, Coupland, Peachy, Durfey, and Henley families. Even the Wallers and Garretts were scraping to pay the undertaker to bury their loved ones and repair their houses. Few could afford to hire either white or black laborers or domestics, causing great hardship to all. A series of crop failures deepened the demoralization. In 1867 Montegu Thompson observed that some people "utterly ruined by the war seem to have lost all energy and hope," and many had become "whiskey drinking loafers." A student arriving in town in 1870 noted the "poverty and paralysis," houses "unpainted and dilapidated," and what few lights were visible emanated "from the numerous bar rooms which lined Duke of Gloucester Street. The suffering and dejection of the inhabitants made them the only enterprises in the town that prospered."[13]

Prosperity continued to elude Williamsburg as the war generation began to pass away. Richard Bucktrout was among the first to die, unexpectedly, in September 1866, and Delia, who married Lt. William Braithwaite of the 32d Virginia on Christmas 1865, took over his undertaking business. During her widowhood some three decades later, the wounded Yankee she had given a drink of water to in Bruton Church returned and "begged her to marry him," but she refused. In September 1868 Robert Saunders succumbed to typhoid fever while serving as Williamsburg mayor, "a warning & awful one to all intemperate persons," Dr. Waller commented in his diary. Dr. Waller's sawmill ultimately failed, and he was forced to sell much of his land to northern specu-

12. Ibid., 26 Nov. 1865, 23 Feb., 1, 3 Mar. 1866; JRC to Juliana Dorsey, 20 Dec. 1865, DCP, MR-CWM.

13. Bucktrout Day Book, 1862–66; P. M. Thompson to William Berkeley, 14 May 1867, P. M. Thompson F/A, UA-CWM; Robert M. Hughes, "Sixty Years Ago: Baccalaureate Address of Robert M. Hughes at the College of William and Mary Final Day, June 12, 1933," *William and Mary Quarterly*, 2d ser., 13 (1933): 195.

lators before his demise in 1872. Sally Galt too had no recourse but to sell her farmland and Richmond property after first trying to rent out rooms in the Galt House. Arena Baker, though remaining with her, so adamantly opposed taking in boarders that Sally gave up the idea. Before her death in 1880, Sally willed Arena the Galt kitchen. Sally's cousin, Gibbie Galt, tried teaching school in partnership with James Griffin, but her struggle with debt led to bankruptcy and the loss of her house to W. W. Vest. "If all the world starved, he would still have enough," Cynthia Coleman characterized Vest when he came back after the war, his fortune intact. Able to support a full staff, he hired Eliza Baker as his housekeeper and upon his death in 1893 bequeathed a corner of his property to her.[14]

A much-reduced inheritance could not stave off the Tuckers' postwar poverty. Lucy, broken in body and spirit, died in February 1867, leaving the Tucker House to son Tom. Having persuaded Charles to return to Williamsburg, Cynthia bought the Griffins' house and attempted to operate a boarding school but was forced to give it up for lack of payment and the arrival of babies. To supplement Dr. Coleman's meager income despite his large practice, Cynthia continued to take in boarders, teach music, rent out the Tucker farm, sell property, and in 1890 sell articles she wrote about the battle of Williamsburg to pay for their winter supply of coal. Bland Taliaferro lost both her babies and in September 1867 became widowed when Edwin succumbed to tuberculosis. Severely debilitated by his war wound, Tom Tucker died on the tenth anniversary of the battle of Williamsburg, "as effectually killed by the ball on the Battle-field of Fredericksburg as if he had fallen on the spot," asserted Cynthia.[15]

14. Waller Diary, 13 Sept. 1866, 11 Sept. 1868, 3 Mar., 24 Apr., 12 May, 29 Sept. 1869, 21 July 1872; Minnie B. Jenkins, "When Delia Bucktrout Ran the Blockade to Richmond," Dorothy Ross Collection; Robert Saunders obituary, 11 Sept. 1868, PSP; Williamsburg City Council resolution, 11 Sept. 1868, PSP; Talbot Sweeney to SMG, 6 Feb. 1866, GFP; Robert H. Armistead to SMG, 10 Feb. 1868, GFP; SMG to Gen. Richardson, 2 July 1869, GFP; SMG Will, 18 May 1869, GFP; Male & Female Classical and English Academy advertisement, 1 Oct. 1869, GFP; notes regarding suit between Vest & Hansford and G. V. Galt, 20 Nov. 1874, GFP; CBT to CWC, 2 Nov. 1865; *(Williamsburg) Virginia Gazette,* 12 July 1893; Mary A. Stephenson, "Palmer House Historical Report," 1960, John D. Rockefeller Jr. Library, CWF.

15. Waller Diary, 18 Feb. 1867; Thomas S. B. Tucker to CBT, 1 Apr. 1867, TCP; "Female Seminary" advertisement, 3 Oct. 1867, TCP; CBT to George P. Coleman, 18 Oct. 1885, 13 May 1886, 18 June 1890, TCP; Mary A. Stephenson, "Tayloe House Historical Report, Block 28 Building 3 Lot 262," 1949, John D. Rockefeller Jr. Library, CWF; Thompson to Berkeley, 15 July 1867, P. M. Thompson F/A; Edwin Taliaferro obituary, Edwin Taliaferro F/A, UA-CWM; Bruton Church Register, Bruton Parish Records, vol. 1; CBT, "Peninsula Campaign."

After Tom's death the Tucker House was rented to Mary Southall Fisher. Because her husband died of disease in Richmond in January 1865, she returned to Williamsburg after the war as simply Mary Southall and married Junior Guard veteran Henley Jones of a once-wealthy local family. The couple's failed attempts at farming brought them into town, where they moved into the Tucker House and operated a drugstore associated with Dr. Coleman's practice. Henley played a leading role in Williamsburg's Magruder-Ewell Camp of Confederate Veterans, and Mary organized the Ladies Auxiliary to the camp. She and Cynthia kept the Confederate flame alive in Williamsburg by decorating the graves of Confederate soldiers in the City Cemetery and Bruton Churchyard every Memorial Day. Included in these honors were the soldiers buried in trenches outside the Baptist church and reinterred, as Isabella Sully had promised, at Bruton after the war. Mary's funeral at the City Cemetery in April 1894 was one of the largest the city had seen, showing "how highly she was esteemed by the citizens of all classes."[16]

Two months after Mary's services, another huge funeral took place. Benjamin Ewell had spent most of his postwar years soliciting funds from northern donors and the U.S. government to reimburse William and Mary's rebuilding. When the college was forced to close in 1881, he continued to lobby and kept the campus alive by tutoring and ringing the school bell at the beginning of every session until it was revived with state funds in 1888. He then retired and worked on a biography of his brother, Richard, until death seized him in June 1894. The train that first arrived on the Peninsula in 1881 stopped at Ewell Station by his farm and picked up his remains to transport into town. A tremendous crowd in procession led by a band and including the Confederate Veterans Camp, Sons of Confederate Veterans, Board of Visitors, mayor, city council, and students accompanied his coffin to the College Cemetery.[17]

Williamsburg witnessed yet a third colossal funeral three months later. After suffering with facial cancer since May 1894, Dr. Charles Coleman, a lieutenant colonel in the Confederate Veterans Camp, expired while seeking treatment in Richmond that September. His body returned home by train and was met at the depot by a "large crowd of citizens of all classes" eager "to show their respect and esteem for one who had done so much for them during his

16. CBT to CWC, 20–22 Jan. 1865, TCP; *(Williamsburg) Virginia Gazette*, 28 Apr. 1894, 19 July 1902; Sully to CBT, 30 Oct. 1890, 16 July 1892, TCP; CBT to George P. Coleman, 9 May 1893, TCP.

17. Godson et al., *College of William and Mary*, 1:352–61, 402–3, 409–11; BSE to Elizabeth S. Ewell, 31 May 1892, EFP; *(Williamsburg) Virginia Gazette*, 22 June 1894.

life." Mourners filled every seat and crowded the aisles at Bruton Church during his funeral service before his burial in the churchyard.[18]

A grief-stricken Cynthia overcame her sorrow in her usual way, by keeping busy. She had been active in preservation projects, beginning with the "Catharine Memorial Society," formed in 1884, after the death of her youngest daughter, to restore the crumbling churchyard. Inspired by the society's work, several ladies joined with Cynthia to establish the Association for the Preservation of Virginia Antiquities, which purchased the old Powder Horn in 1889 and transformed it into a museum. Another dream of hers, to mark the soldiers' graves in Bruton Churchyard with a monument, came true on Memorial Day, 5 May 1893. On the same day in 1908, a Confederate monument honoring all soldiers and sailors of Williamsburg and James City County was unveiled on Palace Green in front of Bruton Church. A stroke ended Cynthia's earthly existence that October, and hundreds from Williamsburg and Richmond attended her funeral at Bruton Church. "One has not lived in vain whose life is given to good works," her obituary eulogized. "Her memory will long be cherished in the hearts of our people."[19]

Several more decades would pass before the entire war generation crossed over the river, but already Williamsburg's focus was shifting to an earlier era. The minister officiating at Cynthia's funeral service, Dr. William A. R. Goodwin, had just finished restoring Bruton Church to its colonial configuration and dreamed of a similar treatment for the entire town. As farming declined in the area, forest began reclaiming much of the battlefield. Soon thereafter, both the battle of Williamsburg and the townspeople who so staunchly defended their homes throughout the Federal occupation would be all but forgotten.[20]

---

18. CBT to George P. Coleman, 5 May 1894, TCP; *Richmond Dispatch,* 18 Sept. 1894; Rouse, *Cows on the Campus,* 70.

19. CBT to George P. Coleman, 26 Feb. 1884, 9 May 1893, TCP; Rouse, *Cows on the Campus,* 83–4; *(Williamsburg) Virginia Gazette,* 9 May, 31 Oct. 1908.

20. Yetter, *Williamsburg Before and After,* 49–51.

APPENDIX A

Confederate Troops at Williamsburg, 4–5 May 1862

COMMANDER: *Joseph Eggleston Johnston*
FIELD COMMANDER: *James Longstreet*

FIRST DIVISION: *Lafayette McLaws*

Brigades

Paul J. Semmes	*Joseph B. Kershaw*
5th Louisiana	2d South Carolina
10th Louisiana	3d South Carolina
10th Georgia	7th South Carolina
15th Virginia	8th South Carolina
	Gracie's Battalion

SECOND DIVISION: *James Longstreet*

Brigades

Ambrose Powell Hill	*Richard H. Anderson*	*George Edward Pickett*
1st Virginia	4th South Carolina Battalion	8th Virginia
7th Virginia	5th South Carolina	18th Virginia
11th Virginia	6th South Carolina	19th Virginia
17th Virginia	Palmetto Sharpshooters	28th Virginia
	Louisiana Foot Rifles	

Cadmus Marcellus Wilcox	*Roger Atkinson Pryor*	*Edward Raleigh Colston*
9th Alabama	8th Alabama	3d Virginia
10th Alabama	14th Alabama	13th North Carolina
19th Mississippi	14th Louisiana	14th North Carolina

FOURTH DIVISION: *Daniel Harvey Hill*

Brigades

Jubal Anderson Early
24th Virginia
38th Virginia
5th North Carolina
23d North Carolina
2d Florida
2d Mississippi Battalion

*Robert Rodes**
5th Alabama
6th Alabama
12th Alabama
12th Mississippi

*Gabriel J. Rains**
13th Alabama
26th Alabama
6th Georgia
23d Georgia

W. S. Featherston
27th Georgia*
28th Georgia*
4th North Carolina
49th Virginia*

CAVALRY DIVISION
James Ewell Brown Stuart
3d Virginia Cavalry
4th Virginia Cavalry
Wise Legion
Jeff Davis Legion
Stuart Horse Artillery

ARTILLERY
Lee (Williamsburg) Artillery
Manley's Battery
Richmond Howitzers
Richmond Fayette Artillery
Fauquier Artillery
Lynchburg Artillery
Virginia Battery
Donaldsonville Artillery*
Kemper's Battery

*Not engaged

APPENDIX B
Union Troops at Williamsburg, 4–5 May 1862

COMMANDER: *George Brinton McClellan*
SECOND IN COMMAND: *Edwin Vose Sumner*

THIRD CORPS: *Samuel Peter Heintzelman*

SECOND DIVISION: *Joseph Hooker*

First Brigade
Cuvier Grover
1st Massachusetts
11th Massachusetts
2d New Hampshire
26th Pennsylvania

Second (Excelsior) Brigade
Nelson Taylor
70th New York (1stExcelsior)
72d New York (3d Excelsior)
73d New York (4th Excelsior)
74th New York (5th Excelsior)

Third Brigade
Francis E. Patterson
5th New Jersey
6th New Jersey
7th New Jersey
8th New Jersey

Artillery
Charles S. Wainwright
1st New York, Battery D
4th New York
6th New York
1st U.S., Battery H

THIRD DIVISION: *Philip Kearny*

First Brigade
Charles D. Jameson
57th Pennsylvania
63d Pennsylvania*
105th Pennsylvania
87th New York

Second Brigade
David D. Birney
38th New York
40th New York
3d Maine*
4th Maine*

Third Brigade
Hiram G. Berry
2d Michigan
3d Michigan
5th Michigan
37th New York

Artillery
*James Thompson**
1st New Jersey, Battery B
1st Rhode Island, Battery E
2d U.S., Battery G

FOURTH CORPS: *Erasmus Darwin Keyes*

FIRST DIVISION: *Darius Nash Couch*

First Brigade
*Julius W. Adams**
65th New York
   (1st U.S. Chasseurs)
67th New York
   (1st Long Island)
23d Pennsylvania
31st Pennsylvania
61st Pennsylvania

Second Brigade
John J. Peck
55th New York
62d New York
93d Pennsylvania
98th Pennsylvania
102d Pennsylvania

Third Brigade
Charles Devens Jr.
7th Massachusetts
10th Massachusetts
2d Rhode Island

Artillery
*Robert M. West**
1st Pennsylvania, Batteries C, D, E, H

SECOND DIVISION: *William F. Smith*

First Brigade
Winfield Scott Hancock
5th Wisconsin
49th Pennsylvania
43d New York*
6th Maine

Second Brigade
*W. T. H. Brooks**
2d Vermont
3d Vermont
4th Vermont
5th Vermont

Third Brigade
Winfield Scott Hancock
7th Maine
33d New York
49th New York
76th New York*

Artillery
Romeyn B. Ayres
1st New York, Battery E
3d New York
5th U.S., Battery F

THIRD DIVISION: *Silas Casey*

First Brigade	**Second Brigade**
Henry M. Naglee*	*William H. Keim*
11th Maine	96th New York
56th New York	85th Pennsylvania
100th New York	101st Pennsylvania
52d Pennsylvania	103d Pennsylvania
104th Pennsylvania	

Third Brigade	**Artillery**
Innis N. Palmer	*Guilford D. Bailey**
81st New York*	1st New York, Batteries A, H
85th New York*	7th New York
92d New York	8th New York
93d New York	
98th New York*	

ADVANCE GUARD

Cavalry
George Stoneman
5th U.S.

Division
Philip St. George Cooke
1st U.S.
6th U.S.

First Brigade
William H. Emory
3d Pennsylvania
McClellan (Illinois) Dragoons

Artillery
Henry J. Hunt
2d U.S., Batteries B, L, M
3d U.S., Batteries C, K

*Not engaged

BIBLIOGRAPHY

Manuscript Sources

Earl Gregg Swem Library, College of William and Mary, Williamsburg, Virginia

Manuscripts and Rare Books Department
Allcot, William P. Papers, 1861–1864
Alfriend, Thomas L. Papers, 1861–1865, 1901
Armistead Papers, 1736–1897
Blow Family Papers, 1770–1875
Brisbin, James S. Letter to wife, 18 August 1861
Brown, Edwin Y. Papers, 1862
Bruton Parish Records, 2 vols., 1868–1903 (on deposit from Bruton Parish Church)
Bucktrout, Richard M. Day Book and Ledger, 1850–1866 (on deposit from Anne H. Cutler)
Bucktrout-Braithwaite Foundation Papers, 1780–1902
Bucktrout-Smith Papers, 1861–1977
Cary, Harriette. Diary, 1862
Civil War Collection, 1861–1865
Dorsey-Coupland Papers, 1840–1876
Eastern State Hospital Papers, 1862–1868, 1956–1957
Ewell Family Papers, 1784–1934
Galt Family Papers, 1789–1876
Garrett Family Papers, 1786–1928
Henry C. Hoar Memorial Collection, 1861–1862
Holt, Samuel E. Diary and Memorandum Book, 1861 (photocopy)
Johnston, Joseph E. Papers, 1825–1891
Page-Saunders Papers, 1790–1932

Tucker-Coleman Papers, 1770–1945
Walker, F. N. Diary, 1862
Waller, Robert P. Diaries, 13 vols., 1858–1872
Williamsburg City Papers, 1700–1991
Williamsburg Historical Records Association

University Archives
Board of Visitors Minutes
Chronology File
Faculty/Alumni File
Faculty Minutes
Goodwin, Mary R. M. "Historical Notes on the College of William and Mary," 1954
 (copy; original in John D. Rockefeller Jr. Library, Colonial Williamsburg Foundation)
Presidents' Papers–Benjamin S. Ewell
William and Mary College Papers

Eleanor S. Brockenbrough Library, Museum of the Confederacy,
Richmond, Virginia

Petty, James Thomas. Diary No. 2, 1862

John D. Rockefeller Jr. Library, Colonial Williamsburg Foundation,
Williamsburg, Virginia

Special Collections
Anderson, Helen M. Papers, 1818–1912. MS89.13
Baker, Eliza. "Memoirs of Williamsburg," 1933. TR00/4 May/1933 (original in Archives and Records Department of the Colonial Williamsburg Foundation)
Charles, John S. "Recollections of Williamsburg, Virginia, as It Was at the Beginning of the Civil War," 1928. TR90 (original in Archives and Records Department of the Colonial Williamsburg Foundation)
Cronin, David Edward. "The Vest Mansion: Its Historical and Romantic Associations as Confederate and Union Headquarters (1862–1865) in the American Civil War," 1908–1910 (typescript copy of original manuscript in the Collection of the New-York Historical Society). TR09
Hooker, Joseph. "Report to Capt. C[hauncey] McKeever," 10 May 1862. MS00/10 May/1862
Lee, Victoria King. "Williamsburg in 1861," 1933. TR00/Feb/1933 (original in Archives and Records Department of the Colonial Williamsburg Foundation)
Munford, M. N. Letter to Gen. H. Naglee, 10 Dec. 1862. MS00/10 Dec/1862

Public Services
Stephenson, Mary A. "Tayloe House Historical Report, Block 28 Building 3 Lot 262," 1949. Research Report Series #1523

————. "Robert Carter House Historical Report, Block 30-2 Building 13 Lot 333, 334, 335, 336," 1956. Research Report Series #1604

————. "Palmer House Historical Report, Block 9 Building 24 Lot 27" 1960. Research Report Series #1131

The Library of Virginia, Richmond

Governor (1860–1863: Letcher). Executive papers, 1859–1863 (Chronological Files). State Government Records Collection

Little Bighorn Battlefield National Monument, Crow Agency, Montana

Custer, George Armstrong. Letter to Lydia Reed, 15 May 1862

National Archives, Washington, D.C.

Southern Claims Commission Case Files, 1871–1883

North Carolina State Archives, Raleigh

Oscar W. Blacknall Papers, 1861–1866

Special Collections Library, Duke University, Durham, North Carolina

Louis Malesherbes Goldsborough Papers, 1827–1877

Virginia Historical Society, Richmond

Chappell, John Taylor. "From Yorktown to Williamsburg," n.d.
Maxwell, David Elwell. Papers, 1862
Meem, John Lawrence. Letter to father, 10 May 1862
Payne, Mrs. William H. "Search for My Wounded Husband," 1910
Payne, William Henry Fitzhugh. Map of James River, 1862
Saunders Family Papers, 1798–1903
Stuart, J. E. B. Letter to Flora Stuart, 9 May 1862
Talcott Family Papers, 1816–1915
Wellford, Beverley Randolph. Papers, 1773–1907

Wilson Library, University of North Carolina, Chapel Hill

Southern Historical Collection of the Manuscripts Department
McLaws, Lafayette. Papers, 1836–1897. 472

PRIVATE COLLECTIONS

Dorothy Ross Collection, Live Oak, California
Will Molineux Collection, Williamsburg, Virginia

Interviews

Judge Robert Armistead, 22 April 1991.
Mrs. Cynthia Barlowe, 11 December 1996.

Newspapers

Daily Richmond Examiner. May 1862.
New-York Daily Tribune. May 1862.
New York Herald. May–August 1862.
Richmond Dispatch. March 1863, September 1894.
Richmond Enquirer. May–October 1862.
The Times Richmond. May 1890.
Weekly Williamsburg Gazette. 1857.
(Williamsburg) Cavalier. June–August 1862.
(Williamsburg) Virginia Gazette. 1853–1856, 1893–1894, 1902, 1908.
Williamsburg Weekly Gazette and Eastern Virginia Advertiser. March 1859–October 1860.
(Yorktown) Cavalier. March 1863–April 1864.

Books, Pamphlets, and Articles

1860–1861, 1865–1866 Catalogue of the College of William and Mary, in Virginia. Richmond: Gary and Clemmitt, 1866.

Alexander, Edward Porter. *Military Memoirs of a Confederate: A Critical Narrative.* 1907. Reprint, New York: Da Capo, 1993.

Allen, James H. "The James City Cavalry: Its Organization and Its First Service." *Southern Historical Society Papers* 24 (1896): 353–8.

Angle, Paul M., and Earl Schenck Miers, eds. *Tragic Years, 1860–1865.* 2 vols. New York: Simon and Schuster, 1960.

Barrett, John G., ed. *Yankee Rebel: The Civil War Journal of Edmund DeWitt Patterson.* Chapel Hill: University of North Carolina Press, 1966.

Battle-Fields of the South, From Bull Run to Fredericksburgh: With Sketches of Confederate Commanders, and Gossip of the Camps. New York: John Bradburn, 1864.

Bell, Robert T. *11th Virginia Infantry.* Lynchburg: H. E. Howard, 1985.

Boatner, Mark Mayo III. *The Civil War Dictionary.* Rev. ed. New York: David McKay, 1988.

Bratton, John. "The Battle of Williamsburg." *Southern Historical Society Papers* 7 (1879): 299–302.

Buck, Alice Trueheart. "Founder of the First Confederate Hospital." *Confederate Veteran* 2 (1894): 141.

Buckley, Cornelius M., trans. *A Frenchman, a Chaplain, a Rebel: The War Letters of Pere Louis-Hippolyte Gache, S. J.* Chicago: Loyola University Press, 1981.

Burns, James R. *Battle of Williamsburgh, with Reminiscences of the Campaign, Hospital Experiences, Debates, Etc.* New York: Published by author, 1865.

"Capt. W. R. Garrett." *Confederate Veteran* 12 (1904): 129.

Carroll, John M., comp. and ed. *Custer in the Civil War: His Unfinished Memoirs.* San Rafael, Calif., 1977.

Carter, W. H. *From Yorktown to Santiago: With the Sixth U.S. Cavalry.* 1900. Reprint, Austin: State House Press, 1989.

Comte de Paris. *History of the Civil War in America.* 4 vols. Philadelphia: Porter and Coates, 1876.

Coxe, John. "With the Hampton Legion in the Peninsular Campaign." *Confederate Veteran.* 29 (1921): 414–6, 442–3.

Crews, Edward R. "The Battle of Williamsburg." *Colonial Williamsburg Journal* 18 (summer 1996): 15–25.

Cummings, C. C. "Confederate Heroine at Williamsburg, Va." *Confederate Veteran* 4 (1896): 91.

Dain, Norman. *Disordered Minds: The First Century of Eastern State Hospital in Williamsburg, Virginia, 1766–1866.* Williamsburg: Colonial Williamsburg Foundation, 1971.

Davis, Jefferson. *The Rise and Fall of the Confederate Government.* 2 vols. New York: D. Appleby, 1881.

Davis, W. W. H. *History of the 104th Pennsylvania Regiment from August 22nd, 1861, to September 30th, 1864.* Philadelphia: Jas. B. Rodgers, 1866.

De Peyster, Watts. *Personal and Military History of Philip Kearny.* New York: Rice and Gage, 1869.

Dickert, D. Augustus. *History of Kershaw's Brigade with Complete Roll of Companies, Biographical Sketches, Incidents, Anecdotes, Etc.* Newberry, S.C.: Elbert H. Auil, 1899.

Donald, David Herbert, ed. *Gone for a Soldier: The Civil War Memoirs of Private Alfred Bellard.* Boston: Little, Brown, 1975.

Donaldson, W. E. "On the 5th day of May, 1862." *Confederate Veteran* 4 (1896): 164.

Dutcher, Salem. "Williamsburg: A Graphic Story of the Battle of May 5, 1862." *Southern Historical Society Papers* 17 (1889): 409–19.

Early, Jubal Anderson. *Jubal Early's Memoirs: Autobiographical Sketch and Narrative of the War between the States.* [1912.] Reprint, Baltimore: Nautical and Aviation Publishing, 1989.

Everson, Guy R., and Edward W. Simpson Jr., eds. *"Far, Far from Home": The Wartime Letters of Dick and Tally Simpson, Third South Carolina Volunteers.* New York: Oxford University Press, 1994.

Ewell, Benjamin S. "The College in the Years 1861–1865." *William and Mary Quarterly,* 2d ser., 8 (1928): 290–6.

Eyland, Seth [David Edward Cronin]. *Evolution of a Life.* New York: S. W. Green's Son, 1884.

Flournoy, H. W., ed. *Calendar of Virginia State Papers and Other Manuscripts from January 1, 1836, to April 15, 1869.* 11 vols. Richmond, 1893.

Floyd, Fred C. *History of the Fortieth (Mozart) Regiment New York Volunteers.* Boston: F. H. Gilson, 1909.

Freeman, Douglas Southall. *Lee's Lieutenants: A Study in Command.* 3 vols. New York: Charles Scribner's Sons, 1942.

Frobel, Anne S. *The Civil War Diary of Anne S. Frobel.* McLean, Va.: EPM, 1992.

Gallagher, Gary N., ed. *Fighting for the Confederacy: The Personal Recollections of General Edward Porter Alexander.* Chapel Hill: University of North Carolina, 1989.

Godson, Susan H., Ludwell H. Johnson, Richard B. Sherman, Thad W. Tate, Helen C. Walker. 2 vols. *The College of William and Mary: A History.* Williamsburg: King and Queen Press, 1993.

Goodwin, Rev. W. A. R. *Historical Sketch of Bruton Church, Williamsburg, Virginia.* N. p., 1903.

Gracie, Archibald. "Gracie's Battalion at Williamsburg in 1862." *Confederate Veteran* 19 (1911): 27–32.

Gregory, G. Howard. *38th Virginia Infantry.* Lynchburg: H. E. Howard, 1988.

Grimsley, Mark, ed., and Bernatello Glod, trans. "'We Prepare to Receive the Enemy Where We Stand': The Journal of the Comte de Paris Revealed." *Civil War Times Illustrated* 24 (May 1985): 18–26.

Grizzard, R. W. "Dr. E. S. Pendleton." *Confederate Veteran* 28 (1920): 177.

Hamilton, J. G. De Roulhac, ed. *The Papers of Randolph Abbott Shotwell.* 2 vols. Raleigh: North Carolina Historical Commission, 1929.

Hamlin, Percy Gatling. *Making of a Soldier: Letters of General R. S. Ewell.* Richmond: Whittet and Shepperson, 1935.

Harvie, E. J. "Gen. Joseph E. Johnston." *Confederate Veteran* 18 (1910): 521–3.

Hastings, Earl C., Jr., and David Hastings. *A Pitiless Rain: The Battle of Williamsburg, 1862.* Shippensburg, Pa.: White Mane, 1997.

Hebert, Walter H. *Fighting Joe Hooker.* Indianapolis: Bobbs-Merrill, 1941.

"Henley T. Jones to the Editor." *William and Mary Quarterly,* 1st ser., 11(1903): 178.

Hewett, Janet B., ed. *The Roster of Confederate Soldiers, 1861–1865.* 16 vols. Wilmington, N.C.: Broadfoot, 1995–1996.

Hewett, Janet B., Noah Andre Trudeau, Bryce A. Suderow. *Supplement to the Official Records of the Union and Confederate Armies.* Wilmington, N.C.: Broadfoot, 1994.

Holzman, Robert S. *Adapt or Perish: The Life of General Roger A. Pryor, C. S. A.* Hamden, Conn.: Achon, 1976.

Hudson, Carson O. *Civil War Williamsburg.* Williamsburg: Colonial Williamsburg Foundation, 1997.

Hughes, Robert M. "Sixty Years Ago: Baccalaureate Address of Robert M. Hughes at the College of William and Mary Final Day, June 12, 1933." *William and Mary Quarterly,* 2d ser., 13 (1933): 195–202.

Hurst, M. B. *History of the Fourteenth Regiment Alabama Volunteers.* Edited by William Stanley Hoole. 1863. Reprint, University, Ala.: Confederate Publishing, 1982.

Jennings, T. D. "Incidents in the Battle at Williamsburg." *Confederate Veteran* 5 (1897): 477–8.

Jensen, Les. *32nd Virginia Infantry.* Lynchburg: H. E. Howard, 1990.

Johnson, Robert Underwood, and Clarence Clough Buel, eds. *Battles and Leaders of the Civil War.* 4 vols. 1887. Reprint, Secaucus, N.J.: Castle, n.d.

Johnston, Joseph E. *Narrative of Military Operations during the Civil War.* 1874. Reprint, New York: Da Capo, 1990.

Jones, H. T. "Wounded at Williamsburg, Va." *Southern Historical Society Papers* 24 (1896): 172–5.

Jones, Terry L. *Lee's Tigers: The Louisiana Infantry in the Army of Northern Virginia.* Baton Rouge: Louisiana State University Press, 1987.

Jordan, Ervin L., Jr. *19th Virginia Infantry.* Lynchburg: H. E. Howard, 1987.

Kearny, Thomas. *General Philip Kearny: Battle Soldier of Five Wars.* New York: G. P. Putnam's Sons, 1937.

Krick, Robert K. *Lee's Colonels: A Biographical Register of Field Officers of the Army of Northern Virginia.* 4th ed. Dayton, Ohio: Morningside, 1992.

"Letters of William Fitzhugh." *Virginia Historical Magazine* 1 (1893–94): 253–77.

[Lively, E. H.] "Williamsburg Junior Guards." *Southern Historical Society Papers* 18 (1890): 275–7.

Lively, E. H. "Williamsburg Junior Guards." *Southern Historical Society Papers* 29 (1901): 175–7.

Loehr, Charles T. "The First Virginia Infantry in the Peninsula Campaign." *Southern Historical Society Papers* 21 (1893): 104–10.

Longstreet, James. *From Manassas to Appomattox: Memoirs of the Civil War in America.* [1896.] Reprint, New York: Mallard Press, 1991.

Love, William DeLoss. *Wisconsin in the War of the Rebellion: A History of All Regiments and Batteries the State Has Sent to the Field.* Chicago: Church and Goodman, 1866.

Lowe, R. G. "The Dreux Battalion." *Confederate Veteran* 5 (1897): 54–6.

———. "Magruder's Defenses of the Peninsula." *Confederate Veteran* 8 (1900): 107.

Manarin, Louis H. *15th Virginia Infantry.* Lynchburg: H. E. Howard, 1990.

Marks, Rev. J. J. *The Peninsular Campaign in Virginia, or Incidents and Scenes on the Battle-fields and in Richmond.* Philadelphia: J. B. Lippincott, 1864.

Martin, Fred R. "Pelham of Alabama." *Confederate Veteran* 29 (1925): 9.

Maury, Richard L. *The Battle of Williamsburg and the Charge of the Twenty-fourth Virginia of Early's Brigade.* Richmond: Johns and Goolsby, Steam Printers, 1880.

———. "The Battle of Williamsburg, Va." *Southern Historical Society Papers* 22 (1894): 106–22.

McClellan, George B. *McClellan's Own Story.* New York: Charles C. Webster, 1887.

McRae, D. K. "The Battle of Williamsburg—Reply to Colonel Bratton." *Southern Historical Society Papers* 7 (1879): 360–72.

Minnich, J. W. "Incidents of the Peninsular Campaign." *Confederate Veteran* 30 (1922): 53–6.

Montgomery, Horace. "A Union Officer's Recollections of the Negro as a Soldier." *Pennsylvania History* 28 (April 1961): 156–86.

Moore, Frank, ed. *The Rebellion Record: A Diary of American Events with Documents, Narratives, Illustrative Incidents, Poetry, Etc.* 9 vols. New York: G. P. Putnam, 1863.

Moore, J. Staunton. *An Address Delivered by J. Staunton Moore at the 50th Re-union of the Fifteenth Virginia Regiment at Williamsburg, Virginia, May 24, 1911.* N.p., n.d.

Morgan, W. H. *Personal Reminiscences of the War of 1861–5.* Lynchburg: J. P. Bell, 1911.

Munford, Beverley B. *Random Recollections.* Privately printed, 1905.

Nanzig, Thomas P. *3rd Virginia Cavalry.* Lynchburg: H. E. Howard, 1989.

Nevins, Allan, ed. *A Diary of Battle: The Personal Journals of Charles S. Wainwright, 1861–1865.* Gettysburg: Stan Clark Military Books, 1962.

Olmert, Michael. *Official Guide to Colonial Williamsburg.* Williamsburg: Colonial Williamsburg Foundation, 1985.

Park, Robert E. "The Twelfth Alabama Infantry, Confederate States Army." *Southern Historical Society Papers* 33 (1905): 193–296.

Peterson, A. G. "Battle of Williamsburg, May 5, 1862." *Confederate Veteran* 20 (1912): 271–2.

Ratchford, J. W. "More of Gen. Rains and His Torpedoes." *Confederate Veteran* 2 (1894): 283.

Rawle, William Brooke, William E. Miller, James W. McCorkell, Andrew J. Speese, and John C. Hunterson. *History of the Third Pennsylvania Cavalry Sixtieth Regiment Pennsylvania Volunteers in the American Civil War, 1861–1865.* Philadelphia: Franklin Printing, 1905.

Reid, J. W. *History of the Fourth Regiment of S.C. Volunteers from the Commencement of the War until Lee's Surrender.* 1891. Reprint, Dayton, Ohio: Morningside, 1975.

Rhodes, Robert Hunt, ed. *All for the Union: The Civil War Diary and Letters of Elisha Hunt Rhodes.* New York: Orion, 1985.

Riggs, David F. *Embattled Shrine: Jamestown in the Civil War.* Shippensburg, Pa.: White Mane, 1997.

Robertson, William Glenn. *Back Door to Richmond: The Bermuda Hundred Campaign, April–June 1864.* Baton Rouge: Louisiana State University Press, 1987.

Rouse, Parke, Jr. *Cows on the Campus: Williamsburg in Bygone Days.* Richmond: Dietz Press, 1973.

Schaff, Morris. *The Spirit of Old West Point, 1858–1862.* Boston: Houghton, Mifflin, 1907.

Sears, Stephen W., ed. *The Civil War Papers of George B. McClellan: Selected Correspondence, 1860–1865.* New York: Da Capo, 1989.

———, ed. *For Country, Cause, and Leader: The Civil War Journal of Charles B. Haydon.* New York: Ticknor and Fields, 1993.

"Sketches from the Journal of a Confederate Soldier (Samuel Elias Mayes)." *Tyler's Quarterly* 6 (1924): 29–33.

Slater, J. L. "Burning of the College in 1862." *William and Mary Quarterly,* 1st ser., 11 (1903): 179.

Sorrell, G. Moxley. *Recollections of a Confederate Staff Officer.* 1905. Reprint, New York: Bantam, 1992.

Stiles, Robert. *Four Years under Marse Robert.* 1903. Reprint, Dayton, Ohio: Morningside, 1988.

Swint, Henry L., ed. *Dear Ones at Home: Letters from Contraband Camps.* Nashville: Vanderbilt University Press, 1966.

U.S. Bureau of the Census. Williamsburg and James City County Records. 1860, 1870. Microfilm.

U.S. Congress. *The Report of the Joint Committee on the Conduct of the War.* Vol. 1. Washington: Government Printing Office, 1863.

U.S. Naval Records Office. *Official Records of the Union and Confederate Navies in the War of the Rebellion.* 30 vols. Washington: Government Printing Office, 1894–1922.

U.S. War Department. *The War of the Rebellion: A Compilation of the Official Records of the Union and Confederate Armies.* 128 vols. Washington: Government Printing Office, 1880–1901.

———. *Atlas to Accompany the Official Records of the Union and Confederate Armies.* Washington: Government Printing Office, 1891–1895.

Wall, H. C. "The Twenty-third North Carolina Infantry." *Southern Historical Society Papers* 25 (1897): 151–76.

Wallace, Lee A., Jr. *1st Virginia Infantry.* Lynchburg: H. E. Howard, 1985.

———. *A Guide to Virginia Military Organizations, 1861–1865.* Lynchburg: H. E. Howard, 1986.

———. *3rd Virginia Infantry.* Lynchburg: H. E. Howard, 1986.

Walther, Eric H. *The Fire-Eaters.* Baton Rouge: Louisiana State University Press, 1992.

Warner, Ezra J. *Generals in Gray: Lives of the Confederate Commanders.* Baton Rouge: Louisiana State University Press, 1959.

———. *Generals in Blue: Lives of the Union Commanders.* Baton Rouge: Louisiana State University Press, 1964.

Webb, Alexander S. *The Peninsula: McClellan's Campaign of 1862.* New York: Charles Scribner's Sons, 1881.

West, George Benjamin. *When the Yankees Came: Civil War and Reconstruction on the Virginia Peninsula.* Edited by Parke Rouse Jr. Richmond: Dietz Press, 1977.

Wheeler, Richard. *Sword over Richmond: An Eyewitness History of McClellan's Peninsula Campaign.* New York: Harper and Row, 1986.

Whittaker, Frederick. *A Complete Life of General George A. Custer.* 2 vols. 1876. Reprint, Lincoln: University of Nebraska Press, 1993.

"William and Mary College as a Hospital." *William and Mary Quarterly,* 2d ser., 19 (1939): 181–6.

Wise, Henry A. "The Career of Wise's Brigade, 1861–5." *Southern Historical Society Papers* 25 (1897): 1–22.

Wise, John S. *End of an Era*. Boston: Houghton Mifflin, 1899.

Wood, William Nathaniel. *Reminiscences of Big I*. Edited by Bell Irvin Wiley. Wilmington, N.C.: Broadfoot, 1992.

Yetter, George Humphrey. *Williamsburg Before and After: The Rebirth of Virginia's Colonial Capital*. Williamsburg: Colonial Williamsburg Foundation, 1988.

Index